Klezmer's Afterlife

Klezmer's Afterlife

*An Ethnography of the Jewish Music Revival
in Poland and Germany*

MAGDALENA WALIGÓRSKA

OXFORD
UNIVERSITY PRESS

OXFORD

UNIVERSITY PRESS

Oxford University Press is a department of the University of Oxford.
It furthers the University's objective of excellence in research, scholarship,
and education by publishing worldwide.

Oxford   New York
Auckland   Cape Town   Dar es Salaam   Hong Kong   Karachi
Kuala Lumpur   Madrid   Melbourne   Mexico City   Nairobi
New Delhi   Shanghai   Taipei   Toronto

With offices in
Argentina   Austria   Brazil   Chile   Czech Republic   France   Greece
Guatemala   Hungary   Italy   Japan   Poland   Portugal   Singapore
South Korea   Switzerland   Thailand   Turkey   Ukraine   Vietnam

Oxford is a registered trade mark of Oxford University Press
in the UK and certain other countries.

Published in the United States of America by
Oxford University Press
198 Madison Avenue, New York, NY 10016

© Oxford University Press 2013

Library of Congress Cataloging-in-Publication Data
Waligórska, Magdalena.
Klezmer's afterlife : an ethnography of the Jewish music revival
in Poland and Germany / Magdalena Waligórska.
p.   cm.
Includes bibliographical references and index.
ISBN 978–0–19–999579–0 (hardback : alk. paper) 1. Klezmer music—Poland—History
and criticism. 2. Klezmer music—Germany—History and criticism. 3. Klezmer music—Social
aspects—Poland. 4. Klezmer music—Social aspects—Germany. I. Title.
ML3776.W35 2013
781.62'924043—dc23

2012048276

9780199314744

1   3   5   7   9   8   6   4   2

Printed in the United States of America on acid-free paper

CONTENTS

ACKNOWLEDGMENTS

Writing this book may have been a lonely pursuit, but a great number of people were involved in making the project happen. It could never have been written without the generosity of my interviewees, who invited me to their concerts, rehearsals, and their homes, and shared their stories with me.

I am extremely grateful to: Wiaczesław Abaszidze, Mark Aizikovich, Michael Alpert, Gigi Backes, Jerzy Bawół, Alan Bern, Jarosław Bester, Martin Borbonus, Paul Brody, Magdalena Brudzińska, Sławomir Cierpik, Christian Dawid, Gennadij Desatnik, Alexandra Dimitroff, Simon Jakob Drees, Sruli Dresdner, Giora Feidman, Walter Zev Feldman, Wlady Ginzburg, Jossif Gofenberg, Gołda Tencer, Hy Goldman, Max Hacker, Henryk Halkowski, Jan Hermerschmidt, Bert Hildebrandt, Jacek Hołubowski, Maciej Inglot, Alex Jacobowitz, Katarzyna Jamróz, Daniel Kahn, Ulrike Kloock, Karel Komnatoff, Leopold Kozłowski, Agata Krauze, Stefan Kühne, Shelly Kupferberg, Tomasz Kurkuba, Franka Lampe, Tomasz Lato, Heiko Lehmann, Grzegorz Lenart, Zdzisław Leś, Lesław Lic, Jasha Lieberman, Barbara Łypik-Sobaniec, Urszula Makosz, Janusz Makuch, Lisa Mayer, Tomasz Michalik, Maria Miodunka, Avia Moore, Sanne Möricke, Jarosław Naliwajko, Wojciech Ornat, Anna Ostachowska, Karol Pacholec, Rabbi Boaz Pash, Detlef Pegelow, Vitaliy Petranyuk, Przemysław Piekarski, Jalda Rebling, Hardy Reich, Roman Reiner, Andrzej Róg, Thomas Römer, Irene Runge, Joachim Russek, Henry Sapoznik, Fabian Schnedler, Anna Schubert, Till Schumann, Chris Schwarz, Snorre Schwarz, Burkhart Seidemann, Rafał Seweryniak, Rabbi Joshua Spinner, David Symons, Roman Ślazyk, Grzegorz Śpiewak, Mariola Śpiewak, Harry Timmermann, Ewelina Tomanek, Karsten Troyke, Irena Urbańska, Carsten Wegener, Michael Wex, Marcin Wiercioch, Jarosław Wilkosz, Henner Wolter, and Katarzyna Wydra.

During the long process of interpreting, processing, and writing I have greatly benefited from the expertise of a number of advisors whom I was lucky to have. I owe much gratitude to Heinz-Gerhard Haupt and Joachim Schlör for guiding me in this work, inspiring my research, and supporting me in matters big and small. I also wish to thank Jay Winter, who mentored me during the first year of my doctoral program; Donatella Della Porta, for invaluable advice on interviewing techniques; and to Giulia Calvi, Arfon Rees, Philipp Ther, and Stephen Smith for comments on my work in progress. I am likewise indebted to Steven Saxonberg, who first gave me the idea of writing about the klezmer revival, as well as to Walter Zev Feldman for illuminating discussions on heritage appropriation and Jankiel the klezmer, and Alan Bern and Michael Alpert for their kind support and sharing their invaluable insights on the klezmer scene. I also benefited enormously from the critical comments and insights of Joanna Tokarska-Bakir, Barbara Kirshenblatt-Gimblett, Michael Brenner, Ruth E. Gruber, Hankus Netsky, Philip Bohlman, and the anonymous reviewers at Oxford University Press, whose constructive criticism and good advice helped me to develop my argument further and strengthen the structure of the book.

While this book was taking shape, I also relied on the help and assistance of many fellow researchers working in the field of Jewish studies. I want to thank, in order of appearance, Małgorzata Pakier and Staś Tyszka for the inspiring conversations, and Gerben Zaagsma, Michał Szulc and Janina Wurbs for inventing and sustaining the beautiful tradition of transnational "Jewish Studies Scholars Dinners." The support and collaboration of Sophie Wagenhofer was both incredibly inspiring and almost medicinal. Finally, Erica Lehrer and Michael Meng, with their insightful comments, guidance and good advice, were my rock throughout the publishing storm.

Over the years spent researching and writing this book, I enjoyed the support of a number of institutions. A doctoral grant from the Polish Committee for European Integration allowed me to pursue the project at the European University Institute in Florence, which offered me superb working conditions, a dreamlike library, and the unwavering support of its staff. A postdoctoral fellowship from the Humboldt Foundation at the Freie Universität in Berlin, under the mentorship of Irmela von der Lühe and Hans Richard Brittnacher, made it possible for me to finish the manuscript. The KlezKanada Youth Scholarship Program supported my research at the KlezKanada festival in 2007, and a number of other Jewish cultural festivals offered their help and assistance, in particular the Jewish Culture Festival in Kraków, Warszawa Singera, Yiddish Summer Weimar, and Jüdische Kulturtage Berlin. Janusz Makuch (Jewish Culture Festival in Kraków), Gołda Tencer (Warszawa Singera), and Jalda Rebling (Tage der Jiddischen Kultur Berlin) deserve my thanks for sharing their archival materials with me, as does Maria Miodunka (TVP Kraków) for supplying me with archival recordings and audience ratings.

Many individuals have also helped me by searching their private archives and hard drives for illustrations that made their way into this book. I am immensely indebted to Christian Dawid, Daniel de Latour, Jacek Dyląg, Albrecht Grüß, Aneta Kaprzyk, Soliman Lawrence, Vitaliy Petranyuk, Jalda Rebling, Marek Sosenko, Przemysław Stachyra, Karsten Troyke, Carsten Wegener, the label Oriente, and the YIVO Archives for granting me permission to reproduce copyrighted material. A very special thanks goes to Marcin Piekoszewski for accompanying me to klezmer concerts in Berlin and capturing their atmosphere in his unique photographs, and to Klementyna Chrzanowska and Szymon Sokołowski for being my special task force of photographers in Kraków.

On the translation, transcription, and proofreading front, Janina Wurbs was invaluable for her help with Yiddish, while Scotia Gilroy and Rachel Harland helped to correct my English. All translations are my own unless noted otherwise.

Finally, on the home front, aides-de-camp, helpers, and supporters have been so many and their assistance so indispensable that it fully escapes the formulaic language of these acknowledgements. Without the love, help, and support of my Polish and German family, the common sense, wit, and sense of humor of my friends, and the endless patience of my husband there would be no book. Thank you. Dziękuje. Grazie. This book is for you.

Klezmer's Afterlife

Introduction

"Jews by Profession"

In his collection of essays *Żydowskie życie* [Jewish Life], the late Jewish historian and writer Henryk Halkowski ponders the phenomenon of what he calls "Jewish life without Jews." Pointing out that Poland has often been described as a land of "anti-Semitism without Jews," he wonders whether non-Jews do not altogether substitute Jews in the Polish public space. For Halkowski, the recent revival of Jewish culture in Poland, unfolding in places where, as in Kraków, the Jewish community is minute, is not a sign of continuity but rather of strenuous and sometimes paradoxical reinvention. Thinking of the irony of performing Jewish heritage in an environment where there is a virtual absence of people who can relate to it in a direct way led Halkowski to note that "being Jewish in today's Poland is not a nationality anymore, nor a religion, but only a profession."[1]

Henryk Halkowski, in 2003, was writing from a place that had become one of the most iconic hubs of the "Jewish revival" in Europe: Kraków's Jewish district of Kazimierz. Exceptionally well preserved and picturesque, Kazimierz started turning into a tourist magnet soon after the fall of Communism in 1989, and today is one of the main European destinations of Jewish heritage travel and Holocaust tourism. But although the quarter buzzes with cultural activity focused on Jewish heritage, the local Jewish community barely exceeds one hundred members. It is not much different elsewhere in Poland. Before World War II, Poland was home to 3.5 million Jews. Today there are four thousand people registered as members of Jewish organizations in Poland, and it is estimated that the population of those who identify themselves as Jewish does not exceed somewhere around ten thousand to thirty thousand.[2] Given the dimensions of loss and absence

---

[1] Ryszard Löw in Henryk Halkowski, *Żydowskie życie* (Kraków: Austeria, 2003), 152.

[2] Konstanty Gebert, "Jewish Identities in Poland: New, Old, and Imaginary," in *Jewish Identities in the New Europe*, ed. Jonathan Webber (London: Littman Library of Jewish Civilization, 1994), 161–67; Stanisław Krajewski, "The Impact of the Shoah on the Thinking of Contemporary Polish Jewry. A Personal Account," in *Contested Memories: Poles and Jews during the Holocaust and its Aftermath*, ed. Joshua D. Zimmerman (New Brunswick, NJ: Rutgers University Press, 2003), 292.

communicated by these statistics, the intensity of Jewish cultural events in Kazimierz might seem paradoxical. The district hosts the biggest European festival of Jewish culture, it has Jewish museums, Jewish cultural centers, Jewish bookstores, tourist agencies offering Jewish heritage trips, and Jewish restaurants holding daily concerts of klezmer music. Most of the people working in these, however, are not Jewish.

Having witnessed this singular revival firsthand, Halkowski muses about the irony involved in the non-Jewish participation in Jewish culture. "Jews have always had it harder in any job," he notes, "but the profession of the Jew in Poland is probably the hardest for a real Jew. . . . How much easier," he speculates, tongue in cheek, "it is to be a professional Jew for someone who is a good Pole and Catholic."[3] Seeing the "real" Jews in Poland still traumatized by the Holocaust and burdened with excessive expectations, he argues that "professional Jews" can be much better at being Jewish.

Halkowski's skeptically humorous concept of "Jews by profession" may be a rhetorical trope, but it brings to the fore an important aspect of what has been termed the "Jewish boom" in Poland. The klezmer scene that emerged in Kraków in the 1990s is probably one of the most striking examples of this non-Jewish involvement in Jewish life. And Henryk Halkowski, a keen observer and critic of the local klezmer microcosm, would have likely considered the non-Jewish klezmer musicians performing in Jewish restaurants "professional Jews" par excellence. To be sure, the epithet is mockingly pejorative, and most klezmer artists would probably find it offensive. Clearly, their job consists in playing Jewish music, not impersonating Jews. And yet klezmer musicians are professionals who make a living from Jewish culture, performing it, often, in lieu of Jews. The role they play has consequences, and this is where Halkowski's category of "Jews by profession" provokes the most interesting questions. Do people who perform Jewish culture in public wish to become Jewish? How does this experience change them? What does their involvement mean to Jews? Even though they might not be Jewish themselves, their engagement with the music of the other gives klezmer revivalists a unique insight into Jewish culture. They play together with Jewish musicians, perform for Jewish audiences, and have Jewish friends. They are even sometimes mistaken for Jews. This proximity to the other not only influences the way they think of their own identity but also has potential for the local Jewish/non-Jewish dialogue. In fact, occupying the position in between Jews and non-Jews, today's klezmer revivalists play a somewhat similar role to that which their historical predecessors held in their local communities.

A Yiddish compound of two Hebrew words: *kley*, meaning a vessel, and *zemer*, meaning a song, klezmer signified initially a musical instrument, later a musician, and finally, also the musical genre. Originally, klezmer was instrumental music of the Yiddish-speaking eastern European Jews, played for private celebrations,

---

[3] Halkowski, *Żydowskie życie*, 152.

religious holidays, and for dancing.[4] Above all, however, klezmer was played at weddings and not necessarily only Jewish ones. Klezmer musicians—the *klezmorim*—together with a wedding jester, called the *badkhn*, were essential for the Jewish wedding ritual both in its spiritual and social dimensions.[5] Their performance generated a feeling of collective identity and had a symbolic status. Accompanying the central events of a Jewish life cycle, the klezmer musician was also "a special kind of Jew."[6] As Freedman notes, klezmer musicians were "liminal characters," "insider/outsiders," and "part of multiple or overlapping social

Fig. 0.1 Klezmer musicians at a Gentile wedding in the village of Lachwa, Poland, 1927. Courtesy of the YIVO Archives.

[4] Walter Z. Feldman, "Remembrance of Things Past: *Klezmer* Musicians of Galicia, 1870–1940," in *Polin: Studies in Polish Jewry*, vol. 16, *Focusing on Jewish Popular Culture in Poland and its Afterlife*, ed. Michael Steinlauf and Antony Polonsky (Oxford: Littman Library of Jewish Civilization, 2003), 29.

[5] More information on the social history of the genre and its recent revival in the United States can be found in: Henry Sapoznik, *Klezmer!* (New York: Schirmer Trade Books, 1999); Susan Bauer, *Von der Khupe zum Klezkamp: Klezmer-Musik in New York* (Berlin: Piranha, 1999); Seth Rogovoy, *The Essential Klezmer* (Chapel Hill, NC: Algonquin, 2000); Mark Slobin, *Fiddler on the Move: Exploring the Klezmer World* (Oxford: Oxford University Press, 2000); Mark Slobin, ed., *American Klezmer: Its Roots and Offshoots* (Berkeley: University of California Press, 2002); Yale Strom, *The Book of Klezmer* (Chicago: A Cappella Books, 2002).

[6] Walter Z. Feldman, "Bulgareasca/Bulgarish/Bulgar: The Transformation of a Klezmer Dance Genre," *Ethnomusicology* 38, no. 1 (1994): 4.

worlds."[7] At times composed of both Jewish and non-Jewish musicians, klezmer bands also often played for Gentiles and incorporated in their repertoire elements of many different eastern European folk genres.[8] Klezmer was, therefore, in many ways a platform of intercultural exchange, a space of ethnic overlapping, both denoting the core of Jewish tradition and marking an openness to external influence. The world of klezmer musicians has always been a world of cultural osmosis. And even though it changed beyond recognition, silenced by the Holocaust to resound in entirely new contexts, it definitely retained some of its original character as a space of encounter, a space in between.

The Return of Music and the Music of Return

"Willingly or unwillingly, Poland will never be able to forget the Jews," wrote Aleksander Hertz, a sociologist of Polish–Jewish relations, in 1988.[9] Soon afterwards, with the upsurge of scholarly interest in Jewish themes, the renovation of synagogues, and the opening of Jewish cultural institutions, his words appeared prophetic. Jewishness returned to claim the collective memory of post-Communist Poland along with popular culture itself. Jewish souvenirs, Jewish food, and Jewish music turned into marketable goods. And the klezmer revival, introducing Jewish music to clubs, discos, and outdoor festivals, became perhaps the most visible symbol of this return.

Around the same time, in the 1980s and '90s, Germany witnessed not only a similar revival of Jewish heritage but also an actual return of Jews. Since 1990, when the East German government allowed entry to Jews from the former Soviet Union (a policy reconfirmed later by the reunified German state), the local Jewish community has been rapidly growing, becoming the third largest Jewish population in Western Europe. The immigration wave, although it posed a great challenge to the Jewish institutions in Germany, gave a new boost and new visibility to Jewish life. And as the Jewish population in Germany started to grow, Germans also discovered a new fascination for Jewish culture.[10]

Klezmer accompanied both comebacks: the return of Polish memory about Jews, and the return of Jews to Germany. Jewish music became a source of inspiration for those seeking traces of the lost Jewish world, and a space where "Jewishness" could be dreamed, reinvented, and performed anew. Secular in nature and not requiring any background knowledge to enjoy it, klezmer appealed to a wide audience

---

[7] Jonathan Freedman, *Klezmer America: Jewishness, Ethnicity, Modernity* (New York: Columbia University Press, 2008), 74.

[8] See, for example: Mark Slobin, "Klezmer," in *Enzyklopädie jüdischer Geschichte und Kultur*, ed. Dan Diner (Stuttgart: J. B. Metzler, 2012), 377; Sapoznik, *Klezmer!* 6–10; Rogovoy, *The Essential Klezmer*, 45–49.

[9] Aleksander Hertz, *The Jews in Polish Culture* (Evaston, IL: Northwestern University Press, 1988), 5.

[10] Peter Laufer, *Exodus to Berlin: The Return of the Jews to Germany* (Chicago: Ivan R. Dee, 2003).

and became a product, which satisfied a wide range of different needs. Given that klezmer was also popular among the Jewish musicians coming to Germany from the former Soviet Union, the genre truly became the soundtrack of the "Jewish boom."

Klezmer as Simulacrum

Following the American klezmer revival of the 1970s and '80s, klezmer became increasingly popular on the world music scene in Europe and around the globe. But while klezmer bands were appearing in such unexpected places as South Africa, Brazil, New Zealand, and China, it was in Germany and Eastern Europe where the klezmer revival roused the most interest, and also the most voices of indignation.[11] As Polish and German audiences turned out in droves at klezmer concerts, with new klezmer bands mushrooming on both sides of the Oder River, many critics began to perceive the klezmer revival in the hands of non-Jews as suspect. Since a significant majority of the creators and consumers of this revival were non-Jewish, and the spaces of klezmer production were also the sites of the Holocaust, the phenomenon provoked a lot of emotions, polemics, and critical writing, which did not refrain from radical formulations such as "Jew Zoo,"[12] "Jewish Disneyland,"[13] or even "cultural necrophilia."[14] Many critics accused klezmer musicians of being impostors; they painted an image of the klezmer scene as an epicenter of cultural theft, where non-Jews not only take over part of Jewish heritage but also aspire to a Jewish identity.[15] The notions of

---

[11] Wiltrud Apfeld, ed., *Klezmer—hejmisch und hip: Musik als kulturelle Ausdrucksform im Wandel der Zeit: Dokumentation zur Ausstellung* (Essen: Klartext, 2004), panel 32.

[12] The filmmaker and Yiddish vocalist Elizabeth Schwartz in Strom, *The Book of Klezmer*, 242.

[13] Iris Weiss, "Jewish Disneyland—the Appropriation and Dispossession of 'Jewishness,'" *Golem: Europäisch-Jüdisches Magazin* (2002), accessed January 13, 2009, http://www.hagalil.com/golem/diaspora/disneyland-e.htm.

[14] Wolf Krakowski, Yiddishe Cup Blog, accessed March 7, 2013, http://www.yiddishecup.com/blog/2009/11/04/over-there/.

[15] Henryk Broder, "Die Konjunktur des Jüdischen an der Schwelle zum 21. Jahrhundert," in *Jüdische Musik? Fremdbilder—Eigenbilder*, ed. Eckhard John and Heidy Zimmermann (Köln: Böhlau, 2004), 368; Michael Birnbaum, "Jewish Music, German Musicians: Cultural Appropriation and the Representation of a Minority in the German Klezmer Scene," *Leo Beck Institute Year Book* 54, no. 1 (2009): 297–320; Rita Ottens, "Die wüste Stadt Berlin: ein Versuch zur Standortbestimmung jiddischer Musik unter den jüdischen Zuwanderern aus der ehemaligen Sowjetunion in Berlin," in *Jüdische Musik und Ihre Musiker im 20. Jahrhundert*, ed. Wolfgang Birtel, Joseph Dorfman, and Christoph-Hellmut Mahling (Mainz: Arc Edition, 2006), 73–132; Rita Ottens, "Der Klezmer als ideologischer Arbeiter," *Neue Zeitschrift für Musik* 159, no. 3 (1998): 26–29; Sylke Tempel, "Alan Bern lehrt die Deutschen das mollige Kuscheln mit Klezmer," *Die Welt*, September 1, 2004, accessed June 20, 2008, http://www.welt.de/print-welt/article337596/Alan_Bern_lehrt_die_Deutschen_das_mollige_Kuscheln_mit_Klezmer.html; Rita Ottens and Joel E. Rubin., "'The Sounds of the Vanishing World': The German Klezmer Movement as a Racial Discourse," accessed December, 14, 2006, http://mki.wisc.edu/Resources/Online_Papers/MusicConfPapers/Ottens-RubinPaper.pdf.

appropriation, authenticity, and legitimacy as well as the memory of World War II and the Holocaust, limned the core of the discourse on non-Jewish klezmer and turned it into an issue, which concerned far more than just music.

One of the most essential questions that the controversy around the klezmer revival in Poland and Germany put into relief concerned, in more universal terms, the status of art originating as an ethnic genre and undergoing cultural appropriation. In particular terms, it is also related to the problem of whether, in post-Holocaust Europe, the borrowing, replication, and consumption of Jewish culture by non-Jews is a morally legitimate endeavor at all. Many scholars commenting on the klezmer revival in places such as Poland and Germany have classified the phenomenon as a simulacrum—a representation, which, within the dichotomy of true/false or real/imaginary, occupies the position of the untrue and unreal. Ruth E. Gruber, for example, identified the klezmer scene as part of "virtual Jewishness," a "parallel universe," which threatens to substitute and eclipse the "authentic" Jewish culture in Europe.[16] Journalists, likewise, frequently decried non-Jewish klezmer as a "simulation,"[17] or a "Potemkin village,"[18] a fake place created with the intention to deceive and mask the truth. Framed in these terms, the klezmer revival has predominantly been seen as misrepresenting the reality.

In his *Simulacra and Simulation*, Jean Baudrillard traces how humans have been growing increasingly suspicious of the power of images, ascribing representations the corruptive capacity to "mask and denature a profound reality" or to "mask the *absence* of a profound reality."[19] This interpretation of simulation as an "evil," distortive force has inspired iconoclasts and continues to determine the discourse of cultural critics today. Thus, many observers of the klezmer revival, especially within the German Jewish community, believe that klezmer "denatures" the image of Jewish heritage, in that it brings to the fore only its folkloristic aspects, neglecting elements of high culture produced by Jews.[20] Other critics fear, too, that klezmer "masks the absence" of Jews. Treated as a token of a vivacious revival of Jewish life, klezmer may actually obfuscate the fact that the local Jewish communities might be small or plagued with serious problems.[21]

Understood as a simulacrum, the klezmer revival is thus seen both as detrimental and as a symptom of more wide-ranging deficiencies in how the German and Polish societies approach their Jewish minority. Connoting "low culture" and

[16] Ruth E. Gruber, *Virtually Jewish: Reinventing Jewish Culture in Europe* (Berkeley: University of California Press, 2002), 50.

[17] Daniel Bax, "Berliner Simulation," *Die Tageszeitung*, November 19, 1999, 15.

[18] Ibid.

[19] Jean Baudrillard, *Simulacra and Simulation* (Ann Arbor: University of Michigan Press, 1999), 6.

[20] Weiss, "Jewish Disneyland."

[21] Sandra Lustig and Ian Leveson, introduction to *Turning the Kaleidoscope: Perspectives on European Jewry*, ed. Sandra Lustig and Ian Leveson (New York: Berghahn Books, 2006), 1–23; Konstanty Gebert, "Nieautentyczność?" introduction to *Odrodzenie kultury żydowskiej w Europie* by Ruth E. Gruber (Sejny: Pogranicze, 2004), 13.

political correctness, "klezmer" has become a metaphor for an excessive interest in Jewish culture gone wrong. Thus, for example, the editor in chief of a major German public TV station warned the German media of clichéd representations of Jewish life, referring to them as "klezmer music and bagel culture."[22] The Jewish journalist Henryk Broder, in turn, in many of his often sarcastic commentaries on current affairs in Germany, used phrases such as "friends of bagels and klezmer music"[23] as a euphemism for philo-Semites who, in his view, cherish Jews "as long as they play klezmer music, eat gefilte fish, and otherwise behave inconspicuously."[24] Listening to klezmer music is also, according to Broder, one of the main characteristics of the German Babbitt, who succumbs to the fashion for Jewish music just as fatuously as he "subscribes to the *Zeit,* without necessarily reading it."[25] These metaphors clearly suggest that "klezmer" has become a synecdoche of oppressive fascination with the other, perhaps even unconscious prejudice.

This rhetorical use of klezmer demonstrates how much the klezmer revival, together with other forms of non-Jewish participation in Jewish culture, has been interpreted as undesirable and illegitimate. Indeed, most of the scholarly debate on the Jewish heritage revival in Germany and in Poland has been dominated by the paradigm of cultural appropriation, which frames phenomena such as non-Jewish klezmer as simulacra and a potential threat to the Jewish community.[26] Scholars adopting this perspective view klezmer within a bipolar system, in which "real" Jewish heritage is understood as made by Jews and for Jews, and simulated Jewishness as produced by non-Jews for non-Jews. Demarcating the realms of authenticity and simulacrum, however, they overlook the fact that the categories that they were taking for granted, such as "Jewish" and "non-Jewish," "authentic" and "inauthentic," are also constructed entities with unstable boundaries. What is more, in the context of the contemporary Jewish heritage boom, these are precisely the categories undergoing the most intensive negotiation and redefinition.

---

[22] Petra Lidschreiber cited in Michael Meyer, "Klezmer und Bagel," *Berliner Zeitung,* June 18, 2001, accessed January 13, 2009, http://www.berlinonline.de/berliner-zeitung/archiv/.bin/dump.fcgi/2001/0618/none/0056/index.html.

[23] Henryk Broder, "Der ewige Gute," *Spiegel,* January 19, 2006, accessed January 14, 2009, http://www.spiegel.de/kultur/kino/0,1518,396116,00.html.

[24] Henryk Broder cited in "Wir sind alle traumatisiert," *tachles: Das jüdische Wochenmagazin,* July 14, 2006, accessed January 13, 2009, http://www.hagalil.com/archiv/2006/07/selbsthass.htm.

[25] Henryk Broder, "Bildungsbürger als Bla-Bla-Blockwarte," *Spiegel,* January 19, 2008, accessed January 13, 2009, http://www.spiegel.de/kultur/gesellschaft/0,1518,529487,00.html.

[26] See, for example: Gruber, *Virtually Jewish*; Rita Ottens and Joel Rubin, *Klezmer-Musik* (München: Bärenreiter, 2003); Birnbaum, "Jewish Music, German Musicians"; Leveson and Lustig, *Turning the Kaleidoscope,* 187–204; Ariane Handrock, "Klischees als Verkaufsschlager: die jüdische Musikszene in Deutschland," in *Music Netz Werke, Konturen der neuen Musikkultur,* ed. Lydia Grün and Frank Wiegand (Bielefeld: Transcript, 2002). One of the few exceptions to this paradigm is Annamaria Orla-Bukowska, "Goje w żydowskim interesie: Wkład etnicznych Polaków w życie polskich Żydów," in *Polacy i Żydzi. Kwestia Otwarta,* ed. Robert Cherry and Annamaria Orla-Bukowska (Warszawa: Więź, 2008), 223–41.

The paradigm of cultural appropriation thus offered static dichotomies to de-scribe a phenomenon in motion. But by concentrating on ascribing legitimacy to the klezmer revival (when performed by Jews), and denying it (especially if staged by non-Jews), the critique of the new klezmer scene in Europe has so far failed to explain the dynamics of encounter, learning, and identification inherent in this cultural phenomenon. Dismissing the non-Jewish klezmer revival as meaning-less, driven by exclusively economic motivations, and detrimental to the "real" Jewish culture, many critics thus have thrown the baby out with the bath water. Disapproving of klezmer as a simulacrum, they have not addressed the question of how the klezmer revival has challenged the very definition of Jewish culture and Jewishness, and how borrowing the art of the other can also breed respect and understanding.

Klezmer as Translation

By contesting the paradigm of appropriation, I am not suggesting the klezmer revival is not a form of cross-ethnic borrowing. Cultural appropriation, however, is a natural process, which takes place at any juncture of cultures. In the case of klezmer, which has always relied on incorporating various folk influences, it was also one that shaped the genre in a decisive way. In fact, it is not an exaggeration to say that klezmer was born of cultural appropriation. What this book proposes, therefore, is an alternative reading of the klezmer revival not as an impoverish-ment of the culture of origin but as a site of cultural translation, which enables new modes of encountering the other and expressing the self.

Understanding the klezmer revival, and the Jewish heritage boom more generally, as a *translation* rather than a *theft* opens up possibilities of seeing cultural appropriation in terms of enrichment and not just deprivation. Still, approximation and at least a partial loss of original meaning are side effects of every appropriation process. Klezmer performed by non-Jews today does not have the same form, significance, or function as klezmer played by Jewish musicians in pre-Holocaust Europe. But instead of interpreting this as a mis-representation of the "original," the klezmer being played today should also be acknowledged as a catalyst of new forms, functions, and meanings, all of which make up the significance of this music in contemporary Polish and German society.

The paradigm of translation, concentrating not on *who* is making use of a cul-tural text but on *how* they are doing it, helps us to understand better what happens in the process of cultural appropriation. First of all, it acknowledges the "transla-tors" as active agents who contribute to the cultural end product, and it brings into relief the fact that cultural appropriation takes place within a condition of intergroup contact. Secondly, it frames cross-cultural borrowing as a procedure of selective and creative adaptation, rather than uncritical and unreflective taking.

One of the ideas that deeply influenced the way this book conceptualizes the klezmer revival was Mary Louise Pratt's concept of a "contact zone."[27] Writing about the way the contact between the colonizers and the colonized enabled new art forms based on creative appropriation, Pratt defined these artistic acts as outcomes of dynamic "contact zones." These spaces of encounter had a dual potential: they were both meeting platforms and sites of violent culture clashes. Pratt's contact zone is one of colonial hegemony, in which a subordinate group creates its own art, selecting and adapting elements of the dominant culture. This process, however, does not entail merely imitation and reproduction but rather reinvention. In the course of absorbing a "borrowed" culture, the other is symbolically "eaten" to nourish a new vernacular art form. The Brazilian modernist Oswald de Andrade, in his 1928 *Manifesto Antropófago*, was probably the first to turn the metaphor of "cultural anthropophagy" into a program.[28] A metaphorical devouring of the other had a concrete function for de Andrade. Writing at the time of the rise of Brazilian nationalism and a collective yearning for a Brazilian vernacular culture, de Andrade paradoxically indicated European heritage as the raw material with which to build the new Brazilian identity. Only by absorbing and digesting the culture of the other, he argued, are we ultimately able to articulate the self. In other words, we need appropriation in order to find our own genuine voice.[29]

Pratt's and de Andrade's visions of turning the culture of the other into a medium for expressing the self are relevant for thinking about today's appropriation of Jewish culture in Poland and Germany, even though they both refer to a historical context so far removed from the klezmer revival. The vector of cultural borrowing in the case of the contemporary non-Jewish klezmer scene is not the same as in the colonial context. It is the ethnic majority, the host society, that adapts elements of a minority heritage here. The process, however, entails similar dynamics. The translation of the Jewish element for Polish and German audiences involves just as much domestication, distortion, and amalgamation as the art emerging in the throes of colonialism and its aftermath. What is more, it also generates an added value and yields a new product, which bears some features of both the source and the target culture but does not really belong to any of them.

However, there is more to the "art of the contact zone" than creative hybridity. As Pratt and de Andrade make clear, appropriation is often directly connected to an identity-building project. The subaltern groups, adopting elements of the dominant culture, seek to express themselves in relation to the hegemonic other.

[27] Mary Louise Pratt, "Arts of the Contact Zone," *Profession* 91 (1991): 34.

[28] Oswald de Andrade, "Cannibalist Manifesto" translated by Leslie Bary, *Latin American Literary Review* 19, no. 38 (1991): 38–47.

[29] Rodica Ilie, "Cultural Anthropophagy: A Poetic Counter-Ideology: Pau Modernism—Futurism's Re-signification," *Caietele Echinox* 14 (2008): 68–78.

An incursion into the cultural territory of the other is here a way of constructing the boundary between "us" and "them." The klezmer revival, located on the fault line between the Jewish and the non-Jewish realms, is not just generating new art, but it is also a space breeding hybrid identities and allowing unconventional patterns of belonging.

This book is the story of people inhabiting this Jewish/non-Jewish contact zone: the "Jews by profession," the Jewish stand-ins, the substitute Jews— klezmer musicians. It is about the voyage into the culture of the other and its sometimes far-reaching consequences for the travelers. Telling the story of one of the most paradoxical musical revivals in recent history, this book is also about narratives of a life in between. Placed at the junction of cultures, klezmer musicians often play the role of middlemen, ambassadors, and commuters across borders. They not only maneuver between different heritages but also exist within the overlapping space between them—not merely translating from one language to another but speaking a creole stemming from both. Indeed, the relation of klezmer professionals to Jewishness often challenges the simplistic dichotomy of Jewish and non-Jewish. The klezmer scene fosters new patterns of Jewish identification, embracing both religious and secular Jews and those who claim to be partially Jewish, temporarily Jewish, conditionally Jewish, or, to paraphrase Barbara Kirshenblatt-Gimblett and Jonathan Karp, "subjunctively Jewish" people.[30]

Based on in-depth interviews with klezmer musicians and cultural organizers promoting klezmer, this book shows the consequences that the so-called "Jewish boom" brings for its non-Jewish participants. Dealing with a very specific case of cultural appropriation, however, it also addresses the broader concern of what happens to people who work creatively in a cultural realm not their own, and how crossing cultural boundaries affects the way individuals come to think of themselves as group members. What this book researches, therefore, is also the possibility that consuming the other, or "cultural anthropophagy," can be an introspective tool for examining the self.

The case of non-Jewish klezmer musicians is also a starting point for investigating how Poles and Germans make sense of their "significant others" via music. Looking at music from the perspective of a cultural historian and sociologist, I am particularly interested in how it offers unique modes of coming to terms with a difficult past. Approaching music as a multitextual cultural product, which signifies not only via sound and notations but also by "visual forms, by the practices and sociality of performance, by social institutions and socioeconomic arrangements [and] by language in different guises,"[31] I see klezmer as a contact zone for

---

[30] Barbara Kirshenblatt-Gimblett and Jonathan Karp, eds., *The Art of Being Jewish in Modern Times* (Philadelphia: University of Pennsylvania Press, 2008), 5.

[31] Georgina Born and David Hesmondhalgh, introduction to *Western Music and Its Others: Difference, Representation, and Appropriation in Music*, ed. Georgina Born and David Hesmondhalgh (Berkeley: University of California Press, 2000), 37.

Jews and non-Jews. It is, therefore, through the prism of encounter that I look at the discourses concerning the klezmer scene and its actual products, examining both the social spaces and representations that it generates.

The story of klezmer in Kraków and Berlin is also part of a larger narrative about the appropriation of Jewish culture in post-Holocaust Europe. Turning the spotlight onto klezmer, which has become the icon of the commercial Jewish heritage boom, might also help us understand the mechanisms behind the return of Jews into the consciousness of Europeans. Many authors have noted the re-surgence of things Jewish, particularly in Germany, heralding "a Jewish renais-sance,"[32] a rise of a "non-Jewish Jewish culture,"[33] or the emergence of a "Jewish Space," where Europeans engage themselves with Jewish culture.[34] Klezmer has, undoubtedly, become a sonic metaphor of this return, which can also serve as a key to comprehending the way this return functions on a micro scale and what the long-term consequences are for those who participate in it.

Jonathan Freedman, in his recent *Klezmer America*, argues that the klezmer re-vival, with its hybridity and revisionism, can serve as a paradigm of cultural criti-cism. For Freedman, klezmer typifies an "antinormative, [and] antigenetic model of cultural reproduction," which draws on the Jewish migratory experience, as-similation, accession to whiteness, and a redefinition of Jewish gendered identity. Considering the art of the klezmer virtuosos in America and their "successors in the klezmer revival," Freedman states that "by its relentless and systematic syn-cretism," their work "challenges simple, reductive predications of national, ethnic, racial, or religious identity across the board (including but not limited to Jewish identity) even or especially because it composes itself out of their raw material."[35] In other words, klezmer stands for a mode of self-expression, which feeds itself on the "raw material" of Jewish culture to transform it in ways that question es-sentialist categories of collective belonging.

This book argues that klezmer serves as such an "antinormative model of cul-tural reproduction" not only on the New Continent, where it is deeply rooted within the Jewish community, but also in Europe, where many of its artists are non-Jewish. The klezmer scene in Poland and Germany offers challenges to the ways we think of Jewish culture or Jewish identity, even though it might do it in different ways than its counterpart in the United States. While migration and the diasporic experience of Jews in America defined the klezmer movement across the ocean, the key aspects feeding into the klezmer scene in Germany and Poland

---

[32] Y. Michal Bodemann, *Gedächtnistheater: die jüdische Gemeinschaft und ihre deutsche Erfindung* (Hamburg: Rotbuch Verlag, 1996), 42.

[33] Michael Brenner, "The Transformation of the German-Jewish Community," in *Unlikely History: The Changing German-Jewish Symbiosis 1945–2000*, ed. Leslie Morris and Jack Zipes (New York: Palgrave, 2002), 54.

[34] Diana Pinto, "The Third Pillar? Toward a European Jewish Identity," 1999, accessed June 2, 2006, http://www.ceu.hu/jewishstudies/pdf/01_pinto.pdf.

[35] Freedman, *Klezmer America*, 93.

are "encounter," "adaptation" and, to borrow a term from Eric Lott, "ventriloquial self-expression through the art forms of someone else's."[36]

Unlike many of the critics of the klezmer revival who have concentrated mostly on the material aspects of appropriation (cultural products that change hands), I prefer to frame the revival as a space of interaction, which enables Jews and non-Jews to engage in particular modes of mediation, including critique, cooperation, and what I call "standing-in." The klezmer scene is a contact zone where Jews and non-Jews enter into conversation about the painful Polish Jewish or German Jewish past, exchange ideas, and work together, but also challenge each other, compete, and articulate their (sometimes conflicting) interests.

Nonetheless, this present book is also about the new "translated" art that they produce. The klezmer revival does not merely resuscitate a historic genre; it adapts it, filtering it through the sensitivities of Polish and German audiences. As a result, the revival generates a vernacular musical language, which follows a new cultural grammar and fulfills new social functions. It is not a simulacrum of the old but a new idiom to express the demands of the present.

Finally, klezmer is a site, which inspires alternative ways of living Jewish identities. As a realm of secular Jewish culture, the klezmer scene attracts people who identify themselves with Jewishness in various, often unorthodox, ways. But the experience of participating in Jewish culture leaves marks on non-Jews as well, and klezmer music has the potential of becoming their medium of self-expression. I argue, therefore, that klezmer, allowing negotiation and contestation of cultural boundaries, has become a realm of shifting categories and risky identity quests, where the very borders of Jewish culture are being constantly defined, questioned, and redrawn.

The anthropophagic framework, adopted as a lens for looking at klezmer, also offers a more holistic approach to cultural appropriation, regarding it simultaneously as a site of artistic creativity, interpersonal dialogue, and consumption. The commodification of klezmer has been one of the main concerns of critics who view the klezmer revival as a source of profit for the tourist industry. But while the economic aspect of the klezmer boom is an important question, the phenomenon should not be reduced merely to consumption, as even economically motivated interest in Jewish heritage does not exclude the possibility that klezmer revivalists identify in meaningful ways with the genre they appropriate and market. Thus, the advantage of using the paradigm of cultural anthropophagy is that it frames cultural borrowing as a unique condition for intercultural dialogue and a legitimate mode of producing new art while it also focuses the lens on instrumentalization and exploitation.

It is the comparative dimension of this book, however, that best puts into relief the fact that cultural appropriation has the potential of enabling interethnic

---

[36] Eric Lott, *Love and Theft: Blackface Minstrelsy, and the American Working Class* (New York: Oxford University Press, 1993), 92.

encounters within one society and across borders. The story of the klezmer revival in Poland and Germany is also the story of how heritage music helps us visualize both the internal and the external other. The comparison between the two countries is interesting for several reasons. Both in Poland and Germany, where klezmer has reached widespread popularity, the revival of Jewish heritage is viewed with particular interest and, sometimes, distrust. Poland and Germany are places meaningful for Jews and for each other. Just as Poles often frame their relationship with Jews by relating to Germans as the perpetrators of the Holocaust, Germans closely follow reports of anti-Semitism in Poland, viewing with a critical eye the engagement of Poles in wartime anti-Jewish violence.

The two places that this book takes us to, Kraków and Berlin, have become the centers of the European klezmer revival. Both cities are important for Jewish history and Jewish art, and are highly symbolic for the Polish and the German national narratives. Kraków and Berlin may differ in size and importance; they have different ethnic and religious composition, and the dynamics of the local Jewish life is hardly comparable. And yet, in the last twenty years, these two very different cities have become not only the two most important strongholds of klezmer on the Old Continent but also crucial destinations of Holocaust tourism. Kraków, as the former seat of the Polish monarchy, and Berlin, as the city whose division and reunification epitomized the history of post-1945 Germany, might be unique for their heritage and not necessarily representative of the whole of Poland or Germany. Still, with their local efforts to pay tribute to the Jewish past, they have provided national models of preserving and memorializing Jewish heritage. Berlin is the central Holocaust commemoration site in Germany, and home to the biggest and most dynamic Jewish community in the country. It is not surprising, therefore, that the local klezmer revival has been concerned both with the troubled past of Jews and Germans and with hopes for a new Jewish future. In Kraków, with its vicinity to Auschwitz and an intact historic Jewish Old Town, klezmer has been a medium between the past and the present, but, more than anywhere else, entangled in the wheels of the Jewish heritage industry. With their specific local character, Kraków and Berlin are also exponents of a larger international klezmer network and two of its crucial junctures, generating creative impulses for the European klezmer scene and beyond. Understanding how klezmer has conquered Kraków and Berlin is therefore also a key to comprehending the mystery of klezmer's return to Europe.

Because the question of how the music of ethnic others becomes significant for those who appropriate it is central for this book, interviews with klezmer musicians from Kraków and Berlin constitute its most important raw material. Between 2004 and 2008, I conducted over eighty in-depth, guided interviews with musicians, cultural organizers promoting klezmer, and representatives of the local Jewish communities. During my fieldwork, I was periodically living in Berlin and visiting Kraków for a series of shorter research stays, documenting the development of the local klezmer scenes, attending concerts, workshops, informal jam sessions, and various events that featured klezmer, from theater productions to Holocaust commemoration events.

My conversations often directly followed these performances and were commentaries on the events I had the privilege of witnessing. I reached virtually all of the klezmer ensembles performing in Kraków at the time of my research and a large number of those working in Berlin. The interviews took place in three different languages: English, Polish, and German. Translations of the transcripts are all mine. I arranged most of the interviews with one interviewee at a time, but when that was not possible, I also met with an entire band at the same time. I met five of the respondents (or groups of respondents) more than once over the course of my research.

Apart from the interviews recorded in Kraków and Berlin, I additionally interviewed several American klezmer musicians at the KlezKanada festival near Montreal. Most of my interviewees from Kraków and Berlin were Poles or Germans, but I also interviewed a few American and Ukrainian musicians who were living and/or performing in Berlin and Kraków. The principle that I followed in selecting my interviewees was to reach as large a group of performers as possible, embracing both Jews and non-Jews, professional and amateur musicians, those who earned their living from klezmer, and those who performed it only as a hobby. Apart from musicians, I talked to producers, organizers of Jewish festivals, and members of Jewish cultural institutions who were, in one way or another, dealing with klezmer music. The artists and cultural organizers that I portray in the book are usually quoted with their full names when speaking of their ensembles and creative endeavors. The exceptions are chapters 6 and 7, and several passages in chapters 2 and 4, which address the more sensitive issues of how my interviewees identify themselves vis-à-vis Jewishness. As their narratives in this part of the book mostly concern their private lives, their names are not disclosed.

I began to explore behind the scenes of the klezmer revival in 2004, but it was not the first time that I had been exposed to this music. Living in Kraków between 1999 and 2003, some of this time in Kazimierz itself, I had the privilege to witness firsthand the rapid changes that the Jewish district was undergoing. As the Jewish quarter, which at that time was still partly a desolate working-class neighborhood, began to attract a steadily increasing number of tourists and face unavoidable gentrification, the klezmer scene turned into a crucible focalizing different, sometimes conflicting, interests, desires, and demands. Klezmer in Kraków, crowning the biggest annual Jewish festival in Europe and defining the soundscape of the historic Jewish quarter for the rest of the year, became for many Poles and foreigners alike the most attractive and accessible way of approaching Jewish heritage. The potential of the klezmer scene as a gateway to the culture of the other fascinated me both as a sociologist and as a Pole who, like many of my compatriots at that time, was only beginning to discover the importance of Jewish culture for Polish history as well as the extent of the Polish complicity in anti-Jewish violence.

Trying to understand the klezmer scene as a cultural space where non-Jews co-create and co-perform Jewish culture, and investigating into the consequences that such an involvement has for non-Jews, I found myself in a position very similar to that which I was researching. Teaching and writing about Jewish history and Jewish heritage, I was confronted with many of the issues that I saw my interviewees struggling with. I strongly believe, therefore, that the position of Polish and German klezmer musicians is also the position of many more "Jews by profession" who, despite being non-Jewish, find themselves in situations in which they perform, impart, and present Jewish culture to others, act as intermediaries between Jews and non-Jews, and venture into a space "in between," where, while approaching the other, they actually have to confront the self.

Organization of the Book

Chapters 1 and 2 set the scene, giving an idea of how the Polish and German klezmer scenes have developed and been perceived by critics. Chapter 1 offers a general introduction to the traditions of klezmer music in Kraków and Berlin, placing the recent Jewish heritage boom in a historical context. Chapter 2 introduces the polyphonic debate on the klezmer revival in Poland and Germany, providing a synthesis of the discussions about the legitimacy of the non-Jewish klezmer revival. It also presents in more detail what I have called here the paradigm of appropriation, pinpointing the most important arguments of writers, journalists, and members of the Jewish community who have been skeptical of the non-Jewish appropriation of Jewish heritage. But, while giving voice to the opponents of the klezmer scene, it also presents the responses of klezmer musicians who counter the accusations and narrate their own part of the story.

If chapter 2 presents the current state of the debate and shows how the klezmer revival has been framed as cultural theft threatening the development of "authentic" Jewish culture, chapter 3 offers a counterparadigm, shifting attention to aspects of the klezmer phenomenon that have been so far neglected by scholars and critics alike. This chapter develops the claim that klezmer, as an easily accessible and enjoyable medium, is one of the most intensive contact zones in Europe, opening a space where Jews and non-Jews have the chance to meet, discuss, and create art together. This section of the book illustrates the modes of what I will call "meeting" and "eating" the other—the exchange and negotiation that includes, apart from learning and communication, also consumption and commercialization. Chapter 3 concentrates on this dual nature of the klezmer revival by investigating the relations between the klezmer scene and local Jewish communities, the connections within the transnational klezmer networks, and the interaction of Jewish and non-Jewish musicians in the scene, viewing these within the context of the commercial success of klezmer.

The remaining chapters present the outcomes of these klezmer encounters. Chapter 4 gives us an overview of the images of Jews that populate the klezmer scene. However, revisiting the most persistent clichés about Jews that the klezmer scene recycles, it also describes the novel ways in which klezmer artists strive to challenge them. Cataloging images and discourses that surround the musical production of the klezmer scene, this section analyzes the strategies of cultural translation that musicians and their managers apply in order to adapt a historic Jewish genre to the needs of its new consumers. It maps out the new language of klezmer that, drawing on its historic sources, melds elements of Jewish heritage with other ethnic legacies. Showing the heterogeneous end product of this creative process of "digesting" the culture of the other, it also demonstrates how the klezmer scene aims to meet the demands of the contemporary world music market and heritage tourism. Chapter 5 shows how klezmer has become instrumentalized and politicized in Poland and Germany, both as a soundtrack to Holocaust commemoration events and a symbol of successful politics of multiculturalism.

But by describing the ways klezmer revivalists remodel Jewish music into a new form of art that has become meaningful to Polish and German society in sometimes unexpected ways, this book also sets out to investigate what the music means to those who make it. Non-Jewish klezmer musicians, whose involvement with Jewish heritage is especially intensive and often long-term, face particular challenges to their identity as Poles or Germans. Scrutinized and often criticized by their Jewish audiences and critics, they seek ways in which they can frame their contribution to the klezmer scene as legitimate. Chapter 6 speaks about the challenge that playing the music of the other poses to the identity of non-Jewish klezmer musicians, presenting their often intimate accounts of how they have come to terms with the dark chapters of the German and Polish past. Chapter 7, in turn, by applying theories of social identity, addresses the question of what kind of identity processes take place in the situation of cultural appropriation, looking at how non-Jewish musicians define themselves vis-à-vis Jewish heritage that they perform.

This book is not a history of the klezmer revival. Instead, it tells the story of how a music revival can become a site of difficult debates on troubled intergroup relations in the aftermath of the Holocaust. Drawing on critical theories from sociology, cultural studies, anthropology, and ethnomusicology, this book offers an interdisciplinary perspective on an example of heritage appropriation, which has had far-reaching implications for the way many Poles and Germans have come to recall their past and imagine their future as multi-ethnic societies. It is a book about how music has become the language with which to speak about a difficult past. It is also a book about individuals who, by confronting the legacy of the other, find ways to rethink their own heritage.

1

The Genealogies

Klezmer Music and Its Traditions in Kraków and Berlin

As a small boy, Frederic Chopin spent his summers in the Polish countryside at the manor of the Dziewanowski family in Szafarnia. It was there that one summer, as the anecdote goes, the young prodigy gave an improvised concert for a group of Jewish corn traders who had come on business from a neighboring town. The medley of wedding dances that he played is said to have been so rousing that the flabbergasted Jews could not resist dancing and, complimenting Chopin by saying that he played like a "born Jew," invited him to perform at a Jewish wedding in a nearby village. Although the musicologist Józef Reiss, who recounts this story, never mentions whether the composer accepted the invitation, evidently klezmer must have been in the air of that nineteenth-century Polish countryside, as Chopin's later *Mazurka a-moll*, also known as "Żydek" ("Little Jew"), is clearly inspired by Jewish dances.[1]

The story of Chopin playing in the Jewish idiom should not be surprising. Poland was for many centuries a home to klezmer music, which left a firm mark on the Polish musical tradition. Jewish instrumental music arrived in Poland with the first Jewish settlers. The first known use of the word "klezmer" occurs in a document of the Jewish community in Kraków dating from 1595.[2] *Klezmorim* played not only for Jewish and non-Jewish weddings but also at inns, markets, and sometimes in the houses of nobility.

Many genres of Jewish music came into being and developed in Polish lands. Poland, considered the birthplace of cantorial music, was home to many excellent cantors who influenced the art of synagogal singing in Europe and beyond. It was also an important center of Yiddish theater, which created its own musical forms accompanying, for example, the *Purim-spiln*, or popular folk plays performed for

[1] Józef Reiss, "Dusza żydostwa w muzyce," *Muzyk wojskowy,* July 1, 1928, 2; Marian Fuks, *Muzyka ocalona: Judaica polskie* (Warszawa: Wydawnictwa Radia i Telewizji, 1989), 23–34.

[2] Feldman, "Remembrance of Things Past," 29.

the holiday of Purim.[3] The Ashkenazi Jews, who started arriving in Poland from German-speaking lands in the second half of the twelfth century, also created a large repertoire of folk songs. Yiddish songs written and composed in Polish lands included love songs, lullabies, and humorous pieces commenting on Jewish everyday life, as well as more politically charged Jewish workers' and revolutionary songs, or songs about war and being a soldier. The Hasidic communities, the followers of the great Ba'al Shem Tov (ca. 1700–1760), also created their own music. The Hasidim, a Jewish sect that believes music is heavenly inspired and provides a unique mode of prayer, composed the *nigunim*, wordless songs, performed collectively *a cappella* as a form of ecstatic prayer, often accompanied by dancing.[4] Their holy songs, usually composed by the *tzadikim*, or the Hasidic spiritual leaders, were believed to be able to "purify the fallen soul, heal the sick, and perform all sorts of miracles."[5] Hasidic courts, such as the ones in Sadogóra or Bobowa in Galicia, would often employ their own klezmer ensembles, which played for their gatherings.

Musical genres developed by Jews, although they had different functions and were often bound to specific ritual or social contexts, influenced each other and drew from other folk traditions. Klezmer has been, in this respect, a particularly receptive genre. An instrumental music most commonly performed at weddings, klezmer had the crucial function as the "organizer" of the whole Jewish wedding ceremony.[6] Klezmer *kapelyes*, usually made up of three to five members, would accompany both the nuptials and the pre-wedding preparations, which could extend over many days. The basic repertoire of klezmer musicians included dance music and music for listening, which accompanied various wedding rituals such as greeting the guests, the "seating" of the bride, and the street procession.[7] The *klezmorim* were usually accompanied by a *badkhn*, a performer who improvised special wedding verses, told jokes, and sang songs of a moralistic character.[8]

The ensemble was hired first for an engagement party and would then play for the family during the four months preceding the wedding. Seven days before the wedding, when the bride and groom were not supposed to leave their houses, the *klezmorim* would play at their homes each night. They would also accompany

---

[3] In the seminal five-volume "Jewish Musical Folklore" by Moshe Beregovski (1892–1961), the major enthnomusicologist of Eastern European Jewish music in the Soviet Union, Jewish folk music is divided into five major fields: (1) workers' and revolutionary songs, (2) love and family songs, (3) klezmer, (4) textless songs, and (5) music for the *Purimspil*.

[4] Some of the *nigunim* do have lyrics in Hebrew, Yiddish, or other languages such as Ukrainian. It is the wordless melodies, however, that are given the greatest significance in the Hasidic tradition.

[5] Abraham Z. Idelsohn, *Jewish Music in Its Historical Development* (New York: Schocken Books, 1967), 414.

[6] Moshe Beregovski, *Old Jewish Folk Music: The Collections and Writings of Moshe Beregovski*, trans. and ed. Mark Slobin (Philadelphia: University of Pennsylvania Press, 1982), 301.

[7] Moshe Beregovski, *Jewish Instrumental Folk Music: The Collections and Writings of Moshe Beregovski* (Syracuse. NY: Syracuse University Press, 2001), 8.

[8] Ibid., 12.

a special meal in honor of the groom before the wedding and the bride's visit to the *mikveh* (ritual bath).[9] Music was, in fact, especially important for the r᷉u᷉als involving the bride. The *kale bazetsn*, (seating of the bride) was a part of ᷉he wedding when female guests gathered around the bride and cut her long hair. The women were accompanied by the band and the *badkhn*, who recited melancholy couplets about the difficulties and pain awaiting the bride in married life. This first part of the ceremony, called in Yiddish *kale baveynen*, (crying with the bride) is meant to bring the woman and her guests to tears. Soon after this highly emotional moment, the musicians swiftly move to the more joyful *bazingen*, or "singing for the bride," with a set of tunes and recitations by the badkhn, which extol the happiness awaiting the newlyweds.[10] Later, the musicians would lead the couple to the *khupe*, the wedding canopy where the actual wedding ceremony took place, and then perform at the ensuing banquet.[11]

The klezmer "core repertoire," as identified by musicologist Walter Z. Feldman, embraced tunes composed by the *klezmorim* themselves and performed only for Jewish wedding ceremonies.[12] An obligatory number on their playlist was the *freylakh*, considered to be *the* Jewish folk dance par excellence and, as such, readily adopted into Moldavian and Ukrainian folk music. The *klezmorim* had more to offer than just dance music, though. Their repertoire also included nondance wedding melodies as well as paraliturgical pieces for such Jewish holidays as Hanukkah and Purim. Klezmer was therefore a multifunctional music, which drew inspiration from many sources. It incorporated not only the Hasidic nigunim, transformed in the klezmer repertoire into the *khosidl* dance[13] or Yiddish folk songs, but it was also influenced by the folk traditions of other eastern European ethnic groups. A part of their repertoire had what Feldman identified as an "Orientalizing" character. In particular, dances such as the hora, sirba, and bulgarish drew on the music of Gypsies from Moldova, the Balkans, and the Crimea. The *klezmorim* were also familiar with "co-territorial" genres such as the Polish mazurka or Ruthenian kolomeyka, and even the "cosmopolitan" repertoire of western and central European dances, such as the quadrille, polka, and waltz.[14]

Even though musicologists admit that it is not possible to individuate the klezmer style as a genre entirely distinct from other musical folk traditions of eastern Europe,[15] they point out several specific characteristics, which give the klezmer

[9] Strom, *The Book of Klezmer*, 86–87.

[10] Ibid., 28; Beregovski, *Jewish Instrumental Folk Music*, 11–12.

[11] Strom, *The Book of Klezmer*, 29.

[12] Feldman, "Bulgareasca/Bulgarish/Bulgar," 3.

[13] Slobin, *Fiddler on the Move*, 102.

[14] Feldman, "Bulgareasca/Bulgarish/Bulgar," 7–10. Details on the particular klezmer dances are given by Strom, *The Book of Klezmer*, 55–58 and 61–66; Beregovski, *Jewish Instrumental Folk Music*, 10–11.

[15] Joel Rubin and Rita Ottens, "Klezmer-Forschung in Osteuropa: damals und heute," in *Juden und Antisemitismus in östlichen Europa*, ed. Mariana Hausleitner and Monika Katz (Berlin: Harassovitz Verlag, 1995), 184–85.

repertoire that unmistakable Jewish inflection. Mark Slobin suggests that it is the ornamentation, or, as he puts it, the musical "diacritical marks" that make for the Jewishness in a repertoire marked by extensive borrowing.[16] Klezmer-specific "diacritical marks" include techniques that imitate the capacities of the human voice: *krekhtsn* (Yid: groans, moans), an ornament which resembles a guttural stop; *kneytshn* (Yid: fold, wrinkle), which produces sharply swallowed notes; or *tshoks* (Yid: lavishness, splendor), which emulates laughter.[17] These ornaments, also known as *dreydlekh*, are more than mere embellishments. Inspired by the Jewish vocal traditions of cantorial singing and Torah cantillation, they constitute the very structure of klezmer music, testifying to the Judaic tradition of relating ritual texts to music.[18] Even the musical scales characteristic for klezmer bear the Hebrew names of Shabbath prayers, which are traditionally accompanied by melodies in those scales. And thus the most popular klezmer mode, the altered Phrygian, known in the world of *klezmorim* as *freygish*, is also referred to as *Ahava-Raba* (Heb: a great love), and the altered Dorian scale is also known as *Mishebeyrakh* (Heb: he who blesses).[19] Both scales were, along with the natural minor, the most common modes of klezmer tunes and determined what Yale Strom calls the "distinct Semitic sound" of the genre.[20] The *freygish* scale (E–F–G#–A–B–C–D#–E), common also in Egypt, Asia Minor, and the Balkans, constitutes the basis of a quarter of all klezmer instrumental tunes.[21] The *Mishebeyrakh* (D–E–F–G#–A–Bb–C#–D), in turn, widespread in Ukrainian, Moldavian and Romanian folk music, is more unevenly represented but also prominent in klezmer melodies.[22]

Klezmer's affinity with vocal music does not end with the scales that the genre inherited from synagogal singing. The cimbalom and the violin, traditional klezmer instruments, have often been seen as extensions of the human voice. String instruments, which until the nineteenth century constituted the main klezmer instrumentation, were believed to be able to affect the listener in a particularly emotional way. In literary accounts, the klezmer fiddle was often anthropomorphized as "speaking" or "crying."[23] The most famous klezmer musician in Yiddish literature, Sholem Aleichem's Stempenju, a klezmer virtuoso and womanizer, was a violinist who could make his fiddle "talk, dispute and sing" like a living person.[24] The Jewish cymbalist Jankiel, a protagonist of the Polish national epic poem "Pan Tadeusz" (1834) by Adam Mickiewicz, brought his spectators to tears with his cimbalom, which could even emulate sounds of battle. Although

---

[16] Slobin, *Fiddler on the Move*, 106.
[17] Strom, *The Book of Klezmer*, 120–21.
[18] Slobin, *Fiddler on the Move*, 106.
[19] Strom, *The Book of Klezmer*, 122.
[20] Ibid.
[21] Beregovski, *Jewish Instrumental Folk Music*, 17; Idelsohn, *Jewish Music*, 84–89.
[22] Ibid.; and Beregovski, *Old Jewish Folk Music*, 564.
[23] Beregovski, *Jewish Instrumental Folk Music*, 20–21.
[24] Scholem Alejchem, *Stempenju* (Leipzig: Reclam, 1989), 10.

in the 1800s klezmer musicians took up many new instruments, and by the end of the century a typical klezmer ensemble encompassed, in addition to string instruments, also the clarinet, flute, cornet, trombone, and Turkish drum with cymbals,[25] the most spectacular klezmer career of all times was still reserved to a cymbalist.

Josef Michal Guzikow (1806–37), a virtuoso of the straw fiddle (a xylophone of his own construction), is acclaimed today as "the grandfather of the modern performing klezmer."[26] Born in 1806 in Shklov (present-day Belarus), he made a truly international career performing both klezmer tunes and contemporary opera pieces. In the 1830s, he traveled to Kraków and Berlin, among other places, and enchanted with his playing even George Sand and Felix Mendelssohn.[27] His charismatic appearance and untimely death during a concert in Aachen, with his cimbalom in his hands, led to his personification as the mythical itinerant klezmer who could captivate his listeners regardless of their ethnic or social background.

The charisma of klezmer musicians, not just of stars such as Guzikow, was related to the special position that the *klezmorim* held in the Jewish community. The klezmer was a broker of emotions and a crucial participant in the central events of the Jewish life cycle. Belonging to the lower social ranks and often considered as licentious and corrupt, he—the klezmer profession was, in general, exclusively male—was also "a special kind of Jew."[28] The *klezmorim* formed castelike family structures and passed the profession on from father to son. Organized in guilds, they made up a specific and autonomous social group, which enjoyed considerable social liberty, if little prestige. The klezmer musicians had the reputation of being "irresponsible, sexually active, and violent." Accompanying the wedding ritual, they came to be associated with the element of sexual taboo and were often perceived as "outsiders to the mores and gender identities of the community."[29] The impenetrability of their group was secured by their own argot, the *klezmer loshn* (Yid: language). This klezmer slang, "filled with sarcasm, disdain, humor, and sexual innuendo,"[30] as Strom puts it, allowed the musicians to communicate in secret about their business and to comment on the women present.

Although the historians of Jewish music mention women active in klezmer bands in the Middle Ages, for a long time their public presence as professional musicians was restricted.[31] Salmen reports that women musicians were usually excluded from musicians' guilds, and their performances were sometimes

---

[25] Beregovski, *Jewish Instrumental Folk Music*, 29–30.

[26] Sapoznik, *Klezmer!* 1.

[27] Fuks, *Muzyka ocalona*, 40–42.

[28] Feldman, "Bulgareasca/Bulgarish/Bulgar," 4.

[29] Freedman, *Klezmer America*, 76.

[30] Strom, *The Book of Klezmer*, 96.

[31] Idelsohn, *Jewish Music*, 456.

prohibited by religious and municipal authorities.[32] Banning the female voice from liturgical services in the early Christian era had a long-lasting effect on the status of music produced by Jewish women.[33] Even today, in strictly Orthodox Jewish communities, women are not allowed to sing in front of men other than their relatives.[34] Female musicians gained acceptance at the time of the Jewish Enlightenment; only later, with the rise of the Yiddish theater, did real career possibilities open up for female singers and instrumentalists.[35]

Although Strom mentions itinerant female musicians performing together with Jewish entertainers across the German lands in the seventeenth and eighteenth centuries, and Sapoznik quotes an example of a klezmer from Volhyn who, in the late nineteenth century, was teaching his daughters and nieces to play various instruments, both authors add that the practice was uncommon.[36] Ottens and Rubin point out that even musically educated Jewish women were not expected to perform professionally.[37] Women trained as klezmer musicians were still a rarity in the late nineteenth century. Only folk songs, which gained popularity particularly in the nineteenth century, became a musical niche for them. Sung *a cappella*, mostly in Yiddish, these songs accompanied various household chores performed by women.[38] Several decades later, though, the klezmer daughters began to form their first klezmer bands. The *froyen kapelyes*, women's ensembles, which appeared in Lvov at the beginning of the twentieth century, were considered as "one of the most striking innovations in the Jewish musical life."[39] Nevertheless, female musicians functioned within a separate circuit and played mostly in restaurants, while Jewish life-cycle celebrations were still the exclusive domain of their fathers and brothers.

The klezmer traditions in eastern Europe, still widespread in the nineteenth century, did not survive intact until the Holocaust. As Russian pogroms against the Jews during World War I triggered a massive emigration wave, klezmer bands in Galicia had already begun to disintegrate. The radio dealt the final blow. There are still records of klezmer bands being active in eastern Galicia, in Lvov and Przemyśl, and also south of Kraków, in Nowy Sącz, at the beginning of the twentieth century, but it was by then a dying tradition.[40] Klezmer made it onto the first Polish phonograph recordings but was much less popular than Yiddish songs

[32] Walter Salmen, " . . . *denn die Fiedel macht das Fest:" Jüdische Musikanten und Tänzer vom 13. bis 20. Jahrhundert* (Innsbruck: Helbling, 1991), 36.

[33] Irene Heskes, "Miriam's Sisters: Jewish Women and Liturgical Music," *Notes* 48, no. 4 (1992): 1196.

[34] Abigail Wood, "The Multiple Voices of American Klezmer," *Journal of the Society for American Music* 1, no. 3 (2007): 383.

[35] Heskes, "Miriam's Sisters: Jewish Women and Liturgical Music," 1200.

[36] Sapoznik, *Klezmer!*, 24; Strom, *The Book of Klezmer*, 9, 17, and 37.

[37] Ottens and Rubin, *Klezmer-Musik*, 136–37.

[38] Ibid., 79.

[39] Feldman, "Remembrance of Things Past," 33.

[40] Strom, *The Book of Klezmer*, 294–95.

or cantorial music.[41] After the war, the world of traditional klezmer bands slowly came to an end.[42]

In the period directly preceding the Holocaust, however, the Yiddish song was still a lively tradition in Poland.[43] Yard players would perform in the streets of the Jewish districts, singing in Yiddish or Polish.[44] Klezmer musicians still played for Purim festivities and for weddings, following the current musical fashion and also performing tangos and foxtrots.[45] The Kraków Yiddish Theater, based in Kazimierz, also drew on the popular traditions, staging Yiddish musicals and operettas and, occasionally, evenings of Yiddish folk songs.[46] Jewish musicians were also active in popular Cracovian jazz bands such as Banda, Szał, and The Jolly Boys. Playing in nightclubs for a mixed audience, musicians such as Zdzisław Gotlib, Stanisław Landau, Henryk Sperber, and Henryk Rosner with his Krakowska Orkiestra Salonowa were, in a certain sense, the heirs of the local klezmer tradition that was then finding modern forms of expression.[47]

Meanwhile, east of Kraków, traditional Jewish instrumental music was still in the repertoire of the local musicians. Lesław Lic, one of the Kraków-based klezmer musicians of the older generation, remembers *klezmorim* as an integral part of the cultural life in prewar Przemyśl, his hometown:

> On Sunday afternoons we had the custom of going out to listen to some music. The music was played by a klezmer band, who performed at the castle. . . . I was maybe four or five years old at that time. The tradition ended, however, when the radio became more widespread. That was the end of that kind of music.[48]

The real blow to the Jewish musicians came with the onset of World War II. The last in the line of the prewar Jewish folk musicians in Kraków was Mordechai

---

[41] Michael Aylward, "Early Recordings of Jewish Music in Poland" in Steinlauf and Polonsky, *Polin*, vol. 16, *Focusing on Jewish Popular Culture*, 59–69.

[42] Walter Salmen, "The Post-1945 Klezmer Revival," in *Yiddish in the Contemporary World: Papers of the First Mendel Friedman International Conference on Yiddish*, ed. Gennady Estraikh and Mikhail Krutikov (Oxford: Legenda, 1999), 110.

[43] Isaschar Fater and Ewa Świderska, *Muzyka żydowska w Polsce w okresie międzywojennym* (Warszawa: Oficyna Wydawnicza, 1997), 12.

[44] Fuks, *Muzyka ocalona*, 31.

[45] Anis D. Pordes and Irek Grin, *Ich miasto: Wspomnienia Izraelczyków, przedwojennych mieszkańców Krakowa* (Warszawa, Prószyński i Spółka, 2004), 17 and 125.

[46] Mirosława M. Bułat, *Krakowski teatr żydowski: między szundem a sztuką* (Kraków: Wydawnictwo Uniwersytetu Jagiellońskiego, 2006).

[47] Biographic notes of these musicians can be found in: Fater and Świderska, *Muzyka żydowska w Polsce*, 260, 279, 301; and in Hankus Netzky, "Three Twentieth-Century Jewish Musicians from Poland: Frydman, Rosner, and Bazyler," *Polish Music Journal* 6, no. 1 (2003), accessed October 23, 2012, http://www.usc.edu/dept/polish_music/PMJ/issue/6.1.03/Netsky.html.

[48] Lesław Lic, interview by the author, Kraków, July 11, 2006.

Gebirtig [Markus Bertig] (1877–1942), a carpenter and songwriter who died in the Kraków ghetto but whose songs entered the world canon of Yiddish music.[49] Gebirtig, who was involved in a Jewish amateur theater group and also in Bundist circles, wrote socially engaged, pacifist songs, which became world-renowned after a star of American Yiddish cinema, Molly Picon, included them in her repertoire.[50] He remains today one of the most popular authors on the scene of Yiddish heritage music and an icon of Jewish socialism, subversive cabaret, and the musical traditions of Jewish proletarian Kraków. Even though Jewish music was still performed in the Kraków ghetto, the Holocaust took its toll on Yiddish-speaking artists. The Yiddish singer Iza Wexler, as well as Mordechai Gebirtig's daughter, Lola, and the members of the Rosner-Reich Brothers Orchestra were among the most prominent Cracovian Jewish musicians murdered in the Holocaust.[51]

As soon as the war was over, the surviving Jewish musicians were in high demand again. "Jews were coming out of their hideouts," recollects Lesław Lic, "There were quite a lot of them in Przemyśl. A lot of these people were getting married at that time to leave to Israel already as a married couple, so there were a lot of Jewish weddings. And I played at them with both Jewish and non-Jewish musicians."[52] The postwar entertainment scene not only relied on Jewish musicians but also drew inspiration from Jewish music. *Klezmerzy*, as they were called in Polish, would perform for dance parties in the cinemas and cafés with an entirely new and contemporary repertoire. Many of the pieces they played were Polish versions of popular Yiddish songs, but their origins, with time, became entirely forgotten. Recordings of Yiddish songs were still appearing in post-1945 Poland, among them Abraham Samuel Rettig's *Z albumu pieśni żydowskich* (1964) with Polish versions of Yiddish folk songs, and Gołda Tencer's entirely Yiddish *Miasteczko Bełz* (1988). At the same time, Jewish songwriters and composers produced many hits of postwar Polish popular music. The tradition of klezmer *kapelyes*, however, had long been history.

In the German lands, Jewish traditional music lost its appeal much earlier. Süsskind of Trimberg, a thirteenth-century troubadour, or *Minnesinger*, is considered the German prototype of the klezmer musician.[53] And although music historians still debate whether this mysterious Jewish bard ever existed, there is evidence that several centuries later, Jewish ensembles in Germany were nothing out of the ordinary. There are reports from the seventeenth century of klezmer musicians based in Berlin and traveling with their performances as far as Leipzig.[54] Jewish traditional music, however, was one of the first victims of

---

[49] Fater and Świderska, *Muzyka żydowska w Polsce*, 73–74.

[50] Natan Gross, "Mordechai Gebirtig: the Folk Song and the Cabaret Song," in Steinlauf and Polonsky, *Polin*, vol. 16, *Focusing on Jewish Popular Culture*, 108–9.

[51] Fuks, *Muzyka ocalona*, 171–72.

[52] Lic interview.

[53] Reiss, "Dusza żydostwa w muzyce," 2.

[54] Salmen, " . . . *denn die Fiedel macht das Fest,*" 57–58.

the Jewish assimilation, with chamber music becoming the preferred genre in the central European Jewish communities.[55] Yiddish folklore, along with the Yiddish language, came to be disregarded as anachronistic and backward. The wind of change generated by the Haskalah movement, also known as the Jewish Enlightenment (1770–1880), produced outstanding musicians, such as Felix Mendelssohn-Bartholdy, but at the same time the shifting value system of the German Jewry disconnected them from Yiddish folklore for decades to come.

A change of attitude toward the Yiddish cultural legacy took place only in the late nineteenth century, when modern anti-Semitism, fueled by the economic crisis of the second half of the nineteenth century, challenged the relationship that German Jews had with German culture. Many began questioning the assimilation project and sought new forms of Jewish identity, which were to be based on the values of modern Europe but rooted in tradition. Folk culture, and folk music in particular, played an important role in this process.[56]

German Jewish scholars began collecting eastern European Jewish folk songs, both in transcription and recorded on wax cylinders. Ethnographers interviewing, among others, prisoners of World War I, collected a wealth of Jewish folk music ranging from Yiddish songs and biblical cantillations to the music of Tunisian and Yemeni Jews.[57] Jewish associations published songbooks, which aimed to foster a new Jewish identity. The new Jew was to be more aware of his or her distinct Jewish cultural background, while at the same time participating in public life, in which social boundaries were slowly dissolving.[58]

The traditions of Yiddish-language popular music in the Weimar Republic were rich. Between 1923 and 1936, Berlin-based labels released the records of as many as twenty-seven Jewish artists. Most of these recordings featured Yiddish songs, but there were also some Hasidic chants, chansons, Jewish tangos, and klezmer tunes. There were at least nine labels in Berlin producing Jewish popular music in the 1920s and '30s, with Artiphon, Lindström, and Brillant among the most prolific ones.[59] The fascination with Yiddish and the culture of east European Jews

---

[55] Philip V. Bohlman, *Jüdische Volksmusik—eine mitteleuropäische Geistesgeschichte* (Wien: Böhlau, 2005); Philip V. Bohlman, "Of *Yekkes* and Chamber Music in Israel: Ethnomusicological Meaning in Western Music History," in *Ethnomusicology and Modern Music History*, ed. Stephen Blum, Philip V. Bohlman, and Daniel M. Neuman (Urbana: University of Illinois, 1991), 259.

[56] Bohlman, *Jüdische Volksmusik*, 16–17; Inka Bertz, *"Eine neue Kunst für ein altes Volk": Die jüdische Renaissance in Berlin 1900 bis 1924* (Berlin: Jüdisches Museum, 1991); Emily D. Bilski, *Berlin Metropolis: Jews and the New Culture 1890–1918* (Berkeley: University of California Press, 1999).

[57] Susane Ziegler, *Die Wachszylinder des Berliner Phonogramm-Archivs* (Berlin: Ethnologisches Museum, 2006).

[58] Bohlman, *Jüdische Volksmusik*, 29; Philip V. Bohlman, "Die Volksmusik und die Verstädterung der deutsch-jüdischen Gemeinde in den Jahrzehnten vor dem Zweiten Weltkrieg," in *Jahrbuch für Volksliedforschung*, ed. Otto Holzapfel and Jürgen Dittmar (Berlin: Erich Schmidt Verlag, 1989), 25–40.

[59] Rainer E. Lotz, *Discographie der Judaica-Aufnahmen* (Bonn: Brigit Lotz Verlag, 2006).

even intensified as Nazism barred Jews from German culture and the focus on *Yiddishkeit* became a remedy for the "loss of Germany."[60]

After the National Socialists took power in Germany and banned Jews from performing for non-Jewish audiences and Jewish audiences from attending "German" cultural events, it was the Jewish Culture League, founded in 1933, that undertook the task of continuing Jewish cultural life under conditions of increasing persecution. Although most of the concerts organized by the league between 1933 and 1941 in Berlin included works by German composers, Yiddish music performances also regularly appeared on their program.[61] Under these extreme circumstances of control, censorship, and a forced separation of "German" from "Jewish" music—the Nazi authorities were gradually banning music by non-Jewish composers from being performed by the league—Yiddish songs became a new musical alternative for the German Jewish audience so far unfamiliar with Jewish folk music. It is telling that a quarter of all records released between 1932 and 1937 by the Berlin label Lukraphon, which was one of the two labels in the city producing Jewish music, contained Yiddish songs.[62]

After World War II, there were still artists who performed Yiddish music on both sides of the Berlin Wall. In West Germany these included the folk singer Peter Rohland, the ensembles Zupfgeigenhansel, espe, and Kasbek, and the duo Hai and Topsy Frankl.[63] East Germany had the state-subsidized Synagogue Choir in Leipzig (*Leipziger Synagogalchor*) and a handful of artists who, like Perry Friedman and Lin Jaldati, devoted themselves to Yiddish song. Interestingly, Friedman, who immigrated to the GDR in the 1950s from Canada, and Jaldati, who moved to East Berlin from Holland, were devoted Communists and viewed Yiddish songs as vehicles for political statements. Lin Jaldati, venerated in the GDR as the First Lady of Yiddish song, performed continuously until 1988, when she gave one of her last concerts at the second festival of Yiddish Culture in East Berlin.

The early 1980s was a time when a new generation of East German musicians became interested in Yiddish songs and klezmer music. Among them was the Berlin-based singer Karsten Troyke, who still performs a wide repertoire of Yiddish songs, ranging from folk songs to Yiddish tangos. In 1984 Claudia Koch and Hardy Reich, two young East German musicians likewise fascinated by folk music, founded the band Aufwind. Like Karsten Troyke, they learned Yiddish, did research into Jewish music in Eastern Europe, and were among the first musicians

[60] Boas cited in Joachim Schlör, *Das Ich der Stadt—Debatten über Judentum und Urbanität 1822–1938* (Göttingen: Vandenhoeck & Ruprecht, 2005), 439.

[61] Lily E. Hirsch, *A Jewish Orchestra in Nazi Germany: Musical Politics and the Berlin Jewish Culture League* (Ann Arbor: University of Michigan Press, 2010).

[62] Horst J. P. Bergmeier, Eljal J. Eisler, and Rainer E. Lotz, *Vorbei/Beyond Recall: Dokumentation jüdischen Musiklebens in Berlin 1933–1938* (Hambergen: Bear Family Records, 2001).

[63] Aaron Eckstaedt, *"Klaus mit der Fiedel, Heike mit dem Bass. . . . ": Jiddische Musik in Deutschland* (Berlin: Philo, 2003), 16–24.

who performed at the Jewish festival in East Berlin, in 1987.[64] Thus, long before the fall of Communism and the reunification of Germany, there were musicians on both sides of the Wall who rediscovered the klezmer repertoire and were successful enough to win an enthusiastic audience. Before long, Aufwind produced their first record on the state-owned GDR label Amiga (1989), and Troyke's *Yiddish Anders* (1992) received the prestigious German Record Critics' Award (*Preis der Deutschen Schallplattenkritik*).

The klezmer boom that appeared in the 1990s did not just show up in a vacuum. Yiddish songs and klezmer music had their history in Berlin and in Kraków, and there were artists in Poland and in both sides of divided Germany who performed the repertoire after 1945, serving as an important point of reference for the new generation of revivalists. These local traditions and resources became an inspiration for the new *klezmorim*, but the impulse for the klezmer boom also came from abroad. The klezmer revival in the United States, in particular, and the popularity that American klezmer bands started enjoying in Europe, was a powerful stimulus for the European klezmer scene.

With the arrival of the American klezmer revivalists to Europe, klezmer music reentered the Old World, returning to its departure point. The music of the eastern European shtetl reached America at the moment when the pogroms in Russia and the growing anti-Semitic atmosphere at the turn of the twentieth century were pushing nearly one-third of eastern European Jewry westward. Migrants traveled via Germany, Holland, and England to make a much-dreamed-of passage to the promised land—America. Among them were also musicians, who usually continued their trade on the new continent. They played at weddings, in Jewish clubs, cabarets, and popular vacation spas. The klezmer repertoire they brought with them expanded and morphed in time to include new American klezmer genres, such as the Romanian-style bulgar, but also elements of the "American pop idiom," such as blues and swing.[65] In the 1920s and '30s, the American Jewish music scene was shaped by Europe-born klezmer masters, such as Abe Schwartz (1881–1963), Naftule Brandwein (1889–1963), and Dave Tarras (1897–1989) and also by Yiddish vaudeville and theater composers, whose Yiddish crossover recordings (such as "Hot Dogs," "Der Yiddisher Santa Claus," and "Yiddishe Charleston") signaled how deeply rooted this music had already become in the American context.[66]

For decades, klezmer in the United States occupied a safe niche in the celebrations of Jewish communities. Areas with a considerable Jewish population, such as Brooklyn, had several specialized klezmer bands who would regularly play at Jewish weddings and other life-cycle celebrations such as bar mitzvahs. But

---

[64] Ibid., 40–44.

[65] Feldman, "Bulgareasca/Bulgarish/Bulgar," 1–35; Sapoznik, *Klezmer!*

[66] Sapoznik, *Klezmer!* 78–82; The contribution of Jewish musicians to the American jazz scene was also considerable, see Peter N. Wilson, "Jazz und 'Jewish roots' " in *Jüdische Musik? Fremdbilder—Eigenbilder*, ed. Eckhard John and Heidy Zimmermann (Köln: Böhlau, 2004), 257–68.

outside of this context, the genre was virtually unknown. It was only the advent of the folk revival that, in the 1970s and '80s, prompted some Jewish musicians and researchers to turn to their own, nearly forgotten Yiddish folklore. New York City became the hub of the movement, with neo-klezmers discovering archival recordings and interviewing old klezmer masters.

The American revivalists started touring Europe at the time of the great changes on the old continent. The New York bands Kapelye and Andy Statman Klezmer Orchestra went on tour in West Germany in 1984, discovering enthusiastic local audiences. They were followed by other prominent American klezmer bands: the Klezmatics (1988), Brave Old World (1990), and the Epstein Brothers (1992).[67] The fall of the Iron Curtain opened whole stretches of Eastern Europe, which had been previously inaccessible to artists from the West. American klezmer revivalists, who came in search of their European roots and to confront the "continent of the Shoah," were welcomed with great curiosity. They soon gained a crucial position on the Jewish heritage scene in Europe as performing artists, artistic directors, and consultants. Alan Bern, for example, a member of the American klezmer band Brave Old World and one of the leading American klezmer revivalists, has worked as program director for festivals such as *Jüdische Kulturtage* (Days of Jewish Culture) in Berlin, the London *KlezFest*, and the Jewish Culture Festival in Kraków. Since 1999 Bern has also been running Yiddish Summer Weimar, one of Europe's most renowned workshops in klezmer music, aimed toward professional musicians. Germany has been particularly fertile soil for the efforts of the klezmer revivalists from the United States. In the 1990s American musicians toured Germany extensively and taught at numerous workshops, a fact that led Heiko Lehmann, one of the insiders of the Berlin klezmer scene, to remark that business was "booming" for klezmer workshops.[68] Soon, however, the American *klezmorim* also became important mentors and role models for the growing Polish klezmer scene.

Only a few of them ventured to Eastern Europe before the fall of Communism, but their contribution to the development of the klezmer revival in Eastern Europe is hard to overlook. The musician, writer, and filmmaker Yale Strom was among the first who came to Poland in the 1980s, doing research on klezmer traditions and giving some informal concerts for the local Jewish communities. The first official stage appearance of an American revivalist band took place in 1990. The Klezmer Conservatory Band from Boston was the first American ensemble invited to the Jewish Culture Festival in Kraków. In 1991 Brave Old World performed during the Days of the Jewish Kazimierz, and their clarinet player, Joel Rubin, became the music director of that edition of the festival. Soon, contact between the festival organizers and the American klezmer scene intensified, and American klezmer musicians became regular guests at other Polish festivals of

---

[67] Eckstaedt, "Klaus mit der Fiedel, Heike mit dem Bass," 45–52.

[68] Heiko Lehmann, "Klezmer in Germany, Germans and Klezmer: Reparation or Contribution," accessed April 21, 2008, http://www.sukke.de/lecture.html.

Jewish culture. Some initiatives, such as the SejN.Y. summer klezmer workshops, organized in the town of Sejny in northeastern Poland, played on the transcontinental connection to New York musicians even in their name.[69]

But although the new, "made in the USA" klezmer had its impact on the Polish and German scene, they also owed their beginnings to a particular post-1989 momentum that differed considerably in Poland and in Germany. In the Polish case, the advent of the klezmer movement was inextricably linked with a "return" of memory concerning Polish Jews into the public sphere and, more specifically, with the "rediscovery" of Kazimierz, the Jewish district of Kraków, which was soon to become the headquarters of the new Polish klezmer revival.

Kazimierz

Kazimierz, which belongs today, along with Kraków's Old Town, on UNESCO's World Heritage List, was founded in 1335 as an independent town near Kraków. It takes its name from Casimir the Great (1310–70), the king known for his particular benevolence toward Jews, as well as for his legendary love affair with Esther, a local Jewish beauty. King Casimir's new town was not meant as a Jewish settlement, as Jews had been living for centuries in the center of Kraków, but rather as a rival town to the capital city, which according to Casimir's plan was to expand into an educational center and, in time, take over the royal functions.

But the new Kazimierz in the shadow of Kraków soon proved of great importance to Jews. In 1495 the Jews of Kraków, accused of arson, were expelled from the city. Their Cracovian ghetto was destroyed, and university buildings were erected on these central and attractive parcels of land. The Jews, in turn, moved to Kazimierz, which at that time was enclosed on an island separated from Kraków by the Vistula River. Around one-fifth of the entire town became the new Jewish district while the rest remained Christian, populated with numerous churches, convents, and monasteries. Jewish Kazimierz thrived over several centuries. It became an important center of Talmudic studies, famous for its yeshiva and the outstanding rabbis who worked there: Moses Isserles (1510–72), Natan Nata Spira (1583–1633), and Joel Sirkes (1583–1640). The imposing synagogues of Kazimierz were designed and decorated by Italian architects. In the sixteenth century the Jewish town even received the privilege of *non tolerandis Christianis*, which were bans on Christian settlements in the area.[70]

---

[69] The Sejny-based Foundation Borderland (*Fundacja Pogranicze*) organized 3 editions of klezmer workshops (2001–2006) under the title of "The Musicians' Raft between New York and Sejny." The latest (4th ed.), titled "New Generation" (2010), dropped the SejN.Y. label and chose young European klezmer artists as its focus.

[70] Majer Bałaban, *Historja Żydów w Krakowie i na Kazimierzu 1304–1868* (Kraków: Krajowa Agencja Wydawnicza, 1991 [1931]).

Jewish Kazimierz prospered according to the changing fortune of the entire kingdom. Weakened by the transferal of the capital to Warsaw, by the numerous wars of the seventeenth and eighteenth centuries, and, finally, by the partitions of Poland, it managed to raise itself from the ruins under the Austrian rule. Even though various tendencies influenced the character of Jewish life in Kraków—from the emancipating impulse of the Haskalah to tradition-oriented Hasidism—Kazimierz retained the character of a distinctly Jewish quarter until World War II. Although by that time the district had become associated with the Jewish lower classes as the affluent Cracovian Jews moved to more prestigious districts, Kazimierz still comprised the heart of Jewish religious and institutional life. The Jewish population of Kazimierz was forced to leave the district in March 1941, as the Nazi authorities forced all of the Jews into the ghetto on the other side of the river, in the Podgórze district. When the Kraków ghetto was liquidated in 1943, the history of Jews in the city virtually ended.

In the postwar period, Kazimierz was in decline and had gained a bad reputation as the city's slum. In 1945, the area turned into a site of violence when an angry mob attacked Holocaust survivors in one of the synagogues.[71] The largely desolate quarter became a reservoir of inexpensive housing for the working classes of Kraków. The low social status of the new inhabitants of Kazimierz coincided with a high crime rate, adding to the negative image of the district. Lack of renovation and deliberate destruction of the quarter took its toll. Synagogues and prayer houses were taken over by state institutions and adapted for new needs, losing their sacral character. The quarter remained in a state of dereliction for many years. One exception was the Remuh Synagogue, which still served the small local Jewish community; it was renovated thanks to the financial support of the Joint Distribution Committee, while the Old Synagogue was adapted into a Jewish Museum and is now one of the branches of the Kraków Historical Museum.

Only in the late 1980s did municipal authorities become alarmed by the dilapidated state of the Jewish heritage in Kazimierz. This coincided with a more general change taking place in the way Polish society began to reflect on Polish Jewish relations. Forty years after the outbreak of the Warsaw Ghetto Uprising of 1943—the final resistance act of the Jews of Warsaw before the ultimate liquidation of the ghetto—the question of the Jewish history of Poland entered the public debate. After more than a decade since the anti-Semitic purges of 1968, when some twenty thousand Jews were forced to leave Poland, Polish intellectuals started breaking the silence that had accrued around the word "Jew." In 1983 the cultural magazine *Znak* dedicated an entire issue to the Warsaw Ghetto Uprising; in 1986 the Jagiellonian University in Kraków opened a Research Center for Jewish History and Culture in Poland. Dealing with Jewish history in prewar

---

[71] See Anna Cichopek, *Pogrom Żydów w Krakowie: 11 sierpnia 1945* (Warszawa: Żydowski Instytut Historyczny, 2000).

Poland also led historians and publicists to pose the question of the moral respon-sibility of Poles as witnesses of the Holocaust. The groundbreaking article by the Polish historian Jan Błoński, "Poor Poles Look at the Ghetto" (*Biedni Polacy patrzą na getto*), addressing the Polish indifference toward the Ghetto Uprising, shook Polish consciences.[72] After decades of silence, it seemed that the new postwar gen-eration was finally ready to face the difficult issues in Polish Jewish relations.

Kazimierz seemed the perfect place to implement these ideas into action. Municipal authorities and grassroots organizations promptly got in touch with international Jewish organizations to fund-raise for a revitalization of Kazimierz. Soon, renovation works in several synagogues and at the Jewish cemetery were under way. At the same time, local intellectuals interested in rediscovering the forgotten Jewish heritage of the district staged the first Jewish Culture Festival in 1988 and brought to life the Judaica Foundation, which opened a pioneering Center for Jewish Culture in 1993.

That same year Steven Spielberg immortalized the Jewish district in his film *Schindler's List*. Spielberg decided to shoot the scenes in the Jewish ghetto in Kazimierz, while in fact the ghetto had been located in the nearby Podgórze area. This pragmatic "artistic" decision—Kazimierz looked much more "authentic" than the area where the real ghetto had been—had long-term consequences for the district.

Wojciech Ornat, who runs a Jewish restaurant and publishing house in Ka-zimierz, remembers that Steven Spielberg's presence had a great impact on the neighborhood long before *Schindler's List* was screened. In 1993 Ornat had just opened a small Jewish café called Ariel in Szeroka Street, when it unexpectedly became the meeting point for Spielberg's actors and guests. "That year was a turn-ing point," recollects Ornat.[73] "The whole of Szeroka Street was one big film set," adds Tomasz Lato of Kroke, the first Cracovian klezmer band, which had their debut in that very café:

> Ariel was then the only place where you could sit down, have a cup of tea and listen to some music . . . so it soon turned into the actors' club. As soon as they arrived here, the big boom happened. Spielberg's wife, Kate, used to come here very often . . . and she was saying all the time "I have to bring my husband here." . . . Finally, at the end of the shooting, Spiel-berg appeared at the café to listen to our concert. The next day we got a proposal: "Boys, we're going to Israel in two days. There's going to be a concert for you to play."[74]

---

[72] Jan Błoński, "Biedni Polacy patrzą na getto," *Tygodnik Powszechny* 2 (1987): 1. In English: "The Poor Poles Look at the Ghetto", in *My Brother's Keeper? Recent Polish Debates on the Holocaust*, ed. Antony Polonsky (London: Routledge, 1990), 34–52.

[73] Wojciech Ornat, interview by the author, Kraków, June 29, 2006.

[74] Tomasz Lato [Kroke], interview by the author, Kraków, June 25, 2005.

Kroke accepted Spielberg's invitation and went to Jerusalem to play their first concert abroad. They performed at a reception that Spielberg had organized for the real-life survivors from the original Schindler's list. Later, Kroke also played at the first screening of *Schindler's List* in Kraków, where Spielberg joined them on the clarinet. The Hollywood adventure of *Schindler's List*, which featured two other local klezmer musicians as actors, Leopold Kozłowski as a Jewish investor and Lesław Lic as a Jewish musician, might have been a short episode, but it made many realize for the first time that the future of Kazimierz lay in the revival of Jewish culture.

Soon after the film was released in cinemas, the first *Schindler's List* tourists appeared in Kazimierz. They were in search of locations where the film was shot, frustrated by the fact that there was hardly any tourist information available to them in the still desolate Jewish district. Zdzisław Leś, owner of a Jewish bookshop in Kazimierz, remembers how the premiere of the film changed people's perception of the actual places in Kazimierz:

> We didn't realize back then that it was such a momentous event. Only later did it become clear. The premiere [of *Schindler's List*] in New York was in December and by January the first tourists started appearing. They would come by taxi, look around, and when they saw the English sign "bookshop" here, they would come in with a huge article from the *New York Times*, with lots of pictures in it, and they asked me: "Where is this gate?" "Where is that?" There were film stills there, as well as real photos, and what they were mostly interested in was the ghetto gate from the film, which does not exist. What they were asking about was a papier-mâché gate, which was only part of the film set and was destroyed immediately afterwards. They were outraged. "What do you mean, it doesn't exist?" one of them said. "The *New York Times* is a serious newspaper and they don't lie!"[75]

Leś estimates that after *Schindler's List* the number of tourists in Kazimierz increased fivefold. His bookstore turned into an information point and a meeting place for many of the heritage tourists. Responding to this tourist demand, in 1994 Leś issued the first small guidebook that listed the places where the film was shot. The booklet quickly became a bestseller, and the bookshop also began offering *Schindler's List* guided tours. Even now, two decades after the film's premiere, there are still tourists who ask the staff of the bookshop how to find the places pictured in *Schindler's List*. "People see Kraków through the eyes of Spielberg," concludes Leś.[76]

[75] Zdzisław Leś, interview by the author, Kraków, June 10, 2006.
[76] Ibid.

But it was already several years before Hollywood ventured into Kazimierz that the Jewish district started attracting the attention of cultural organizers and entrepreneurs. The forlorn atmosphere of the district had charm, but Kazimierz was not a place that promised good revenues. Wojciech Ornat, one of the pioneer businessmen in Kazimierz, recollects:

> That Kazimierz, in the beginning, was completely extraordinary . . . and it will never come back. [Our café] was the only place where something was going on, it was completely silent around, there were fewer people around, and you could feel some metaphysics in the air. When you were entering Kazimierz from the Main Market Square, it was as if you were crossing an invisible boundary. In Kazimierz you found yourself in a different world. It was not just a question of the buildings, but the silence that you were entering. It was a different space: both material and immaterial. You could feel it on your skin. At eight or nine o'clock in the evening, there was a perfect silence. You could even hear people talking in their houses.[77]

Szeroka Street, which Ornat still remembers as desolate and quiet, is now the heart of the klezmer scene in Kazimierz. Forming a rectangular square with limited traffic and bordering on three synagogues and an old Jewish cemetery, Szeroka Street quickly became the center of Jewish heritage tourism. The first venue for Jewish music was a café opened for the duration of the Jewish festival in 1992, in one of the unused synagogues. With time, a group of entrepreneurs opened a full-fledged café and restaurant, located in one of the historical houses of Szeroka Street. Other similar venues quickly followed. Ornat, the founder of this prototypical Kazimierz café, several years later opened Klezmer Hois: a combination of a restaurant, hotel, and publishing house specializing in Jewish heritage and history. Klezmer Hois, which occupies the building of a former mikveh and community jail, has become both a popular tourist destination and a meeting point for local Jews. Leopold Kozłowski, a descendant of a klezmer dynasty from Przemyślany (now in Ukraine) considered to be the "last klezmer of Poland," not only has his own table in the restaurant but also supervised the kitchen so that the prewar traditional Jewish dishes could be re-created as authentically as possible.

The Jewish-style restaurants in Kazimierz, which proliferated as the Jewish district was undergoing revitalization, represent a very particular business model combining catering with music performances and the sale of Jewish-themed souvenirs. Offering a packaged Jewish heritage experience, they have become an integral part of the Cracovian tourist industry. Their beginnings, which coincided with the advent of the klezmer revival, took place in not necessarily auspicious conditions, though. In the early 1990s, Kazimierz did not offer much in terms of

---

[77] Ornat interview.

entertainment and still suffered from a negative reputation. The klezmer musicians who performed in the first Jewish-style café in Kazimierz had to take care of the promotion of their concerts themselves. They printed leaflets and distributed them by bicycle among the main tourist information points and in pubs. Their families helped them in this, and if their efforts were successful, the weekly Saturday concert would gather around thirty to fifty spectators.[78]

Kroke, the pioneers of the Kraków klezmer scene, started performing Jewish folk music in 1993, during the time when it was virtually unknown in Poland. After graduating from the Kraków Music Academy, the musicians of Kroke formed the band and played in streets and restaurants. The graduates of the prestigious academy playing Jewish folk music were a curiosity to their colleagues. The band members remember that many fellow classical musicians were skeptical of their choice, believing that playing klezmer was "degrading" and that it was a "profanation" of their classical education.[79] With time, as Kroke became successful, and the tourist industry in Kazimierz started growing, playing klezmer music became an attractive option to the graduates of the academy. More and more classical musicians taught themselves klezmer in order to perform in Kazimierz, mostly in the new Jewish-style restaurants.

To understand how much Kazimierz has changed in the last two decades, it is enough to have a look at the statistics. In 1989 there were no tourist accommodations in Kazimierz; while in 2004 there were twenty-two hotels, hostels, and guest rooms. By 2004, the number of restaurants increased seven times, and the amount of tourists coming yearly to Kazimierz to visit Jewish heritage monuments was estimated at around 120,000.[80] In 2006, every tenth tourist in Kraków visited a Jewish heritage monument, and in 2011 tourists ranked Kazimierz as the third most impressive site in Kraków, preceded only by the royal castle and the Main Market Square.[81]

There were more than a dozen klezmer bands in Kraków in 2013, most of them regularly performing in Kazimierz. Virtually all of the bands consist of professional musicians, most of them non-Jewish. Many openly admit that their main incentive to start playing klezmer was pecuniary. Marcin Wiercioch of the Klezzmates makes a straightforward statement: "In my case, my first contact with klezmer music was based on financial considerations. It turned out that one could play this music and earn money from it."[82] Magdalena Brudzińska of the Quartet

[78] Kroke, interview by the author, Kraków, June 25, 2005.

[79] Ibid.

[80] Monika Murzyn, *Kazimierz: Środkowoeuropejskie doświadczenie rewitalizacji* (Kraków, Międzynarodowe Centrum Kultury, 2006), 259–73.

[81] Krzysztof Borkowski, "Ruch turystyczny w Krakowie w 2011 roku," Kraków, Małopolska Organizacja Turystyczna, 2006, accessed October 20, 2012, http://www.mot.krakow.pl/index,a,b,c,16.html; Murzyn, *Kazimierz: Środkowoeuropejskie doświadczenie rewitalizacji*, 282.

[82] Marcin Wiercioch [Klezzmates], interview by the author, Kraków, June 30, 2006.

Klezmer Trio states that klezmer is a midway genre between classical and popular music, and saves classical musicians from being forced to play more mainstream and less sophisticated music. "This music gives us a lot of satisfaction," she says. "Apart from that, it gives us the possibility to survive and support ourselves in much better conditions than if we were playing classical music today in Poland."[83]

Polish musicians were not the only ones to join the klezmer scene in Kazimierz. One of the first klezmer bands in the district, Kuzmir, was founded by Ukrainians who came to Kraków from Donetsk in 1994. Wiaczesław Abaszidze, who was teaching at the Music Academy in Donetsk and had his own band, at first came to Kraków only periodically to play in Kazimierz. After some time he moved to Kraków permanently with his wife and daughter, who also play in Kuzmir. "We don't want to go back to the Ukraine," Abaszidze confesses, "because it's hard for people in our profession. There is one revolution after another and no stability."[84] Indeed, the klezmer scene in Kazimierz can offer a promise of financial stability for professional musicians because it is intrinsically bound to the microeconomy of Jewish heritage tourism, which has been stimulating the development of the district for the past two decades.

By 2013 there were four Jewish-style restaurants in Szeroka Street employing klezmer ensembles. All of them function on a similar basis. Evening klezmer concerts take place daily in the tourist season and on weekends during the rest of the year. The guests are charged an additional fee for the music. Most of the customers are tourists, for whom dinner in Szeroka is the leg of their sightseeing day. The restaurants take care of the steady influx of guests by making arrangements with travel agencies, which make a klezmer evening in a Jewish restaurant a highlight of their organized tours. Between April and October the restaurants, which usually have several dining halls, manage to stage up to four concerts simultaneously, often in two or three shifts. Thus, the klezmer bands of Kazimierz, which are usually affiliated with one restaurant, give between twenty and thirty concerts per month.

Off season, very few klezmer concerts take place in Kazimierz. During that time, the musicians usually try to look for other concert possibilities. Playing outside of Kazimierz is usually more profitable, but the concerts in Szeroka Street secure them a regular income. There are, however, drawbacks. The restaurants sometimes arrange the evening gigs with the musicians on very short notice. The boom of cheap airlines and the rise of independent traveling have disrupted the stable flow of bookings from travel agencies. Now that the concerts are contracted just shortly before the customers arrive at the restaurant, the musicians are expected to be on standby.

Given that musicians do not have permanent employment contracts but are paid per performance, their employers do not pay insurance or social security for

---

[83] Magdalena Brudzińska, interview by the author, Kraków, January 23, 2008.

[84] Wiaczesław Abaszidze, interview by the author, Kraków, June 30, 2006.

Fig. 1.1 Klezmer concert in a Jewish-style restaurant in Kazimierz, 2008.
Photo by Soliman Lawrence.

them and, in cases of illness or pregnancy, the musicians are left to their own devices. One of the musicians from Szeroka Street comments bitterly on this precariousness: "[Working here] is like a great canyon over which someone stretched a thread, and you balance on this thread, singing about peace and love."[85] To get insurance, some musicians find additional employment as school teachers, even though Kazimierz remains an important, albeit seasonal, source of income for them. In 2012 the restaurants hired bands at a fixed rate of 400–450 PLN (around 140 USD) per performance. Given that most of the bands are trios, with an average of twenty-five concerts per month, each musician was able to earn up to 3,750 PLN (1,100 USD), which was around the average salary in Poland.[86]

Jewish-style restaurants are the principal venues of most of the klezmer concerts staged in Kraków, but they are by far not the only ones. Klezmer bands also perform at the Center for Jewish Culture, which has produced CDs for local ensembles and stages regular concerts, and at the Galicia Jewish Museum. The Alchemia club in Plac Nowy, one of the first entertainment venues opened outside of Szeroka Street, has also had a long tradition of avant-garde klezmer concerts, hosting since 1999 the most prominent Polish klezmer bands and co-organizing the late-night klezmer jam sessions during the Jewish festival. But although Cracovian klezmer bands also perform outside of the Jewish district, and some of them even tour abroad, klezmer and Kazimierz remain inseparable.

---

[85] Maciej Inglot [Sholem], interview by the author, Kraków, July 1, 2006.

[86] The average gross salary in Poland in 2011 was 3399 PLN. Główny Urząd Statystyczny, accessed October 27, 2012, http://www.stat.gov.pl/gus/5840_1630_PLK_HTML.htm.

Fig. 1.2 A Jewish-style restaurant in Kazimierz with Christmas decoration, 2012.
Photo by Szymon Sokołowski.

What makes Kazimierz such a perfect backdrop for klezmer is the old, dusty, and otherwordly aura that surrounds the Jewish district. The extent to which this aura is becoming exploited by the tourist industry in Kazimierz resembles, indeed, some of the urban utopias visualizing the so-called time tourism. In the early 1970s Kevin Lynch, an urban planner and author, developed the idea of a "time enclave," which "retarded in technology" would be a space where the pace of life could slow down and daily routines be retained as they were in the past.[87] With its architectonic substance left almost intact, Kazimierz also lures visitors into believing that they step into a time enclave. But although the patina of time is quite palpable in Kazimierz, many of the district's revivalists do not stop themselves from creating it anew. The historic walls of the Jewish quarter have become the background for a new performance of the Jewish past, which can be gaudy, ostentatious, and preponderant. With new Yiddish shop signs and repainted Yiddish inscriptions, Kazimierz has turned into a site of what Svetlana Boym calls "urban theatricality."[88] "Restorative nostalgia," which Boym so compellingly defines in *The Future of Nostalgia* as an attempt at a "transhistorical reconstruction" drives the revivalists of Jewish Kazimierz to literally "patch up the memory gaps" with a fresh layer of paint.[89]

[87] Kevin Lynch, *What Time Is This Place?* (Cambridge, MA: MIT Press, 1993), 237–38.
[88] Svetlana Boym, *The Future of Nostalgia* (New York: Basic Books, 2001), 76–77.
[89] Ibid, 41.

The new-old Kazimierz today is the main destination of Jewish heritage tourism in Poland, and one of the trendiest areas of Kraków. It bustles with activity day and night, with scores of cafés, clubs, and restaurants. There is an incessant flow of guided tours marching through the district, but it is also a favorite night-life destination for local Cracovians. This revitalized Kazimierz does not so much freeze the past as offer its custom-tailored version. The Jewish quarter adapted for the needs of time tourists is more colorful, harmonious, and readable. Shop signs adorning cafés, restaurants, and ice-cream parlors use transliterated Yiddish names and are antiqued, made to look as if they were old. At times, they also use mock Yiddish, such as in the case of the Bąbelstein pub, whose name (*bąbel* is a bubble or blister in Polish) outlived the actual establishment and remained on the wall long after the pub closed down. The Long Ago in Kazimierz café, located directly opposite the old Jewish cemetery, is a time enclave in a nutshell. Its exterior is decorated to look like a row of four old shops. Each of them, adorned with shutters with peeling paint, has the name of a fictitious shop owner above the entrance. Walking into the café, picturesquely filled with vintage bric-a-brac, the visitor goes back in time to an idealized harmonious Polish Jewish past. Szymon Kac, the tailor, and Benjamin Holcer, the carpenter, are here door-to-door neighbors of Stanisław Nowak, the grocer. Kazimierz of this undefined "long ago" age is both quaint and arcadian.

Klezmer music plays an important role in the Kazimierz time enclave. Bands with names such as Kuzmir (Yid: Kazimierz), Kroke (Yid: Kraków), or Di Galitzyaner Klezmorim (referring to the region of Galicia that formed one of the largest

Fig. 1.3 The former *Bąbelstein* café in Szeroka Street, Kazimierz, during the Jewish Culture Festival, 2010. Photo by Soliman Lawrence.

Fig. 1.4 Café "Long Ago in Kazimierz," 2006. Photo by Soliman Lawrence.

settlements of Jews in eastern Europe) invoke a nostalgic topography. Their music, too, often addresses an imaginary Kazimierz of the past. The Cracovian Jewish district thus becomes *the* authentic klezmer space for local *klezmorim* and for musicians from abroad. The Danish klezmer band Mazel, for example, made a shooting for their CD cover in the backyards of Kazimierz.[90] These snapshots, set in sepia tones, were meant to give their record the flavor of a bygone time. The musicians, who also posed in front of the Long Ago in Kazimierz café, were more than time tourists. They were time pilgrims, venerating the illusion of a reinvented past.

Not only visitors but some of those who co-author this utopian vision of Kazimierz believe in the authenticity of their creation. Jasha Lieberman, leader of one of the local klezmer bands, claimed in a press interview that what is happening in Kazimierz is "a reflection of what there was here before the war. There are galleries, cafés, and hotels here now. People who used to live here have come back; the music has come back too. Kazimierz is beginning to live."[91] Understanding revitalization as a return of what was lost in the Holocaust is, nonetheless, a delusion. But the creation of spaces that employ the "reset button technique," promising the experience of an encapsulated past, responds to a strong demand. Wojciech Ornat, the owner of Klezmer Hois, knows a lot about it. His restaurant is a time enclave too, with its retro interiors, klezmer concerts, and traditional food on the menu. To Ornat, Jewish food is an element of heritage that requires

[90] Mazel, *Un brukhe*, Tylkomuzyka, 2006.
[91] Jasha Lieberman, cited in Dorota Gonet, "Jesteśmy sentymentalni," *Gazeta Wyborcza Lublin*, April 23, 2001, 5.

preservation. "You won't find such food in Israel anymore," he points out. "People often come to us with recipes and then we cook according to them. . . . I often see people from Israel weeping over the food! For the first time in fifty years they eat like they used to at home."[92] Capturing the smells, tastes, and sounds of the past is, for Ornat, a service salable to time tourists and a way of preserving Jewish heritage. The Jewish-style restaurants that have proliferated in Kazimierz, he argues, play an important role beyond catering to the needs of tourists: "They remind you with their style about what this place used to be. Of course, you can frown at them, saying that certain things are wrong with them, or even very wrong. Nevertheless . . . it is also a form of memory."[93] This "memory," however, is rather a conscious reenactment, which recombines elements of Jewish heritage into a cultural product attractive to its new, not necessarily Jewish, consumers. For a long time, commercial establishments such as the Klezmer Hois were the only places in Kazimierz that offered a participatory experience of Jewish food and music. Unlike the cultural institutions in the district that educated about and displayed artifacts of Jewish heritage, the restaurants are spaces that allow a daily and consumable "Jewish practice." They attract both non-Jews, who can, often for the first time in their lives, directly face the image, however approximated or misrepresented, of a culture that once flourished in Kazimierz, and Jews, who find an informal and secular place to meet. Today, new Jewish spaces in Kazimierz such as the Jewish Community Center, opened in 2008, and two kosher restaurants offer additional alternatives.

In 1939 Jews made up a quarter of the city's population. Immediately after the end of World War II in 1945, there were only five hundred Jews in Kraków. This number rose to twenty thousand in 1947, only to plummet to four thousand in 1950. Since then the local Jewish community has been steadily decreasing in numbers. After the catastrophe of the Holocaust, Kraków lost its remaining Jewish population due to the emigration waves after the Kraków pogrom of 1945, the foundation of the State of Israel in 1948, and the anti-Semitic purges of 1968.

Today 97 percent of Kraków's population is Roman Catholic.[94] The Orthodox Jewish community in Kraków has around one hundred registered members. They hold services at the Remuh synagogue, and occasionally at two other synagogues, which usually open only for larger visiting groups. Members of the local community are mostly elderly and often require assistance. The congregation therefore runs a kosher dining place and a Jewish home for the elderly. It is estimated that there are only around four hundred people in Kraków who identify themselves as Jewish. A group of reformed Jews now meets for Friday evening Kabbalat

[92] Ornat interview.

[93] Ibid.

[94] Główny Urząd Statystyczny, *Wyznania religijne, stowarzyszenia narodowościowe i etniczne w Polsce 2009–2011* (Warszawa: Zakład Wydawnictw Statystycznych, 2013), 36.

Shabbat (welcoming the Shabbat) celebrations at the Galicia Jewish Museum, and they offer courses preparing for a conversion to Judaism.

"Building a Jewish Future in Kraków" is the motto of the new Jewish Community Center, situated next to the historic Tempel synagogue. Built with the assistance of World Jewish Relief and the American Jewish Joint Distribution Committee, the center accommodates a seniors' club, a mini-nursery, a Jewish Sunday School, and the Jewish Students' Association. It also hosts a wide range of events from Hebrew lessons and computer courses to belly dancing and psychological counseling. Most importantly, however, it is a place where the whole community can celebrate Jewish holidays. Kazimierz has always been the seat of Jewish institutions, but the shrinking number of community members after 1945 led to a relative stagnation of Jewish life. The new Cracovian Jewish institutions, in turn, attract people who only recently rediscovered their Jewish roots. Revivalists of Jewish life from abroad are also becoming active in Kazimierz. The Hasids of the Chabad Lubavitch movement, for example, who moved into the Isaac synagogue in 2006, run a small day-care facility, have opened a kosher shop, and supervise a mikveh. And although the number of registered members of the Jewish community has not risen significantly, the community of people who identify themselves as Jewish is growing and becoming more and more conspicuous.

"Had there been no Holocaust," speculated the late Chris Schwarz, a British photojournalist and founder of the Galicia Jewish Museum, "you'd have Jewish discotheques, Internet cafés, Jewish people doing house music, jazz clubs, strip clubs, cabarets, weird performance artists, the same music that you get among Jews in Israel and America. Why should it be different in Kraków?"[95] Following his own motto, Schwarz opened the Galicia Jewish Museum in 2004 in Kazimierz to provide a progressive space for new manifestations of Jewish life. The museum, which has an overtly secular profile and is also open on Saturdays, uses contemporary artistic means to present Jewish culture. "I'm trying to do the opposite to what everybody else seems to be doing in Kazimierz, which is creating a pre-1939 space," said Schwarz in a 2006 interview. "You have two options in Kazimierz: you can either put a fence around it, and say: 'right, nothing should change after 1939.' I don't know if this is realistic, that's certainly not what happened. Or you say: 'culture is evolving, and any culture that's static is going to die.'"[96] Although it does not seem likely that Jewish culture made by Jews is going to dominate the cultural production in Kazimierz anytime soon, places such as the Jewish Community Center and the Galicia Jewish Museum, promising "a contemporary look at the Jewish past in Europe,"[97] without a doubt will take part in shaping the district's future.

---

[95] Chris Schwarz, interview by the author, Kraków, July 5, 2006.

[96] Ibid.

[97] "Galicia Jewish Museum," accessed May 21, 2007, http://www.galiciajewishmuseum.org/en/muzeum.html.

Everything that has taken place in Kazimierz since the late 1980s, including the rise of Jewish heritage tourism and the revival of Jewish life, has been a result of relatively rapid changes in Polish society, which began in the final years of the Communist period and accelerated after 1989. Although the Berlin klezmer revival has developed, in some respects, in a context similar to the Polish case, it has had at the same time a longer and more complex genealogy.

Berlin

The Berlin klezmer revival began while the city was still divided by the Wall and emerged against the background of two different historical narratives. While the Holocaust constituted the central event defining the approach to Jewish culture in both German states after 1945, the German Democratic Republic, building its legitimacy as an antifascist state, considered only the Federal Republic of Germany as the direct heir of the Third Reich and hence the state bearing the sole moral responsibility for the Holocaust. The process of *Vergangenheitsbewältigung* (coming to terms with the past), and in particular with the period of National Socialism, has had its own turbulent and relatively long tradition, but it took place with a different intensity and emphasis in the two German states before 1989.

In West Germany, the context in which the first wave of interest in klezmer music unfolded was quite specific. In 1984 the renowned clarinetist Giora Feidman, later avowed as the "king of klezmer," appeared in Joshua Sobol's play *Ghetto* at the Freie Volksbühne theater in West Berlin. His virtuoso performance, which hugely contributed to Feidman's later popularity in Germany, was welcomed enthusiastically by the press, heralding a new interest in Jewish folk music and linking klezmer to the German debates on the Holocaust and the boundaries of its representation.[98] The 1980s were, indeed, a time of particularly intensive disputes concerning the Shoah. The 1979 screening of the American TV series *Holocaust* in West Germany proved to be a "Catharsis of a Nation."[99] After decades of absence, the Holocaust entered popular culture with such an impetus that some even went as far as to speak of a "Holocaust inflation."[100] Other observers saw a clear cause-and-effect relationship between the representations of the Holocaust that mushroomed in the media, literature, and even advertising in West Germany, and the rise of interest in Yiddish culture.[101]

---

[98] On reception of Sobol's "Ghetto" in West Germany see Kerstin Mueller, "Normalizing the Abnormal: Joshua Sobol's *Ghetto* in West Germany," *Seminar. A Journal of Germanic Studies* 45, no. 1 (2009): 44–63.

[99] Siegfried Zielinski, "History as Entertainment and Provocation: The TV Series 'Holocaust' in West Germany," in *Germans and Jews Since the Holocaust: The Changing Situation in West Germany*, ed. Anson Rabinbach and Jack Zipes (New York: Holmes and Meier, 1986), 259.

[100] Ibid., 273.

[101] Ibid., 277.

This intensive coming to terms with the Holocaust was also at times interpreted as an attempt at normalizing the past. The famous *Historikerstreit*, the dispute of German historians that flared up in the 1980s, concerned precisely the question of what position the Holocaust occupied in German history. The sociologist and philosopher Jürgen Habermas was one of the leading figures of the controversy and one of the main voices speaking out against the whitewashing of the German past by apologetic historians such as Ernst Nolte. The intellectual debate was also counterpointed by highly contested political gestures, such as the 1985 visit of President Reagan and Chancellor Kohl to the Bitburg military cemetery, where members of *Waffen-SS* were buried. Many saw these episodes as marking what Henri Lustiger-Thaler called the "decline of the philosemitic bonus and the ascendance of German memory."[102] To be sure, in the 1980s the Holocaust became a subject that resonated enormously.

The question of whether it was acceptable to commemorate also those who endorsed the Nazi regime, such as the SS officers in Bitburg, was accompanied by the issue of what representations of Jews are now appropriate in German cultural productions. The 1985 staging of Rainer Werner Fassbinder's play *Garbage, the City, and Death* in Frankfurt, which was halted by a group of protesters who considered the play anti-Semitic, provided another controversy that sparked public debate in West Germany. The open and fervent manifestation of local Jews, who opposed the play, marked something of a "coming out" of the Jewish community in the German media. Contemporary German Jews as agents in public life now became a counterweight to the "historical" Jews.

German authorities launched several major enterprises to commemorate the Holocaust. In 1989 Daniel Libeskind won the competition for the design of the new Jewish Museum in Berlin, and around that same time a group of intellectuals put into motion the initiative of erecting the Memorial to the Murdered Jews of Europe in the center of Berlin. Both projects triggered extensive public debates, but on their completion they turned into important landmarks of the German capital. Many, however, remained skeptical of this outburst of commemorative zeal, fearing that establishing ultimate national monuments to the victims of the Holocaust might only facilitate forgetting.[103] The klezmer movement in Berlin thus began at a turbulent time when, on the one hand, German memory of the Holocaust was being institutionalized in large-scale commemorative projects; on the other hand, the German public was negotiating not only the way they wish to remember the Holocaust but also the possibility of leaving the burdensome memory-load behind.

---

[102] Henri Lustiger-Thaler, "Remembering Forgetfully," in *Re-situating Identities: The Politics of Race Ethnicity and Culture*, ed. Vered Amit-Talai and Caroline Knowles (Peterborough, ONT: Broadview Press, 1998), 197.

[103] Ibid., 193.

While in Kraków the revitalized Jewish district has been the main axis of the local klezmer revival, the Berlin klezmer scene lacks such particular spatial coordinates. This is partly so because the city has no single area that could be called the Jewish district. Jewish spaces in Berlin are numerous, and they are dispersed all around the city. One of these, in particular, stirs the imagination of artists and tour operators as a shtetl in the middle of a metropolis. The centrally located Scheunenviertel, or Barn District, might have little semblance to the traditional Jewish districts of eastern Europe, but it remains a reference point for contemporary klezmer revivalists as the space where Yiddish culture was once at home.

At the turn of the twentieth century, as the burgeoning Jewish middle classes were living all around Berlin, poor Jewish refugees from eastern Europe began their exodus westwards. Berlin became an important node of these migrations. Many Jews, escaping pogroms and waves of anti-Semitic violence in Russia, headed to the United States. For others, the Scheunenviertel had to suffice as a temporary promised land.[104]

In the first decades of the twentieth century, every tenth Jew in Berlin came from Russia, Galicia, or Romania. With Silesia, Pomerania, Posen, and East Prussia included, eastern European Jews accounted for up to 40 percent of Berlin's Jewry.[105] In 1925 the number of Jewish citizens in Berlin peaked. There were 172,672 registered Jews, while some estimated that the real number oscillated between 200,000 and 250,000. Many of the new Jewish immigrants were residents of the Scheunenviertel, where they lived according to Old World customs imported from eastern Europe. Their traditional dress, the Yiddish they spoke, and the folklore they practiced made them much more conspicuous as Jews. Frowned upon even by many assimilated German Jews, they became targets of anti-Semitic violence. The 1923 pogrom that swept across Berlin began right in the Scheunenviertel.[106]

For many assimilated Berlin Jews, the Scheunenviertel had the reputation of an unsafe and crime-ridden area. Coco Schumann, a renowned Berlin jazz musician and Auschwitz survivor, recollects in his autobiography how sinister, but at the same time exciting, the prewar Scheunenviertel was:

> The Scheunenviertel had a thrilling atmosphere for hanging out; it was a poor but lively quarter where people made themselves busy to survive the day. . . . At the same time, the *Mulackei,* named after the notorious Mulackstraße, . . . was a home to all the demimonde and the underworld. . . . As a young boy, I asked myself why so many women were hanging around

[104] See: Anne-Christin Saß, *Berliner Luftmenschen: Osteuropäisch-jüdische Migranten in der Weimarer Republik* (Göttingen: Wallstein, 2012).

[105] Schlör, *Das Ich der Stadt,* 106.

[106] Ulrich Eckhardt and Andreas Nachama, eds., *Jüdische Orte in Berlin* (Berlin: nicolai, 2005), 33.

there by night, standing in front of the house doors, but since I kept my eyes open, I soon figured it out on my own.[107]

Walter Mehring wrote in 1929 that Berlin bordered on Galicia, so powerful was the impression of the foreignness of the district. Scheunenviertel, with its cheap rents, attracted Jews and poor immigrants from the German countryside who hoped for a new life in the capital city as domestic servants, artisans, and prostitutes. The area, where the local underworld lived side by side with pious Hasidic Jews, stood in clear contrast to the wealthy Jewish areas in nearby Oranienburger Street and around the New Synagogue, a lavish Moorish-style Reform temple, inaugurated in 1866. Although eastern European Jews performed many important functions in the Jewish communities of Berlin, from rabbis and cantors to Torah-scribes and producers of ritual objects, the Berlin Jewry shunned the "backward" district and its inhabitants, considered the "confessional proletariat" of Berlin. Many assimilated Jews in Berlin felt that the immigrants from the East disrupted the process of full acculturation of Jews into German society.[108]

Nonetheless, the "exotic" and "authentic" eastern European Jews were also a source of fascination. Many viewed them as bearers of unspoiled Jewish tradition and sought to connect with it. The *Jüdisches Volksheim*, Jewish People's Home, established in the Scheunenviertel in 1916, played the role of one such meeting platform for eastern and western Jews. Founded by the Zionist physician and pedagogue Siegfried Lehmann, the institution offered educational activities to immigrant Jews and an opportunity for its teachers to confront "what they could not find in themselves: Jewish authenticity."[109]

The shtetl in the center of Berlin also became an inspiration for many artists. The Yiddish theater and cabaret was among the liveliest offspring of the Yiddish renaissance, unfolding at the beginning of the twentieth century. The Scheunenviertel itself, between 1901 and 1918, had three official as well as many more "underground" Yiddish theaters.[110] In 1929 the district itself was immortalized on stage with Walter Mehring's *Merchant of Berlin*, loosely inspired by Shakespeare's *Merchant of Venice* but set in the Scheunenviertel. By then, however, entertainment in Yiddish had long left the boundaries of this immigrant quarter. The eastern Jewish cultural association *Progreß*, founded by a group of enthusiasts in the early 1920s, organized concerts of Yiddish, Polish, and Russian songs.

---

[107] Coco Schumann, Max Christian Graeff, and Michaela Haas, *Der Ghetto-Swinger: Eine Jazzlegende erzählt* (München: Deutscher Taschenbuch Verlag, 2005), 20–21, trans. from German by the author.

[108] Ludger Heid, "Ostjüdische Kultur im Deutschland der Weimarer Republik," in *Juden als Träger bürgerlicher Kultur in Deutschland*, ed. Julius H. Schoeps (Stuttgart: Burg Verlag, 1989), 329–55.

[109] Michael Brenner, *The Renaissance of Jewish Culture in Weimar Germany* (New Haven: Yale University Press, 1996), 187.

[110] Peter Sprengel, *Populäres jüdisches Theater in Berlin von 1877 bis 1933* (Berlin: Haude & Spener, 1997).

The first Yiddish cabaret, Kaftan, opened in 1930 and quickly became a meeting point for a very mixed audience. Among the cabaretgoers were not only the poor refugees from the Scheunenviertel but also the burgeoning Jewry from the western districts of Berlin, who still felt attached to Yiddish, and even some Zionists, who wanted to manifest their solidarity with the east European Jews.[111] The Scheunenviertel thus became, if not *the* Jewish district of Berlin, at least a symbolic space, which witnessed the greatest changes and the greatest catastrophes for the Jews of Berlin.

In the 1920s and '30s the Berlin police, and later the SS, frequently raided the Scheunenviertel, arresting many immigrant Jews without a valid permit of stay. In 1938 Jews who were Polish citizens were expelled from Germany and deported to the Polish border, where they were granted entry only after a long and humiliating wait. This was a prelude to the mass deportations of Jews from Scheunenviertel and the rest of Berlin in the years to come. Out of more than 170,000 Jews living in Berlin in 1933, nearly half left Germany before the outbreak of the war; around 50,000 were deported to ghettos in farther east and later to concentration camps; and only 9,000 survived the war in the city.[112] After 1945, the Scheunenviertel found itself under the Soviet jurisdiction and later was made part of East Berlin. By then there was little left of the original architectural substance of the district. Affected by the urban changes of the 1920s and, later, Hitler's destruction and the Allied bombings, the Scheunenviertel transformed beyond recognition. With the New Synagogue destroyed in the war, the center of Jewish life in East Berlin moved to the synagogue in Rykestraße in the northern district of Prenzlauer Berg. In West Berlin, the much more numerous Jewish congregation was centered around the *Gemeindehaus* (Jewish Community House) built in 1959 on the site of a destroyed synagogue in Fasanenstraße. It was only in 1995 that the New Synagogue in Oranienburgerstraße became once again a functional space for the reunited Jewish community. After the fall of the Berlin Wall, what used to be the Scheunenviertel quickly experienced gentrification. Designer shops and art galleries moved into the quarter, often capitalizing on the area's more recent past as part of East Berlin, rather than the more distant in time and less tangible Jewish heritage. The Jewish past, however, continued to inspire heritage revivalists, historians, and artists.[113]

Although the Scheunenviertel itself remains a symbolic reference point rather than a space that can be recognized as Jewish, the budding Berlin klezmer scene

---

[111] Ibid.; Heid, "Ostjüdische Kultur im Deutschland der Weimarer Republik."

[112] Kurt Jakob Ball-Kaduri and Michael Berenbaum, "Berlin 1933–39" and "Berlin 1939–1945" in *Encyclopaedia Judaica*, vol. 3 (Detroit: Thompson-Gale, 2007), 448–51.

[113] The 1980s witnessed the first publications about the Scheunenviertel, such as Eike Geisel's album *Im Scheunenviertel* (Berlin: Severin und Siedler, 1981), reprints of old novels set in the district, like Adolf Sommerfeld's *Das Ghetto von Berlin* (Berlin: Verlag Neues Leben, 1992), and artistic projects, such as Shimon Attie's *Sites Unseen* (Heidelberg: Umschau/Braus, 1998).

used the myth of the metropolitan shtetl quite intensively. The Hackesches Hoftheater, which opened in 1992 just off the historic Scheunenviertel, was for many years, until its closure in 2006, the headquarters of the local klezmer revival. Staging Yiddish plays and scheduling regular klezmer concerts, the theater, advertised as being located "at a historic venue," understood itself as the heir of the Yiddish theater and cabaret of the Scheunenviertel. The mid-1990s were the heyday of the Berlin klezmer revival, and the theater contributed immensely to the genre's popularity. Virtually every klezmer band in Berlin regularly performed there. In 1998 the Berlin cultural bimonthly *Zitty* advertised as many as 302 klezmer concerts, most of which were staged by the Hackesches Hoftheater. Ten years later, when the theater had been closed for two years, the number of klezmer concerts dropped by more than 50 percent.[114] The Hackesches Hoftheater was more than just a concert venue, though, and the artistic network it helped to create outlived the institution. Jalda Rebling, who performed Yiddish songs and acted in many of the theater's stage productions, remembers that the small venue was a meeting point for very different groups interested in Jewish culture, both non-Jewish Germans, Germans "who were a little bit Jewish," and Jewish immigrants from Eastern Europe who were discovering what it meant to be Jewish in Germany.[115]

Fig. 1.5 Mark Aizikovich and band during a performance at the Hackesches Hoftheater, 2005. Photo by Albrecht Grüß.

[114] The author's own calculation based on concerts advertised as "klezmer" or *"jiddische Lieder"* in the daily music program of *Zitty: Illustrierte Stadtzeitung*, nos. 1–26, 1998, and nos. 1–26, 2008.

[115] Jalda Rebling, interview by the author, Berlin, February 6, 2006.

Fig. 1.6 Foyer of the Hackesches Hoftheater, 2002. Photo by Albrecht Grüß.

In 2013, there were more than twenty professional and semiprofessional klezmer bands performing in Berlin, comprised of both German and foreign musicians, both Jewish and non-Jewish. There are a number of clubs, bars, and cafés, as well as churches, that have klezmer in their concert repertoire. Regular klezmer dance events are also held in an old ballroom in Lübars, on the outskirts of Berlin, and in the popular Cafe Burger in the city center. A restaurant at the Jewish Museum offers a weekly "oriental buffet" accompanied by klezmer music, and the museum itself occasionally organizes klezmer concerts as events accompanying their temporary exhibitions.

Klezmer music also features in the program of the Bimah Jewish Theater, which opened in 2001. Although it stages mostly light German-language repertoire, including Kurt Tucholsky's cabaret and Ephraim Kishon's humoresques, Bimah also produces musicals with Yiddish songs and klezmer. Jewish folk music is also on the program of their New Year's Eve parties, as well as at their Shabbat evenings, during which spectators are invited to participate in a traditional Friday night ritual "with a Jewish family."[116]

Quite a unique klezmer venue in Berlin is the monthly get-together of both professional and amateur klezmer musicians called the Klezmer Stammtisch (regulars' table). The local klezmer "regulars" first organized themselves after a klezmer workshop in Bad Pyrmont run by the American revivalists from the Brave Old World band in 1996. Ever since, musicians who in the meantime founded

---

[116] "Bimah Theatre in Berlin," accessed August 24, 2011, http://www.juedischestheaterberlin.de/Stuecke.php?Bereich=Aktuelles&Stueck=ShabatShalom.

Fig. 1.7 Klezmer dancing event at Lübars, near Berlin, 2006. Photo by Marcin Piekoszewski.

their own klezmer bands and play together in various constellations, have been meeting to exchange ideas and jam together.

Unlike in Kraków, klezmer concerts in Berlin are not part of a highly organized Jewish heritage industry. Instead, local klezmer bands perform, for example, in schools as part of educational programs about Judaism, as well as during seminars, conferences, and book presentations related to Jewish culture. They are hired for weddings, funerals, and even divorce parties. At times, klezmer musicians are also asked to play at political rallies (the Social Democrats and the Greens seem to have a liking for klezmer), antifascist demonstrations, promotional parties, or on the ships cruising the Spree River. On certain anniversaries, such as November 9 (Kristallnacht) or 27 Nissan (Yom HaShoah), klezmer musicians are often invited to play during commemorative celebrations on the sites of deportation or in concentration camps. Finally, Berlin also has a few small festivals of Jewish music: the annual *Pankower Klezmertage* (the Pankow Klezmer Days) in the northeast of Berlin, and a Klezmer Festival organized by the Berlin Philharmonic. The major klezmer event remains, however, the annual *Jüdische Kulturtage*, which is one of the oldest such events in Europe.

Jewish Festivals

Two years before the fall of the Wall, as the end of the Soviet bloc loomed near with perestroika and glasnost, a group of East Berlin artists and intellectuals gained permission to stage a three-day festival of Yiddish culture (*Tage der jiddischen Kultur*). The dream of Jalda Rebling, daughter of Lin Jaldati and one of the organizers of the festival, was to turn Berlin into a meeting point for artists and scholars of Yiddish from the West and the forgotten East. Following up the first Yiddish Song Festival in Wuppertal and the first European Yiddish Folk Festival in Zurich in 1984, the small Berlin festival drew considerable media attention. *Neues Deutschland*, the official newspaper of the Socialist Unity Party of Germany (SED), reported on the festival events, including concerts of the pioneers of the klezmer scene, noting that they were concluded with "roaring applause."[117] The success of the first edition secured the continuation of the festival in the following years and even won the organizers the support of UNESCO, which listed the event in its program of the World Decade for Cultural Development 1988–97.

With editions dedicated to Yiddish culture in Poland, Romania, Vilnius, and Ukraine, the festival expanded year by year and became more and more international. And as soon as the Wall came down, bands from the former West Germany, America as well as freshly immigrated Soviet Jewish artists such as Mark Aizikovitch joined in. It quickly became clear that it was the music that attracted most of the spectators. "In the 1980s, I found it just great that there was such a great interest in Yiddish," Jalda Rebling recollects. "At the same time, as far as Yiddish literature was concerned, when we invited for instance Yiddish poets, there were

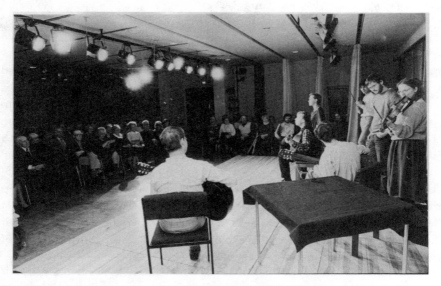

Fig. 1.8 Jewish music concert at the first festival of Yiddish culture in East Berlin, 1987. Photo by Ulrich Rödiger. Courtesy of Jalda Rebling.

[117] "Tage der jiddischen Kultur wurden beendet," *Neues Deutschland*, January 29, 1987, 7.

maybe sixty people in the audience, but when we had a klezmer concert it was three hundred people filling a big hall."[118] Providing space for music and highlighting the links between Eastern European Jewish heritage and Germany, the Days of Yiddish Culture anticipated and to a degree also nurtured the wave of interest in Yiddish song and klezmer that was to peak in the following years.

This "made in the GDR" Jewish festival was promptly followed by its western equivalent. The same year that the East Berlin festival had its first edition, in 1987, the Jewish community in West Berlin launched their own Jewish Culture Days (*Jüdische Kulturtage*). Staged at first as part of the celebrations of Berlin's 750th city anniversary, the "western" festival was initiated under the motto of "the best of Jewish culture" and actually outlived its "eastern" counterpart (which had its last edition in 1997).

The Jewish Culture Days in Berlin, organized under the auspices of the Jewish Community and generously supported by the municipal authorities of Berlin, is an event important to the image of the city, with the list of public figures visiting the festival and addressing the participants including even Chancellor Angela Merkel. The festival has been housed by a number of prestigious cultural venues in Berlin, such as the Philharmonic Hall, the Academy of Arts, Deutsches Theater, and the Jewish Museum, but most of its events usually take place in the local synagogues. Unlike its predecessor from East Berlin, where the Jewish minority amounted to only about five hundred people, the Jewish Culture Days from the beginning has been an event addressing a more numerous and constantly growing local Jewish community. Shelly Kupferberg, who has co-organized a few editions of the festival, states that the agenda of the festival organizers is to address the issues that are important to the Jewish community today and to attract younger community members.[119] Its program, featuring Israeli popular culture and music, has also included ballroom dance events with live music and the *Fest der Gemeinde* (community party), staged at the Jewish Community House. After the fall of the Wall, as the Berlin Jewry became more heterogeneous, multicultural, and multilingual, and still struggling to absorb a large number of Jewish immigrants from the former Soviet Union, the Jewish festival, by including, for example, Russian-language events in the program, came to play the role of a social binding force.

Although the repertoire of the *Jüdische Kulturtage* does not limit itself to heritage music like its eastern counterpart did—the highlight of the 2007 edition for instance was a series of concerts of Israeli and Palestinian hip-hop staged in a popular rock club—both festivals promoted the growing local klezmer scene. It was at the Days of Yiddish Culture in East Berlin that the first klezmer musicians in the GDR could meet Yiddish revivalists from different parts of the world,

---

[118] Rebling, interview by the author, Berlin, February 6, 2006.

[119] Shelly Kupferberg, interview by the author, Berlin, April 12, 2007.

and it was the Jewish Culture Days that staged many highly popular klezmer concerts and dance events such as, among others, the "Long Night of Klezmer" in 2003.

Despite this synergy between the festivals and the local klezmer scene, the Jewish Culture Days in Berlin have never really become a mainstream cultural event. Enclosed in spaces under constant police protection and requiring spectators to go through baggage searches and metal detectors, the festival has a special status as a space potentially fraught with violence. This, and the festival program that, due to problems with financing, shrank drastically in the last few years, might be the reason why this Berlin festival has remained a niche event. While in 2007 around twelve thousand spectators total attended various events of the festival, there were twice as many attending the Jewish festival in Kraków. This festival gathers more than ten thousand spectators every year for its final open air concert alone.

Initiated by Janusz Makuch and Krzysztof Gierat, two non-Jews fascinated by Jewish culture, the first edition of the Cracovian Jewish Culture Festival took place in 1988, when the country was only beginning to regain the memory of its Jewish past. Makuch and Gierat, who belonged to an informal group of Jews and non-Jews learning about Judaism and related to the *Solidarność* movement, were driven by a pioneer enthusiasm and curiosity about a world, which appeared to them like a forgotten Atlantis. The festival was their way of responding to the need of getting to know a culture, which in postwar Poland was surrounded by taboo. "We created a valve to release the tension which had been building up in previous years and which concerned a return to the past," Krzysztof Gierat said retrospectively about the first festival. For him, the interest in Jewish culture in the 1980s was a symbolic return to the period of the Polish Lithuanian Commonwealth, a return to the time "when we were rich owing to this multitude of cultures."[120] The first festival in 1988, organized in a small cinema by the local film discussion club, featured Yiddish films, lectures on Jewish culture, a photo exhibition, and a walking tour around Kazimierz. Soon, Makuch and Gierat made contact with other revivalists of Jewish heritage in Europe. The second festival in 1990, however, organized in co-operation with a number of German institutions and with a German musical director, raised some controversies. A journalist for the newspaper *Jüdische Rundschau* asked dramatically, "Where are the Jews?" and the German Jewish journalist Henryk Broder wondered whether the festival was not a "macabre idea" altogether.[121]

---

[120] Krzysztof Gierat cited in Anna Dodziuk, *Druga dusza: O dwudziestu Festiwalach Kultury Żydowskiej w Krakowie* (Warszawa: Czarna Owca, 2010), 74.

[121] Judith Glass, "Flowers on the Grave," *Jüdische Rundschau*, no. 22, 1990, cited in *3. Festiwal Kultury Żydowskiej w Krakowie* (Kraków: Graffiti, 1992), 151; Henryk M. Broder, "Die toten Juden von Kazimierz," *Themen der Zeit*, no. 21, 1990, cited in *3. Festiwal Kultury Żydowskiej w Krakowie* (Kraków: Graffiti, 1992), 145.

The critical voices led the organizers to reflect on how far the non-Jewish contribution to a Jewish festival could go. "It all came down to the fact that if I, as a *goy*, dare to organize a Jewish festival in the biggest Jewish cemetery in the world," says Janusz Makuch, "I cannot invite only German, French, Dutch, and Belgian artists, without inviting, first of all, Jews. If this is a festival of Jewish culture, Jews must create it, with all their pain, and joy, memory, and hope for the future."[122] Although the festival originated as a way for Poles "to learn about Jewish traditions and overcome negative stereotypes,"[123] with time, it became an important destination for Polish and foreign Jews.

During ten days in summer, cultural institutions, synagogues, and the streets of Kazimierz turn into festival venues. It is one of the rare moments when all of Kraków's synagogues are open. The festival program is incredibly rich, and expands every year. Its twenty-fifth edition in 2010 embraced some 250 events, including thirty-three concerts, fifty lectures, book promotions and panel discussions, and twenty-one different workshops. The festival organizers invited 254 artists and lecturers from various countries, including the United States, Israel, Lithuania, Cuba, Kurdistan, and others.[124] The festival is the biggest cultural event in Kraków and one that is particularly important for the city's image. Municipal authorities subsidize it, and almost a third of its budget comes from the Polish Ministry of Culture and Heritage. The president of Poland is the honorary patron of the event.[125] With thousands of people participating in workshops and concerts, more than ten thousand attending the final open-air concert and a million watching its televised broadcast, the festival has the public acknowledgment and appreciation enjoyed by hardly any other event of this kind.[126]

Kazimierz is both the logistic and spiritual center of the festival. The organizers and visitors alike often speak of the hidden energy of the district. "You feel really connected to your past here," said the American musician Andy Statman, a frequent guest of the festival. "There is also, particularly on Shabbes, an incredible energy of hominess, *kiddush* and sweetness, because the great *tzadikim* are buried here and you can actually feel their presence and their holiness enhancing the Shabbes. It's very very special. If you're sensitive to it, you can experience it."[127]

---

[122] Janusz Makuch, interview by the author, Kraków, May 3, 2007.

[123] Krzysztof Gierat in *3. Festiwal Kultury Żydowskiej w Krakowie* (Kraków: Graffiti, 1992), 148.

[124] "20 Festiwal Kultury Żydowskiej w Krakowie, 24 czerwca-4 lipca 2010 roku: Raport," accessed August 26, 2011, http://www.jewishfestival.pl/upload/downloads/a1eb00a8523a639.pdf.

[125] Statistical data: Jewish Festival Office, Robert Gądek, personal communication, May 15, 2007.

[126] Statistical data: Telewizja Polska Kraków, Maria Miodunka, personal communication, June 8, 2007.

[127] Andy Statman, in *Klezmer Musicians Travel "Home" to Krakow*, directed by Curt Fissel (Jem/Glo, 2004), DVD.

Fig. 1.9 Participants of a Jewish dance workshop staging a Jewish wedding during the Jewish Culture Festival in Kraków, 2008. Photo by Soliman Lawrence.

Fig. 1.10 "Shalom in Szeroka Street." Final concert of the Jewish Culture Festival in Kraków, 2008. Photo by Soliman Lawrence.

The head of the festival, Janusz Makuch, goes so far as to state that the festival exists only thanks to the "mystical consent" of the spirits of Kazimierz:

> The context of this festival is extremely important. . . . I am internally convinced that there is something beyond the concept of *genius loci*, that this place is mystically permeated with the energy of the people, events, history, and religion which flourished here for over seven centuries. . . . Now that all the living are returning here, with the consent of those who died, but whose presence is still perceptible to those who are sensitive to it, a certain symbiosis is taking place—a resonance between the living and the culture which is gone. Without this mystical consent, I don't think we would have been able to organize this festival.[128]

In recent years, the festival has begun to reach out into the region, offering tours to former Jewish towns and organizing concerts in the local synagogues. Since 2009, the festival office also runs the Cheder Café, a meeting space for Jews and non-Jews, which hosts concerts and other cultural events both during the festival and throughout the year.

Although the festival in Kraków offers a wide selection of events, ranging from workshops in Jewish paper-snipping to Sephardic belly dancing and lectures on Yiddish slang, music occupies a central place. Labeled by journalists a "Jewish Woodstock," the festival attracts the most prominent contemporary Jewish musicians worldwide, and the avant-garde of the American klezmer revival are its regular guests. Staging two ticketed evening concerts daily in the beautifully renovated Tempel Synagogue and a free final concert in Szeroka Street, the festival has become a mecca for klezmer fans from all around the world and a mass event, which entirely transforms the Jewish district.

Surprisingly enough, the local klezmer musicians from Kazimierz are not very frequent guests of the festival. Although many of the local bands performed during the early editions of the festival, and the stars of the Polish klezmer scene, Kroke and the Bester Quartet, make regular appearances, the festival and the Kazimierz klezmer scene are largely parallel worlds. One of the reasons is that the festival, which has grown into a prestigious event and attempts to provide performances of high quality, invites internationally renowned musicians. The other, however, is that the festival's director Janusz Makuch believes that Jewish culture at the festival should be performed by "those for whom it is in their bloodstream and their soul—that is the Jews."[129] These two requirements can also be in conflict, since what the festival's director regards as "non-authentic" culture does not automatically have to be of aesthetically low quality, just as the "authentic" productions do not guarantee artistry.

[128] Makuch interview, May 3, 2007.

[129] Janusz Makuch, cited in Dodziuk, *Druga dusza*, 73.

The first editions of the Berlin and Kraków festivals were among the first such events in Europe and blazed the trail for dozens of other local Jewish festivals, which proliferated in Europe after 1989. While Germany hosted some of the earliest Jewish festivals in Europe and still boasts a significant number of annual local events, in the 1990s Jewish festivals spread also to Italy, Holland, Hungary, and Russia. Since the establishment of the European Day of Jewish Culture in 1999, more local initiatives have joined this framework and, in 2008, more than 230 cities in twenty-seven European countries organized small festivals of Jewish culture, attracting at least 140,000 visitors.[130] An important model for the European festivals of this kind was, however, the American KlezKamp: Yiddish Folk Arts Program, which opened in the New York's Catskills Mountains in 1984. An extended workshop program scheduled over Christmas, KlezKamp became a meeting point for American and European klezmer revivalists and a prototype for many other klezmer music festivals from Canada to Russia. And although many of these events, like the ones in Kraków and Berlin, have grown out of local initiatives of often very small groups of activists and cultural organizers, many festivals cooperate now and form something of a North Atlantic "kleznetwork," which nurtures the transnational character of the klezmer scene.[131]

One might ask, however, to what extent the klezmer phenomenon, and for that matter also the Jewish festivals in places such as Kraków and Berlin, should be seen as a revival of the local legacies and to what extent they are manifestations of "invented traditions" serving a particular historical or political moment. Both Kraków and Berlin have a history of klezmer music that constitutes a crucial point of reference for contemporary klezmer revivalists. This has both a material and a more metaphysical dimension. On the one hand, the rich collections of Yiddish songbooks and archival recordings collected in Berlin, or the legacy of the Kraków-based songwriter Mordechai Gebirtig, are important material resources for local musicians. But perhaps more importantly still, it is the emotional bond of today's revivalists to the spaces where Yiddish language culture once flourished, such as Kazimierz and the Scheunenviertel, which enables them to see their work in terms of performing an inherited tradition.

At the same time, the klezmer revival is clearly not a mere excavation of historic musical material performed at historic sites. Even less is it a continuation of prewar musical traditions. In Kraków, klezmer was already undergoing dynamic changes and adapting to the new demands of the entertainment market at the turn of the twentieth century. In Berlin, the klezmer boom can even be seen as a

---

[130] "Report of the Workshop on the European Itinerary of Jewish Heritage, 2008," accessed May 20, 2009, http://www.jewishheritage.org/jh/upload/publications/JH_19.pdf.

[131] See Magdalena Waligórska, "*Kleznetworks*: The Transnational and the Local Dimension of Jewish Culture Festivals," in *Jewish Spaces: Die Kategorie Raum im Kontext kultureller Identitäten*, ed. Petra Ernst and Gerald Lamprecht (Innsbruck: Studienverlag, 2010), 137–56.

meta-revival, as it feeds on the pre–World War II rediscovery of Yiddish culture and the post-1945 work of musicians such as Lin Jaldati, who were revivalists themselves. Post-1989 klezmer in Kraków and Berlin is neither a resurrection nor a reinvention of the historic Jewish soundscapes in these cities. Even if some musicians attempt to revive an old style in a historically accurate manner, the function that this new klezmer fulfills and the context in which it is performed are entirely different from the genre's social role, for example, in a nineteenth-century Polish shtetl. The new klezmer that contemporary musicians in Kraków and Berlin play is rather an adaptation: a creative and selective recombination of elements of the local musical heritage in new contexts and for a new audience. The new klezmer scene echoes the klezmer of the past in that it celebrates heterogeneity, freely drawing from various musical sources such as jazz or even hip-hop, but also in that it defines anew the liminal position of the klezmer musician, who today, just like a hundred years ago, is operating at the very boundary between "Jewish" and "non-Jewish." This echo is not the original, but it is equally real.

2

The Controversy

Appropriated Music

The klezmer revival has frequently made headlines in Germany. Journalists have spoken of a "klezmer cult,"[1] a "*Klezmeritis*"[2] that is afflicting Germans, and a boom of "philo-Semitic shtetl romanticism,"[3] often framing the phenomenon as a suspicious and unhealthy public frenzy. The klezmer scene quickly gained the epithets of "simulation,"[4] "*Massen-Klezmatis*,"[5] and "fakelore."[6] The very first public appearance of non-Jewish klezmer musicians at the East Berlin Days of Yiddish Culture in the late 1980s had already instigated some controversy. The periodical of the Association of Jewish Communities in the GDR promptly questioned the eligibility of non-Jewish musicians to play Jewish music and the authenticity of such performances.[7] With time, as the klezmer scene grew, the appropriation discourse became more and more heated. Rita Ottens and Joel Rubin, authors of *Klezmer-Musik*, titled a chapter on the subject of klezmer in Germany "Music

---

[1] Bax, "Berliner Simulation."

[2] Michael Wuliger, "Schweig, Klezmer, schweig," *Allgemeine Jüdische Wochenzeitung*, August 25, 1994, 2, cited in Ottens, "Der Klezmer als ideologischer Arbeiter," 29.

[3] Tim Schomacker, "Zeichen der Zeit; Notizen vom 4. Klezmer Festival im Vegesacker KITO," *Die Tageszeitung*, May 2, 2000, 23.

[4] Bax, "Berliner Simulation."

[5] Viktoria Tkaczyk, "'Wir sind die Indianer Europas,'" *Die Welt*, August 6, 2001, accessed September 20, 2006, http://www.welt.de/data/2001/08/06/509284.html?prx=1.

[6] Frank London cited in Thomas Groß, "Der Auserwählte Folk," *Die Zeit*, June 24, 2003, accessed June 21, 2009, http://www.zeit.de/2003/31/Klezmer. The term "fakelore" comes from the folklorist Richard Dorson in *Folklore and Fakelore: Essays toward a Discipline of Folk Studies* (Cambridge, MA: Harvard University Press, 1976).

[7] Peter Zacher, "Erfolgreicher Versuch der Wiederannäherung an Unaufgebbares: Drei Tage jiddischer Kultur in Berlin," *Nachrichtenblatt der Jüdischen Gemeinden in der Deutschen Demokratischen Republik*, June 1987, 10–12; Peter Zacher "Erneute Wiederannäherung: Möglichkeiten und Grenzen der Darstellung jiddischer Kultur heute," *Nachrichtenblatt der Jüdischen Gemeinden in der Deutschen Demokratischen Republik*, June 1988, 12–14.

of the Grandchildren of the Victims for the Grandchildren of the Master Race."[8] Clearly, the central anxiety of this klezmer debate concerns not only the manner of representation but also a taboo-breach, and the klezmer revival often has been interpreted as a perverse aftereffect of the Holocaust.

Music is probably the most common object of cultural appropriation. Suitable for mass consumption, well marketable, and capable of generating considerable profit, other cultures' music is especially desirable for borrowing. Yet, at the same time, there is a widespread notion that ethnic music is really "owned" by one group of people and cannot "belong" to others. As Radano and Bohlman note, we tend to think of music in terms of "metaphysics of ownership," believing that a particular genre of music can only be truly understood by those who speak its "language."[9] It is perhaps for this reason that these musical "thefts" often trigger particular indignation.

Klezmer in Germany, from the very beginning, constituted a controversial case, and the 1990s witnessed a heated public debate about whether non-Jewish Germans had the moral right to perform klezmer music at all. The discussion, which unfolded together with the rise of the klezmer revival movement, reflects the anxieties of a minority group that fears the commodification and misrepresentation of their heritage. It also indicates the complexities of Jewish identity in contemporary Germany and brings attention to some of the thorny issues in Jewish/non-Jewish relations.

The appropriation discourse is, indeed, the dominant framework through which the klezmer revival in places such as Germany and Poland has been described, interpreted, and criticized both in journalistic and scholarly writing. Since the very beginning of the klezmer boom in the early 1990s, performances of Jewish music by non-Jews have attracted the attention of publicists and commentators as a particularly morbid, indecent, and a morally suspect case of cultural theft. Branded by the German musicologist Rita Ottens in 1998 as an attempt at a "dejudification of Yiddish music,"[10] the klezmer revival in Germany was soon interpreted as an essential part of what Ruth Ellen Gruber in 2002 labeled "virtual Jewishness."[11] The anxiety that both authors articulated concerned the fact that many of the klezmer revivalists in Germany were non-Jewish, and the contention was that the cultural products they offered were not only deprived of authenticity but also marginalized, and perhaps even threatened, "authentic" Jewish culture. This chapter revisits

---

[8] Ottens and Rubin, *Klezmer-Musik*, 299. The title is a paraphrase of a passage in the *Stuttgarter Zeitung*, reporting a concert of an American klezmer band in Germany in the 1980s, as Ottens and Rubin point out on p. 301.

[9] Ronald Radano and Philip Bohlman, "Introduction: Music and Race, Their Past, Their Presence," in *Music and the Racial Imagination*, ed. Ronald Radano and Philip Bohlman (Chicago: University of Chicago Press, 2000), 6.

[10] Ottens, "Der Klezmer als ideologischer Arbeiter," 28.

[11] Gruber, *Virtually Jewish*.

the arguments used in the controversy around the klezmer boom in Poland and Germany, probing into the set of assumptions about heritage and group boundaries that the framework of cultural appropriation, as such, rests upon.

Cultural appropriation might take very different forms, and appropriation debates concern conflicts over physical objects, sites, traditional music recorded and sold without acknowledging the original source, symbols and patterns, photos of tribal life taken without permission, as well as stories and narratives reproduced and circulated in the media. Typically, these conflicts refer to heritage, but it is not always the indigenous or native heritage that becomes the object of dispute. For example, when the art of Parkour, or freerunning past, over or through obstacles in the urban landscape by means of climbing, jumping, and vaulting, made its way into a James Bond film, Parkour practitioners accused the filmmakers of stealing and profiting unjustly from their "heritage."[12] Likewise, Serdar Somuncu, a German cabaret artist of Turkish background, was accused of appropriation by neo-Nazi circles when he performed a show containing readings of Hitler's *Mein Kampf.*[13] In both cases, the problem was not only *how* a given "heritage" material was tackled, but *by whom.*

The very definition of appropriation lends itself to various interpretations. Though it may denote taking something "illegally or without permission,"[14] it can also be understood as creative incorporation. Appropriation art, in fact, professes even a "direct duplication" of images which, presented in a different context, acquire a different meaning, thus "questioning notions of originality and authenticity."[15] While the definition of appropriation as trespassing prevails among those bent on heritage protection, artists see in it a necessary element of inspiration.

The act of appropriation, regardless of its form, always implies the existence of certain incontestable boundaries between groups. Appropriation might involve tangible or intangible property; it can be literal or figurative. Apart from the classic case of land dispossession, it can also take place through processes such as ventriloquy or translation. In the most basic terms, however, we have to say that cultural appropriation occurs "when a member of one culture takes a cultural practice or theory of a member of another culture as if it were his or her own or as if the right of possession should not be questioned or contested."[16]

---

[12] "James Bond und Le Parkour," accessed May 6, 2009, http://www.reticon.de/nachrichten/james-bond-und-le-parkour_1529.html.

[13] Oliver Link, '"Dann sterbe ich eben,'" *Stern,* February 8, 2006, accessed June 20, 2009, http://www.stern.de/politik/deutschland/:Karikaturen-Streit-Dann/555187.html.

[14] *Collins English Dictionary,* s.v. "Appropriation."

[15] Ian Chilvers, "Appropriation Art," in *A Dictionary of Twentieth Century Art* (Oxford: Oxford University Press, 1998), 473.

[16] Jonathan Hart, "Translating and Resisting Empire: Cultural Appropriation and Postcolonial Studies," in *Borrowed Power: Essays on Cultural Appropriation,* ed. Bruce Ziff and Pratima V. Rao (New Brunswick, NJ: Rutgers University Press, 1997), 138.

Lack of legitimacy of the appropriating agent is one of the defining features of cultural appropriation. This, however, must be understood in the context of cultural boundary, exclusion, and power relations. Although cultural appropriation is ubiquitous and multidirectional, and cultural goods can be simultaneously possessed by more than one party (e.g., intellectual property), appropriation often entails exploitation, marginalization, and subordination. The mission of nation-state building in particular is a task that has often required "nationalizing" the heritage of others in order to maintain the legitimacy of the ruling ideology. The economic dimension is also crucial. Appropriation concerns money, and thus branches of economy, such as tourism, often "hijack" the heritage of a powerless minority for mere economic profit.

The discourse on cultural appropriation has become particularly audible in the media in recent decades. The legal regulation of appropriation poses a new challenge not only to the music industry but also to international lawmakers. This new sensitivity is connected with the increase of attention being given to minorities and political correctness, and with the fact that modern technology has made appropriation more ubiquitous than ever before.

The Appropriation Boom

The fashion for heritage is not new. The problem of a "heritage overload" was already recognized in the nineteenth century, when museums started to accumulate more than they were able to process and display. But these days, claims David Lowenthal, the heritage boom has turned into a "sacred cow" and has become "suffocatingly unmanageable."[17] Modern media, with their heightened potential of transmission, produce an unprecedented number of representations, which float freely from one corner of the world to another. The mimetic capital created by the accumulated and reproduced images from various cultures feeds on and further facilitates appropriation. Bent on providing a vicarious experience of the distant and exotic world of "others," global media are in frenetic pursuit of a new and more thrilling mixture of styles and cultures. In other words, stealing somebody's culture has never been as easy as it is now.

Heritage has moved from the domain of the elite to the vernacular and the quotidian. It has also become less material and more intangible. But its main function remains the same: celebrating the past and professing faith in what Lowenthal calls "a past tailored to present-day purposes."[18] An idealized past serves as a cure against atomization, isolation, uprootedness, and the anxieties of the modern world in the age of massive migrations. Cherishing heritage, we are "clinging to

[17] David Lowenthal, *The Heritage Crusade and the Spoils of History* (Cambridge: Cambridge University Press, 2005), 12.

[18] Ibid., x.

the remnants of stability."[19] Insecurity about the future is, therefore, grist to the mill of heritage revivalists. What makes somebody else's tradition appealing? Lowenthal accounts for this fascination with the principle of "ethnic empathy," or the willingness to express solidarity with powerless minorities. But as the price for celebrating the heritage of minorities/indigenous peoples is also the admission of historical guilt toward them, might this mean that interest in the heritage of persecuted minorities is motivated only by the need of atonement?

George Lipsitz, an American Studies scholar, believes there is something beyond a postcolonial sense of guilt in the cultural appropriation of a minority's heritage. The art of ethnic minorities, bred in a situation of powerlessness and exclusion, contains the irony and ambiguity that have become important elements of postmodern aesthetics. Paradoxically, the culture of the marginalized minority expresses particularly well the anxieties of post-traditional societies. Lipsitz argues:

> Because their marginality involves the pain of exclusion, minority group culture speaks eloquently about the fissures and frictions of society. Because their experience demands bifocality, minority group culture reflects the decentered and fragmented nature of contemporary human experience. Because their history identifies the source of their marginality, minority group cultures have a legitimacy and connection to the past that distinguishes them from more assimilated groups. Masters of irony in an ironic world, they often understand that their marginality makes them more appropriate spokespersons for society than mainstream groups unable to fathom or address the causes of their alienation.[20]

The culture of the other has the potential of becoming a means of self-expression, but what if minorities, rather than "masters of irony," are seen as exotic, satisfying the need for the authentic and pre-industrial? Pictured in simplistic and traditional terms, for example in travel advertisements, indigenous people or minorities might find it more difficult to assert their identity as part of a modern society with diverse lifestyles.[21]

 Musical borrowings can caricature the other, as well. Falling into the pitfalls of representational reductionism, pop productions based on appropriations often romanticize, patronize, and "diminish" the other.[22] Hybridization is reckoned as

---

[19] Ibid., 6–9.

[20] George Lipsitz, "Cruising Around the Historical Block": Postmodernism and Popular Music in East Los Angeles," in *Popular Music: Critical Concepts in Media and Cultural Studies*, vol. 4, *Music and Identity*, ed. Simon Frith (London: Routledge, 2004), 326.

[21] Constance Classen and David Howes, "Epilogue: The Dynamics and Ethics of Cross-Cultural Consumption," *Cross-Cultural Consumption: Global Markets, Local Realities*, ed. David Howes (London: Routledge, 2000), 187.

[22] Steven Feld, "The Poetics and Politics of Pygmy Pop," in Born and Hesmondhalgh, *Western Music and Its Others*, 273.

yet another danger. The common argument is that although it might bring to-gether various culturally distinct groups in a multicultural society, blending indig-enous motifs with other traditions can also lead to the marginalization of native peoples, who become "neutralized" as their heritage enters the mainstream.[23] The other side of the coin is that indigenous people often play on stereotypes and commodify their culture themselves, according to the expectations of the con-sumers. But this conscious and voluntary adoption of the constructed traditional image is, nevertheless, related to the market conditions generated by the demand of the majority.[24]

Heritage = Property?

The paradox is that in order to curtail abusive heritage theft, lawmakers have not been able to work out a more nuanced definition of cultural appropriation than that of property. While appointing an institutionalized "owner" of a given heri-tage makes it easier to prosecute acts of misappropriation, it also reifies culture, assuming fixed boundaries in a realm of endless negotiations.

The United Nations Educational, Scientific, and Cultural Organization (UNESCO) has been among the most active parties in sanctioning the protection of cultural heritage. The UNESCO Model Law, if adopted at the national level, would be quite harsh toward misappropriating artists. It would criminalize not only the failure to acknowledge the source of heritage production but also the elements of prejudice in the artistic rendition of a given group's folklore.[25] Thus, artists who deal with the heritage of cultures that they barely know would be treading on thin ice indeed; if the community from which the heritage originates were able to find the representation in any way offensive to their dignity, the artist could face charges.

The premise of the UNESCO Model Act is, however, that the appropriating artist can use a given heritage, provided that they pay the required fees. More-over, the whole procedure would be controlled by the state, not by the community that it concerns.[26] At the present moment, with the Model Act a dead letter at the national level, offended communities can still resort to the regulations of their respective national codes. There are some possibilities of prosecuting artists who

[23] Michael F. Brown, *Who Owns Native Culture?* (Cambridge, MA: Harvard University Press, 2004), 63.

[24] Certain Native American tribes, such as Hopi and Navajo, have taken advantage of the commercial value of their name and image by selling their own art. See Howes, "Cultural Appropriation and Resis-tance in the American Southwest: Decommodifying 'Indianness,'" in *Cross-Cultural Consumption*, 155.

[25] Brown, *Who Owns Native Culture?*, 217.

[26] Bruce Ziff and Pratima V. Rao, "Introduction to Cultural Appropriation: A Framework for Analy-sis," in *Borrowed Power: Essays on Cultural Appropriation*, ed. Bruce Ziff and Pratima V. Rao (New Bruns-wick, NJ: Rutgers University Press, 1997), 20.

misrepresent ethnic or religious minorities in their performances. According to Polish law, for example, messages of racial hatred, insulting behavior, or the abuse of a personal image can be prosecuted on the basis of either the civil or penal code.[27] However, there are no specific regulations concerning cultural heritage, which requires of the complaining communities more flexibility and interpretational skills to make use of the existing regulations.

On the one hand, applying a law to protect heritage seems to be problematic not only because of the inadequate regulations but also because it would force ethnic groups to redefine and reify their culture, if they wanted to employ legal resources. And certain oral narratives, elements of mysticism, or performative devices, which in their original context may have other functions than mere entertainment or transfer of information, do not lend themselves easily to categorization in legal or economic terms.[28] On the other hand, legal intervention seems to be the only way to prevent power inequality and domination in cases of appropriation.

The definition of heritage in terms of property raises many questions. How can we draw boundaries of culture? How can we decide whether an individual belongs to a given *culture* when establishing whether she belongs to a given *group* might already be problematic? How can we state whether a given culture has actually been damaged through appropriation? Would the absence of standards lead to some exaggerated complaints of damage from hysterical defenders of heritage? Would total heritage protection lead to the claim that only the members of a given group should deal with that group's culture? Although many groups demand more effective protection against heritage theft, some observers also doubt whether a general, all-embracing *legal* solution can successfully protect native heritage against misappropriation without enclosing it in an iron cage of bureaucratic language.[29]

Appropriation and Ethnic Boundaries

Heritage provides a compass of group identities and helps mark the borders between groups. For this reason, heritage appropriation is seen as a disruption of an intricate system of intergroup relations. Cultural production mediates the mutual conception of groups and, through the stereotypes that it employs, helps

---

[27] Personal goods are protected by article 23 of the civil code. Racial and ethnic hatred or slandering an ethnic or national group is covered by articles 256 and 257, and unlawful menace toward an ethnic group by article 119 of the Polish penal code.

[28] Elizabeth Burns Coleman, Rosemary J. Coombe, and Fiona MacArailt, "A Broken Record: Subjecting 'Music' to Cultural Rights," in *The Ethics of Cultural Appropriation*, ed. James O. Young and Conrad G. Brunk (Chichester: Wiley-Blackwell, 2009), 173–210.

[29] Brown, *Who Owns Native Culture?*, 205ff.

individuals to classify the world. If we accept Robert Cantwell's argument that representations of culture help maintain the "insulating lines" between groups, the appropriation of a cultural content of one group by an outsider can be interpreted as a violation of the established cultural scripts.[30]

The belief in this crucial, boundary-sustaining role of heritage feeds an entire set of arguments against appropriation. Walter Benjamin, for example, saw the authenticity of an art object in its embeddedness in a given tradition. "[T]he unique value of the 'authentic' work of art," he wrote, "has its basis in ritual, the location of its original use value." The very reproduction of a work of art, therefore, is a threat to tradition.[31] In a similar vein, Born and Hesmondhalgh argue in favor of what they call "strategic essentialism" in music, believing that retaining boundaries and distinctive aesthetic traditions in the age of hybridities could actually bring new creative impulses into music making, stimulating cultural diversity and celebrating distinct social identities.[32]

Given that the performance of heritage is a way of flagging group identities, heritage appropriation can also have an aspect of impersonation. Cases of assuming the identity of an ethnic minority are, in fact, not new. As early as 1920, a group of businessmen in Arizona created a "tribe" resembling the Hopi, who were engaged in their own version of Indian rituals. What began apparently as a racist parody eventually consolidated a group identifying itself more and more with Native Americans.[33] There are more such examples, where self-ascribed "natives" aspire to the title of "traditionalists" and strive to be more "picturesquely native" than those who have practiced Indian customs for generations.[34] Such hobby-Indians, or philo-Indians, who appropriate Native American traditions, are, according to some observers, a greater danger to Native Americans than those who demand their assimilation. A borrowed identity is seen as a threat to the ethnic boundary.[35]

"[C]onfirming possession to some while excluding others is the raison d'être of heritage," notes David Lowenthal. The exclusivity secures the group's cohesion and enforces solidarity against outsiders. This results in the common belief that "only our own flesh and blood can cherish heritage intact; newcomers and colonials erode or debase it."[36] What happens, though, when there is no "flesh and blood" left to carry on with the enactments of heritage?

---

[30] Robert Cantwell, *Ethnomimesis: Folklife and the Representation of Culture* (Chapel Hill, NC: University of North Carolina Press, 1993), 6–7.

[31] Walter Benjamin, *Illuminations* (London: Pimlico, 1999), 217 and 215.

[32] Born and Hesmondhalgh, introduction to *Western Music and Its Others*, 42.

[33] Howes, "Cultural Appropriation and Resistance," 141–42.

[34] Brown, *Who Owns Native Culture?*, 187.

[35] Howes, "Cultural Appropriation and Resistance," 138.

[36] Lowenthal, *The Heritage Crusade and the Spoils of History*, 230–31.

Discontinuity of Inheritance

Heritage without heirs abounds in history. Genocides, forced migrations, and other abrupt or lengthy demographic processes disrupt the continuity of cultural inheritance and leave the fate of a given legacy in the hands of outsiders. The fate of Jewish heritage in post-Holocaust Central and Eastern Europe provides a particularly powerful illustration of a ruptured chain of inheritance. The transmission of the pluralist and locally diversified Jewish heritage has certainly never followed the rigid and dogmatic patterns of the church-sanctioned transmission of Christian heritage. However, the existence of the central reference point of all Jewry, the Torah, has always allowed Jews to retain distinctive traditions and the legacy of learning, which continued even under the conditions of dispersion in the Diaspora. It was only the tragedy of the Holocaust, together with Stalinist purges and post–World War II persecution of Jews, that left the Jewish material culture of vast areas of Central Europe in the hands of ethnic others.

Heritage without heirs runs the risk of being either ignored as irrelevant by locals or, if the authorities try to preserve it, becoming a thorn in the side of those who oppose giving priority to the legacy of the absent ethnic group. However, as soon as advantages of cultivating the abandoned heritage appear, the past of a minority group can be easily hijacked by another group and used as a cultural, political, or economic resource.[37] It is not uncommon that the heritage of an ethnic minority changes its status in the host communities from undesired "pollution" to an economic asset.[38] Particularly with the rise of heritage tourism, local communities might choose to capitalize on the heritage of their absent minorities, selling it to foreign tourists. In some cases, tour-operators might even promote to visitors from abroad their own abandoned heritage, as in the case of German tourism in Gdańsk.[39]

Whether such an economically motivated continuation of the heritage of absent minorities is a positive or a negative phenomenon is debatable. While Tunbridge and Ashworth are convinced that a "sensitive tourist-historic appropriation of minority heritage also generates a positive spin-off for international relations,"[40] the tone of the debates over Jewish heritage in Germany and Poland suggests that cultural appropriation in this context often meets with a complete lack of acceptance.

[37] Ibid., 153–54 and 34–69.

[38] John Urry, *Consuming Places* (London: Routledge, 1995), 188–89.

[39] John E. Tunbridge and Gregory J. Ashworth, *Dissonant Heritage: The Management of the Past as a Resource in Conflict* (Chichester: Wiley, 1996), 155–60.

[40] Ibid., 274.

The Klezmer Revival as a Case of Appropriation

The universal arguments against cultural appropriation are usually centered around three concepts. The key idea is the assumption that appropriation might destroy the integrity of the community of origin in misrepresenting the culture in question.[41] Since a group identity is shaped by our recognition by others, "[n]onrecognition or misrecognition can inflict harm, can be a form of oppression, imprisoning someone in a false, distorted, and reduced mode of being."[42] The argument of misrepresentation implies too that artists coming from outside of the community do not have what Young and Haley call insiders' "privileged knowledge," and are likely to produce a distorted image of the culture they are dealing with.[43] The second danger of appropriation is the propensity to damage or transform an element of culture. If a traditional artifact circulates outside of its original context, it might undergo hybridization or even lose its inherent spiritual meaning. Replacing an original with a merely approximated copy becomes also a metaphor for displacing the other in the process of what bell hooks terms "consumer cannibalism."[44] Here, the other whose heritage is appropriated and consumed is denied the specificity of his voice in that his difference becomes commodified to satiate the majority's appetite for ethnic "spice." Finally, yet importantly, when appropriation has an economic purpose, it generates benefit for the appropriators to the material detriment of the community where the culture originated.[45]

The klezmer revival in Germany came to be considered by many as a classic case of cultural appropriation, and its counterpart in Poland also generated many controversies. The debate on the moral aspects of entertaining non-Jewish audiences with Jewish popular culture, however, is older than that. In 1908 the Berlin Jewish weekly *Jüdische Rundschau* alarmed its readers about a vaudeville theater run by two comedian brothers, Anton and Donat Herrnfeld, both converted Jews, who were staging plays featuring comical Jewish characters for a prevalently non-Jewish audience. What the indignant journalist, who saw the Herrnfeld Theater productions as nothing less than anti-Semitic and scandalous, bemoaned the most was that Jews attended the questionable performances too.[46]

---

[41] Ziff and Rao, "Introduction to Cultural Appropriation," 9.

[42] Charles Taylor, *Multiculturalism: Examining the Politics of Recognition* (Princeton: Princeton University Press, 1994), 25, cited in Ziff and Rao, 11–12.

[43] James O. Young and Susan Haley, "'Nothing Comes from Nowhere': Reflections on Cultural Appropriation as the Representation of Other Cultures," in Young and Brunk, *The Ethics of Cultural Appropriation*, 275.

[44] bell hooks, "Eating the Other: Desire and Resistance," in *Media and Cultural Studies: Key Works*, ed. Meenakshi G. Durham and Douglas M. Kellner (Oxford: Blackwell, 2006), 373.

[45] Ziff and Rao, "Introduction to Cultural Appropriation," 8.

[46] See "Die antisemitischen Gebrüder Herrnfeld," *Jüdische Rundschau*, August 28, 1908, accessed September 16, 2011, http://www.filmportal.de/material/die-juedische-rundschau-ueber-das-herrn-feld-theater.

A century later, some of the preoccupations about the way Jews are represented in popular culture remain the same. Many critics of the German klezmer scene see it as an outright abuse of Jewish heritage or even an essentially anti-Semitic phenomenon.[47] The critical voices come mainly from the Jewish press, such as the *Allgemeine Jüdische Wochenzeitung*, or *European-Jewish Magazine Golem*, but not only. The arguments used in the dispute about the legitimacy of non-Jewish musicians playing klezmer have touched upon generic issues such as the commercialization of heritage, as well as more specific problems such as depriving Jewish music of its spiritual dimension. What makes this debate particular, though, are the questions probing into the history of the relations between Jews and non-Jews in Germany and Poland, and the moral and philosophical significance of the Holocaust for the performance of Jewish heritage today.

The argument that the klezmer scene stereotypes Jewish culture is a common indictment in both Germany and Poland. Iris Weiss, a Berlin-based journalist, was among the first to speak of the "Disneylandization" of Jewish heritage, claiming that klezmer artists are often uninformed about Jewish culture and present it via clichés that falsify the history of the Jews. This falsification, according to Weiss, consists in presenting Jews as the exotic "others" who, as the misled spectator might conclude, were annihilated *because* they were so different. Weiss finds it crucial for the understanding of the Holocaust in Germany that most of the pre–World War II German Jews were entirely assimilated, and it was their similarity to their German persecutors that constituted the real tragedy of their predicament. The nostalgia for the shtetl Jewry, which is, in Weiss's opinion, inherent in the klezmer revival, leads only to the proliferation of stereotypes about Jews and a misinterpretation of history.[48] The reservations that Weiss presented—both in her essay and during the "Jewish Disneyland" walking tours she used to lead in the center of Berlin—grew out of an anxiety that popular representations of Jews serve non-Jewish artists and spectators as an ersatz encounter with Jews. In her opinion, just as Eastern European Jewish folklore has replaced German Jewish heritage, klezmer musicians have replaced Jews.

Similarly, the German literature scholar Leslie Morris believes that the klezmer phenomenon has affected the realms of popular culture and also German memory. "[W]hat is remembered with the ubiquitous strains of Klezmer in Germany," she claims, "is not the experience of German Jews . . . nor that of other cosmopolitan European Jews, but rather a simulacrum of a displaced and fetishized Jewishness."[49] Klezmer thus functions as a metonymy of Jewish experience, an

---

[47] See Rita Ottens, "Ikonografie der Andersartigkeit: Rassismus und Antisemitismus in der deutschen Popularmusik," *Neue Zeitschrift für Musik* 163 (2002): 54–57.

[48] Weiss cited in Kirsten Kueppers, "Marketing mit Davidstern," *Die Tageszeitung*, November 20, 2000, 19; Weiss, "Jewish Disneyland."

[49] Leslie Morris, "The Sound of Memory," *German Quarterly* 74, no. 4 (2001): 376.

association that Morris sees as "illusory, fictive, invented, or 'hyperreal.'"[50] Like Weiss, she considers the displaced and metonymic nature of the klezmer revival as distorting and homogenizing Jewish culture.

Journalists from the Polish Jewish magazine *Midrasz* felt inspired by the debate initiated by Weiss and, reprinting her article, argued that some of the stereotypes used by the klezmer revivalists in Poland also border on anti-Semitism. It is the simplification present in many heritage productions, and the reduction of the diversity of Jewish life to an immediately recognizable cliché that, according to *Midrasz*, disturbs the Jewish audiences of the revival. The journalists also bemoaned the fact that only Jewish folklore, not Jewish high culture, attracted the attention of the revivalists. This imbalanced representation of Jewish cultural heritage has turned klezmer into *the* musical image of Jewishness.[51] In addition, the daily newspaper *Gazeta Wyborcza* commented on the representational reductionism of the klezmer revival in Kraków. Klezmer forms part of a commercialized cliché of Jewishness, argued one journalist, illustrating his point with a comparison addressed to the Polish reader preoccupied with the condition of Polish heritage in today's Ukraine and Lithuania: "It is as if all that was left of the Polish Vilnius and Lvov were kitschy figures of the stereotypical Pole in a Łowicz folk costume manufactured by the locals."[52] What this interesting parallel brings into relief is not only the problem of the reduction of the complex heritage to one image, but also the identity of the authors of such artifacts.

Apart from the argument that klezmer misrepresents Jewishness, reducing it to a set of clichés, klezmer revivalists also face the accusation of hybridizing Jewish traditional music and thus distorting its original form. While many klezmer bands mix the genre with other styles, to klezmer purists this crossover is nothing other than a contamination. Ottens and Rubin, in their *Klezmer-Musik*, claim that hybridization of klezmer reduces it to "neo-primitivism" and destroys the essence of this music.[53] The authors see the very willingness of musicians to contribute something new to klezmer as detrimental. In their view, klezmer should be retained by its revivalists in the traditional form.[54] A related argument is raised by Assaf Talmudi of the Israeli klezmer band Oy Division. In a discussion on the future of Yiddish culture organized by the KlezKanada festival, he argued that the displacement of klezmer, as a folk genre, from the context of community life into a formalized concert-hall context endangers the core qualities of the music.

---

[50] Ibid.

[51] Alina Cała et al., "Koza ze styropianu, pejsy z pakuł," *Midrasz*, March 2006, 9–13.

[52] Wojciech Orliński, "Szanuj menela swego," *Duży Format: Gazeta Wyborcza*, June 30, 2008, 4.

[53] Ottens and Rubin, *Klezmer-Musik*, 309.

[54] Ibid., 9–10.

Everything that we like about this music, all the nuances, the intricacies, evolved because of the music being close to the community. . . . Folk music, in order to breathe, needs to be within a community . . . you can say it doesn't matter if these are Gentiles or Jews, but if it becomes an artifact of representation, it's finished.[55]

The protective instincts of the purists are also dictated by the fear that Jewish life might be entirely marginalized by what Ruth Gruber calls "virtual Jewishness."[56] The journalist Konstanty Gebert, in his introduction to the Polish edition of Gruber's *Virtually Jewish*, claims that this has already taken place in Poland, where the Jewish heritage boom overshadows the small, assimilated Jewish communities.[57] Gruber herself argues in a press interview that the klezmer revival is part of a wider interest in the dead Jewish culture, while the living Jews and their contemporary problems do not attract enough attention.[58] This has led to the situation, according to Gebert, where there is nobody to defend the authentic Jewish culture.[59]

There are also pessimists who warn that Jews have been made redundant as non-Jews take over the cultivation of Jewish heritage: If *anyone* can be an expert on Jewish culture, what place do Jews hold?[60] The literary scholar Liliane Weissberg, reflecting on the German klezmer scene, was alarmed about what she interpreted as an impersonation of Jews by non-Jews: "[German klezmer musicians] are not just playing music. They are playing Jews. This role-play has become very successful, and gives apparent satisfaction to the actors and listeners."[61] The fear that such public representations of Jewishness will supplant the Jewish voice in society is becoming more common. The recent German feature film *Ein ganz gewöhnlicher Jude* [Just an Ordinary Jew] written by Charles Lewinsky, a Swiss Jewish author and scriptwriter, brought it to the attention of a wider public. The protagonist of the film, a Jewish journalist Emmanuel Goldfarb, frustrated by his family life and exasperated with examining his own Jewishness, leads a prolonged monologue directed at Mr. Gebhardt, a German school teacher who has invited him to speak about Jewishness in his class. With biting sarcasm and rising vexation, Goldfarb exposes the revival of Jewish heritage as a manifestation of

---

[55] Assaf Talmudi, "The Future of Jewish Culture," a debate organized within the program of the KlezKanada festival, Montreal, August 25, 2007.

[56] The term "virtual Jewishness" was coined by Ruth E. Gruber in her book *Virtually Jewish*.

[57] Gebert, "Nieautentyczność?," 13.

[58] Ruth E. Gruber, "Wierzchołek nieistniejącej góry," *Tygodnik Powszechny*, July 3, 2005, accessed August 1, 2005, http://tygodnik.onet.pl/1548,1235372,0,354087,dzial.html.

[59] Gebert, "Nieautentyczność?," 16.

[60] Cała et al., "Koza ze styropianu, pejsy z pakuł," 10.

[61] Liliane Weissberg, "Reflecting on the Past, Envisioning the Future: New Perspectives in German-Jewish Studies," Lecture LBI/GHI Washington, October 2003, 3.

suffocating philo-Semitism, which in its fascination for enacted folklore, marginalizes real Jews:

> We have become fashionable; most of us only posthumously, but anyway. In every respectable Jewish center you can learn Israeli folk dances. At every town-fair there is a stand with Jewish cuisine: latkes and gefilte fish. Is that not enough Jewishness for you? What do you need *me* for? A real Jew can only disturb you in your efforts to find Jews great. Why don't you take your pupils to Fürth for the klezmer festival? There will be some band on the stage called All-Stars-Klezmer-Something, or whatever they call themselves, and none of the musicians will be Jewish. . . . Sometimes I feel like coming up to those world-saving musicians, and saying right in their faces: "If you have already killed our musicians, why can't you at least leave our music in peace?" But they wouldn't understand, because out of all that philo-Semitism they have already long become the better Jews. What do you need me for, Mr. Gebhardt? What do you need a real Jew for? There are, after all, enough artificial ones![62]

Goldfarb labels non-Jewish klezmer revivalists not just as fake Jews who appropriate the cultural space due to Jews but as the offspring of the perpetrators of the Holocaust. As such, their relation to Jewish music is ambiguous. Goldfarb, as the voice of ordinary Jews in Germany, sees this musical appropriation through the prism of guilt and quasi-colonialist behavior—with the conclusion that the perpetrators should not profit from the music of their victims.

The idea that the grandchildren of those who staged the Holocaust are fascinated with the music of their victims has led some observers to suspect that Jewish heritage is being instrumentalized. For the publicist Henryk Broder, reviving the shtetl-image is an attempt at bringing back the status quo ante in post-Holocaust Europe, a means of self-reassurance, and a national therapy for Germans.[63] Iris Weiss speaks of "Jewish Disneyland" as an easy version of Jewishness, one that allows bypassing all unpleasant confrontations with the past.[64] She also claims that instead of dealing with the German heritage of atrocity, Germans instrumentalize klezmer in order to "identify with Jewish victims rather than the perpetrators."[65] Sylke Tempel, in *Die Welt*, argues, similarly, that klezmer festivals deliver a "soft experience" of Jewishness, helping to ease guilty feelings toward Jews,[66] and Leslie Morris asks whether the fabrication of Jewish sound fills the spaces of the Jewish absence in Germany.[67]

---

[62] *Ein ganz gewöhnlicher Jude*, directed by Charles Lewinsky and Oliver Hirschbiegel (NFP Marketing and Distribution, 2005), DVD. Translation by the author.

[63] Broder, "Die Konjunktur des Jüdischen."

[64] Weiss, "Jewish Disneyland."

[65] Weiss cited in Jeremy Eichler, "Klezmer's Final Frontier," *New York Times*, August 29, 2004, 1.

[66] Tempel, "Alan Bern lehrt die Deutschen das mollige Kuscheln mit Klezmer."

[67] Morris, "The Sound of Memory," 374.

Michael Birnbaum goes even farther, claiming that the "prevalence of Eastern European klezmer images in German culture impedes possibilities for dialogue and exchange between the Jewish community and the German community as a whole." Although Birnbaum does not name any instances in which the existence of the klezmer scene in Germany actually has hindered communication between Jews and non-Jews, he is confident that the popularity of klezmer induces Germans to treat Jews as "wholly distant and foreign," which eventually allows them to "lessen their guilt about the Holocaust."[68]

Beyond the argument of the therapeutic function of klezmer, several scholars of German Jewish relations have observed that the interest in Jewish folklore marks a process of redefinition of the German national identity. Ottens and Rubin claim that the fraternization with Jews through their music is a way for Germans to detach themselves from the devalued concepts of nation and fatherland.[69] Likewise, Karen Remmler puts forward a hypothesis that the appropriation of klezmer and other forms of Yiddish folklore represent the yearning of a part of German society to return to the vision of German heritage as cosmopolitan.

> The attempt by some Germans to recover an international, cosmopolitan tradition by harking back to German-Jewish tradition as an integral part of *German*, not just German-Jewish history, counters a more nationalistic movement among some Germans to revive traditional customs and traditions that hark back to a notion of German *heimat*. This revival, which I would argue includes an appropriation of klezmer music and Yiddish theater as ersatz German folk culture, expresses a German desire to return to a pre-Shoah period in which a mythic cosmopolitanism coincided with a particularly unstable brand of democratic civic society.[70]

Remmler identifies the klezmer boom as part of a return to "a sense of normalcy," even though the mythologized cosmopolitanism that it invokes never really existed. The engagement of Germans with Jewish culture is therefore an introspective process, self-serving, and bordering on impersonation and the subsumption of the other. Morris and Zipes even note that "Germans cannot operate without the Jews within them."[71] Remmler, however, warns that intergroup dialogue through cultural appropriation is dangerous:

> A dialogue or encounter between an I who can only engage with an other by identifying does more harm than good. . . . How might one encounter

---

[68] Birnbaum, "Jewish Music, German Musicians," 319.

[69] Ottens and Rubin, *Klezmer-Musik*, 299.

[70] Karen Remmler, "Encounters Across the Void: Rethinking Approaches to German-Jewish Symbioses," in *Unlikely History. The Changing German-Jewish Symbiosis 1945–2000*, ed. Leslie Morris and Jack Zipes (New York: Palgrave, 2002), 21.

[71] Leslie Morris and Jack Zipes, "German and Jewish Obsession," in *Unlikely History*, xv.

another human being face-to-face? This would not consist of Germans appropriating the supposed culture of the other (klezmer music, conversion, and so on) but rather a form of empathy that would recognize the difference of the other and take responsibility for that person's well-being, while acknowledging the impossibility of becoming the other.[72]

Apart from the argument of the potentially invasive nature of appropriation, another frequently made point is that cultural borrowing infringes on the sphere of the sacred. The spiritual dimension of some Jewish music, particularly of the Hasidic *nigunim* and the fact that klezmer music originally accompanied the wedding ritual, provides some controversy here. For some critics the use of musical material charged with religious meaning outside of its original context and without the knowledge of its spiritual connotations is, at least, inconsiderate. For Alex Jacobowitz, without the connection to God, the performance of klezmer is empty, meaningless, and "vulgar."[73] Similarly, Jalda Rebling, singer and cantor in the liberal synagogue in Berlin, is of the opinion that without an understanding of Jewish liturgy, klezmer musicians of today are not able to perform Jewish music in a competent and fully respectful way.[74]

The argument about the element of the sacred in klezmer suggests that the genre deserves particular respect and protection from profane use. This taboo status relates also to the fact that for many, the Holocaust marks a moral caesura for entertainment featuring Jewish humor or parody. As the journalists of the Polish *Midrasz* observe, Jewish jokes and cabaret songs with self-derogatory humor sound "ghastly" after the Holocaust. Even though they may have been an important part of pre–World War II Jewish popular culture in Poland, performed today in the absence of Jews they are offensive and might fuel anti-Semitic clichés.[75]

The ethnomusicologist Philip Bohlman notes that some Jewish cabaret songs did indeed contain anti-Semitic lyrics.[76] Walter Zev Feldman observes that parody was inherent in many of the American recordings of klezmer music from the 1920s and earlier. Likewise, a number of Yiddish songs sung by Hasidim originated as parodies aimed against them. The parody in Jewish music was usually generated by Jews themselves, but sometimes also the host societies employed Jewish music in parody aimed against the Jewish minority.[77] An infamous example from Poland is the travesty of the traditional Jewish Sabbath song "mayufes,"

---

[72] Remmler, "Encounters across the Void," 26.

[73] Jacobowitz interview.

[74] Rebling, interview, February 6, 2006.

[75] Cała et al., "Koza ze styropianu, pejsy z pakuł," 9–11.

[76] Philip V. Bohlman, "Music, Modernity, and the Foreign in the New Germany," *Modernism/Modernity* 1, no. 1 (1994): 141.

[77] Walter Zev Feldman, e-mail communication, November 5, 2006.

popular particularly in the nineteenth century. Polish gentry who delighted in this mockery would summon "their Jews" to sing to the melody and perform a humiliating choreography. This form of entertainment was so popular that it soon inspired the appearance of professional impersonators of Jews, who would dress up as Jews and, entertaining the audience with jokes in mock-Yiddish, perform the "mayufes" dance. This demeaning practice eventually caused the original "ma-yufes" song to disappear from many Sabbath hymn anthologies and alienated it from its original religious context.[78]

Last but not least, the arguments against the klezmer boom touch on the subject of the financial benefits of the appropriators. Rokhl Kafrissen, columnist of *Jewish Currents,* in her "Jewish Cultural Manifesto," addressed this issue in relation to the klezmer revival in Germany. She stated in her opening sentence that "Jewish culture belongs to Jews. . . . Forget Holocaust reparations. I'd like to see every Jew in the world get a piece of the exploitation of Jewish culture. It wouldn't be much, I admit; in fact, it would be infinitesimal. But all I want is the tiniest little symbolic recognition that we have something that they want."[79] Although it might not always be so boldly formulated, the question of who draws profits from the performance of Jewish heritage also makes its way to the debate on the appropriation of klezmer.

The case of klezmer in Poland and Germany inspired an entire range of arguments against the appropriation of Jewish heritage by non-Jews. The issues raised in this public discourse refer to, next to the universal problems of stereotyping, misrepresentation, and economic exploitation, also to the unique character of the Holocaust and therefore to the distinctiveness of the appropriation of Jewish heritage. However, not all of the voices in this heated debate do, in fact, condemn the non-Jewish involvement in klezmer.

The historian Diana Pinto believes that the interest in Jewish heritage coming from outside of the Jewish community has a chance to create "an open, cultural and even political *agora*" where non-Jews encounter Jews.[80] The resulting "Jewish Space" would be beneficial for Jews in helping them to form a new Jewish identity vis-à-vis non-Jews:

> Rather than perceiving this reality as an impoverishment, Jews should consider this structural condition as a major positive challenge, indeed a challenge unique to Europe. For it is only here that Jews must confront

---

[78] Bret Werb, "Majufes: A Vestige of Jewish Traditional Song in Polish Popular Entertainment," *Polish Music Journal* 6, no. 1 (2003), accessed September 19, 2011, http://www.usc.edu/dept/polish_music/PMJ/issue/6.1.03/Werb.html#[4]; Bret Werb, "Majufes" in *Enzyklopädie jüdischer Geschichte und Kultur* (Stuttgart: J. B. Metzler Verlag, forthcoming).

[79] Rokhl Kafrissen, "A Jewish Cultural Manifesto," in *Jewish Currents,* November 2005, accessed May 19, 2008, http://www.jewishcurrents.org/2005-nov-kafrissen.htm.

[80] Pinto, *The Third Pillar?*

historically charged "others," whose ancestors were very much present, if not always responsible, during the Holocaust and before that during the centuries of European anti-Semitism.[81]

While stressing the special condition of Jewish heritage revival, Pinto sees the involvement of non-Jews in Jewish culture as an advantage. "Jewish Space," even though it might be based on cultural appropriation, is an important place of interaction between Jews and non-Jews, where painful issues from the past can be debated and tensions relieved.

Konstanty Gebert, despite his reservations, does not refute non-Jewish artists who promote and propagate Jewish culture. He believes that cultural transfer might allow non-Jews to familiarize the unknown other and thus bridge the gap between the two groups.[82] Philip Bohlman also looks at the klezmer revival with optimism. Although he finds it paradoxical that some actors of this revival are Gentiles, he points out that the revival has managed to win for Jewish music a prominent place on the global music market, and that it would not be fair to consider the Jewish folk music of reunited Central Europe as artificial or dissociated from its counterpart a century ago.[83] In his view, promoting Jewish music from Eastern Europe on the European cultural scene is important not only to Jewish identity but also to European identity, which would remain incomplete without its Jewish components.[84]

A number of researchers of Jewish folk music also make a point that the history of klezmer as a genre must be understood within a context of constant interethnic cultural appropriations. Walter Zev Feldman, as a musicologist, supplies numerous examples of this exchange.[85] Ruth Rosenfelder notes, too, that direct appropriation of folk repertoire from other cultures has been a frequent practice in Hasidic music. Thus, not only Eastern European or Caucasian folk tunes in time became adapted for the Hasidic *nigunim*, but also the Marseillaise, for example.[86] Conversely, as Feldman points out, the repertoire of the *klezmorim* also made its way to other Eastern European genres: the Jewish dance *sher* was adopted by Ukrainians and the Jewish *khosidl* tunes featured at Christian weddings in northern Bucovina.[87] In the first half of the twentieth century, traces of

[81] Ibid.

[82] Gebert, "Nieautentyczność?," 14.

[83] Philip Bohlman, "Historisierung als Ideologie: die 'Klesmerisierung' der jüdischen Musik," in *Jüdische Musik? Fremdbilder—Eigenbilder*, ed. Eckhard John and Heidy Zimmermann (Köln: Böhlau, 2004), 255.

[84] Bohlman, *Jüdische Volksmusik*, 344–47.

[85] Feldman, "Bulgareasca/Bulgarish/Bulgar," 1–35.

[86] Ruth Rosenfelder "Whose Music? Ownership and Identity in Jewish Music," presented at the conference "Jewish Culture in the Age of Globalization" held at the University of Manchester, July 22, 2008.

[87] Walter Z. Feldman, e-mail communication, November 5, 2006.

klezmer music were also discernible in Moldavian folk music (*jidancuta*) and in Russian popular music.[88]

The history of mutual Jewish/non-Jewish appropriation in folk music testifies also to the fact that klezmer was historically performed also by non-Jews and for non-Jewish audiences. As Henry Sapoznik, a klezmer revivalist and the initiator of The Yiddish Folk Arts Program KlezKamp, points out: "Klezmer existed also partially in the non-Jewish world, and there has always been a sizable non-Jewish minority in klezmer. That says something. That's a true reflection of the status of klezmer."[89]

Apart from the fact that there is a history of non-Jewish engagement in Jewish folk music, the argument of legitimate curiosity toward the other also gains currency in the klezmer debate. Beyle Schaechter-Gottesman, a Yiddish poet and Holocaust survivor living in New York, notes that the klezmer revival among non-Jews should be seen also through the prism of the history of Jewish interest in non-Jewish mainstream culture. In an interview for the *New York Times*, she said: "The Jewish participation in the non-Jewish world was so overwhelming through the years, it's only right that they should come to find out about us."[90]

The Musicians' Response

Regardless of the single voices of encouragement, non-Jewish klezmer musicians often encounter accusations that they are usurpers of Jewish folklore. It doesn't take long for novices on the klezmer scene to find out that journalists, reviewers, and even their audiences might question their involvement. Hardy Reich, of the East German group Aufwind, realized this for the first time when his band traveled to Israel in 1990. Invited to a klezmer festival in Safed, the band spent some time in the country, busking in the streets. "We had one really striking experience in Jerusalem when we played in the street for money," recalls Reich:

> When we stopped playing, two orthodox men came up to us, very religious types, with yarmulkes on their heads. They started talking to us and they asked us where we were from. When they found out that we were from Berlin and not Jewish they asked us if they could take back the money they had put into the box for us. What can you say to something like that? I was speechless . . . but this is when I realized that you have to be prepared to face such situations.[91]

[88] Walter Z. Feldman, "Klezmer as 'Other Music' for American Jews, 1950–1980," a lecture held at the symposium "Klezmer and other 'other' musics" at Yiddish Summer Weimar, July 14, 2007.

[89] Henry Sapoznik, interview by the author, KlezKanada Festival, August 23, 2007.

[90] Beyle Schaechter-Gottesman in Eichler, "Klezmer's Final Frontier," 24.

[91] Hardy Reich, interview by the author, Berlin, June 2005, 13.

By now, non-Jewish German klezmer musicians seem to be prepared for tł
troversy. "Are you Jewish?" is one of the most frequent questions that k
musicians face after a concert. These queries, tedious as they are, make them realize how much klezmer audiences bind the idea of authenticity to the ethnic background of the musicians. The challenge, however, is the question that follows:
namely, why they, as non-Jews, play Jewish music. Snorre Schwarz of *Di Grine
Kuzine*, who came to the band with a punk-rock background, very soon became
aware that playing klezmer is different:

> There is no chance to escape that. . . . Everybody asks you: Why? Why
> this? Why not? Are you? Are you not? Why can you? How can you? How
> do you feel? When I was doing music before nobody was interested in
> that, nobody was asking: "Why do you play this music?" Since then, of
> course, I've had to think about why I do this.[92]

Confronted with such questioning on an everyday basis, many German musicians
have been forced to reflect at great length on whether what they do is cultural appropriation and, if so, whether there is anything wrong with it.

Burkhart Seidemann, who for twelve years managed Hackesches Hoftheater,
the headquarters of klezmer and Yiddish music in Berlin, is exasperated with
what he calls "authenticity mysticism." He discards questions about whether his
artists are Jewish as irrelevant. The ethnic or religious origins might matter in the
Jewish community but not in a theater, he says. "People look for authenticity that
they connect to blood. But the blood of culture is its quality."[93]

Similarly, Detlef Pegelow, a tuba player who performs in several klezmer bands,
believes that the authenticity of the genre does not depend on the person of the
performer: "What I believe in is that a klezmer song which is interpreted in a
certain moment is Jewish because it is played by a Jewish person, or by somebody who knows how to play in the Jewish style. They don't need to be Jewish, as
long as they know how to play in the Jewish style." Reducing an artist to playing
only the genre that he was brought up with, continues Pegelow, is absurd: "I'm a
German and I would just have to play Berlin songs, nothing else. Because I was
born in Berlin and my father was born in Berlin!"[94]

Many German klezmer musicians refute the notion of culture as the property
of the ethnic group where it originated, and they point out that appropriation is
a very natural phenomenon in music. "I would actually accuse myself of stealing
music all over the place," says Max Hacker from *Di Grine Kuzine*. "If they think
that taking music from somewhere else is a bad thing then they know pretty

---

[92] S. Schwarz, interview by the author, Berlin, January 2006, 23.
[93] Burkhart Seidemann, interview by the author, Berlin, January 4, 2006.
[94] Detlef Pegelow, interview by the author, Berlin, January 18, 2006.

damn little about music" he counters the critics.[95] To Detlef Pegelow, klezmer, a compound of different Eastern European genres originally performed also by Gypsy and Christian musicians, is not just a "Jewish issue." Klezmer played for entertainment does not, in his view, belong to the Jewish sphere of the sacred and can be freely appropriated.[96] Christian Dawid, one of the most successful klezmer clarinetists, sees musical appropriation in terms of learning a foreign language. Klezmer can be mastered, regardless of one's ethnic background, and, even though Dawid admits he "speaks" it with an accent, it has long become his own medium of expression: "I'm not in contact with a Jewish grandmother on stage when I'm playing it . . . [but] I think more of the human language in that music."[97] Klezmer is thus in the eyes of the German musicians both a legitimate source of inspiration and a medium that they relate to in an emotional way, incorporating it into their personal musical idiom.

As ethnic music circulates increasingly and finds new markets beyond the group that produced it, the question about its future "owners" becomes more and more complicated. "How will one define klezmer music in fifty years?" asks accordionist Franka Lampe. "Will it still be the music of Yiddish-speaking Jews, or Germans who are interested in Jewishness, or the music of the English-speaking Jews from America who have their roots in Europe?" On the one hand, Germans are among those who secure the continuity of klezmer in post-Holocaust Europe, and their contribution should be taken seriously in the historical perspective. On the other hand, though, Lampe, like many of her colleagues, is aware of ethnic boundaries when she says: "What I won't ever do is to say that I want to develop a new form of klezmer music, because then it will be rather a new form of German music, because I'm German."[98]

A sense of uneasiness is not uncommon to many of the German klezmorim, who realize they cannot fully identify with the music they play. To avoid accusations that they impersonate Jews, some bands put an extra emphasis on the fact that they are not Jewish. The Bremen-based Klezgoyim is a case in point. Their guitarist Stefan Kühne is straightforward as to why the band decided on such a name: "We chose it to avoid all possible accusations that we are committing cultural theft as the offspring of the perpetrators of the Holocaust, and that we are using the culture of the annihilated people."[99] An appropriate label, therefore, serves as a disclaimer.

Naming issues aside, some non-Jewish klezmer musicians report a sense of not truly belonging to the music they make. Ulrike Kloock, who plays in a klezmer

---

[95] Max Hacker, interview by the author, Berlin, January 16, 2006.

[96] Pegelow interview.

[97] Christian Dawid [Khupe], interview by the author, Berlin, May 9, 2005.

[98] Franka Lampe, interview by the author, Berlin, January 7, 2006.

[99] Stefan Kühne, interview by the author, Berlin, March 12, 2005.

orchestra, admits, "I have always realized that klezmer music is part of Jewish culture . . . and that I am only a guest there. Sometimes I feel like more than a guest, and sometimes completely alien."[100] Some musicians feel that the fact that they might always be judged as mere "guests" of the Jewish tradition affects their artistic freedom. Detlef Pegelow, who planned on adapting a story by Isaac Bashevis Singer into a klezmer musical, was discouraged by someone who told him: "Well, it's a very good idea, but the problem is that you're German and if you do it, it will always turn its back on you, because you're trying to do the schmaltzy kind of shtetl thing."[101] The constant pressure from the audience who, as one of the musicians put it, expects to "touch the aura"[102] of real Jews, gives some bands an uncomfortable feeling. *Di Grine Kuzine*, annoyed with the artificiality of what they call the "Berlin klezmer hype," ultimately decided to abandon the klezmer label and play more Balkan, Eastern European, and German music. For Snorre Schwartz, *Di Grine Kuzine*'s drummer, this retreat from klezmer felt like a good decision: "I feel like I'm back home now. I can sing in German now, I'm making the music, and I know now what I'm doing."[103]

The feeling of treading upon alien ground is, however, by no means a dominant attitude among the German *klezmorim*. While some feel the discomfort of dealing with such an emotionally charged genre, others contest them. The bassist Carsten Wegener notes, "A lot of people are very cautious with the music. They say: 'Watch out that you don't change the tradition, for God's sake, because the Jews might not accept it.'"[104] Many musicians disagree, however, that somebody's Jewish background should give them the authority to judge the quality of non-Jewish klezmer:

> We played during a street festival and after the concert there was an elderly lady, maybe seventy years old, who came up to us, and said to me: "I was very skeptical if you could play this music at all, but yes, it sounded Jewish! Respect!" Then she said she was Jewish. On the one hand it was beautiful to get such friendly feedback, but on the other, I asked myself the question: Does any Jew really believe that they can judge what is good klezmer and what is not just because they are Jewish, without having any musical or artistic education? Is it really so that a Jew is automatically an expert on klezmer? I don't think so. Many of them have no idea about this music at all. And it is OK, but to think that if one is Jewish they have the right to decide what is right, what is wrong, and what sounds Jewish, or not, already borders on reversed racism.[105]

---

[100] Ulrike Kloock, interview by the author, Berlin, January 19, 2006.
[101] Pegelow interview.
[102] S. Schwarz interview.
[103] Ibid.
[104] CarstenWegener, interview by the author, Berlin, February 27, 2006.
[105] Kühne interview.

Most non-Jewish klezmer musicians believe that they are just as competent in what they are doing as their Jewish colleagues and, therefore, should not be discriminated against as inauthentic appropriators. Some of them go so far as to say that as Germans, they have a very special connection to Yiddish culture that Jewish American klezmer musicians lack. Martin Borbonus of Tants in Gartn Eydn, who attended klezmer workshops in the US, points out that Germans have a certain advantage because they can understand Yiddish songs much better:

> We come from Europe where Jewish life was blooming fifty–sixty years ago and then you go six thousand kilometers and you're sitting there in West Virginia in the cornfields listening to Americans trying to learn Yiddish. The Americans are so far away from this culture and from this language that I had the feeling that we know Jews better and we're nearer to this music.[106]

Likewise, Stefan Kühne, of the band Klezgoyim, is skeptical about the proclaimed superiority of Jewish American revivalists: "They *learned* Yiddish late in life at workshops, and I *understand* Yiddish."[107] Although they might be forgetting that many American klezmer revivalists come from Yiddish-speaking Ashkenazi communities and have an incomparable wealth of Yiddish archival resources at their disposal, there is some validity in the argument that German artists have a privileged access to Yiddish as a Germanic language.[108] This linguistic proximity also helps them to relate to klezmer as "their" music.

Apart from asserting their competence, some musicians, however, also resort to the argument that Jews are grateful to them for continuing Jewish heritage in Europe. The positive feedback that they receive from their Jewish audience makes them believe that their contribution to Jewish culture is not unwelcome:

> At the concerts that we play there are a lot of non-Jews, but sometimes Jews come as well, and there is a sense of a certain thankfulness that we play their music in Germany. It is also striking for me when Jews come

[106] Martin Borbonus, interview by the author, Berlin, February 27, 2006.

[107] Kühne interview.

[108] The New York YIVO Institute for Jewish Research has one of the most extensive sound collections, frequently consulted and curated by the pioneers of the American klezmer revival. The musician and researcher Henry Sapoznik, for example, founded the Max and Frieda Weinstein Archives of Recorded Sound at YIVO, and later initiated KlezKamp. For an account of Sapoznik's research, see Henry Sapoznik, "Klezmer Music: The First One Thousand Years," in *Musics of Multicultural America: A Study of Twelve Musical Communities*, ed. Kip Lornell and Anne K. Rasmussen (New York: Schirmer Books, 1997), 49–71; Sapoznik, *Klezmer!* A notable archival project, which delivered a particular impulse to the American klezmer scene, was also the publication of the papers and musical transcriptions of the Soviet ethnomusicologist Moshe Beregovski, edited and translated by Mark Slobin in cooperation with Michael Alpert of *Brave Old World*.

and say that they had heard something similar in the 1920s. . . . [At one
of the concerts] an elderly Jewish photographer from Warsaw came up to
me and said: "You're playing in the style from Warsaw of 1928!"[109]

The positions that German non-Jewish klezmer musicians take in the appropriation debate are often ambiguous and self-contradictory. Accused of misappropriating Jewish heritage, they justify their right to use Jewish folklore with artistic
freedom. However, while many are self-confident on the scene of Jewish music,
and believe they have the skill for it and a deep understanding of Jewish culture,
there are also those who feel uncomfortable about tackling the heritage of others.
In extreme cases, this uneasiness can lead musicians to abandon the genre and
move on to something they can better identify with, or at least that evokes less
controversy.

The Jewish musicians performing klezmer in Germany often agree with their
non-Jewish colleagues that ethnicity has nothing to do with the right to play
Jewish music. The "king of klezmer," Giora Feidman, who frequently performs in
Germany and also leads klezmer workshops, represents one of the most unorthodox stances on the question of klezmer appropriation. The Hebrew *kley* (vessel)
and *zemer* (song), composing the word "klezmer," symbolize to Feidman the
human body as an ultimate "instrument of song." Challenging ethnic and national
boundaries in music, Feidman subsumes all music making under his definition of
"klezmer" and strongly disagrees with the opinion that only Jews should perform
it.[110] On the other hand, he does recognize ethnic divides, emphasizing that his
concerts contribute to a healing process between Germans and Jews, or Jews and
Palestinians. His performances of Wagner in Auschwitz, or of a piece sampling
German, Israeli, and Palestinian national anthems, provoke many controversies
and lead some Jewish observers to conclude that Feidman himself is also misappropriating Jewish music.

Daniel Kahn, a young Jewish American musician who founded a klezmer band
in Germany and performs with both Jewish and non-Jewish musicians, addressing in his songs also the difficult issues, such as the Holocaust, contests the very
concept of authenticity:

> The idea of authenticity in music is extremely reactionary and problem-
> atic. It has predicated a lot of bad ideas: the idea of authenticity as a com-
> modity, as something that can be quantified. The only authenticity that
> I am interested in is a personal authenticity, an authenticity of intention
> rather than whether or not somebody is a real Jew, a real whatever. It's
> perverse, the idea that I would be entitled to compose and sing a song
> like "Birkenau" simply because I am Jewish. I wasn't there. I am not a

[109] Harry Timmermann, interview by the author, Berlin, November 8, 2006.
[110] Giora Feidman, interview by the author, Berlin, December 4, 2006.

Holocaust victim. We are all entitled to it. It's a fictional perspective; it's art.[111]

Kahn believes, too, that the protectionist behavior of some Jewish critics who oppose the non-Jewish klezmer revival is detrimental to the development of the genre:

> In my experience, living in Germany and playing with a *lot* of non-Jewish musicians . . . I find that the more we can reach out and bring people in, and also bring ourselves to them, [the better]. I mean, these people who are making klezmer music in Germany and Poland are . . . not the ones who bring hip-hop and death metal into this music, but they're also not necessarily the ones who turn this music into a dead museum. They bring intelligence, they bring respect, and they bring creativity. The more xenophobic we are, the more protectionist, the sooner this will turn into just a boring museum item.[112]

While some Jewish klezmer musicians are supportive of the non-Jewish klezmer scene, others show skepticism. Jossif Gofenberg, who grew up in a Yiddish-speaking family in Czernowitz, and lives in Berlin today, believes that ethnic background provides for an authentic touch in music:

> You can play the music—but it's only notes. What is important for me is that the people feel what I sing. If I sang a song about a Chinese mother, I don't know if I would have the same feeling that I have when I sing "Yiddishe Mame." I know what it means: a Jewish mother. I haven't read about it in a book, I know it myself! I know what a Jewish father is, because I am one. I imagine this Jewish mother when I play. And I play this song almost crying inwardly. You have to have a feeling for these songs. You can't just play the notes and put the money in your pocket. If you're not Jewish, how can you have this feeling?[113]

Gofenberg points out the (illegitimate) financial gain of the non-Jewish performers of Jewish music, but his main argument concerns the "privileged knowledge" that Jewish musicians possess. In his mind, only life experience as a Jew can allow an artist to fully comprehend Yiddish songs and perform them with true emotion.

---

[111] Daniel Kahn in Anette Stührmann, "Six Million Germans!" *Exberliner*, July 2007, accessed July 7, 2007, http://www.exberliner.net/verbatim.php?action=inthisissue.

[112] Daniel Kahn, "The Future of Jewish Culture," a debate organized within the program of the KlezKanada festival, Montreal, August 25, 2007.

[113] Jossif Gofenberg, interview by the author, Berlin, January 23, 2006.

Apart from the intangible emotional veracity, some artists also worry about the dominating presence of non-Jewish musicians on the klezmer scene, wh̄ h̄ some believe marginalizes Jewish artists. Commenting on a German artist, a revivalist of Mordechai Gebirtig's songs who has gained recognition in Poland, Jalda Rebling states:

> When a German musician goes to Kraków and says, "I'm bringing Mordechai Gebirtig back to Kraków," it's difficult for some people—there is a *goy*, a German, a *daytsh*, who goes so deep into history that he wants to save pieces of culture that seem to be lost. But you can also say: "I'm sorry, but there was a singer from Warsaw, Gołda Tencer, who was singing Mordechai Gebirtig long before this German. Why doesn't he look into his own history? Why does he need this history?"[114]

Harsh, skeptical, or polemical as the arguments in this debate can be, the fact remains that Jossif Gofenberg, Jalda Rebling, and many other Jewish musicians in Germany frequently work together with non-Jewish artists. The same is true in Poland, where the debate on the appropriation of klezmer is at the same time much less embittered than in Germany. In spite of several unfavorable articles in the Polish press about the Kazimierz klezmer scene, or Yale Strom's critical documentary *Klezmer on Fish Street* (2003), where he voices reservations toward the local klezmer scene, many Polish klezmer musicians are not even aware that the non-Jewish participation in the klezmer scene stirs so much emotion among international commentators.

At the same time, Polish klezmer musicians do face the same probing questions from the audience as their German colleagues. "'If you're not Jewish, why are you dealing with it?' Or . . . 'Since you are Polish, why don't you play Polish folk?'"[115] are the typical queries, states one Polish musician. Many artists are visibly vexed by the fact that the audience asks them so often about their ethnic background:

> If you start dealing with Irish music, and form a band . . . nobody asks you whether you have Irish roots. But when you play Jewish music, the first question is: "Do you have any Jewish roots?" You can hit the roof! It's a heritage that I like, whether I know it well or not is a different question, but let's say: I play the music because I like it, I prepared a repertoire—so leave my roots alone![116]

---

[114] Rebling interview, February 6, 2006.

[115] Brudzińska, interview, June 30, 2006.

[116] Jarosław Wilkosz [Klezzmates], interview by the author, Kraków, June 30, 2006.

Others see the questions about their ethnic background as a disguised value judgment:

> When we have groups from Israel here, they are usually Orthodox Jews. They ask whether we are Jewish or not, whether we are one of them, or not. Because a Jew supports another Jew. And they might like what we play, and they applaud, but [think] . . . "you are not one of us" . . . they might be very satisfied, but they believe that if we were Jewish, we would have done it better.[117]

Facing this sometimes implicit critique, some musicians take a defensive tone, occasionally even invoking old stereotypes, such as this one about Jewish solidarity. Sometimes they also resort to an argument that Jews were neglecting their own heritage in Poland: "Why don't they come here and play this music themselves? Why don't they come here and settle down and live in this reality? They should try, but instead they escaped to the United States. Let them cultivate here their own Jewish culture. Why do they ban us from doing it?"[118]

Such outright defensive reactions suggest ignorance but also insecurity. Framing the Jewish absence in Poland as opportunist migration thus permits the interviewee to present her legitimacy as a Jewish heritage revivalist on a rescue mission. By omitting the reasons for postwar Jewish emigration from Poland, among which, as in 1968, anti-Semitism in Poland played the main role, the speaker is able to present the Polish attitude toward Jewish heritage as unambiguously noble. Although statements betraying anti-Semitic stereotypes were rare during my field research, they reveal how much the appropriation debate feeds on preexisting prejudices and clichés that the participants might fall back on while formulating their arguments.

The assertion that klezmer revivalist work sustains Jewish heritage in a country almost devoid of Jews is, of course, an argument that does not necessarily have to be tinged with anti-Semitism, and it is, indeed, commonly quoted by numerous klezmer musicians in Kraków. Jarosław Bester of the former Cracow Klezmer Band (now Bester Quartet) is aware of the role of his band in popularizing Jewish music and bringing klezmer to prestigious concert halls:

> We, as a band, have introduced klezmer onto big stages, such as philharmonic halls, theaters, the world's most beautiful concert halls. What can we be blamed for in this case? That we propagate klezmer music in the best possible way? If we commercialized it in an extreme way and played

---

[117] K01 (See list of coded interviews in the appendix).
[118] K08.

it at some drinking parties, I would understand if the Jewish community said that we desecrate their culture. But it's the other way round; we make it even more elevated. They should be glad about it.[119]

That klezmer is a way to promote Jewish culture was also the argument of the late Chris Schwarz, director of the Galicia Jewish Museum. The Jewish heritage revival in Kazimierz, commercialized as it is, might be the only alternative in a place like Kraków: "The Jews here are not going to start any project, because they're all old. Who is going to do it? Entrepreneurs, and somebody with better taste! I don't think we should be too critical of these people," Schwarz said in 2006.[120]

The Polish Jewish author Stanisław Krajewski also believes that the continuation of Jewish culture by non-Jews is a better alternative than a total cultural void:

I see [the revival of Jewish heritage by non-Jews] as a completely positive thing. I know many Jews who are ambivalent, or even bitter about it. They say: "Well, there are no Jews, and there is Jewish culture flourishing." My answer is: basically, there are two possibilities: either there is nothing, and we'd be very unhappy if there was nothing Jewish, no Jewish culture, no Jewish continuity, or there is whatever is realistically possible. It's not possible to have full-fledged Jewish life in Kraków, or in Poland. There can only be little pockets of Jewish life.[121]

Krajewski brings up the contention, relatively common in the heritage appropriation debate, that even if cultural appropriation may be questionable, omission of a minority group's heritage in the mainstream culture also does harm to the group.[122] Clearly, if the majority ignores a minority and does not represent it at all in the popular culture, it leads to a misrepresentation of reality—a situation not unknown to the postwar Jewish community in Poland, where for decades Jewish victims of concentration camps were being listed by nationality and marginalized as only one of many "national" groups of prisoners.

The mission of preserving Jewish heritage is one of the main arguments that Polish klezmer revivalists use in the appropriation debate, but it is not the only one. Like their German colleagues, some Polish artists also position themselves as the "insiders" of Jewish folklore. "[Klezmer] is Polish, because it's from Poland!" states Jarosław Bester. "It was created here, on this spot; it was born here, so it's Polish."[123] While for the American klezmer revivalists reaching back to the musical traditions of the Old World has been a way of examining their ethnic roots, some

---

[119] Jarosław Bester, interview by the author, Kraków, April 17, 2004.

[120] C. Schwarz, interview.

[121] Krajewski in *Klezmer on Fish Street*, directed by Yale Strom (Castle Hill Productions, 2003), DVD.

[122] Young and Haley, " 'Nothing Comes from Nowhere,' " 275.

[123] Bester interview.

Polish klezmer musicians identify with the genre via its spatial roots. They recognize klezmer as their own because it comes from the same place as they do. Defining klezmer music as part of Poland's folklore also permits musicians to dismiss accusations of appropriation. If Jewish culture is subsumed into the category of Polishness, boundaries of ownership also become reinterpreted.

For some klezmer revivalists, however, the boundaries are still well in place. Jarosław Wilkosz of the Klezzmates, who was among the first musicians to play klezmer in Kazimierz, eventually abandoned traditional Jewish music and moved on to playing new pieces, only distantly inspired by Jewish music. "One day it dawned on me that I cannot play Jewish music the Jewish way," he states, "so I want to play something else, and treat Jewish music as a serious inspiration."[124] Apparently, finding one's own voice is not always easy in conditions of musical borrowing.

Although some musicians do not comprehend why Poles should be accused of misappropriating Jewish culture, there are also those who are sympathetic to the position of the critics. "If we reversed the situation, and assumed that Poles had been treated in the Second World War like Jews were," hypothesizes Maciej Inglot of Sholem, "then we would be sitting here today and analyzing each foreigner dealing with our heritage. I'm one hundred percent sure of it!"[125] Taking in stride the fact that occasional Jewish spectators at their concerts might be judging them in this way, the musicians of Sholem say they try to perform in a possibly "traditional" and "respectful" way.

Leopold Kozłowski, one of the few Jewish musicians performing in Kazimierz and a descendant of a famous family of klezmorim, is much more laidback about the issue of appropriation. Even though he enjoys being acknowledged as the last authentic klezmer in Galicia, he does not see cultural borrowing as a problem. That even the spectators critical of non-Jewish involvement in Jewish music are confused about who is Jewish in his band makes him conclude that ethnic background does not matter in playing good music:

> Once, when we had a concert in Copenhagen, a Jewish woman came to talk to one of my singers, who isn't Jewish, and she said: "It is obvious that you Jews sing these Jewish songs so beautifully, but how did this Polish nobleman with a moustache, this Kozłowski, this goy, how did he come to play it so well?"[126]

The amusing misunderstanding over the identity of Kozłowski's band members represents well the predicament of both the Polish and German klezmer scene, where the provenance of the artists is often not what the audiences imagine it to be. Although the appropriation of klezmer seems to be less of a controversy

---

[124] Wilkosz interview.
[125] Maciej Inglot [Sholem], interview by the author, Kraków, July 1, 2006.
[126] Leopold Kozłowski, interview by the author, Kraków, April 20, 2004.

in Poland, many of the arguments used in the debate on klezmer are the same in Kraków and Berlin. Some of the klezmer conflicts are also, in fact, transnational. The bitter exchange between Berlin-based Rita Ottens and Joel Rubin and the Polish band Kroke, whom they criticized as impostors in their book *Klezmer Musik*, is a case in point.

Kroke, the first Polish klezmer band, founded in 1992, plays world music, touring internationally and publishing their records on a German label. Although the trio has developed their own original style and no longer advertises their music as klezmer, Jewish music and the image of *klezmorim* is very important to the band. They feel that they continue the tradition of itinerant performers, and they draw inspiration from Jewish heritage music with which they feel a particular affinity ever since two of the musicians discovered their Jewish ancestry.

In 1999, when Kroke was releasing its fourth record, *The Sounds of the Vanishing World*, Rita Ottens and the renowned klezmer clarinetist from the United States, Joel Rubin, published the book *Klezmer-Musik* in Germany. The book was highly critical of the klezmer revival taking place outside of its original Jewish context, and the authors bemoaned what they saw as a suspicious and detrimental excess of goodwill toward the genre from the audience and media. In one of the chapters, the authors also criticized Kroke (unnamed in the book) for misusing cabbalistic symbols on their record cover and aspiring to contribute something new to Jewish music. Since Ottens and Rubin considered hybridization in Jewish heritage music as damaging, they also disapproved of Kroke's attempts at experimenting with the genre. On top of that, they pointed out that the band members were not Jewish.[127]

The musicians and Kroke's producer, Till Schumann, read the remarks in Ottens and Rubin's book as an attempt to ban them from playing klezmer on ethnic grounds, and an effort to discredit the band on the klezmer market. Schumann, who considers the band members as Jewish, resented the fact that Ottens and Rubin put an emphasis on the musicians' ethnicity while judging their artistic merits. In response, the label issued an open letter under the ironic title "A Non-Arian Certificate for Polish Klezmer Musicians?" [*"Nicht-Arier-Nachweis für polnische Klezmer Musiker?"*], addressed to journalists and cultural organizers who were interested in the group. The statement spoke of a targeted attack against a *Jewish* band, which had been involved for years in the revival of Jewish cultural life in Poland, against the opposition of conservative Catholic circles. Gigi Backes, Reiner Jordan, and Till Schumann, who signed the letter, criticized the authors of *Klezmer-Musik* for assuming the role of "cultural popes" and refuting the musical production of Kroke because of their ethnicity. At the same time, they made it clear that Kroke was a Jewish band and hence had a right to cultivate *their* cultural traditions.

---

[127] Ottens and Rubin, *Klezmer-Musik*, 9–10.

The controversy attracted some media attention, which, as the band reports, resulted in even more people coming to Kroke's concerts in Germany. The musicians
even recount that some fans, amused by the debate, brought Ottens and Rubin's
book and asked the members of Kroke to autograph it.[128] The unpleasant exchange
over appropriation did not, therefore, turn out to be damaging to the band.

Although the statement made by Kroke's label strikes one, first of all, as a disclaimer about the band being non-Jewish, in personal communication, Kroke's
producers deny that as having been the main motive of their leaflet. Till Schumann
declares that his purpose was rather to protest against Ottens and Rubin's clear-
cut dichotomy of Jewish versus non-Jewish, which disregarded the complicated
situation of Jews in post–World War II Poland, where they often chose to conceal
their identity and to assimilate. "This reminded me of Goebbels [sic!]:[129] 'I decide
who is Jewish,'" states Schumann:

> Ms. Ottens cannot decide who can play [klezmer] and who can't, and
> she cannot decide if somebody is Jewish enough to play it . . . And this is
> exactly what we didn't want to do, we were not going to ask Kroke to pull
> down their trousers to show if they were circumcised or not. We didn't
> want to supply the proof that Kroke is Jewish, or that two of them are
> Jewish, or that two of them come from Jewish families, or however one
> wants to define it. In Poland after 1945, there were so few Jews, and a lot
> of them did not manifest their Jewishness.[130]

The indignation of Kroke's producers was twofold. They contested not only the
idea that non-Jewish musicians commit an unacceptable act of appropriation if
they play Jewish music, but also the very definition of Jewishness that Ottens
and Rubin applied. The owners of Kroke's label, acknowledging the difficulty of
unambiguously defining the band's hybrid identities, treat the band as Jews.
When Till Schumann recollects the beginnings of his work with Kroke, he admits
that he was slightly preoccupied by whether the band would mind working with a
German label: "I asked them if they had any problems as Polish Jews with working
with a label from Berlin. Then they smiled mildly and said, 'If there is any, it's only
your problem.'"[131] This short exchange made it clear for both sides that although
the musicians of Kroke do not consider their ethnicity as a crucial factor in their
relations with the label, their producers take their Jewish identity for granted.

To make the issue even more complex, the two Kroke musicians who have a
Jewish background do not regard themselves as primarily Jewish. They admit that
the discovery of having Jewish ancestors did not change much in their everyday

---

[128] Tomasz Lato [Kroke], interview by the author, Kraków, April 17, 2004.
[129] It was Karl Lueger (1844–1910), the mayor of Vienna, who said "Wer ein Jud ist, bestimm' ich."
[130] Till Schumann, interview by the author, Berlin, December 12, 2006.
[131] Ibid.

lives, and they see the idea of ethnicity-based judgments of artistic performance as a "dead-end street."[132] Nevertheless, they do refer to their Jewish roots in the context of Ottens and Rubin's publication. Tomasz Lato, a double-bass player, recollects that the suggestion that Kroke is not Jewish upset the band:

> It's ridiculous anyway, this sort of peeping into people's pants and deciding if they can play this music or not. It's like forbidding a white person from playing the blues! But the consciousness of our Jewish roots made us feel really hurt by what she had written. If we didn't have any Jewish roots whatsoever, I don't know, I guess that we might wonder whether we were perhaps trespassing over certain borders, religious or other, whether we were indeed doing something we shouldn't.[133]

Tomasz Kurkuba, a violinist, felt an initial urge to go to Berlin to present Rita Ottens and Joel Rubin with the documents proving his Jewish origin, but the band decided to abandon this idea. Although Kroke rejects the validity of ethnic boundaries in music, their Jewish roots gain saliency for them once questioned. What is more, the band names boundaries of appropriation that they would not trespass. For the accordionist, Jerzy Bawół, the unacceptable begins with the use of elements of religious rites: "You just don't use certain liturgical elements. For instance, we've always liked Hasidic music, but we don't play it because we don't want to encroach on somebody else's territory."[134] In other words, while the appropriation of ethnic music adds to a natural and desirable cross-cultural exchange, "liturgical" music, because of its special function, should not undergo this process.

Although the band positions themselves in this debate in the borderland of ethnic Jewishness, using the notion of "roots" and their family histories—but not Judaism per se—as a cultural referent, they define their opponent in terms of her national identity. Since, based on an earlier exchange, both the label and the musicians assumed that it was Ottens and not Rubin who stood behind the critique, they addressed their response personally at her. Two of the musicians admit that the criticism from a German author was particularly difficult for them to accept: "My grandfather was in a German concentration camp and now a German has some objections toward us!"[135] "The fact that she is German hurt us even more. What right does she have [to criticize]? Didn't they do enough during the war? And now they want to segregate [the musicians] saying who is entitled to play and who isn't?"[136] The question that arose was not whether non-Jews are entitled to

---

[132] Jerzy Bawół [Kroke], interview by the author, Kraków, April 17, 2004.

[133] Lato interview, April 17, 2004.

[134] Bawół interview, April 17, 2004.

[135] Tomasz Kurkuba [Kroke], interview by the author, Kraków, April 17, 2004.

[136] Lato interview, April 17, 2004.

contribute to Jewish culture but whether Germans have the right to voice their opinion in this respect.

The language that the musicians use is heavily marked with the vocabulary of World War II. Ottens is presented primarily as a member of a hostile group, one of "them," Germans, responsible for concentration camps and racial segregation. Identifying the author as German serves the purpose of disqualifying her as a legitimate adversary in this debate. But Ottens and Rubin also rely on racial and national categories when they respond to the statement made by Kroke's label, which they call an anti-Semitic "hate pamphlet."[137]

In their unpublished article from 2004, Ottens and Rubin put forward a hypothesis that the German klezmer movement is in essence antagonistic to Jews. To illustrate their point, they use the case of Kroke, which they categorize as a German band. The authors justify their peculiar methodology with the argument that Kroke produce their records in Berlin and that "the psycho-social situation of Polish society in the early 1990s could be compared to Germany in the mid-1960s when the first recording with Yiddish music appeared and found a wide echo of reactions."[138] Leaving aside the validity of such a comparison, it is interesting to see that Ottens and Rubin, again, put the (postulated) ethnicity of the artists at the center of their argument. Asking the rhetorical question: "Do two Jewish grandmothers of three Polish musicians make the group a Jewish group playing Jewish music?" They go on to say that Kroke's self-definition as Jews abuses the halachic laws, in trying to replace them with racial criteria used by the Nazis.[139]

Ottens and Rubin define Jewishness in terms of Jewish religious law. They also insist that klezmer music should be "rooted in traditional Jewish religion and culture" and should not be treated as an "empty shell that can be filled with random terminology and charged with new meanings."[140] Having been alienated from the Judaic tradition, in their view, klezmer music in Germany falls prey to those who "appropriate and instrumentalize these traditions for their nation-building processes." Kroke, subsumed into the category of "German" and "non-Jewish," fits into Ottens and Rubin's framework of historical guilt and perpetual anti-Semitism, which supposedly fuels the klezmer revival.[141]

The debate between the two musicologists and Kroke is striking in how much it focuses on ethnic categories. The ethnicity card is played on both sides of this controversy, reflecting the prejudices and myths present in this tangled triangle of Polish/Jewish/German relations, but also leading the debate on appropriation *ad absurdum*. The question of who is Jewish monopolizes the exchange, leaving

---

[137] Ottens and Rubin, "'The Sounds of the Vanishing World'," 3.
[138] Ibid., 27.
[139] Ibid., 35–36.
[140] Ibid., 26.
[141] Ibid., 19.

almost no space for other relevant issues such as, for example, whether the artists acknowledged the sources of their music, or whether the local Jewish community feels offended in any way by their performances. Most importantly, however, the Ottens/Rubin vs. Kroke debate reveals the major weakness of the appropriation framework, that is, the assumption that we can always view cultural products in terms of insiders who own them, and outsiders.

All arguments against cultural appropriation, including those put forward by Ottens and Rubin, rest on the premise that each "culture" has clean-cut boundaries, and that there is an essential difference between those who belong to the group and therefore possess a "privileged epistemic access"[142] to it, and those who do not. The case of Kroke illustrates how inadequate the frame of appropriation is for the analysis of the revival of Jewish music in post-Holocaust Poland, where concepts such as "Jewish identity" or "Jewishness" are all but straightforward.

After 1945, many Jews who decided to remain in Poland despite massive emigration waves in the late 1940s, 1950s, and, finally, 1968 made the decision not to disclose their Jewish identity. Some, who survived the war "on the Aryan side" having assumed a Catholic Polish identity and facing the postwar pogroms and hostility toward returning Jews, decided to continue living under their false names. Others were Communists and lived a fully atheist life, not cultivating any Jewish traditions in their families. Finally, many lived in mixed marriages and had their children baptized and raised as Catholics. Living in hiding, assimilation, and intermarriage all contributed to the situation that many children and grandchildren of Polish Holocaust survivors grew up not knowing that they were Jewish, with the family's past surrounded by the impenetrable silence of their parents or grandparents, who still feared anti-Semitism. According to Stanisław Krajewski, a Polish Jewish philosopher and publicist who coined the term "marginal Jews" to denote this group of people, the number of those who have Jewish roots in Poland far outnumbers the registered members of the Jewish community.[143]

The 1990s, with the rise of popular interest in Jewish culture in Poland, witnessed many "return stories," with Poles of various ages researching their Jewish roots, becoming engaged in Jewish cultural initiatives, and even converting to Judaism. The appearance of new institutions such as the progressive Jewish Community *Beit Warszawa* in 1999, or the *Czulent* Jewish Association in Kraków in 2004, both of which address the needs of Polish "marginal Jews," have facilitated for many a means to regain their newly discovered Jewish identity. In the case of this specific Jewish revival, correlated in important ways with the non-Jewish interest in Jewish culture, the essentialist approach to group identity simply fails. The complexities of patterns of Jewish identification after 1945, and the existence of individuals whom Krajewski describes as "marginal Jews" and the American cultural anthropologist

---

[142] Young and Haley, "'Nothing Comes from Nowhere,'" 285.
[143] Krajewski, "The Impact of the Shoah," 292.

Erica Lehrer as "Jewish-identified Poles,"[144] challenge the claim that insiders of a group are necessarily in possession of "privileged knowledge" about their heritage. As both Krajewski and Lehrer make clear, many people who identify as Jewish in Poland do not initially know much about Judaism and have to arduously study Jewish culture, not uncommonly starting from the position of complete "outsiders." The case of the musicians of Kroke, who learned about having Jewish ancestors during their klezmer career, requires us to think of heritage not as a lump sum of directly inherited knowledge but rather as a process of discovery and accumulation of cultural capital, in which the knowledge of one's culture becomes layered upon and interacts with the knowledge of other cultures. The complexity of the Polish and, for this matter, also the German klezmer revival can be fully comprehended only when we move beyond the essentialist dichotomies of "Jewish" or "non-Jewish," and "authentic" or "inauthentic." To be able to understand the true significance of the klezmer revival, we need to approach it as a dynamic network of social relations, emerging out of a quest for, rather than a straightforward bequest of, traditions. Also, we have to view it as a social context, which enables simultaneous, hybrid, and transitory identities (see chaps. 6 and 7).

In view of these complexities, the concept of authenticity deserves some more attention. What much of the critique of the klezmer scene quoted in this chapter implies is that the "outsider artists" are not able to create an authentic expression of a culture that is not their own. Authenticity as a quality of an insider's experience of culture is no doubt a value in itself, but it ceases to be a useful tool of analysis in a situation when the boundary between "in-group" and "out-group" becomes blurred. Rather than arbitrarily granting or denying authenticity to artists, it seems more fruitful, as Young and Haley postulate, to consider authenticity as veracity of artistic expression and hence inherent in every work of art.[145] Thus, the work of an ideal type of "outsider" should be treated as an authentic expression of a particular perspective on a given culture. Klezmer music played by a non-Jewish klezmer band in Kraków is, consequently, authentic, and the music of Kroke is an authentic expression of artists, some of whom identify as both Polish and Jewish. As long as non-Jewish artists, marketing their music to their audiences, do not try to pass themselves off as Jews or misrepresent Jewish culture in their performances, Jewish heritage music that inspires their artistic work cannot be treated as morally suspect. What is more, although the two are often conflated by critics of cultural appropriation, authenticity, or a lack thereof, does not automatically entail or exclude aesthetic quality. It is equally conceivable that there are Jewish musicians who play mediocre klezmer, as non-Jewish musicians who become klezmer virtuosos. In fact, concrete examples of both can be found.

---

[144] Erica Lehrer, "Bearing False Witness? 'Vicarious' Jewish Identity and the Politics of Affinity," in *Imaginary Neighbors: Mediating Polish-Jewish Relations after the Holocaust*, ed. Dorota Glowacka and Joanna Zylinska (Lincoln: Nebraska University Press, 2007), 87.

[145] Young and Haley, "'Nothing Comes from Nowhere,'" 281.

Concentrating on the perils of misrepresentation or commercial exploitation, the framework of cultural appropriation overlooks the possible positive effects of intercultural borrowing. As Young and Haley argue, the "fashionableness" of minority groups in the mainstream culture might draw attention to their concerns and allow their voices to be better heard in the public sphere. Thus, interest from outside of a group can even contribute to a cultural revival of a minority culture. In fact, some observers who have been deeply engaged in a Jewish revival in contemporary Poland confirm that the Jewish heritage boom initiated by non-Jews has created some positive stimuli for the revival of Jewish life. Jonathan Ornstein, head of the Jewish Community Center in Kraków, stated in a 2011 interview with the *Guardian* that the current "Jewish renaissance" in Kraków is the second stage of a process which was made possible by the interest of non-Jews in Jewish culture.[146] Stanisław Krajewski also notes that the popularity of Jewish heritage in Polish mainstream culture has made it easier for many people who were hiding their Jewish identity to "come out" and "admit their Jewishness."[147] Making Jewish culture "fashionable" has also had consequences for the host culture. By exposing Poles and Germans to a heritage that they might not be familiar with, the klezmer movement has opened new avenues of communication between Jews and non-Jews. These intercultural encounters within the klezmer scene might not always have been easy or successful, but the klezmer scene has been able to offer what Erica Lehrer has termed "organic sites of truth-telling and listening," where Jews and non-Jews can meet and interact in an informal setting, creating conducive conditions for dialogue.[148]

Interpreting the klezmer revival only in terms of cultural theft and impoverishment of the culture of origin reduces a complex phenomenon to the question of cultural ownership. But concentrating only on *whom* klezmer *belongs* to, we overlook the question of *what* klezmer *does*. Viewing the klezmer scene as an environment of dialogue, cultural translation and negotiation of identities allows us to see the genealogy of klezmer as the traditional music of Ashkenazi Jews along with its new functions and the social consequences of the revival in German and Polish society. The next chapters set out to map these new functions of the klezmer revival, focusing, first of all, on klezmer as a site of communication and a unique contact zone.

---

[146] Jeevan Vasagar and Julian Borger, "A Jewish Renaissance in Poland," *Guardian* (UK), April 7, 2011, accessed September 20, 2011, http://www.guardian.co.uk/world/2011/apr/07/jewish-renais-sance-poland.

[147] Krajewski, "The Impact of the Shoah," 301.

[148] Erica Lehrer, "Can There be a Reconciliatory Heritage?" *International Journal of Heritage Studies* 16, nos. 4–5 (2010): 278.

3

Meeting the Other, Eating the Other

Klezmer as a Contact Zone

Jewish weddings in Kraków are rare. With the local Jewish community small and predominantly elderly, they are all the more events of singular importance. Jarosław Wilkosz, a double bass player, and the accordionist Marcin Wiercioch, both non-Jewish, recall how they were hired for a Jewish wedding in Kraków in the late 1990s. The rabbi of Kraków at the time, Sasha Pecaric, assisted by a few Jewish cultural activists, was involved in the organization, hoping to stage a model traditional ritual that many in the community had not witnessed for decades. To stay in line with the local custom, the presence of a klezmer band was of utmost importance. Given that not only in Kraków, but in the whole of Poland there was not a single Jewish klezmer band, the rabbi decided to engage a non-Jewish group from Kazimierz.

The musicians of the band Yarehma accepted the job with apprehension. They had never played for a Jewish wedding and were unsure of the appropriate repertoire. Rabbi Pecaric agreed to hold a rehearsal in one of the Jewish-style restaurants. Jarosław Wilkosz recollects that the rabbi's invitation posed a real challenge:

> I remember when Sasha suggested that we play for this wedding, we were scared like hell. We thought we didn't have enough repertoire for it, that we might not know about something, that we would mess something up, that we wouldn't manage to do it properly. So I remember that we made an appointment with Sasha in Klezmer Hois, to play three pieces for him so that he could give us some feedback, help us somehow. We played a number, and another one, and he said, "Well, this *is* Jewish but it is not *Jewish.*" . . . And it turned out that this was not entirely how it should be.[1]

Rabbi Pecaric, however, offered help, bringing the band a video tape of his own wedding. Wilkosz remembers that the musicians studied the video carefully,

---

[1] Wilkosz interview.

memorizing the elements of the ritual and learning some of the recorded tunes. After this unusual preparation, the band accompanied the entire wedding ritual, starting with the separate receptions for the bride and the groom, and finishing under the traditional *khupe* at the Remuh Synagogue in Kazimierz. According to an old custom, the musicians led the newlyweds and the guests in a procession around the main square of the Jewish district, and then, finally, played for the wedding party.[2]

The story of these uncommon wedding arrangements is more than merely an anecdote. The interaction between the members of the Jewish community and the non-Jewish *klezmorim* illustrates, on the one hand, the new/old functions of klezmer in post-Holocaust Central Europe, where it still occasionally accompanies Jewish weddings. On the other hand, it reveals some of the dynamics of the klezmer scene as a contact zone, where non-Jews learn from, interact, and negotiate with Jews in a creative context.

Mary Louise Pratt, in her influential essay on the art of communication across cultures, defined contact zones as "social spaces where cultures meet, clash and grapple with each other, often in contexts of highly asymmetrical relations of power, such as colonialism, slavery, or their aftermaths."[3] A "contact zone" as understood by Pratt is a space where a subordinated or marginal group negotiates a language of their self-expression, appropriating the modes and genres of the dominant culture (see Introduction). This process of appropriation, however, does not merely proceed along lines of acculturation or assimilation, but rather of what Fernando Ortiz, a Cuban sociologist, termed "transculturation," which is the adapting of elements of the dominant culture via selection and invention.[4]

This process of selective absorption of the culture of the other into one's own has at times been framed by means of the metaphor of cannibalism. One of the most influential texts in this vein is Oswald de Andrade's 1928 *Manifesto Antropófago*, which lays out the principles of cultural anthropophagy. Written by one of the most outstanding representatives of Brazilian modernism as a critique of colonial domination, the manifesto calls for a return to the values of the pre-imperial period and warns against cultural import from Europe. Paradoxically, de Andrade's recipe for a new Brazilian national culture was the "devouring" of Western civilization. The act of eating the other, however, implied absorption of the admired values but also rejection of the undesired elements.[5] The "regurgitated" product was to be both new and vernacular.[6] Important to note here is that the anthropophagous approach to the culture of the other precluded disdain. It

[2] Wilkosz and Marcin Wiercioch [Klezzmates], interview by the author, Kraków, June 30, 2006.

[3] Pratt, "Arts of the Contact Zone," 34.

[4] Ibid., 36.

[5] Ilie, "Cultural Anthropophagy," 68–78.

[6] Alamir Aquino-Correa, "Immigration and Cultural Anthropophagy in Brazilian Literature," *Passages de Paris* 2 (2005): 273–80.

is only the worthy who are devoured so that their strength and heroism can be transfused. Cultural anthropophagy must therefore be understood not merely in terms of appropriation but also as a form of veneration and abolishing of distance, which opens up one culture to the other.

Rosana Kohl-Bines, who adopts the framework of cultural anthropophagy to discuss the use of Holocaust imagery at the famous Rio de Janeiro carnival, applies the theory in a very compelling way in the ambit of Jewish cultural studies. Analyzing the controversy around a float of one of the samba groups that depicted Hitler on top of naked mannequins representing Holocaust victims, Kohl-Bines notes that absorbing the experience of the Jewish minority into a popular form of self-expression—the samba—was a way for Brazilians to reflect on their own national identity.[7] This Brazilian desire to abolish distance and absorb the other can also become a serious challenge to the local Jews, as they are expected to sacrifice their memory for a performance celebrating national coherence. The "anthropophagic model of cultural interaction," as Kohl-Bines terms it, appears therefore as having both strengths and weaknesses.

One of the aspects that the framework of cultural anthropophagy puts in relief particularly well is the interlacement of cultural transfer and consumption. Cultural appropriation viewed from this perspective always entails an encounter with the other and the creation of a cultural product that can be marketed. The other becomes eaten not just metaphorically; the "devoured" becomes performed, sold, and consumed by an audience. And as long as this process, performed by a minority, of absorbing and processing the mainstream culture can be seen in terms of cultural resistance or subversion, it immediately brings up the suspicion of exploitation if carried out by the majority. Indeed, the idea of "eating the other," laden with negative connotations of violence, has often served in cultural studies as a metaphor of exploitation. In her essay "Eating the Other: Desire and Resistance," bell hooks uses the idea of cannibalism to criticize the commodification of ethnic difference via mass culture.[8] Commenting on the white fascination with African American culture in the United States, she argues that what she terms "consumer cannibalism" eradicates "whatever difference the Other inhabits" and "denies the significance of that Other's history" by decontextualizing the culture of origin.[9] Focusing on consumption, bell hooks is skeptical of the positive potential of "eating the other." In her view, it is only the search for new sources of pleasure fueled by a crisis of identity that stimulates the fascination with the other. She is also pessimistic as to whether this interest in the other can actually challenge the patterns of racist domination.[10] Personal interaction across the ethnic divide,

[7] Rosana Kohl-Bines, "Samba and Shoah: Ethnic, Religious and Social Diversity in Brazil," *European Review of History* 18, no. 1 (2011): 101–9.

[8] hooks, "Eating the Other: Desire and Resistance."

[9] Ibid., 373.

[10] Ibid., 367.

according to hooks, can only work on the premise that racism and its legacy are recognized by both parties and the relationship emerges "through mutual choice and negotiation," not out of one-sided desire.[11] Notably, however, hooks herself looks only at the representations of the black other in popular culture, not at the individual encounters that led to the creation and distribution of these images.

The concepts of a "contact zone" and "cultural anthropophagy" provide a perspective on cultural appropriation that opens the door to both the question of legitimate agency and the end products of the process of appropriating. Conceptualizing appropriation as an interactive and creative process, which results in the production of new, vernacular art, neither tantamount to the culture of origin nor that of the target culture, gives us a chance to analyze the *functionality* of cultural appropriation. What is more, the anthropophagic framework offers a more holistic approach to the phenomenon of cultural appropriation, regarding it simultaneously as a site of artistic creativity, interpersonal dialogue, and consumption.

Although Pratt and de Andrade both deal with the predicament of a minority, or a colonized people, who is appropriating the language of a majority, their models are still relevant even when the vector of appropriation is reversed. The klezmer revival in Poland and Germany is a "contact zone" *à rebours*—backwards, as it were. Although the power relations are reversed here, the encounter it triggers still takes place via similar modes of interaction, including mediation, collaboration, and critique. In other words, Jews and non-Jews who play a part in the klezmer movement "meet, clash, and grapple with each other," trying to negotiate their own space and find their own voice in this encounter.

Undoubtedly there are many more possible "contact zones" that enable exchange between Jews and non-Jews in post-Holocaust Europe. They have different functions, though, and not all of them create conducive conditions for generating new art forms. Diana Pinto, who coined the term "Jewish Space" to denote contexts in which non-Jews explore their interest in the Jewish past and heritage, has distinguished among six types of spaces, governed by different rules, where Jews and non-Jews can meet. Thus, while in what she called "Jewish-friendly neutral spaces" non-Jews are "free-standing active equals who are entitled to bring their own views and 'part of the story,'" inner-Jewish community life is a space where non-Jews "do not belong as such."[12] In fact, it is the contention of some observers of the non-Jewish fascination with Jewishness that not all aspects of Jewish life and not every Jewish site should be available to the public as a "Jewish Space." Worried about the "almost voyeuristic"[13] or "uncanny"[14] interest of non-Jews in

---

[11] Ibid., 371.

[12] Diana Pinto, "The Challenges of Progressive Jews in Twenty-first-century Europe," accessed September 28, 2011, http://www.eupj.org/paris-2010/69-dr-diana-pinto.html.

[13] Remmler, "Encounters Across the Void," 23.

[14] Lustig and Leveson, "Introduction," in Lustig and Levenson, *Turning the Kaleidoscope*, 20.

Jewish culture, these critics advocate that Jewish sites of worship, for example, should be protected from the intrusive curiosity of non-Jews.[15]

Long before the klezmer revival, the musical realm already functioned as a "contact zone" for Jews and non-Jews. Philip Bohlman, who discusses the social capacity of the cantorate in the nineteenth-century Austria, notes that cantors "changed the nature of the spaces that musically defined the Jewish community and then became an extension from the community into the non-Jewish world."[16] The popularity of cantors who entered the public sphere and performed on the prominent stages of Western music contributed to the "westernization" of Jews in the eyes of non-Jewish Austrians. Thus, synagogal music became an intermediary space in which the majority and the minority group could negotiate the boundary between them via a musical practice, which had both a symbolic significance for the in-group and allowed external participation. A century later, the klezmer revival is performing a similar role. However, rather than an extension from the Jewish community into the public space, it often functions as a bridge from the non-Jewish public into the Jewish space. Not surprisingly, this "bridge" is often perceived as an incursion.

Klezmer and Jewish Communities: Worlds Apart?

Although the klezmorim always lived on the borderline of the Jewish and non-Jewish spheres, cooperating with non-Jewish musicians and playing for a mixed audience, the principal functions of klezmer music were essentially embedded in Jewish life. This has changed with the revival of Jewish heritage music in post-Holocaust Europe. While in many places klezmer might still accompany Jewish rites and celebrations, the music has also gained new functions in the non-Jewish world. Entering concert halls, clubs, and discos, performed for predominantly non-Jewish audiences and attracting many non-Jewish musicians, klezmer, in the eyes of many Jews, has become alienated from the Jewish context. Ruth Ellen Gruber gave this disaffection a name: "virtual Jewishness."

Gruber's analysis of the rising non-Jewish interest in Jewish culture is based on the assumption that "the public idea of Jewish culture—or what is 'Jewish'—is shaped very much from outside as well as from within the Jewish community." This outside agency, however, generates representations which might distort and dominate what she calls an "inherited tradition."

> Given the post-Holocaust lack of flesh-and-blood Jews and visible social, cultural, and religious Jewish environments in much of Europe, the resulting collective vision is quite frequently the product of literary

---

[15] Ibid., 19.

[16] Philip V. Bohlman, "Composing the Cantorate: Westernizing Europe's Other Within," in Born and Hesmondhalgh, *Western Music and Its Others*, 192.

imagination. . . . This virtual Jewishness or virtual Jewish world is a realm, thus, in which Jewish cultural products may take precedence over living Jewish culture; a realm in many senses constructed from desire rather than from memory or inherited tradition.[17]

Ruth Gruber is not alone in classifying klezmer within the realm of the "virtual" that competes with and threatens to overshadow the "living" Jewish culture. Leibl Rosenberg, a German-based Jewish author, argues that klezmer music appeals to the Jewish community only secondhand, as a cultural product that "the *environment* believes to be genuinely Jewish."[18] The German Jewish publicist Henryk Broder goes further, claiming that klezmer precludes the existence of "real" Jewish culture: "Jewish culture, its renaissance and revival are proclaimed everywhere, where there are no Jews."[19] But are the klezmer scene and the Jewish communities really worlds apart?

In 2003, the journalist Judith Kessler surveyed members of the local Jewish community about religious and cultural events they attended, trying to map Jewish cultural practices in Berlin. She discovered that by far the most popular form of pastime for local Jews was going to concerts, and that almost a quarter of her respondents craved more folklore-oriented entertainment, such as klezmer. Only 10 percent expressed disapprobation of klezmer music.[20] The tendency is also acknowledged by cultural organizers within the Jewish community. In 2007 the Central Council of Jews in Germany, in their annual cultural review under the rubric of "Entertainment," recommended to the local Jewish communities thirteen music ensembles. Seven of them specialized in Jewish heritage music and consisted mostly of Jewish musicians.[21]

The Jewish community of Berlin, with its eleven thousand registered members, is the biggest in Germany. Thanks to the influx of Jews from the former Soviet Union, the Jewish community in Germany has more than tripled in number since 1989, with Germany unexpectedly becoming home to one of the most dynamic Jewish diasporas in Europe. This rapid change has entirely transformed Jewish life in Berlin. For many decades after 1945, Jewish communities in Germany perceived their role only as a temporary support to the Jews who were, eventually, going to leave the country since there seemed to be no future for them there. Today, their future has very concrete dimensions.

[17] Gruber, *Virtually Jewish*, 27.

[18] Leibl Rosenberg, "Jüdische Kultur in Deutschland heute," in *Juden in Deutschland nach 1945: Bürger oder "Mit"-Bürger?*, ed. Otto R. Romberg and Susanne Urban-Fahr (Frankfurt: Tribüne, 1999), 240; italics mine.

[19] Broder, "Die Konjunktur des Jüdischen," 362.

[20] Judith Kessler, "Kultus- oder Kulturjuden?" hagalil.com, May 8, 2003, accessed April 26, 2009, http://www.berlin-judentum.de/gemeinde/mitgliederbefragung-2.htm.

[21] "5. Kulturprogramm des Zentralrats für die jüdischen Gemeinden, Januar-Dezember 2007," accessed April 9, 2008, http://www.zentralratderjuden.de/down/kulturprogramm_2007.pdf.

The life of the Berlin Jewish community centers around nine synagogues. Orthodox, conservative, liberal, and liberal-egalitarian rites are represented, as well as an independent community of *Adass-Jisroel* with its own synagogue and cemetery. The Jewish community manages an extended infrastructure, including Jewish schools, a kindergarten, a seniors' residence, three cemeteries, a community house, and a hospital. There are kosher shops, bakeries, and cafés. There are six Jewish newspapers and magazines. There is a Jewish bookstore, a theater, a tourist agency specializing in Jewish heritage in Berlin, as well as a family center with a *mikveh* and a library recently opened by the *Chabad* community. The Jewish adult education center, *Jüdische Volkshochschule*, offers courses in Hebrew and Yiddish, and the Jewish Gallery located next to the New Synagogue exhibits works by local Jewish artists. A number of Jewish associations are also represented in Berlin, such as the Ronald S. Lauder Foundation, the *B'nai B'rith* Youth Organization, and the sports club Makkabi. In 1999, a seminary for rabbis and cantors opened in nearby Potsdam. The city authorities actively support Jewish community life and institutions. In 2008, 85 percent of the yearly budget of the Jewish community, some 25 million Euros, came from the city of Berlin.[22]

These profound changes within the local Jewish community coincided with the beginnings of the klezmer boom in Berlin, which certainly did not make relations between the local Jews and the emerging klezmer scene easier. Massive immigration of Jews from the Soviet Union, and the necessity to organize a reunification of the East and West Berlin communities, brought with them new challenges that made the non-Jewish interest in Jewish heritage an issue of secondary importance to Berlin Jews. While the Jewish community of pre-1989 East Berlin initially welcomed the non-Jewish contribution to a Jewish culture revival, the situation was soon bound to change. "We had very good cooperation with the Jewish community in the GDR," recollects Jan Hermerschmidt of Aufwind:

> They were all elderly people there, and they were totally happy that somebody young was interested in the music, in the old library. We played a couple of times in the synagogue in the Rykestrasse, but the whole situation changed dramatically after the fall [of the wall]. The western *Gemeinde* was a very wealthy community, the establishment. They didn't want to have anything to do with us and vice versa. It was a totally different community. We tried to play there a couple of times, but we didn't really establish a connection to them.[23]

Although, still in the 1990s, a Jewish businessman from West Berlin supported the musicians of Aufwind by sponsoring their plane tickets to a klezmer festival

---

[22] "Haushaltsloch bei Jüdischer Gemeinde," *Der Tagesspiegel*, April 5, 2008, 11.

[23] Jan Hermerschmidt, interview by the author, Berlin, December 1, 2006.

in Israel, the invitations to play for the Western Jewish community soon ceased. Clearly, as Jewish Berlin underwent its metamorphosis, few were interested in the cultural developments taking place on the margin of Jewish life. "The last members of the original community," says Karsten Troyke, who also performed for the Jewish community in the early 1990s, "are interested in keeping the remnants of a Jewish identity, and not in Germans who sing Yiddish songs."[24] Likewise, Gennadij Desatnik, a Ukrainian musician who also performs klezmer with his band, comments succinctly that the local Jewish community is simply "cooking their own borscht."[25]

Another reason for this disinterest, according to Peter Sauerbaum, who from 2005 to 2007 coordinated the Days of Jewish Culture in Berlin on behalf of the Jewish community, is that the klezmer revival generates an image of Jewish life that is too "cuddly." "Klezmer music is something for weddings!" he comments in an interview for *Jüdische Zeitung*, campaigning for more variety in cultural productions dealing with Jewish heritage.[26] Similarly, Irene Runge, head of the Jewish Cultural Association in Berlin, is convinced that the klezmer scene is, in the long run, not able to offer attractive entertainment to the Jewish community. In her view, at venues that regularly stage klezmer concerts, such as the Hackesches Hoftheater, "when you have Jewish performances every evening then, at some point, you don't get the Jewish audience any more." "They are all good musicians," she comments on the local klezmer revivalists, "but there is no development and there *can* be no development for such a small audience."[27] Where "non-Jews dress up and play what they think is klezmer music," there is a risk that people receive a false impression of a booming Jewish cultural life. This "true" Jewish cultural revival is, however, according to Runge, still missing.

Some leaders of the Jewish communal life in Berlin see the klezmer revival as monochromatic and belonging to the non-Jewish realm. Rabbi Joshua Spinner from the Lauder Foundation argues that "the klezmer scene is clearly perceivable from the Jewish perspective as a non-Jewish phenomenon." What is more, the Jewish heritage boom, which has, in his view, nothing to do with Jewish cultural life, is "not only a parallel track, [but] it's a parallel track existing in a different universe."[28] A joke circulating among Berlin klezmer musicians plays on the same conviction: "Two Jews in Berlin are deciding which party to go to on a Saturday night. One of them says: 'There are two parties—at one of them, they'll be playing klezmer.' 'Let's go to the other one,' responds his friend. 'This one will be full of *goyim*.'"[29]

---

[24] Karsten Troyke, interview by the author, Berlin, January 12, 2006.

[25] Gennadij Desatnik, interview by the author, Berlin, November 30, 2006.

[26] Peter Sauerbaum, "Ich fordere die Zwänge heraus!" *Jüdische Zeitung*, no. 4, December 2005, 22.

[27] Irene Runge, interview by the author, Berlin, January 16, 2006.

[28] Rabbi Joshua Spinner, interview by the author, Berlin, January 13, 2006.

[29] I heard the joke from Paul Brody, interview by the author, Berlin, March 8, 2005.

But are the klezmer scene and the Jewish community really two parallel universes? The experiences of many klezmer musicians in Germany, Jewish and non-Jewish alike, show that there are more points of contact between the two than critics assume at first glance. Klezmer is popular with non-Jewish heritage tourists and local Jews alike. And since the Jewish communities in Germany are numerous enough to create a demand for music for Jewish occasions, local klezmer bands are among ensembles that service this segment of the market too. Jews are not only consumers of klezmer but also producers.

The VonGinzburgBand, based in Berlin, is a good example of a Jewish ensemble that broke into the German klezmer scene. The Ginzburgs, who come from Ukraine, form a family band with long traditions. Wlady Ginzburg arrived in Berlin after a ten-year stopover in Israel together with his father Igor and brother Jenia, both of whom are also performing klezmer musicians. "In our family, there has actually been no klezmer revival, because there was no interruption," he says. "The same way that my grandfather played at weddings, my father has been playing for already twenty-five years and now I do the same: in the Ukraine, in Israel, and in Germany."[30]

The Ginzburgs, who play at Jewish weddings, bar and bat mitzvahs, and Jewish anniversaries, learned klezmer by ear, passing down the repertoire from generation to generation. The name of the Ginzburg family has by now become a trademark. Wlady Ginzburg compares their ensemble to the legendary Epstein Brothers from New York, who could stage three concerts simultaneously under the label of their family band. On the weekends, the Ginzburgs usually give two or three performances, often with different musicians co-opted according to the particular requirements of the concert. The gigs within the Jewish communities are not their only ones, but they make up an important part of their performances. Apart from klezmer, they also play classical music, jazz, and various kinds of dance music, which makes them popular at Jewish community festivities all around Germany, where, as Wlady assures, they are invited to play for most of the Hanukkah balls.

Also in Kraków, where the Jewish community is just a fraction of that in Berlin, a few of the most crucial protagonists of the klezmer scene are Jewish. Leopold Kozłowski is, unquestionably, a towering figure of the local klezmer revival and an authority to many musicians performing in Kazimierz. Born in Przemyślany, near Lvov, the son of a klezmer musician, Hersch Kleinman, and nephew of the legendary American "king of klezmer" Naftule Brandwein, Kozłowski enjoys a particular status as "the last klezmer of Galicia." During World War II, he was imprisoned in a forced labor camp, where he played in the camp orchestra. After his escape from the camp he joined a Jewish partisan unit and later the Polish People's Army. Deciding to remain in Poland after the Kielce pogrom in 1946, he changed his name

---

[30] Wlady Ginzburg, interview by the author, Berlin, August 9, 2007.

from Kleinman to Kozłowski and pursued a career as a musician and conductor. He was an artistic director of a military orchestra until 1968, when, due to anti-Semitic purges, he lost his job in the army. For many years he performed Roma music and was a musical director of the Jewish Theater in Warsaw before, in the early 1990s, he formed his own ensemble in Kraków performing traditional Yiddish songs, mostly in Polish translation.[31]

Today Kozłowski, who has performed worldwide with his band, is an honorary guest of every edition of the Jewish Festival in Kraków and enjoys a certain amount of attention from the media. In 1994 Yale Strom made a documentary about Kozłowski titled *The Last Klezmer*, and in 2006 he was awarded a prize from the public television station (TVP2). The Klezmer Hois restaurant in Szeroka Street, adorned with his portrait and many pictures documenting his career, is the place where his myth is venerated and where he is available to his fans. As one of the last witnesses of the living klezmer tradition, Kozłowski has become an icon of the Polish klezmer revival.

The potential of the klezmer scene as a contact zone, however, does not depend only on the number of Jewish musicians who take part in the revival. The encounters between Jews and non-Jews within the klezmer scene take place on several different levels and in various constellations involving the artists, audiences, critics, and observers. The klezmer scene thus becomes a space of communication, which, just like the colonial contact zone described by Pratt, enables critique, but also cooperation and different modes of mediation.

Testing the Ground

The encounter of Jews and non-Jews in the klezmer scene entails a negotiation of space. Facing the other, acknowledging the presence of the other, and defining one's own position, function, and responsibilities is the prerequisite for a creative exchange. This initial testing of the ground serves as a way of establishing boundaries, and it sometimes takes place during the klezmer concert itself.

For Harry Timmermann, who has been playing klezmer in Berlin for more than a decade, performing for a non-Jewish audience is different than performing in front of Jews. His attempt to be considerate toward Jewish spectators, who might have different associations with klezmer music than do non-Jews, translates into a distinctive style of playing. "I do not have these considerations when I play in front of a non-Jewish audience," confesses Timmermann, "but when I know that there can be someone in the audience for whom this music might have some particular associations, I try to be careful." He remembers one particular situation

---

[31] Kozłowski interview; Jacek Cygan, *Klezmer: Opowieść o życiu Leopolda Kozłowskiego-Kleinmana* (Kraków: Austeria, 2010).

when the gaze of a Jewish person in the audience directly influenced the way he was playing:

> It happened to me once, in Königs Wusterhausen, at a commemora-
> tive event for the fiftieth anniversary of the end of the war. . . . One day
> before the event, I was told by the mayor of Königs Wusterhausen that
> somebody who had been in this concentration camp during the war was
> going to be there. I was told before the concert, and there I was, with this
> maybe eighty-year-old man right in front of my clarinet. Only then did I
> really realize that I was playing in a very careful way. I was watching how
> he was reacting, because I didn't really want to encroach on the world of
> his feelings. Sometimes you can steer a little bit with the clarinet. You
> can bring people to tears, or you can play in a joyful way. And when I
> know about something like that, I play in a more restrained way. But in a
> concert, I feel quite free to play whatever I feel like.[32]

The situation narrated here illustrates some of the most challenging contexts in which klezmer musicians perform. Playing at Holocaust commemoration events, and in particular facing Holocaust survivors, the musicians confront both a gen-erational distance, and one between a contemporary artistic act and a historic event that escapes representation. For non-Jewish musicians, it is also the dis-tance between the self and the other. Wishing to fulfill the expectations of their Jewish audiences, or seeking their acceptance, some klezmer musicians actively look for the means of expression that they perceive as adequate and appropriate.

This heightened attentiveness that Harry Timmermann describes accompa-nies some klezmer musicians not only during the performance but also in its preparation. Ulrike Kloock, who manages the concerts of the biggest klezmer band in Germany, the Klezmer Orchester, tries to pay special attention to the sensitivities of local Jewish communities. "When I make the schedule for our con-certs," she says, "I download a Jewish calendar, and I have a look at it to make sure that there is no Jewish holiday on the day when we want to organize a concert, so that we don't get on the nerves of the local Jewish community."[33] Consulting the Jewish calendar is also a way of negotiating space. Planning the concerts so that they do not conflict with Jewish holidays means acknowledging the pres-ence of the other and the fact that the klezmer scene is a place co-created by and frequented by Jews.

Needless to say, the expectations of Jewish audiences who attend klezmer con-certs in Germany or in Poland are not always met. Many Jewish spectators sup-pose or hope that the artists performing for them are also Jewish. Right after a concert or during the break is thus often the moment when audiences can "test the

[32] Timmermann interview.
[33] Kloock interview.

ground" and find out about who the musicians are. Irena Urbańska, who performs with a program of Yiddish songs in Kazimierz, recalls many such encounters:

> Two weeks ago, there was a married couple from California at my concert in Ariel Café. The gentleman approached me and said: "You are singing it really well. *Ekht yidish!* Where did you learn to sing like that?" And some American or Israeli Jews start speaking Yiddish to me after the concert, because they are convinced I am Jewish and I speak this language fluently. But . . . I don't know it in the sense of, you know, being able to speak Yiddish in a normal conversation. But do I know what I am singing? Of course I do. I understand it, I know what it means. I know all Jewish traditions and rituals, but I don't know Yiddish well enough to be able to speak it in everyday life.[34]

These failed conversations in Yiddish are not failed attempts at communication. They help the speakers to define the boundaries between them and to acknowledge that along the boundaries that they are taking for granted, there are also some anomalous niches and gray zones. A non-Jew who can flawlessly perform in Yiddish but is unable to have a casual conversation in this language marks a category that challenges many assumptions. And it is this constant questioning of the expected patterns of encounter that marks out the central capacity of a contact zone.

Testing the ground of intergroup relations also implies infringing on the boundaries of what is considered acceptable and proper in order to discover new limits. Henry Sapoznik, one of the pioneers of the American klezmer movement and the founder of the Klezkamp festival, recalls one such exchange with non-Jewish klezmer musicians in Germany that left an alienating impression on him:

> I just have this memory that we were playing somewhere in Germany and there was another klezmer band opening before us. At some point they came over to us to buy some records and I said it was this much, and they said: "Oh, come on, give it to me for the Jew price." And he assumed that, like two black guys call each other "nigger," he assumed that . . . you can do that when you're a member of a group . . . it's to presume friendship, to presume there is no space between us. That was weird.[35]

The German musician assumed proximity between himself and his Jewish American colleague. But his positioning of himself as an in-group member was a step too far for Sapoznik. Alluding to Jewish solidarity is perceived here as improper, as a

---

[34] Irena Urbańska, interview by the author, Kraków, July 10, 2006.
[35] Sapoznik interview.

violation of the unspoken boundary between the Jewish and non-Jewish participants of the klezmer scene. Although the musicians are professional colleagues,
the ethnic boundary remains relevant and becomes salient as soon as it is crossed.

The klezmer scene thus functions as a space where Jews and non-Jews face
each other, test each other's sensibilities, and negotiate their position within a
shared professional space. And although this encounter might result in heightened attentiveness to the needs of the other, it also leaves space for voicing critique. And as a contact zone stretching over a particularly sensitive terrain, the
klezmer scene is also, not surprisingly, a space of friction, conflicts, and misun-
derstandings.

Critique

Places like the Hackesches Hoftheater, offering possibilities of creative cooperation between Jewish and non-Jewish musicians and actors, soon became
the epicenters of the klezmer contact zone. Opening an accessible space for
discussion, they took over the role of an informal forum, where critical questions concerning the motivations behind the German klezmer revival could be
posed. Jalda Rebling, one of the theater's core actors, remembers that the mixed
troupe sometimes engaged in disputes, which put in relief the ethnic boundaries within the group. At one occasion, as non-Jewish musicians performing for
the theater realized that the Jewish community in Berlin had lost interest in
hiring them for its events, Rebling recollects that many of her colleagues felt
frustrated:

> One of the female musicians said to us, "If they don't accept me in the
> community, I will invent myself a Jewish grandmother." Anna, who
> was standing next to me, turned pale, I was feeling a bit sick, and Anna
> said: "You know, one of my grandmothers died in Theresienstadt and
> the other one in Auschwitz, I have not invented them. It's not funny to
> have a grandmother who came back from a concentration camp." From
> then on, nothing worked any more. No conversation was possible any
> more . . . there was suddenly a split taking place, we, the Jews, realized
> our Jewishness much more than before.[36]

The perceived lack of acceptance from the Jewish community gives salience to
tensions within the Jewish/non-Jewish troupe. A crisis occurs when one of the
artists questions the cult of authenticity related to the ethnic background of the
musician. If the legitimacy to play Jewish music is reserved for Jews, one can
automatically gain it by "discovering" Jewish roots in one's family, according to

[36] Rebling interview, February 6, 2006.

the provocative claim. Jewish musicians interpret this argument as lacking respect toward the experience of the Holocaust in their families. The attempt to discuss the question of how the politics of identity feed into the debate on cultural appropriation ends here at a failed attempt at communication. Still, the critical exchange is a gain. Bringing together Jewish and non-Jewish artists, the klezmer scene serves as a site where musicians can make each other aware of their different sensibilities.

Simon Jakob Drees, who likewise performed at the theater with his band Ahava Raba, remembers that the debates over the legitimacy to play Jewish music also engaged the audiences:

> We had a couple of concerts, and then some people from the Jewish community came and attacked us very fiercely, saying that we were dealing with the material so disrespectfully. We didn't play the music in a traditional way, but we chopped it into pieces and built our own language out of it. We took inspiration from it, and we made our own material from it. However, we did it with a very deep knowledge of the music. Our clarinet-player and I had been dealing very intensively with this music. I had also been learning Yiddish, so we had respect toward this music and we didn't mean to disregard the music. . . . The people from the Jewish community asked us if any of us were Jewish, and they simply attacked us during the break. They went out after the concert and were waiting for us in the hall to discuss with us as soon as we came out.[37]

As an open space for the creation of art, and what Diana Pinto would call a "Jewish-friendly neutral space," the theater was a venue where Jews and non-Jews could come to grips with each other. It is not surprising that the topics handled in these spaces were not limited solely to music. In her study of the interactions between Jews and non-Jews in Kraków's Kazimierz, the anthropologist Erica Lehrer designates the Jewish district as a space of dialogue and critical "truth-telling."[38] The spaces of klezmer performances seem to catalyze this process in an even more intensive way because they offer a space for particular forms of sociability. Small groups of people meeting in the circumscribed space of a concert or workshop are likely to engage in an exchange, especially in reaction to the stimulus they directly experience: the music. Klezmer events, then, attracting Jews and non-Jews of various nationalities and political views, and from different generations, become sites of this critical truth-telling, where music is the starting point but by no means the only issue.

---

[37] Simon Jakob Drees, interview by the author, Berlin, February 10, 2006.

[38] Lehrer, "Can There Be a Reconciliatory Heritage?" 269–88. See also Erica T. Lehrer, *Jewish Poland Revisited: Heritage Tourism in Unquiet Places* (Bloomington: Indiana University Press, 2013), 140ff.

Daniel Kahn, who moved from Detroit to Berlin in 2006, where he founded his own klezmer band, recalls such an instance of critical truth-telling directly following a concert. After having attended Brave Old World's performance of "Song of the Lodz Ghetto" in Weimar, Kahn found himself exchanging impressions with several of his German colleagues. As the conversation developed, he witnessed an emotional reaction from one of the German spectators:

> "Who do these people think they are, these Americans from the big"—
> and she made this gesture—"USA, who come to Germany to make us
> feel guilty about what Germany did sixty years ago! When they killed
> all of the Indians, and they are killing Iranians"—she said Iranians, but
> she meant Iraqis—"they're over there killing all the people in Iran, and
> doing all of this genocide and war. When every country has done this,
> why should we feel like we're the worst? But we're guilty! Who the hell do
> they think they are, these big American Jews!" . . . I didn't know how to
> respond to that. Everybody was like: "crap, she said this!" Everyone was
> quiet; you could hear the crickets outside. . . . And I said to her: "First of
> all, I want to say that you're absolutely right about what's going on in Iraq
> and what my government is doing is a source of shame for me . . . and
> you're right: genocide has no residence, Germany certainly doesn't have
> a monopoly on that, it's happening right now in Sudan, it happened ten
> years ago in Rwanda, in Cambodia, in the former Yugoslavia. . . . But, the
> real issue is not whether or not there are all of these other comparisons,
> the issue is, why are you bringing them up? What does it serve in you to
> bring them up? Is it a way for you not to take your own responsibility,
> for you not to deal with the part that you play?" . . . And this piece, they
> didn't come to Germany to make her feel guilty, they came to Germany
> because we need to talk about these things!

Reflecting on the significance of performing ghetto songs in today's Germany leads the speakers to discuss questions such as the uniqueness of the Holocaust and collective guilt. But most importantly, the debate forces them to take up the positions of group members (here: German non-Jews vs. American Jews), asking each other questions of critical importance.

Perhaps unavoidably, the German klezmer scene has become a space of engagement with German history. The Holocaust looms in the background for the German musicians who play klezmer, German audiences, and for those foreign artists who come to perform there. For many Jewish American klezmer revivalists, coming to Germany means confronting the contradiction between the country's heritage of genocide and the present-day fascination with Jewish culture. In the accounts of many of them, visions of death and annihilation dominate their perception of the country. Henry Sapoznik of Kapelye remembers that Berlin had a "macabre attraction" for him and that, thinking of the history of the sites where he was performing, he experienced a physical reaction: the food he was served "tasted like ashes."[39] Alex Jacobowitz, who has been performing in Germany for more than ten years, also views Berlin primarily as a site of death: "I don't feel at home here, just down the road is the Memorial for the Murdered Jews of Europe," he notes. He also adds that his coming to Germany had a symbolic dimension for him. "I was afraid," he says, "and I think that's why I came here in the first place: because I was working on the fear of death at the hands of the Germans. I wouldn't have come here out of my own free will. I came here because I needed to. I needed to fix what was broken. I needed to understand how this whole thing could happen; I needed to confront my fear."[40]

It was the band Brave Old World that first translated this confrontation with Germany into their music. Michael Alpert's "Berlin 1990," which he wrote in Yiddish, is both a confession of how difficult it is for a Jewish artist to perform in Germany and a critique of German society witnessing the rise of the extreme right-wing and xenophobia:

Kh'ob geshpilt do in daytshland
   sheyn eftere mol
	I've played here in Germany
	   many's the time

'Hamavdil, hamavdil
   beyn keydesh lekhol.'
	"he who divides the sacred
	   from the worldly"

Nor ikh shver bay mayn muze,
   to hert vos ikh zing,
	But I swear by my muse,
	   mark well what I sing

Az keyn eyn mol iz mir geven
   laykht do, un gring . . .
	That not once has it been easy
	   to be here

Kh'halt shtark fun mayn yikhes,	I'm proud of my heritage,
Nor ikh bin aykh mekane,	yet I envy you

Ir, hayntike kinder
   fun nekhtikn faynt,
	Today's children
	   of yesterday's enemy,

Vayl aykh iz di tsukunft,	Because yours is the future,
Eyn land un a shprakh,	one land and a language
Beys mir haltn shtumerheyt do . . .	While we're left here speechless . . .

S'iz shoyn undzer a velt,
   do fargangen in flamen,
	Our world has already gone
	   done in flames here,

Opgezundert di tsvaygn fun
   Yidishn boym,
	Branches severed from
	   the Jewish tree,

Nor nokh a mol boyt men
   uf moyern, tsamen,
	Yet again walls and fences
	   are being built,

[39] Sapoznik, *Klezmer!*, 225–26.
[40] Jacobowitz interview.

Faryogn di, nebekh, vos zukhn a heym.	And you persecute those poor souls seeking a home.
Af s'nay traybt ir yene avek fun di tirn,	You drive them anew from your gates,
Me yogt zay shoyn vider durkh nekht fun krishtal	Hunting them through nights of broken glass.
Oy, vos far a khutspe, azoy zikh tsu firn,	What chutzpa you have to act like that—
Mir zoln in aykh den tsuzetsn di gal?	Are we supposed to forgive you?[41]

Germany inflicts speechlessness: the sound of German recalls the demise of Yiddish and the present-day anti-immigrant violence in Germany stirs up the old anxiety. The new violence in Germany is an echo of the old. The events of the 1990s, when radical right-wing groups attacked asylum seekers' housing centers in Germany, represent a sinister repetition of the 1938 *Kristallnacht*—Night of Broken Glass. History seemingly repeating itself relentlessly gives no hope that the relation of Jews toward Germany can ever be unproblematic. There is no lesson learned from the Holocaust, suggests Alpert, and its memory will always haunt the "love-hate" relationship of Germans and Jews.

History itself overshadows the klezmer scene. For some American klezmer musicians, coming to Poland was perhaps as difficult as confronting Germany. Yale Strom, a musician and filmmaker, was among the first American klezmer revivalists who traveled to Poland in the 1980s. In his travel diary, *A Wandering Feast* (2005), Strom conveys the dominant sensation of fear that accompanied him during his trip. One of the episodes he narrates shows it in a very vivid way. Hosted by a non-Jewish family in Kraków, the musician is invited to join them for a small family get-together. At the table, served a roasted pig, he suddenly intuits a Jewish joke being told and the laughter that ensues makes an alienating impression on him. Strom's dramatized narrative indicates his preconceptions about Poland as an unsafe place for Jews, and illustrates some of the anxieties that visiting Jews might have:

> Everything seemed to go into slow motion as I got up from the table to walk to my room. All I could see were their mouths agape, distorted and sinister as the laughter seemed to grow in volume. And even though I didn't fully understand the joke, the fact that they didn't even suspect

---

[41] Michael Alpert "Berlin 1990," Brave Old World, *Beyond the Pale*, Rounder Select, 1994, CD. Transcription from Yiddish: Janina Wurbs.

me of being Jewish somehow made it worse. I wanted to shout: "Ja jestem Zyd!" (I am a Jew!) Instead, I walked resolutely to my room, finally understanding why many of the Polish survivors I had met back home (and even some of their children) had vowed never to set foot on Polish soil again.[42]

Although the situation he finds himself in is ambiguous, since he understands only a few words of what his Polish hosts are saying, it marks a moment of epiphany in Strom's travel report. Poles appear to him as essentially anti-Semitic, and any kind of understanding between them and the Jews seems impossible.

Janusz Makuch, who has invited many American Jewish musicians to Poland to perform at the Jewish festival, has encountered some of this apprehension too. One of the artists even asked for two bodyguards on his first visit.[43] Indeed, many American klezmer revivalists are poignantly aware of the fact that they are coming to the site of the Holocaust, and a country still notorious for its anti-Semitism. "Poland for a lot of Jews represents a cemetery," explains Alex Jacobowitz, interviewed by Yale Strom in his documentary *Klezmer on Fish Street*. Jacobowitz, who first visited Kazimierz to attend the Jewish festival, remembers that he hesitated before he finally made the decision to come to Poland:

> The largest part of our people was killed here, and the pain associated with that historical fact makes many Jews very sour about the Polish experience. And I must say that I wasn't completely immune to that. I don't think I would have easily come to Poland by myself, but with the Jewish festival in Kraków, I thought that would be a possibility to close an open wound.[44]

This sentiment of the musicians makes its way also to the new music inspired by their experience of Poland. Joshua Waletzky, a Yiddish songwriter and filmmaker from New York, upon visiting Kazimierz during the Jewish festival, wrote his elegiac "Ikh heyb mayn fus" ["I Lift My Foot"]. The song, opening his 2001 album *Crossing the Shadows*, speaks of the impossibility of dancing and singing "over the trampled stones" and "under the disgraced trees" of Kazimierz, where the narrating voice still hears the screams of the murdered Jews:

---

[42] Yale Strom and Elisabeth Schwartz, *A Wandering Feast: A Journey through the Jewish Culture of Eastern Europe* (San Francisco: Jossey-Bass, 2005), 141–42.

[43] Makuch interview.

[44] Alex Jacobowitz in *Klezmer on Fish Street*.

Ikh heyb mayn fus,   I lift my foot,
nor zi vil nit tantsn   but it doesn't want to dance
iber di farbrente beyner;   over the incinerated bones.
ikh her nokh dayn geshrey,   I still hear you screaming,
bruder-lebn, shvester-lebn,   dear brother, dear sister,
iber di tsetrotene shteyner.   over the trampled stones.[45]

Asking the question whether music is actually not misplaced on historic sites tinged with death, Waletzky's song could also be interpreted as a critique of the Jewish festival, or the klezmer scene in Kazimierz. And although the creators of the festival have been looking for ways of producing music events that respect the aura of the historic Jewish places, Kazimierz remains a space laden with symbolism.

For this reason, much of the critical truth-telling within the Polish klezmer scene concentrates on conflicts of space. While artists make their claim to the historic Jewish space as the venue of their concerts, some local Jews find it difficult to find their own place in the district overwhelmed by heritage tourism. Przemysław Piekarski, a member of the Jewish community and lecturer of Yiddish at the Jagiellonian University, sees the klezmer revival in Kazimierz as part of what he calls "pseudo-Jewishness," which is at best irrelevant for the local Jews. The real Jewish preoccupations, he says, lie somewhere else. "There is no kosher restaurant, apart from food served in containers and warmed up in the microwave in the Eden hotel," he complains.[46] He is also disappointed that klezmer musicians are not interested in learning Yiddish and that they are sometimes inconsiderate toward the worshipers in the local synagogue. "There used to be a kosher restaurant right next to the [Remuh] synagogue," he recounts:

The eastern wall of the synagogue was adjacent to the restaurant's beer garden. When we were initiating the Shabbat prayers, a concert of pseudo-Jewish klezmer music would be starting on the other side of the wall. You know that Jews cannot even touch a musical instrument on Shabbat, not to mention play it or listen to it, and here we had these quasi-Jewish sounds, "ay ay ay." . . . And this is how it is: they play klezmer music and what do they care about the Shabbat?[47]

Przemysław Piekarski notices the problem areas, or even conflicts of interest, between the Jewish community, worshiping in Szeroka Street, and the local

---

[45] Joshua Waletzky, "Ikh heyb mayn fus," cited in Abigail Wood, "Commemoration and Creativity: Remembering the Holocaust in Today's Yiddish Song," European Judaism 35, no. 2 (2002): 52.

[46] Przemysław Piekarski, interview by the author, Kraków, July 4, 2008. A kosher restaurant was opened in Kazimierz in 2010.

[47] Ibid.

Jewish-style restaurants that schedule their concerts during Shabbat, but he also points out instances of symbiosis. One of the most popular Jewish restaurants in Kazimierz, Klezmer Hois, closes on Yom Kippur, and one of the Yiddish singers performing in Kazimierz, Urszula Makosz, runs Yiddish workshops both at the Jewish festival and, during the rest of the year, at the Jewish Community Center.

Negotiating the spaces of Jewish life and Jewish-style consumption in Kazimierz might be one of the most critical areas in the exchange between Jews and non-Jews in Kraków, but it is not the only problem. The fact that the klezmer scene in Kraków emerged as an autarchic space, responding to the immediate demand for Jewish music in the economy of the revitalized Jewish quarter rather than, like in Berlin, through an intensive exchange with the American klezmer revivalists, leads also to some tensions over hegemony.

Unlike in Germany where many klezmer musicians have attended workshops with Jewish American revivalists, only a few Polish klezmer musicians have worked more closely with the Americans. In fact, the only local band that has had intensive dealings with the American klezmer scene is the Bester Quartet, which has issued six of their records in the Radical Jewish Music series on John Zorn's label, *Tzadik*, and performed, among other places, at one of the cult venues of the American klezmer revival: the Knitting Factory, now located in Brooklyn. At the same time, Jarosław Bester, leader of the group, is critical of what he believes is an aura of authenticity that the American *klezmorim* enjoy in Europe: "A set of artists has emerged, American musicians, who tour all the festivals worldwide and constitute the so-called base. They are considered OK, while all the others are so-called fakes. They are evidently closer to the old sources, and they try to replay the music of Tarras and Brandwein, sometimes without any changes. If Tarras improvised something, and someone repeats exactly what he played, then it doesn't make sense any more."[48] It is not only the method, but also the question of authority that provokes the skepticism of some Polish musicians toward their American colleagues.

Although klezmer workshops for musicians have been on the program of the Jewish festival since 2006, the artists performing klezmer in Kazimierz do not usually participate in them. A Cracovian musician, asked whether he was going to take part in the klezmer workshops offered by an American musician during the festival in Kraków, answered: "As we are educated and professional musicians ourselves, we know how well we play. If our band had more publicity in the world, we would be leading these workshops and you would be asking them if they felt like going there."[49] Another performer from Kazimierz said: "We take it

---

[48] Bester interview.
[49] Inglot interview.

professionally: if we're interested in something ... we consult the greatest authority. If we want to find out something more about Jewish singing and ornamentation, we ask Leopold Kozłowski."[50] Although there are artists who do participate in joint projects with the American musicians and take part in their workshops, for most of the professional musicians based in Kazimierz, the strong presence of the American klezmer revivalists at the Jewish festival has a hegemonic dimension that they resent.

This fact does not pass unnoticed by the American *klezmorim*. Michael Alpert of Brave Old World believes, for example, that Polish musicians could use more of the resources that they have at their disposal in Poland. "There is somewhat this attitude: 'This music comes from Poland, so it's ours and we don't have to learn it,'" he states.

> There is some of that. It's not the only answer. Also, at the Kraków festival, we started having workshops only three years ago, while in the Soviet Union it has been going on for thirteen years now, in Germany even longer. That also sows lots of seeds and brings people in contact, teaches people both technical skills and what to listen for, and how to understand the music. It's not only about music, it's about the culture. This is only beginning to grow there.[51]

The question of how Jewish music should be studied and which role models should be followed touches also upon the question of the legitimate manner of dealing with Jewish heritage. Undoubtedly, motivations behind the American and the Polish revival have been different. The American klezmer movement, which has involved mostly Jewish musicians, is closely correlated with the will to save from oblivion a part of Jewish heritage, which many of its participants can identify with and relate to their own family history. This dimension of rediscovering klezmer as a means of asserting an ethnic identity has been virtually absent in Poland. This ultimately means that for most Polish *klezmorim* their adventure with klezmer is, indeed, only about the music. At the same time, many Polish musicians feel that because of the commonalities between klezmer and Eastern European folk music, they do have special access to the music they play. The debate reflects here anxieties that extend beyond the mere methodology of a music revival. On the one hand, it raises the problem of misrepresentation if klezmer is handled in an incompetent and superficial way; on the other, the uneasiness of the non-Jewish musicians that their contribution might be marginalized.

[50] Jasha Lieberman [Jasha Lieberman Trio], interview by the author, Kraków, July 5, 2006.
[51] Michael Alpert, interview by the author, KlezKanada Festival, August 25, 2007.

Cooperation

Despite the apprehensions, tensions, and conflicts that come to the fore in the klezmer scene, the revival movement is defined by mutual inspiration, exchange of ideas, and a large dose of cooperation between Jewish and non-Jewish musicians. And the microworld of Jewish heritage revival in Kazimierz creates perfect conditions for intensive interactions between Jewish and non-Jewish artists, cultural organizers, residents, and visitors. Unlike in Berlin, where klezmer performances are quite dispersed, Szeroka Street in Kraków has become the hub of the klezmer contact zone, where Jews and non-Jews "grapple with each other" on a daily basis. The Jewish festival is the high point in the yearly schedule of these various intergroup encounters: a time that is exceptional for the sheer quantity of cultural events that bring together Jews and non-Jews, and that focalizes Kazimierz's inherent potential as a meeting space.

For Janusz Makuch, the head of the festival, the acceptance of the Kraków Jewish community for the festival is very important. Although he remembers that, at first, the representatives of the Jewish community were skeptical about the initiative of two non-Jews to launch a Jewish festival, with time the idea won their full support.[52] For years now, the Jewish community has cooperated with the festival foundation, allowing it to use the synagogues for concerts, lectures, and workshops. The community members, in exchange, receive free tickets to some of the events.

Boaz Pash, the chief rabbi of Kraków, who participated in the festival in 2008 as a lecturer and also as a guest performer in a concert of Ladino songs, admits that the event is crucial for the self-definition of the local Jewish community. "The recognition of society is important," he explains, "recognition as an important other culture. It's important for them that people know: 'Hey, you exist, and we know that you exist.' It's important on the level of self-esteem. At least for ten days you can be in Kazimierz and be proud: 'We are here and we're important.'"[53] This affirmation of the Jewish presence is significant in particular because the future of the Kraków community seems so uncertain. For the same reason, the klezmer concerts that take place in Kazimierz on a daily basis, Rabbi Pash believes, can also have a positive value for the local Jewish community. Jewish folklore circulated in Kazimierz may be only like the "outer skin" of Judaism, he says. "[It's] the lowest, simplest, the most exterior part," but it also offers a way for non-Jews to show their respect toward Jews.[54]

Even though the Jewish Culture Festival in Kraków is organized by non-Jews for a prevalently non-Jewish audience, its creators realize that it is only through the cooperation of non-Jews and Jews that the festival can truly fulfill its role

---

[52] Makuch interview, May 3, 2007.
[53] Rabbi Boaz Pash, interview by the author, Kraków, July 4, 2008.
[54] Ibid.

and make an impact. For Janusz Makuch, it is therefore important that the festival not only hosts renowned Jewish artists but also enables a learning process through which non-Jews can find out about Jewish culture and traditions from those who know them best: Jews themselves. The format of the KlezKamp festival in the New York's Catskill Mountains, which Makuch visited for the first time in the 1990s, influenced to a large extent the way the Cracovian event developed. "When I took part in KlezKamp," recalls Makuch, "I finally understood the dimension of Jewish culture rooted in the tradition of Yiddish. . . . It was like a catharsis for me. . . . Suddenly, it was no longer like in the beginning when I was sitting at my desk, trying to come up with something I had no idea about, but we were generating [festival] ideas together."[55] This cooperation had concrete consequences for this first Polish Jewish festival and others that followed. Working closely with Michael Alpert and Alan Bern, both of Brave Old World, Makuch added workshops of Jewish culture to the festival format and in time expanded the offer to include twenty-one different thematic series from "klezmer for beginners" to "Yemenite jewelry making."

But even though the festival is an annual high point in international Jewish/non-Jewish encounters, everyday life in Kazimierz has enough potential for intensive exchange. Although the Jewish community in Kraków is not that large, two Jewish personages have inspired and sustained a critical dialogue with the local klezmer scene from its inception. The Jewish historian and publicist Henryk Halkowski, who passed away in 2009, was a frequent guest of the Jewish restaurants in Szeroka Street and, with his knowledge of Yiddish, a reference point for some of the klezmer musicians performing there. Although not sparing in his criticism of the local klezmer scene, he is also credited with having given a name to one of the oldest Kazimierz bands, Di Galitzyaner Klezmorim, who asked him for help in this matter.[56] Leopold Kozłowski, in turn, apart from being a teacher for a whole generation of klezmer revivalists in Kraków, belonged to the first musicians who performed Jewish music in postwar Kazimierz. Wojciech Ornat, the owner of the Jewish restaurant where Kozłowski first performed with a program of Jewish songs, remembers that the beginning of the klezmer boom in Kazimierz was made possible by a particular synergy. "Us and Leopold, it was like positive feedback," says Ornat:

> Before we became close friends, he was not performing so much, he didn't have his venue or his band; he was a pensioner after he left the Jewish Theater in Warsaw. My first apprehensions that he would not agree to perform in a restaurant were not confirmed though. It was all arranged in a way that didn't collide with his ambition and his self-expression. And

[55] Makuch interview, May 3, 2007.

[56] Henryk Halkowski, "Rodzinny dom w knajpę przemieniony, czyli o kiczu na Kazimierzu," *Midrasz*, no. 3 (2006): 16–19.

there was this one concert, then another one with Sława Przybylska, and then with the actors with whom he is still performing to this day.[57]

Indeed, Kozłowski instructed many musicians who later chose to continue their careers as klezmer musicians in Kazimierz. Irena Urbańska, who performs and records with her own klezmer band, was one of them. She recalls that when, in 1992, Kozłowski approached her with an offer to prepare a concert of Jewish songs for the Days of Jewish Kazimierz, the music was an entirely unknown genre for her. "I am a classical singer," she says, "I didn't have anything to do with Jewish music. Besides, at that time, there was no Jewish music in Poland. It was just not there."[58] The small semiprofessional radio ensemble with whom she performed at the time had to be first introduced to the very basics of Yiddish song:

> My small vocal ensemble, twelve or fourteen people, obtained notation and lyrics from Leopold Kozłowski. And we prepared our first five Jewish songs. He taught us about what this music was, about how to read it and how to sing it. And then we performed it as a matinee in the Popper Synagogue in Kazimierz. This was the first Jewish music that was played in Kazimierz.[59]

Even today, when the Jewish district accommodates a dozen of more or less established klezmer bands, many musicians still refer themselves to Leopold Kozłowski when in doubt in matters of execution or pronunciation of Yiddish. "With every new song that we work with, I go to Mr. Kozłowski first," says the vocalist of Quartet Klezmer Trio, Magdalena Brudzińska, "and he makes sure that I'm not making some terrible mistakes in the pronunciation."[60] The authority of Leopold Kozłowski, however, extends not only to musical matters. With his concert at the Jesuit basilica in Kraków during the "Day of Judaism in the Catholic Church" in 2000, Kozłowski made an important statement for local Jewish/non-Jewish relations.

For Jarosław Naliwajko, the Jesuit priest who invited Leopold Kozłowski to perform in the church, klezmer music is a medium that in a particularly poignant way expresses the sufferings of the Jewish people. Father Naliwajko, who also works as a psychotherapist and is a member of the Polish-Israeli Association for Mental Health (*Polsko-Izraelskie Towarzystwo Zdrowia Psychicznego*), heard klezmer for the first time during a concert by Kozłowski, and remained deeply impressed. Believing that the experience of listening to klezmer music might induce Catholics to reflect on the anti-Semitism contained in the past teachings of the Catholic Church, Father Naliwajko wanted the Jesuit church to host a concert by

[57] Ornat interview.
[58] Urbańska interview.
[59] Ibid.
[60] Brudzińska interview, June 30, 2006.

Kozłowski's ensemble. "Leopold Kozłowski was glad, but also full of apprehension," recalls Naliwajko:

> There is this stereotype, based on two thousand years of Jews experiencing aggression on the part of the Church, or, generally speaking, Poland. And if a priest comes and asks to do a concert in a church, then it is the most you can symbolically do for the relations between our nations. Because it is something else to organize it in a . . . cultural center, than in a church, in which they had the idea that Jews, that Leopold Kozłowski, killed Christ. . . . Maybe this invitation was a kind of fulfillment; the fact that he could perform in a place where he was not expecting it. One of the results of this concert is also the fact that we are friends now, we meet, have a drink together and talk about all kinds of things. Then it turned out that his wife was Catholic. And when she died two years ago, I conducted the funeral. This translates to private issues. Some children were born in the ensemble and I baptized them and slowly I became something of a chaplain. This is the only klezmer band which has a Catholic "chaplain."[61]

Klezmer can exist as a site of dialogue on a microscale and also as the site of many friendships that reach across ethnic and religious boundaries. At times, however, cooperation between Jews and non-Jews on the klezmer scene brings about projects that have an institutional form. One of the most outstanding is the Klezmer School in Berlin, run by Jossif Gofenberg. Gofenberg, a performing klezmer musician and a teacher of Yiddish song at the Jewish Community House (*Gemeindehaus*), came to Berlin in 1990 from Czernowitz. He grew up in a family in which Yiddish was spoken and in a town with very rich traditions of Yiddish culture. Ever since his arrival in Berlin, he has been performing with his band Klezmer Chidesch, touring Jewish communities across Germany. The participants of his hands-on workshops at the Jewish Community House are mostly middle-aged and elderly. They sing together once a week, and occasionally perform in public and go on excursions. Gofenberg is convinced that Jewish music is an important tool of integration, and he attempts to reach out with his project to both Jews and non-Jews. His Klezmer School, which opened in 2000 as a nonprofit enterprise, is an extraordinary project meant, among others, to help integrate the Russian-speaking Jewish musicians in Germany.

The idea behind the Klezmer School was initially, on the one hand, to offer musical education free of charge to children from underprivileged families, and, on the other, to activate some otherwise unemployed Jewish musicians. The teachers, who were, like Gofenberg, immigrants from the former Soviet Union and often already pensioners, would receive a low salary for their teaching, but they had the opportunity to exercise their profession and stay in German-speaking

[61] Fr. Jarosław Naliwajko, interview by the author, Kraków, April 21, 2004.

surroundings. Today, Gofenberg's Klezmer School is part of the music school Berlin-Mitte, and it offers classes to both children and adults. The students get here a unique opportunity to learn not just about klezmer but about Jewish holidays, customs, and traditions. Gofenberg believes that his Klezmer School serves an important function for Jewish identity:

> It's important for them [the teachers] to perform their profession. . . . They become integrated not only through the speaking of German, or the work-experience, but also through the experience of Jewishness. They teach not only about Jewish music, but also about some customs. This is the main task of my school, integration for everyone: pupils, teachers and also the parents who come to our concerts, bringing friends and family. I tell them about Jewish holidays, and they receive information that they would not get otherwise.[62]

Located in the Kulturhaus Mitte, a public cultural institution in the center of Berlin, the Klezmer School had, in 2013, roughly fifty pupils who were learning to play instruments such as piano, violin, and accordion, and attending classes of music theory. The school had also its own ensemble of hobby musicians, Klezmärchen, which occasionally gave concerts.

Fig. 3.1 Jossif Gofenberg (accordion) and the Klezmärchen rehearsing at the Klezmer School, Berlin, 2013.

[62] Gofenberg interview.

Although Gofenberg's initiative might be the only undertaking of this kind in Germany, there are more contexts in which musicians can learn the klezmer style from Jewish and non-Jewish teachers. The largest and most prestigious institution of this kind is the Yiddish Summer in Weimar, which, since 2000, has gathered advanced klezmer instrumentalists and singers. Yiddish Summer Weimar, growing out of the summer klezmer workshops that the musicians of the American band Brave Old World first organized in 1999, is today an institution that organizes two yearly editions of workshops in Yiddish expressive culture and language, including instrumental and vocal music, dance, and storytelling. What is crucial for the director of the festival, Alan Bern, is that the festival examines Jewish music in relation and in opposition to other genres of folk music, such as Greek, Turkish, or Bessarabian. The juxtaposition, according to Bern, provides a creative tension for the musicians, and serves to produce a definition of Jewish culture in constant relation to the other:

> I do not believe in a definition of not only Jewish culture, but anything per se. I believe that everything can only be defined in relation to a certain set of questions, a certain set of purposes, a certain set of functions. So if somebody says something is Jewish, I say: "Compared to what and for whom?" These social categories don't exist intrinsically; they're dynamic categories, comparative categories. For that reason, I would say Weimar is an interesting place because the idea of situating a Jewish festival here is already in a kind of dialogue and correlation with something which is non-Jewish, or there is a certain self-other dialectic already going on and it has been positioned here.[63]

One of the most ambitious projects that the Weimar festival launched in this vein was "The Other Europeans," which investigated the historical and contemporary connections between klezmer and lautari (Roma) music. Carried out between 2008 and 2009 in cooperation with two other European festivals, the KlezMore in Vienna and the Jewish Culture Festival in Kraków, the project included intensive music workshops for klezmer and Roma musicians, a series of concerts and a research trip for both groups to Moldova. Although Alan Bern put particular emphasis on empowering group identity within the "Jewish" and the "Roma" group as a prerequisite for the creative musical negotiation of both groups, this collective identification was not understood here as an equivalent to ethnic identity. The fourteen musicians taking part in the project came from a number of different countries, and among the languages they spoke (English, Russian, Romanian, German, Hungarian, French, Yiddish) there was not a single one common to them all. The so-called klezmer sub-ensemble consisted of Jewish musicians in

---

[63] Alan Bern, interview by the author, Weimar, June 16, 2007.

addition to a non-Jewish German clarinetist, Christian Dawid. This Jewish-Roma search for the common Bessarabian roots of lautari and klezmer has outlived the research project itself. The joint ensemble issued their first CD, *Splendor*, in 2011, and performs today as the Other Europeans Band.[64]

If "The Other Europeans" project was a cutting-edge initiative, it also grew out of the potential for Jewish/non-Jewish (musical) dialogue already inherent within the klezmer scene. Many joint teaching and performing projects have grown out of this fertile ground. Some of the Jewish American klezmer musicians have also decided to move to Germany, becoming key members of the budding klezmer scene.

Stefan Kühne of the German band Klezgoyim remembers that the 1988 tour of the American band The Klezmatics was like an epiphany to him: "The Klezmatics concert was like lightning, because it was both rock and Yiddish songs."[65] Kühne, who attended their concerts three times, finally decided to play klezmer himself. Many other German musicians did not stop at merely listening to Americans. Martin Borbonus of Tants in Gartn Eydn went as far as Virginia to learn the style from Brave Old World and The Klezmatics, who taught at the klezmer workshops there. Being German, meeting Jewish musicians at the American workshops was an important test of acceptance for Martin. "Most of them said that it's great that we were there," he recounts, "but we were not sure because of Germany and Jews, and the history of WWII, and the Holocaust. We were afraid of some people maybe saying, 'Oh no, Germans here,' or something."[66] Franka Lampe, who also attended klezmer workshops in the United States, also feared that at an event "made by Jews and for Jews" a German non-Jewish musician might be seen as a "disturbing factor." But her initial apprehensions were not confirmed. She took accordion classes from Alan Bern of Brave Old World, and later became a klezmer teacher herself at the workshops in Weimar.[67]

In fact, many of the German revivalists learned from Americans and even recorded with them. As Heiko Lehmann, a klezmer musician, observed in 2000, "[t]he more bands that were founded, the greater the longing to receive the imprimatur of an American or Israeli klezmer musician."[68] The American-German klezmer transfer, however, was not reduced to seeking approval, and it was by no means one-directional. German artists, such as the clarinetist Christian Dawid, who regularly performs with the American band Brave Old World, have won international recognition. Some of them, such as the Berlin-based Aufwind or the clarinetist Helmut Eisel, have given concerts even in New York—the American stronghold of klezmer—and others teach at various international klezmer

---

[64] The documentary film *Broken Sound* (2011), dir. Wolfgang and Yvonne Andrä, pictures the development of The Other Europeans project.

[65] Kühne interview.

[66] Borbonus interview.

[67] Lampe interview.

[68] Lehmann, "Klezmer in Germany, Germans and Klezmer."

workshops.[69] Eventually, Berlin has become such an important klezmer location
that it is not unusual that musicians from outside of Germany, including Jews,
come to learn the style in the German capital.

The klezmer scene, however, enables cooperation between musicians and also,
at times, between the artists and their audiences. Karsten Troyke, one of the first
singers to perform at the Days of Yiddish Culture in East Berlin, has such a story
to tell. During the first edition of the festival, in 1987, a woman from the audience approached him after his concert. It was Sara Bialas-Tenenberg, a Holocaust
survivor and a native speaker of Yiddish, born in Częstochowa, Poland. Troyke's
concert of Yiddish songs received a warm reception at the festival, but Sara Bialas-
Tenenberg believed that his Yiddish could still be improved. "Sara was sitting in
the audience, deeply moved, happy to listen to songs in her beloved language after
such a long time," recollects Troyke. "She wanted to help me make my Yiddish
more Yiddish and less German."[70] With time, Sara became Karsten's tutor, but also
a friend and a source of inspiration. She was not only one of the few people with
whom Troyke could speak Yiddish in an everyday context, but she also knew many
Yiddish songs from her childhood in Poland. Troyke started to record her singing
and to do research into the songs, some of which had never been documented.
Ten years after their first meeting, in 1997, Sara's Yiddish songs appeared in new
arrangements on his CD *Forgotten Yiddish Songs* (*Jiddische Vergessene Lieder*).

Fig. 3.2 Forgotten Yiddish Songs by Karsten Troyke, Raumer Records 1997.
Photo by Stefan Meyer. Courtesy of Karsten Troyke.

[69] Helmut Eisel, *Klezmer at the Cotton Club*, Indigo, 2006, CD.
[70] Karsten Troyke, liner notes to *Jiddische Vergessene Lieder*, Raumer Records, 1998, CD, 8.

The CD, which features on the cover a photo of Sara and Karsten, is a compelling presentation of a very special musical oral history project. Troyke not only made sure to carefully document the provenance of the songs, noting the events in Sara's life that they were related to, but he also let the listeners hear Sara's own voice. Sara opens the record in a duo with Karsten singing "Surele," a song she learned as a child in the ghetto, and the record closes with her powerfully touching "Treblinka," performed *a cappella*. Incorporating inherited knowledge, Troyke manages here to create a new form of expression, which does not merely document little known and unknown Yiddish songs. Rather, he sets out to narrate a life story musically, giving us a unique glimpse into a musical dialogue across generational and ethnic divides.

Standing In

The friendship between Sara Bialas-Tenenberg and Karsten Troyke extended beyond speaking Yiddish and singing together. At one point, the two of them also traveled together to Treblinka. "I traveled to Treblinka to visit the commemorative stone for Częstochowa, together with Sara," explains Troyke, "because she wanted to commemorate her parents." Wanting to honor her murdered family, Sara asked Karsten to sing the Hebrew song "Osse Shalom" inside the actual death camp.[71] Taking part in such a private commemorative act of a Holocaust survivor implies stepping into the inner circle of in-group intimacy. This situation of standing in, taking over a capacity that would usually be reserved for a Jew, is relatively common for non-Jewish klezmer musicians. Because of their profession as performers who can be hired for Jewish occasions, and also because of their special knowledge of Jewish culture, and, last but not least, their command of Yiddish or Hebrew, some klezmer musicians often find themselves in the position of insiders by proxy.

Jan Hermerschmidt of Aufwind recollects that when the band went for the first time to Israel to perform at the festival of Safed, their ability to speak Yiddish made it possible for them to socialize within the community of Orthodox Jews. "It was great to meet all these people there," says Hermerschmidt, "people who speak Yiddish! Children who speak Yiddish! We saw them there for the first time. That was a great experience!"[72] Performing Yiddish songs and holding conversations in Yiddish, the musicians from Germany attracted a lot of attention and raised curiosity among the Israelis they met. "They were all laughing at us when they heard us speaking Yiddish for the first time, because it sounded so German," remembers Hermerschmidt. At the same time, however, their concert got a very good reception. "They were one hundred percent impressed with us," he notes with satisfaction. "They said we played like their grandparents and were stunned

---

[71] Troyke interview.
[72] Hermerschmidt interview.

where we knew that all from, [asking] whether we knew anyone who spoke Yiddish. But we didn't. There was hardly anybody in Germany who spoke Yiddish!"[73] The Israeli experience seems to have been a consequential event for the band not only because they had a chance to perform in front of a Yiddish-speaking audience, but also because they found themselves in a position of insiders extraordinaire. Sometimes, however, this function has also been ascribed to them during their regular concerts in Berlin.

After one of Aufwind's performances in the Hackesches Hoftheater, the band was approached with a very singular request. Two visibly moved elderly Jewish American women, twin sisters, came to thank the band for the concert. "They said that it was something very special for them, because it reminded them of their parents and their Jewish family," remembers Hermerschmidt.

> It came out that they were on a European trip, and it was actually their last trip together because one of the twins had cancer and a death sentence had already been given to her by doctors. Then she said: "I want you to play for me in New York when I die. That was the biggest experience that I have ever had in my life; it made me go through my entire life wondering how to come to terms with a sickness like that." In the beginning we were all sitting there like you're sitting now, completely shocked and asking ourselves how could this be true. We were in contact with her afterwards and when she died we really did give a concert in New York. It was quite a big concert, not at the funeral, but a real concert. They organized everything. She was already dead, but it wasn't like there was her picture hanging on the stage, it was a pretty normal concert and we did it because she found us great.[74]

The music of Aufwind becomes here a medium through which the two women try to reconnect with their family history. The non-Jewish musicians, as brokers of Jewish heritage, become agents in a deeply emotional and intimate Jewish act of commemoration. Their music becomes meaningful to Jews qua Jews.

What this function of "standing in" also implies is that non-Jewish musicians are occasionally conceded trust and confidence that they would otherwise, as non-Jews, not likely be granted. Karsten Troyke's experience in Poland illustrates this well.

> I was in Tarnów a couple of times and performed in the square where the synagogue used to be. There is a remaining fragment of the *bimah* there. And I gave the concert there, next to the *bimah*. There were probably no Jews there, apart from one woman, who always came to the concerts and afterwards told me [in Yiddish] "Don't tell anybody that I speak Yiddish,

[73] Ibid.
[74] Ibid.

nobody knows that." She told me that she survived the Holocaust in a hole, in a hole in the ground.[75]

A German musician who performs (and speaks) in Yiddish becomes the confidant of a Pole who is concealing her Jewish identity. As a fellow Yiddish-speaker, he becomes a holder of the secret that is, conceivably, meant only for Jewish ears. Being able to understand the Yiddish-speaking woman, Troyke is identified as belonging to the inner circle of those deserving to know who she really is and how she survived the Holocaust. Her trust designates him as an insider.

Much like their German colleagues, Polish musicians also constantly find themselves in this mediating role, both when they perform for Jewish audiences in Kazimierz, and when they tour abroad. One of the first klezmer bands to give a concert for Jewish audiences outside of Poland was Kroke who, having met Steven Spielberg during the shooting of *Schindler's List* in Kraków, was invited to go to Israel to play at a reunion of Schindler's Jews. Tomasz Lato of Kroke recalls that the concert, and especially meeting a Cracovian entertainer and cabaret artist Leopold Rosner (1918–2008), was crucial for the band. Encountering Rosner, who was forced to play for Amon Goeth in the Płaszów concentration camp and later saved by Oscar Schindler, was very emotional for both parties:

> Poldek Rosner sat down next to us and asked us: "Jurek, Tomek, why are you doing this?" "Are you the only ones doing this now?" "Are there more?" "How did it come about?" "Do you play in Kraków?" "You're kidding me! In Kraków?" . . . And then he said: "Pass me the accordion!" He had his own small accordion with him. "Gentlemen, I'm going to play you the most famous klezmer melody from Kraków." And he played *Hejnał Mariacki*.[76]

This unmistakable tune known to every Pole and immediately associated with Kraków—the melody of the hourly bugle call played from the tower of St. Mary's Church—provides a common frame of reference. Playing the *hejnał* as a klezmer melody, Rosner inverts the musical symbols of Polishness and Jewishness. His playful appropriation points out how unstable and permeable the imagined boundary really is between what is Polish and what is Jewish. The meeting with the old musician plays here the role of a rite of passage for Kroke. The young

---

[75] Troyke interview.
[76] Lato interview [Kroke], June 25, 2005. *Hejnał Mariacki* is the hourly bugle call played by a trumpeter from the highest tower of St. Mary's Church in Kraków, historically sounded to warn citizens about fire or invasion.

Polish artists feel that they receive an imprimatur as legitimate *klezmorim* from the hands of a musician who has the status of a legend. "We understood one thing there," recalls Lato:

> something that many people told us . . . that this whole issue with klezmer music . . . is only about whether you love it, or not, this is the only thing that counts. . . . If this is what you want to do, if you have a heart for it, . . . everything else that people around us say does not matter. This is as if you repeated exactly the words of Poldek Rosner. Word by word. What he said, and the meeting with those people, and their reaction to our music was a confirmation for us that we should go on doing what we are doing. We got a kind of certificate from them.[77]

Touring klezmer bands, like Kroke, often meet Jews who emigrated from Poland at various points in time after World War II. Many of them left only in 1968, when the anti-Semitic purge staged by the Polish Communist Party forced around twenty thousand Polish Jews out of the country. Encounters with expatriate Polish Jews are moving experiences for both sides, as Polish klezmer bands performing abroad are sometimes the first Poles in years that the Jewish émigrés have contact with. For Polish musicians, in turn, who might have very little exchange with the minuscule Jewish community in Kraków, it is the exiled Jews who represent the "Jewish voice" for them. Jerzy Bawół of Kroke believes that such meetings with the Jewish audience abroad have a great potential for enabling open dialogue. "These people left Poland and never wanted to go back," he says, "but the sentiment [for Poland] remained in them":

> On the one hand, their families were killed, or expelled in 1968, so these people often don't want to even hear the word "Poland." But on the other hand, Polish is their mother tongue and they were brought up here. . . . Once, when we played in England, nobody spoke Polish to us, everyone was speaking only English. After the concert, however, it turned out that most of them spoke, or at least understood, Polish. The people opened up, forgot about the past for a moment.[78]

Language, indeed, plays an important role for these particular encounters. The choice of speaking one or the other marks the distance that the participants wish to maintain and the common ground that they want to meet on. These Jewish/non-Jewish meetings are therefore also acts of translation and negotiation of meanings. Magdalena Brudzińska of the Cracovian band Quartet Klezmer Trio

---

[77] Ibid.
[78] Bawół [Kroke] interview, April 18, 2004.

remembers one concert that made her realize that her whole manner of communicating with the audience has to change:

> We were playing a concert in a Jewish club in Denmark. Most of the people who were there were Polish. I think even ninety percent of them. They were all around sixty, seventy years old, and they were all Jews who had escaped from Poland. The tears were running in streams at that concert because some of these people had never returned to Poland, . . . so these were all childhood memories for them and it was really terribly moving. . . . Whenever we play a bigger concert, or when I see that people are interested in the music during a restaurant concert, which is not always the case, I translate the lyrics and tell the people what the song is about. And this is what I was doing in Denmark as well. And then, in the break, the owner of this Jewish club comes over to me and says: "Magda, are you translating these songs out of habit?" "What do you mean? I always translate." "But everybody speaks Yiddish here!"[79]

Performing for Polish Jews abroad, Polish artists take on a double role. As klezmer musicians, they find themselves in the awkward situation of performing Yiddish folklore for native speakers of Yiddish. At the same time, as Poles, they become for their audiences living links to their former home country, and an important source of information about contemporary Poland. As Tomasz Lato recounts, Polish Jewish émigrés from Kraków sometimes approach the musicians after the concert to ask whether the street where they used to live still exists, or whether the buildings they knew are still standing.[80] At times, they also request tunes that they know from their childhood. Urszula Makosz, who performs Yiddish songs in the Galicia Jewish Museum in Kazimierz, makes it clear that it is not always easy for musicians to satisfy these requests. She recalls one such time when, during her rehearsal at the museum, a visitor approached the band:

> A woman who was visiting the exhibit came over to me as she heard me singing Jewish songs. And she asked me to play a very well-known song called "Oifn pripechik." We did not really have it in the repertoire; my pianist had never heard it before. But she hummed the song for us; he started accompanying it a bit. And I saw that this woman started crying, she was so moved.[81]

The acceptance and acclaim of Jews from abroad means a lot to Polish musicians. Ewelina Tomanek of Sholem remembers a Jewish woman who wanted to talk to

---

[79] Brudzińska interview, June 30, 2006.
[80] Lato [Kroke] interview, April 18, 2004.
[81] Urszula Makosz, interview by the author, Kraków, July 8, 2006.

her, moved by the song "Yiddishe Mame" the band had just performed in a concert. "She said: 'I am a Jewish mother,' and she said that she had never expected
it, that [Jewish music] was an incredible surprise for her, at this time and place,"
recounts Tomanek. "'You are heaven-sent, my angel,' she said, and kissed me."[82]
Irena Urbańska, a singer of Yiddish songs, also remembers a concert in Tel Aviv
where Jews from Poland and the former Soviet Union gave her a warm welcome:
"They invited us to their homes; we sold a great mass of records. They said that the
way we played reminded them of their childhood, their youth. Their parents used
to sing that way too."[83] By performing klezmer for Jewish audiences and satisfying this particular demand for nostalgia, Polish musicians do indeed gain professional fulfillment along with a sense of belonging that is uniquely rewarding.

"Stand-in acts" belong to one of the most interesting features of the klezmer
contact zone because they radically put into question the stability of the boundary
between Jews and non-Jews. In Pratt's taxonomy, arts of the contact zone embrace
genres such as parody or imaginary dialogue, which suggest an attempt of the sub-
jects at putting themselves in the position of the other. Klezmer "stand-in acts"
follow a slightly different pattern than what Pratt finds so characteristic of the
postcolonial contact zone. Non-Jewish musicians, who, in place of Jews, perform
Jewish culture, do not impersonate the other. Rather, finding themselves in the
position of mediators and brokers of Jewish culture, they might occasionally be
granted by their audiences a special status of almost-insiders. The act of occupying
the position of the other is, however, not always intended; it is rather situational
and contingent. "Standing in" involves finding a common language with the other,
manifesting empathy or participating in commemorative rituals of the out-group.
Situations in which it occurs, however, are transient. Their scope is subject to negotiation, and they usually do not serve the purpose of impersonation or satire.

Considering all the modalities of contact and negotiation taking place on the
klezmer scene, we cannot forget that the inter-ethnic encounter is evolving here
in the context of consumption. The klezmer revival, offering unique opportunities for expressing critique, cooperating or "standing in," is, at the same time, a
phenomenon that has economic implications. How does it impact the relations of
Jews and non-Jews on the klezmer scene?

Consumption

Berlin is often described as the European capital of klezmer and a particularly
lucrative market for Jewish music. Journalists speak of a "shopping frenzy"[84]
for klezmer CDs or "marketing with the Star of David"[85] on the sites of Jewish

---

[82] Ewelina Tomanek [Sholem], interview by the author, Kraków, July 1, 2006.

[83] Urbańska interview.

[84] Tkaczyk, "'Wir sind die Indianer Europas.'"

[85] Kueppers, "Marketing mit Davidstern," 19.

heritage. A German journalist, Henryk Broder, who sees the klezmer revival as part of a more general economic boom for Jewishness in Germany, goes so far as to say that the interest in Jewish culture is the domain of con artists who appropriate Jewish identity in order to profit financially.[86] But is the klezmer economy a fact or a myth?

The heyday of the klezmer revival in Germany seems to have reached its peak in Berlin in the late 1990s. This was when the Hackesches Hoftheater staged several klezmer performances weekly and posters advertising klezmer concerts were a common sight in the city center. Sales of klezmer records confirm this. A major music department store in the center of Berlin reported that after a steep rise in sales of klezmer CDs between 1997 and 2001, the trend has been stable and a heightened interest in the genre is no longer perceptible.[87] "There is a certain saturation, there is too much of it, people want to listen to something else,"[88] observes Jan Hermerschmidt of Aufwind. "You can play anywhere, if you don't want to play for money," sums up Bert Hildebrandt, who has performed with several klezmer ensembles.[89] Although Berlin is still considered one of the biggest klezmer scenes in the world, it is clear that the klezmer boom is long over.

Disappointed with these developments, some musicians who once played klezmer have turned to other genres. Heiko Lehmann, who belonged to the pioneers of the revival and performed Jewish music for more than twenty years, has switched to writing songs in English. Di Grine Kuzine, once marketing themselves as "the sexiest klezmer band in Berlin," have turned to Balkan and other kinds of folk music, dropping the klezmer label from their records. According to Lehmann, the world music industry, constantly requiring new varieties of musical fusions, has lost interest in klezmer.[90] Clearly, klezmer still occupies a niche on the music market but can not really claim to being more than that.

For many German musicians this means that klezmer has become for them more of a hobby than a profession. This is definitely the case in Berlin, where many klezmer bands consist of amateur musicians. The high standards of musical education in Germany and the relative ease with which nonprofessional musicians can find opportunities to perform in public has fuelled the klezmer revival from its beginnings. Franka Lampe of the band Schikker-wi-Lot even believes that it was the many "homemade bands" that made up the success of klezmer in Germany.[91] Many klezmer musicians began as amateurs, while others never ceased to hold another profession. Carsten Wegener of Tants in Gartn Eydn, for

[86] Broder, "Die Konjunktur des Jüdischen," 373.

[87] Sven Gniesewitz, head of the department of popular music in Dussmann, personal communication, April 14, 2008.

[88] Hermerschmidt interview.

[89] Bert Hildebrandt, interview by the author, Berlin, January 12, 2006.

[90] Heiko Lehmann, interview by the author, Berlin, October 6, 2007.

[91] Lampe interview.

example, was a tennis player before he started playing electric bass in rock bands, and eventually found his way to klezmer.[92] Harry Timmermann, the founder of Harry's Freilach, in turn, discovered klezmer while working as a watchman in a bread factory, where he practiced the clarinet during his night shifts.[93] There is a physicist, a teacher, a stage-set designer, and a tennis coach among the musicians of Tants in Gartn Eydn, while the band Kasbek admits that the ensemble, consisting of a physician, a pastor, an architect, and a journalist, has never lived off of its music alone.[94]

Only a few bands in Berlin declare that they can sustain themselves with klezmer. Audiences attending klezmer concerts are not large, and many artists play so-called door gigs, from which they receive 70 percent of the money from ticket sales. Given that most of these concerts take place in relatively small pubs and cafés, the income for the musicians can be meager. Playing at private parties or at festivals and workshops, in turn, is a source of more substantial income, but requires good managing skills.

Harry Timmermann, who has been earning his living from klezmer music for more than ten years, admits that playing door gigs is hard because sometimes very few people come to the concerts. "But if you risk it, and hang on, you build your network and are hired also for private parties." Timmermann, who with his band Harry's Freilach plays a wedding party almost every weekend in the summer, also performs for birthday parties, vernissages and exhibitions, in schools and in churches.[95] His colleague, Gennadij Desatnik, after he immigrated to Berlin from the Ukraine in 1994, busked with his band in the streets and subway stations. The beginnings were not easy for Desatnik's Trio Scho, and he remembers that before the band "worked their way up" from the subway tunnels "into the light of day," their economic situation was indeed precarious: "It's not easy to earn your money like that, especially in the winter. You sit there for hours and then your fingers can't move any more."[96] Today, however, the Ukrainians have established themselves on the klezmer scene, also playing Eastern European folk music, and they even give occasional concerts at the Philharmonic Hall.

The klezmer scene in Berlin, seen from the perspective of musicians, has little to do with the "Jewish Disneyland" painted by some critics. Far from being part of the mainstream entertainment industry, klezmer is a niche economy, accommodating, next to professionals, also amateurs and hobby musicians. The situation is markedly different in Kraków, where the klezmer scene is organically bound with Jewish heritage tourism. The context in which most klezmer concerts take place does not leave any doubts that the music is in quite a literal way part of a process

---

[92] Wegener interview.

[93] Timmermann interview.

[94] "Kasbek's website," accessed January 6, 2006, http://www.kasbek-ensemble.de/.

[95] Timmermann interview.

[96] Desatnik interview.

of consumption. Not surprisingly, it creates a certain dissonance and makes many musicians from Kazimierz feel frustrated. "Some of the performances are fantastic," says a female performer, "but there are also those from which you leave with a headache and are happy that no one threw a potato at you. This is what you have to put up with in the profession of a gastronomical musician."[97] Another musician complains that the audiences are sometimes not prepared for listening to a concert and "talk, shout, make noise with the cutlery, smoke, and are completely uninterested in the music."[98] Some ensembles, unable to continue, have been known to interrupt their concerts. Others try to play despite the noise, trying to stay out of the way of the waiters in the busy dining rooms. "It's hard work," states Magdalena Brudzińska of Quartet Klezmer Trio. "Sometimes you work until midnight . . . in general, we work day in, day out. Sometimes I don't know what day of the week it is any more. For the last four years we haven't gone on holiday, because we have played every day."[99] Other musicians speak also of the tedious daily routine in the repertoire: "We play the same material, the same one-hour-long program. . . . We have a fixed list of pieces, the audience changes, and we still play the same. Sometimes, it happens that we play the same program two or three times a day."[100] In the machinery of Jewish heritage tourism, music has its specific, determinate, and instrumental role.

The patterns of consumption in Kazimierz assign to Jewish music the role of an attractive background for dining. At the same time, klezmer itself is also a form of "eating the other." In this most basic function, as music accompanying consumption, klezmer in Kazimierz does to a certain extent play the role of a "spice," boosting the appeal of a tourist experience that centers on Jewish culture.[101] The coupling of music and consumption might produce here a routinized repetitiveness, forcing musicians to respond to the demand for entertainment that meets the expectations of the audience, but it also has implications beyond the purely musical dimension. Like every other kind of music, klezmer is a product that is being marketed and sold. In this particular case, however, ethnicity becomes a factor in the marketing process and, with Jewish and non-Jewish musicians competing against each other, an ethnic divide across the klezmer scene becomes at times especially salient.

Both Jewish and non-Jewish klezmer musicians in Berlin admit that the klezmer market offers different performance possibilities for Jewish and non-Jewish artists. According to Wlady Ginzburg, both groups do not even compete directly, because, while the bands consisting of Jewish musicians are usually hired

---

[97] Brudzińska interview, January 23, 2008.

[98] Tomasz Michalik [Sholem], interview by the author, Kraków, July 1, 2006.

[99] Brudzińska interview.

[100] The Saints interview.

[101] hooks, "Eating the Other," 366.

for Jewish occasions, "the non-Jewish bands never get these gigs."[102] Non-Jewish musicians realize that the engagements for the Jewish communities are off-limits for them. Stefan Kühne from the Bremen-based Klezgoyim reports: "It happened to us twice that we were invited to play there [for the Bremen Jewish community] and then the invitation was withdrawn. And then some of the community leaders, I don't know if it was the rabbi, or the lay leaders, said that they just did not want to have non-Jewish musicians playing for the community."[103] Franka Lampe of the Berlin-based Schikker-wi-Lot has already resigned herself to the fact that performances in the Jewish community are not accessible to her ensemble: "The Jewish community in Berlin . . . they are not klezmer-music oriented at all. And if so, they have their own musicians, all of them Russian Jews, and they perform at such events. They would never look at the semiprofessional, non-Jewish klezmer scene of Berlin to look for musicians who could play for them."[104]

And indeed, it seems that at least part of the Jewish community in Germany is not at all interested in hiring local klezmer musicians. Rabbi Spinner from Berlin explains that the local Orthodox Jews, when it comes to their wedding parties or bar mitzvahs, often engage bands from Israel or the UK:

> We normally have a specific kind of music for the Orthodox Jewish scene: it's a rock beat with guitar and drums and so on, but it's with religious content. So it's like a totally different music scene. . . . At Orthodox Jewish events, . . . especially weddings, we like to have a lot of dancing, the men and the women dance separately, but we have a lot of dances, so it's important to have good *simcha* music.[105] And so the guys in town are not good at it, because they don't know it. We usually bring in somebody from the outside.[106]

Sometimes the division in the Jewish music market is justified not only with the specific needs of the audience or the lack of skills among the musicians, but also with arguments of heritage appropriation. "Some people feel like they own this territory, and that non-Jews should have no right whatsoever to play this music," says Hardy Reich of Aufwind.[107] Other musicians see the problem in terms of pure economic competition. "It's always about business," notes Jan Hermerschmidt also of Aufwind, "The [Jewish] musicians don't want us to play there [for the Jewish community], so they say: 'They're not Jewish, don't invite them.' There is

---

[102] Ginzburg interview.
[103] Kühne interview.
[104] Lampe interview.
[105] Hebrew for gladness, or joy, used also to denote a festive occasion.
[106] Spinner interview.
[107] Reich interview.

a lot of competition. No one wants to offend anybody, so this is the easiest argumentation."[108] Facing this competition from non-Jewish musicians, it is conceivable that the Jewish klezmer bands, who are well represented on the local klezmer scene in Berlin, will market themselves as authentic or better qualified for playing for Jewish occasions. This is not to say, however, that Jewish and non-Jewish bands do not share the same audiences, or even play together.

On the contrary, some Jewish communities across Germany do engage non-Jewish musicians or invite them to festivals of Jewish culture. Even in Berlin, several non-Jewish bands have performed at Jewish weddings and bar mitzvahs. There are also numerous klezmer bands in which Jews and non-Jews play together, such as Paul Brody's Sadawi, Daniel Kahn's The Painted Bird, and the multinational Forszpil. What is more, Jewish musicians who specialize in playing for innercommunity occasions, like the Ginzburgs, have considerable success performing for non-Jewish audiences. In Kraków, where the Jewish community itself does not really generate a demand for music for Jewish celebrations, this ethnic divide in the klezmer market is practically nonexistent. Although among the klezmer musicians in Kraków several are Jewish or have a Jewish background, virtually all bands perform for the same audience in the Jewish-style restaurants.

The klezmer revival undoubtedly makes up part of the local economy both in Kraków and Berlin, where Jewish and non-Jewish musicians compete on the same market. This can potentially lead to some tensions or to a segmentation of the klezmer scene. At the same time, though, the "klezmer economy" has not reached the dimensions of mass consumption and is not a mainstream phenomenon that generates any considerable profits. Thus, although consumption does shape, to a certain degree, the conditions of artistic expression and inter-ethnic exchange on the klezmer scene, it does not constitute the only raison d'être behind the klezmer scene, nor does it provide the sole explanation for its dynamics.

Conclusion

The klezmer scene is, on the one hand, a space where the consumption of Jewishness often takes place quite literally. Klezmer as part of the Jewish heritage package in Kazimierz is probably the most emblematic example of the commodification of Jewish culture in contemporary Europe. On the other hand, there is much more to "eating the other" in the context of klezmer than the actual act of consumption. As a music scene that is autonomous but accessible, and to an extent parasitic but also creative, klezmer is a "Jewish Space" of exceptional appeal and singular outreach. Emerging at the crossroads of pilgrimage and tourism, the sacred and the profane, the Jewish and the non-Jewish, klezmer spaces

---

[108] Hermerschmidt interview.

are more than sites where Jewish culture is marketed. Rather, they open new topographies of Jewishness beyond the obvious ethnic boundaries and patterns of self-identification, enabling modes of participation and exchange that transcend the broad-brush category of "dialogue."

Cooperation, critique, and "standing in" are forms of interaction between Jews and non-Jews growing out of a specific social space. Contrary to what many critics have sustained, the klezmer revival is by no means an exclusively non-Jewish realm. Jews act on the klezmer scene as performers, audiences, teachers, reviewers, and patrons. Co-created by Jews and non-Jews, the klezmer scene has become the ground for difficult "truth-telling" and critique, for the imaginative exploration of juxtapositions between the self and the other, and for finding one's own voice in response to and through the art of the other.

Finally, klezmer is also a space where non-Jews occasionally take over the role of "stand-ins" for Jews. In fact, the theatrical metaphor of the stand-in, replacing actual actors under extraordinary conditions when they cannot perform themselves, captures the singularities of the klezmer revival in Poland and Germany particularly well. A stand-in is not the one expected on stage by the audience, but merely a substitution for somebody else who is missing. Their presence is by definition temporary, contingent, and improvised. Stand-in actors are called for by a specific situation and respond to a particular demand. Non-Jewish klezmer musicians thus occasionally find themselves in a position where they become brokers of Jewish heritage for Jews, triggering personal memories, participating in private commemorative acts, or becoming the addressees of untold Jewish life narratives. This standing in, however, takes place solely *within* the framework of performance. Even though they are at times granted by their audiences a special insider's status, stand-ins for Jews are not Jews, and participating in this kind of Jewish/non-Jewish encounter is not tantamount to a claim on the identity of the other.

This is not to say that the particular modes of interaction that the klezmer revival scene enables do not affect the ways in which its protagonists identify themselves. The klezmer contact zone leaves an imprint both on the individuals who inhabit it and the cultural products that they create. The transculturation of the Jewish element into contemporary Polish and German art involves domestication, distortion, and amalgamation, so emblematic of de Andrade's idea of cultural anthropophagy. The klezmer movement, however, is not only about translating Jewish culture into the vernacular but about the potentialities inherent in a marginal space. The klezmer scene, located on the fault line between the Jewish and the non-Jewish realms, is both a site where new art emerges and a space breeding hybrid identities and allowing unconventional patterns of belonging. The next two chapters explore these borderlands in more detail, looking at the new kinds of art and new patterns of identity generated there.

4

The Grammars of Vernacular Klezmer

Representations of Jews on the Klezmer Scene

In the fall of 2007, Polish public television (TVP1) launched one of its most expensive and broadly advertised Saturday night shows, *Hit Night* [Pol: Przebojowa Noc], which featured covers of popular songs from different countries. The "Jewish Night," viewed by an audience of over two million, was placed in the series between the British and the Latino episodes. Although most of the songs were performed in the Polish translation, or were simply Polish songs written by Jewish authors, the "Jewish" edition was distinctly separate from the "Polish Night," which chose patriotic songs as its focus.

The "Jewish Night," consisted of a colorful succession of dance acts choreographed to a mixture of music ranging from "Hava Nagila" through pieces from *Fiddler on the Roof* and klezmer to the performance of the Israeli Eurovision star Dana International. An indisputable highlight of this versatile show, however, was the staging of one of the most emblematic songs from *Fiddler on the Roof:* "Sunrise Sunset." The performance, which made it to the "best of" edition of the show, was an exuberant production with carefully designed costumes and many extras. The singers posed as a young couple under the *khupe*, surrounded by a host of dancers dressed like Hasidim, with *peyes* and burning candles in their hands. The shtetl-aesthetics of the production seem to have appealed to the Polish viewers; many of them rated the show on the program's website as "moving," "romantic," and even "divine."[1] The "Jewish Night" clearly spoke to the mass audience with images that it recognized as essentially Jewish and enjoyed as such. It was, at the same time, a model product of cultural anthropophagy.

The "Jewish Night" is merely one of many musical representations of Jewishness that accompany the klezmer revival in Poland. It is, however, emblematic in how it transposes the idea of Jewish music into an opulent and dreamlike vision of the shtetl that belongs specifically to Polish imagery. The "Jewish Night" might not tell us much about Jewish music that was historically played in Poland, but it

---

[1] "Przebojowa Noc," accessed December 3, 2007, http://v1.itvp.pl/blog/i.tvp/idb/24/idk/277.

betrays a great deal about the way contemporary Polish pop culture domesticates elements of Jewish culture for the needs of a prevalently non-Jewish audience.

The klezmer revival is a product of a dynamic process of encounter, in which an ethnic majority relates itself to the heritage of its minority. Unlike in the colonial context, however, this act of cultural anthropophagy is not taking place in the context of intensive intergroup contact or cohabitation. It is unfolding, instead, in a situation in which the community from which the appropriated culture originated—Eastern-European, Yiddish-speaking, traditional Jews—is no longer there to be directly observed or consulted. And as a generation of young Poles and Germans, who have had only limited interaction, if any, with contemporary Jews, have become interested in traditional Jewish music, their image of the Jew has often relied on stereotypes, which can no longer be adjusted by the experience of interpersonal contact. Due to the lack of a living memory of Jews, the third generation after World War II can resort only to "post-memory": the narratives passed down by the older generations or the representations of Jews circulating in the popular culture.[2] This is particularly the case in Poland where, after the Holocaust, post-World War II pogroms and Communist purges, the Jewish community is extremely small. What *has* influenced the images of Jews circulating on the klezmer scene are hence the old cultural paradigms that klezmer musicians have been exposed to and the new cultural demands of the Jewish heritage boom. The end products of the klezmer revival thus reflect the process in which Poles and Germans reproduce, counter, and come to grips with stereotypes, all the while translating the culture of the other into a new kind of art.

Cultural anthropophagy postulates that inspiration from the culture of the other yields a new vernacular art based on fragments of the heritage of the venerated other, selected and amalgamated into a cultural product that responds to the specific needs and values of the target culture. The process in which the "vernacular klezmer" takes shape reveals, therefore, (apart from the new functions assigned to the appropriated genre), also a value judgment inherent in the selective absorption of the other. In other words, what makes its way into the "new klezmer" are aspects of Jewish music, mythology and imagery that contemporary Poles and Germans ascribe a positive value to. The omissions are in this case equally significant. The selection marks here the boundaries of desire and disinterest toward the other, disclosing, ultimately, the yearnings and anxieties of the self.

This chapter examines the images of Jews generated on the klezmer scene, addressing both their etymology and their new uses. The typology here revisits topoi that have a longer tradition, but rather than seeing them as mere repetitions, it frames them as outcomes of a dynamic process of constructing the self/other boundary. Images such as that of the romanticized shtetl Jew are not only echoes

---

[2] See Marianne Hirsch, "Surviving Images: Holocaust Photographs and the Work of Postmemory," *Yale Journal of Criticism* 14, no. 1 (2001): 5–37; Marianne Hirsch, "The Generation of Postmemory," *Poetics Today* 29, no. 1 (2008): 103–28.

of older clichés but new, expedient reconfigurations, which emerge as a response to immediate challenges. The paradigms of the magical, the incorporated, the syncretic, and the political Jew that I sketch here need to be read both as figurations of the other fostered by the history of representing Jews in Poland and Germany, and as means for articulating the self. Looking at these modes of representation through the lens of what Kohl-Bines termed the "anthropophagic model of cultural interaction,"[3] I see them, rather than as simulacra, as products of cultural translation, transcending the binary opposition of copy versus original. The klezmer scene, with its potential for generating a contact zone, is a space of negotiation, or what Homi Bhabha termed the "third space," where the rearticulation of cultural dichotomies enables the emergence of something new that is "neither the one nor the other."[4] The "vernacular klezmer" is thus neither a reproduction of the old-style Eastern European klezmer nor a fully indigenous Polish/German genre. It is a space where the Jewish element enriches and broadens the mainstream culture of the dominant society, enabling a hybridized art that represents, and responds to, the current cultural anxieties. Having in mind the topography of the "third space" as a creative "space between frames,"[5] it is essential not to lose sight of the major frames that have delineated this space in the past. And for Poland, one of the most dominant topoi that has framed the cultural representations of Jews is the shtetl.[6] Today, more than any other Jewish space, it inspires popular culture and becomes, not surprisingly, the favorite backdrop for klezmer.

The Magical Jew

The popularity of the shtetl in the Polish representations of Jewishness in TV, theater, and cabaret productions has turned it into an essential Jewish location. But its growing appeal has also led to its transplantation into the urban space. The visitors of the "Singer's Warsaw" Festival, the second biggest festival of Jewish culture in Poland, can experience the shtetl atmosphere outdoors. During the weeklong festival, artists affiliated with the local Jewish Theater turn the last surviving street of the Warsaw ghetto, forlorn Próżna Street, into a filmset-like representation of a little Jewish town. Próżna Street, adorned with Yiddish-language shop signs and populated with actors dressed as Orthodox Jews, is the main venue of the festival. Gołda Tencer, the director of the event, explains that the

---

[3] Kohl-Bines, "Samba and Shoah," 102.

[4] Homi K. Bhabha, *The Location of Culture* (London: Routledge, 1995), 25.

[5] Ibid., 214.

[6] See Eva Hoffman, *Shtetl: The Life and Death of a Small Town and the World of Polish Jews* (London: Secker and Warburg, 1998); Eugenia Prokopówna, "The Image of the Shtetl in Polish Literature," in *Polin: Studies in Polish Jewry*, vol. 4, *Poles and Jews: Perceptions and Misperceptions*, ed. Władysław Bartoszewski (Oxford: Littman Library of Jewish Civilization, 1990), 129–42.

Fig. 4.1 Theater performance in Próżna Street during the Warsaw Singer Festival, 2007. Photo by Aneta Kaprzyk.

staged Próżna Street "is not the one from before the war . . . but rather a piece of the shtetl."[7] What defines the shtetl-like atmosphere of this invented space is what Tencer describes as the *heymish* feeling. This "hominess" relies on the use of symbols, gestures, and costumes meant to reconstruct a phantasma that is familiar to Jews and non-Jews alike.

Tradition, the musical production that crowned the 2007 edition of the festival, featured the universe of the Jewish village as a blissful and gaudy microcosm of many cultures. The lost Jewish world also accommodated Ukrainian and Roma artists, happily dancing along with the actors of the Jewish Theater clad in Jewish caftans and *shtreimels. Tradition,* which aimed to "remind" the spectators of how different communities in pre-1945 Poland "shared their fate, their joys and sorrows,"[8] made heavy use of hyperbole. The actors, equipped with oversized "Jewish" props, such as golden watches, roosters, and fishes, resorted to a specific set of gestures, which the Jewish monthly *Midrasz* labeled as "pseudo-Jewish elbow-contracture."[9] Simplified and hopelessly romanticized, the aesthetics of the shtetl is, nevertheless, making a breathtaking career.

---

[7] Gołda Tencer, interview by the author, Warsaw, January 18, 2008.

[8] Jerzy Sokołowski, theater critic, cited in *Festiwal Kultury Żydowskiej Warszawa Singera* (Warszawa: Fundacja Shalom, 2007), 39.

[9] Dorota Szwarcman, "Czy muzyka żydowska musi być kiczowata?" *Midrasz*, no. 3, 2006, 21.

Representations of romanticized, be it benign or caricatured, shtetl Jews circulate not only in the realm of popular culture but form part of consumer culture in Poland. The images of bearded Jews in traditional garb are used, for example, in the advertising of products related to stereotypically Jewish fields of expertise. Thus, in 2009, a plum-flavored tea with "a hint of alcohol" was marketed with an image of a klezmer musician on its packaging—a clear allusion to the old stereotype of the Jewish innkeeper driving Polish peasants into alcoholism.[10]

The same picturesque and quaint images of Jews, colorful but at the same time endowed with a retro quality, also populate Jewish heritage music. A musical titled "Oy Vey, or Stories with Cinnamon" [Pol: *Aj waj! Czyli historie z cynamonem*] was one such prominent production. Combining Yiddish songs with Jewish humor, it pictured sketches from the life of a Jewish village. The performance, directed by Rafał Kmita, which consisted of short cabaret-like musical episodes, was peppered with unsophisticated humor, introducing a whole spectrum of shtetl "types." Kmita's Jews—haggling merchants, housewives, and a prostitute, involved in comical everyday situations—are in fact archetypical. With their unmistakable costumes, their emphatic gestures, and marked speech, they look and sound "Jewish." Although *Midrasz* accused the Cracovian ensemble that staged the show of spreading "Stürmer-like stereotypes,"[11] the musical has been successfully performed more than two hundred times and listed by the conservative daily *Rzeczpospolita* as the fourth best production of 2005.[12]

The Polish klezmer scene, especially in its beginnings, relied heavily on this folklorized aesthetics. The cover of Kroke's first record from 1996, for instance, featured three bearded and caftan-clad Jewish *klezmorim*. For many years, the band performed in white shirts and black hats, and although recently both their music and the design of their records have changed, the black hats remain the key element of Kroke's image. Asked whether their early outfit was meant to imitate Hasidic Jews, they dismiss the question jokingly, saying that they buy their hats in a shop for priests.[13] However, musicians from another Cracovian band, Jasha Lieberman Trio, admit that they consciously make reference to the traditional Jewish apparel with their black-and-white outfits and hats.[14] Orthodox Jews, fiddlers on the roof, and Chagallesque villages feature on the covers of many klezmer records. Sława Przybylska's compilation of Yiddish and Hebrew songs (*Alef-Bejs*, 2005) is decorated with Hebrew-stylized font and a motif from an Abraham Stein painting of Orthodox Jews. Similarly, all of Irena Urbańska's records, including

---

[10] See Joanna B. Michlic, *Poland's Threatening Other: The Image of the Jew from 1880 to the Present* (Lincoln: University of Nebraska Press, 2006), 37ff.

[11] Szwarcman, "Czy muzyka żydowska musi być kiczowata?" 20–21. *Der Stürmer* (1923–45) was an anti-Semitic German weekly, notorious for its racist caricatures of Jews.

[12] "Aj Waj," accessed November 3, 2007, http://www.kmita.art.pl/ajwaj.html.

[13] Kroke, interview by the author, Kraków, April 18, 2004.

[14] Lieberman interview.

Fig. 4.2 Cover of Kroke's first CD *Trio*, 1996. Courtesy of Oriente.

Kołysanki Żydowskie (*Jewish Lullabies*, 2008) use nostalgic, pastel-colored images that communicate warmth and comfort.

Theoreticians of popular culture have defined romance as "imaginative reconstruction."[15] Its appeal relies on a dreamlike and idealized vision of reality, but its function is often understood as that of "reminding" the spectator of the past. The aesthetics of romance thus makes the claim to "reconstructing" a lost world. Such reconstructivist zeal can, however, also imply a canon-bound and uncreative approach to the repertoire. And some of the musicians who play in Jewish-style restaurants and cafés of Kraków indeed only limit themselves to reproducing the klezmer evergreens. This is also, of course, conditioned by the expectations of the market. When the tourist industry commodifies Jewish heritage in an attempt to reenact the nostalgic shtetl, innovation or new compositions are redundant. The romance, after all, is based on recognition.

When attempting to bring the shtetl to life some artists recycle images, which are not only clichéd but resemble anti-Semitic caricatures. *Piosenki Żydów z Odessy* (2000) [*Songs of the Jews of Odessa*] by the Kraków-based Teatr Zwierciadło is a case in point. Against the background of golden coins, the CD cover depicts two personages, immediately recognizable as Jews by their clearly visible red yarmulkes, counting Polish banknotes. The leader of the band, who also posed for the cover photo, explains that his intention was to represent the "atmosphere of the

---

[15] Georgina Born in discussion of the writings of Iain Chambers and Angela McRobbie, see Georgina Born, "Modern Music Culture: on Shock, Pop and Synthesis," in Frith, *Popular Music*, vol. 4, *Music and Identity*, 305.

Fig. 4.3 Kroke in Kazimierz. Photo by Jacek Dyląg.

Odessa bazaar."[16] However, what to the musicians of Teatr Zwierciadło seemed a comical image is received with perplexity by some Jewish tourists who come across the record.[17]

The pairing of Jews and money, which abounded in pre–World War II Polish caricatures and jokes, is still common today. Images of Jews holding or counting money, a popular motif on the Polish market of souvenirs and mass-produced

---

[16] Vitaliy Petranyuk, interview by the author, Kraków, January 21, 2008.

[17] The CD was brought to my attention by Stuart Brotman of the band Brave Old World, who came across it during his visit to Kraków.

Fig. 4.4 Cover of Irena Urbańska's *Kołysanki Żydowskie*, 2008. Design by Daniel de Latour.

Fig. 4.5 Cover image of *Piosenki Żydów z Odessy* by Teatr Zwierciadło, 2000. Courtesy of Vitaliy Petranyuk.

"Judaica," picture usury, one of the traditional professions accessible to Jews in the Middle Ages. Unfortunately, these images also evoke the anti-Semitic stereotype of the Jew as a financial exploiter.[18] The very restaurant that hosts the performances of Teatr Zwierciadło in Kazimierz offers a wide range of carved wooden figures and paintings of Jews holding golden coins. In the popular perception, shared by some Kraków klezmer musicians, these images are not understood as anti-Semitic but rather as performing a certain amulet function. For example, paintings of Jews counting money are common gifts to newlyweds, treated as lucky charms meant to bring good luck and prosperity to the household.[19]

This magical function of the image of the Jewish usurer or banker might also have been in the minds of the artists of Teatr Zwierciadło, who certainly did not intend to offend their partly Jewish audiences in Kazimierz with anti-Semitic clichés. Rather, they placed on their cover an image that was familiar to them,

Fig. 4.6 Paintings of Jews counting money on sale in Kraków, 2012. Photo by Klementyna Chrzanowska.

[18] Janusz Dunin, "Postać żyda w polskiej kulturze popularnej do 1945 roku," in *Wszystek krąg ziemski—prace ofiarowane profesorowi Czesławowi Hernasowi*, ed. Piotr Kowalski (Wrocław: Wydawnictwo Uniwersytetu Wrocławskiego, 1989), 317–23.

[19] Joanna Tokarska-Bakir "Żyd z pieniążkiem podbija Polskę" *Gazeta Wyborcza*, February 18, 2012, accessed October 21, 2012, http://wyborcza.pl/1,75475,11172689,Zyd_z_pieniazkiem_podbija_Polske.html.

unaware of the fact that what they read as humorous echoed anti-Semitic caricatures. This somewhat ingenuous belief that representations of Jews holding money have an exclusively positive connotation seems to be more common on the klezmer scene. In 2006 I recorded an exchange between two musicians working in Kazimierz, who commented on the wooden figurines of Jews holding money.

> MUSICIAN 1: "Buying such a Jewish figure brings good luck. A Jew must be in the house for protection."
>
> MUSICIAN 2: "Yes, in a Polish house, a painting of a Jew counting money, or of a Jew in general, brings good luck, so that there is always money in the house."
>
> MUSICIAN 1: "Even if I didn't know about this custom that Jews bring good luck, I would still prefer to buy myself such a little Jew than, for example, a little Eiffel Tower in Paris . . . I love these little Jews!"[20]

Erica Lehrer, who interviewed manufacturers of such figurines and researched their reception among visitors in Kraków, concludes that even Jewish tourists have an ambivalent reaction to such souvenirs. While some approach the phenomenon as "evidence of Polish anti-Semitism," others find the wooden figurines "melancholy," with their "sad eyes" and "haunted faces" prefiguring the Holocaust.[21] As Lehrer points out, the ways buyers interpret the Jewish figurines vary significantly, and the possible readings range from repulsion to wonder.

The representations of shtetl Jews on the klezmer scene are characterized both by ambiguity and by a touch of the uncanny. The video clip accompanying Nina Stiller's rendition of the song "Mayn shtetele Belz" (2006) is a case in point. The singer, clad in a black dress, with her hair dramatically blowing in the wind, is posed against the image of a village shrouded in dark clouds. The clip, using Tadeusz Rolke's photographs of former Hasidic sites in Poland, builds up a poignant aura of absence, loss, and anxiety. The shtetl in the background of the song is a space beyond time, disquieting, grim, and forbidding. As a result, the arrangement of this pre-Holocaust Yiddish song evokes the atmosphere of impending catastrophe, conveying also a mood of mystery.

The uncanny dominates not just covers of old Yiddish songs but new Polish songs inspired by Jewish themes. Many of these pieces exploit the motif of the supernatural, drawing either on Jewish mythology or anti-Semitic imagery. The "folk metal" band Żywiołak, pursuing what they call Polish "folk demonology," takes inspiration from Jewish tradition, dedicating one of their songs to the figure

---

[20] K13 and K25. Please see appendix for these codes.

[21] Erica Lehrer, "Repopulating Jewish Poland—in Wood," in Steinlauf and Polonsky, *Polin: Studies in Polish Jewry*, vol. 16, *Focusing on Jewish Popular Culture*, 336 and 349.

of the dybbuk.[22] "The Dybbuk's Eye" [*Oko Dybuka*] is a romance written in the convention of a folk song. It tells the story of a rustic couple, Kasia and Jaś, whose love affair becomes disrupted by the malevolent dybbuk, who snatches the man's soul.[23] Interestingly, in this process of adapting the Jewish motif into the Polish genre, Żywiołak transposes the qualities of the dybbuk. Unlike in the Jewish tradition, the dybbuk is no longer the wandering soul of a damned sinner, which "cleaves" to the soul of a living person, possessing the body, but a corporeal creature, which kills its victims and takes over their souls.[24] Żywiołak's dybbuk resembles a monster from a typical Central European fairy tale: the evil is contained in a body, and the beast does physical harm (breaking bones, ripping eyes out), but at the same time, it can be tricked. There is also a moralizing dimension to the song. The dybbuk kills Jaś in punishment for premarital intercourse with Kasia. But even though the evildoing of the dybbuk seems to have a didactic purpose, Jaś emerges as the ultimate winner. In the final verses of the song, he promises his lover that he will come back to her *inside* the body of the dybbuk. And it is at this point that the Jewish concept of the dybbuk undergoes a full reversal: the spirit of the murdered boy (Jaś) possesses the monstrous body of the material dybbuk. This finale can also be read as the victory of love over evil, a usual fairy tale trope. Polish listeners, even though they might not know what a dybbuk is, perceive the "Jewish flavor" of the story and follow the narrative, which they recognize as culturally familiar. The Jewish monster thus becomes domesticated and visualized through a Polish lens.

A similar principle, though to a much more troubling effect, guides the composition of "Rabin Hood," another song in Polish dedicated to a demonic "Jewish" character. The piece, written by Michał Zabłocki, comes from a successful musical dedicated to the Cracovian Jewish district, *Pan Kazimierz* [Mr. Kazimierz] (2007). The CD is based to a large extent on urban legends of the Jewish district in Kraków. The Jewish protagonists of the songs are, however, marginal, grotesque, and comical. Prefaced with a somewhat puzzling introduction stating that "[w]e are all a bit anti-Semitic, just as we are all a bit Jewish," "Rabin Hood" is a ballad about a Jewish beast plaguing the Polish population of Kazimierz. The malevolent Rabbi Hood (*rabin* is Polish for rabbi), who is an amalgamate of all Polish prejudices against Jews, combines, among others, the attributes of a vampire and capitalist exploiter. Clad in a black caftan, Rabin Hood drinks human blood; he also lends money at usurious rates, causes non-Jews to fail exams, and even inspects penises

---

[22] I am indebted to Michel Steinlauf for drawing my attention to "The Dybbuk's Eye" in his lecture "Something Lost that Seeks Its Name: Dybbuks in Post-Communist Poland," presented at the "Modern Jewish Culture: Diversities and Unities" conference, University of Wrocław, June 26, 2008.

[23] Lyrics and music by Robert Wasilewski, "Oko Dybuka," *Nowa Ex-Tradycja*, AKW Karrot Kommando, 2008, CD.

[24] The word "dybbuk" or "dibbuk" comes from the Hebrew verb "to cleave," which stands for the modus operandi of the evil spirit attaching itself to a living body. See Gershom Sholem, "Dibbuk," *Encyclopaedia Judaica*, vol. 5, 2nd ed., 643–44.

in public toilets in search of his next uncircumcised victim. In short, the Jewish "Robin Hood" is an antihero who is both demonic and, because of such a hyperbole, ridiculous.

Chodzi po nocy i czyha na cię	Walking by night, he's waiting for you
postać upiorna w czarnym chałacie	Ghastly black figure cloaked in a caftan
Jak cię przydybie w jakiej ulicy	If out in the street you fall into his hands
to ci upije kwartę krwawicy	Lo, he will feast on a quart of your blood
Jak cię w podworcu jakim przyłapie	If you encounter him in the yard
to ci niechybnie oczy wydrapie.	He'll surely scratch your eyes out
Refrain:	Refrain:
Rabin Hood, Rabin Hood	Rabbi Hood, Rabbi Hood
gnębi kazimierski lud	pesters the Kazimierz folk
Bo się pasie polska bidą	'Cause he milks the Polish poor
i oddaje wszystko Żydom[25]	to give everything to the Jews

The figure of Rabin Hood embodies various malevolent traits ascribed to Jews by anti-Semitic discourse, but the motif of the vampire is central and it reinforces his demonic otherness. As Maria Janion notes, the vampire stands for what is considered impure and unacceptable in society. He is an outcast and a scapegoat, the focus of collective hatred and violence.[26] Rabin Hood the vampire is a double outcast. His beastly practices echo not only the myth of ritual murder but also of Jewish conspiracy against Poles, turning the figure into the ultimate and fearsome other.

The author of the lyrics, Michał Zabłocki, declared in a press interview that with the "Rabin Hood" song he wished to comment on the "obsession of anti-Semitism,"[27] but the liner notes actually relativize the problem, speaking of an "anti-Polish obsession" among Jews being an equally burning issue.[28] Ultimately, repeating the most absurd prejudices against Jews circulating in Polish urban legends, the song does not really achieve any ironic effect but instead perplexes listeners with its content.

[25] Michał Zabłocki, "Rabin Hood," *Pan Kazimierz*, Poemat, 2007, CD, translated into English by the author.

[26] Maria Janion, *Niesamowita Słowiańszczyzna: fantazmaty literatury* (Kraków: Wydawnictwo Literackie, 2006), 65–66.

[27] Michał Zabłocki, interviewed by M. Kozłowski, *Karnet*, no. 2, 2008, accessed June 1, 2009, http://karnet.krakow.pl/?action=,3656,2,20090526,150,view_event.

[28] *Pan Kazimierz*, Poemat, 2007, liner notes, 17.

The elements of the fantastic that appear on the klezmer scene and in its periphery are closely related to the specifics of this particular music revival. Inte‑ st in the music of the other (klezmer), as well as interest for the other as reflecteu in new music, marks the return of memory concerning Jews to the Polish consciousness. As Renate Lachmann notes in her considerations on the literature of the fantastic, "the fantastic confronts culture with its oblivion."[29] It is, in other words, a portal that allows the return of the repressed, forgotten, and the very "unconscious of culture."[30] Emerging as a counterresponse to the unifying discourses, which ban otherness to the margins of the official culture, the fantastic mode challenges the totalizing system and subverts the clear-cut dichotomy between the self and the other. According to Lachmann, the fantastic is a "literature of desire," which diagnoses lack and supplies a remedy, turning to "that which has been silenced, made invisible, covered over and made 'absent.'"[31] The forgotten, however, becomes visualized by means of the mysterious, the marvelous, or the monstrous.[32] The other becomes a phantasma, so that a culture, trying to come to terms with its other, can eventually reflect on "the own in the guise of the foreign and strange."[33]

These ambivalent, partly romanticized–partly demonized images of the Jew picture in a very poignant way the throes of remembering in Poland. The fact that the Jew occupies the continuum between the marvelous and the monstrous suggests that the return of the repressed Jewish narrative poses a challenge to the collective self-interpretation. After all, what we project onto the other is what we fear in ourselves. Thus, the figures of the dybbukim, Jewish vampires, and usurers can be read as guised manifestations of the Polish people's anxiety about facing their own prejudice and violence toward Jews.

The images of the Jew, which draw heavily on shtetl aesthetics, might be uncanny, but, at the same time, they operate with visual attributes immediately recognizable as Jewish (yarmulkes, peyes, long caftans). This device makes such representations readable to a mass audience and, by the same token, qualifies them as kitsch—which, in Clement Greenberg's definition, embraces "the vividly recognizable, the miraculous, and the sympathetic."[34] The key to decoding these images lies, however, in the history of representations of Jews. Folk beliefs, literary tradition, and educational policies over centuries circulated clichés that were often negative or downright anti-Semitic. These core images, however, do not necessarily survive in the same form and might also undergo a reevaluation, in which they are transposed into more "sympathetic" ones. Thus, the representations of

---

[29] Renate Lachmann, "Remarks on the Foreign (Strange) as a Figure of Cultural Ambivalence," in *The Translatability of Cultures: Figurations of the Space Between*, ed. Sanford Budick and Wolfgang Iser (Stanford: Stanford University Press, 1996), 289.

[30] Ibid.

[31] Rosemary Jackson, cited in Lachmann, 287.

[32] Ibid., 291.

[33] Ibid., 292.

[34] Clement Greenberg, *Art and Culture: Critical Essays* (Boston: Beacon Press, 1961), 14.

Jews that circulate on today's klezmer scene might contain remnants of negative stereotypes that become recombined into images that purport to be benign, or amusing. The supposed extraordinary Jewish talent in business, widely exploited in anti-Semitic propaganda, is now portrayed not in terms of a threat, but, as on the *Teatr Zwierciadło* cover, an exotic element of the shtetl-romance.

According to recent surveys on Polish anti-Semitism, such a reinterpretation of the stereotypical features of Jews is common in Polish society at large. The more pro-capitalist attitude of Poles after the fall of Communism is responsible for the revision of the stereotype of the Jew as a capitalist. Hence, Poles list talent for trading and success in finance as positive characteristics of Jews, even though the same features used to be assessed negatively in the past.[35]

A similar reevaluation also took place in relation to the image of the shtetl. The romantic shtetl Jew might bear the same external features as the once ridiculed stereotype of the unenlightened and poor rural Jew, but he is now endowed with intriguing, mystic qualities. The belief in the magical properties of Jews has, in fact, a very long history and reaches back to the beginnings of Christianity. Christian folk tradition placed Jews as the "sacral others" on the borderline between the earthly world and the world of the supernatural. The Jew as the biblical participant in the mystery of Christ's death was simultaneously terrifying and fascinating, damned and holy. The Jew was, in this sense, akin to the devil, who, in the rural tradition, was not only the god of evil but also of the natural vegetative cycle of the earth. The figure of the Jew was required in many rural customs and rituals to secure the vital powers, fertility, and good fortune during the wedding ceremony, for example, where the figure of the Jew was meant to supervise the passage of the bride from her family to the family of her husband.[36]

These old folk customs reverberate even in post-Holocaust Poland. Ethnographic research from the 1980s shows that Polish peasants still believed that rabbis or older Jews could heal, curse, or predict the future.[37] Likewise, some of the folk rituals using the figure of the Jew survived for decades after the real Jews disappeared from the Polish countryside. These folk practices, stigmatizing the Jewish element as "impure," have even been identified as a source of what Marian Pankowski called "magical anti-Semitism," which might be more influential in Poland than its ideological variety.[38]

The long reign of symbolic-romanticism in Polish art was crucial for generating some of the most enduring images of Jews. It was Mickiewicz, the bard of partitioned Poland, who in his national epic *Pan Tadeusz* (1834) created probably the most popular image of a Jew in Polish literature. Jankiel, who is a key figure of

---

[35] Alina Cała, "Autostereotyp i stereotypy narodowe," in *Czy Polacy są antysemitami? Wyniki badania sondażowego*, ed. Ireneusz Krzemiński (Warszawa: Oficyna Naukowa, 1996), 199–228.

[36] Alina Cała, *Wizerunek Żyda w polskiej kulturze ludowej* (Warszawa: Wydawnictwa Uniwersytetu Warszawskiego, 1992), 178–79.

[37] Ibid., 109–20 and 178–80.

[38] Marian Pankowski, cited in Maria Janion, *Bohater, spisek, śmierć* (Warszawa: WAB, 2009), 169.

this lengthy narrative poem, is a patriot and an advocate of the messianic union of Poles and Jews. Though distinct in his beliefs and customs from other Polish protagonists, Jankiel the Jew becomes the mouthpiece of Mickiewicz himself who, in the 1850s, was trying to organize a Jewish legion in Constantinople, dreaming that it could fight against Russia in the Crimean War and subsequently help liberate Poland from Russian occupation.[39] Interestingly enough, Jankiel is a klezmer, as Walter Z. Feldman notes—a character endowed both with diplomatic skills derived from his position between the Jewish and the Gentile world, and with a "charismatic and shamanic aspect" related to his musical virtuosity.[40]

The figure of Jankiel the klezmer has a historical prototype. Berek Joselewicz, a colonel of the Polish army who led a Jewish unit in the Kościuszko Uprising in 1794, was immortalized both in painting and in one of the oldest series of Polish postcards (1902), portraying his heroic death in battle.[41] The common denominator of Joselewicz and Jankiel is the virtue of patriotism, but while Joselewicz functions as the epitome of the "first modern Jew in Poland," the literary Jankiel has something essentially pre-modern, mysterious and magical.[42]

Fig. 4.7 Jankiel the klezmer on a pre–World War II Polish postcard. Courtesy of The Sosenko Family Collection. Photo by Wojciech Sosenko.

---

[39] See M. Janion, *Do Europy tak, ale razem z naszymi umarłymi* (Warszawa: Sic!, 2000), 74–75.

[40] Walter Zev Feldman, *Klezmer Music: History, Memory, and Musical Structure, ca. 1750–1950* (work in progress).

[41] Eugeniusz Duda and Marek Sosenko, eds., *Dawna pocztówka żydowska* (Kraków: Muzeum Historyczne Miasta Krakowa, 1997), 11.

[42] Isaac B. Singer, cited in Janion, *Bohater, spisek, śmierć*, 12 and 46ff; Dunin, "Postać żyda w polskiej kulturze popularnej do 1945 roku," 318–19.

Although most of the popular representations of Jews on the klezmer scene portray men, the Polish tradition also contains romantic images of the Jewish woman. Esterka, the legendary concubine of King Casimir the Great (1310–70), inspired generations of novelists, playwrights, and painters as well as the modern tourist industry.[43] Believed to have been the inspiration for Casimir's privileges for Jews, Esterka is the "ideal Jewess": educated and patriotic, believing Poland to be the promised land for Jews. At the same time, Esterka is also emotional, beautiful, and seductive. Like the biblical Esther, she is perceived as the savior and protector of Jews, and venerated as the Jewish queen.[44]

The romantic and magical Jewish characters have actually outlived the romantic period and still populate Polish literature and theater. The renowned Polish avant-garde theater director, Tadeusz Kantor (1915–90), was perhaps the most prominent artist who introduced enigmatic figures of Hasids into the new postwar theater. But there were more highly successful works in Polish haunted by the figure of the mysterious Jew. Paweł Huelle's prize-winning novel *Weiser Dawidek* (1987) featured a Jewish boy endowed with inexplicable paranormal abilities. And the adaptation of *The Dybbuk* by Krzysztof Warlikowski in 2003 earned international acclaim. Just these few examples indicate that the figure of the magical Jew is well anchored not only in Polish folklore but also in high culture.

It is therefore no wonder that the klezmer revival, likewise, makes use of romanticized images of Jews, generating representations that are dreamlike but distorted. The trope of the "magical Jew," is also noteworthy because of what it eclipses. Oscillating between the familiar and the exotic, the folkloristic and the carnivalesque, it supersedes the image of the urban, assimilated Jew who cherished and co-created Polish culture. The romanticized reconstruction produces an image of the Jew that might be readily recognizable but is not representative. It is familiar but not faithful.

Although the developments on the Polish and German klezmer scenes are in many respects parallel, the romanticized shtetl imagery has a decidedly different status in Germany. Idyllic images of Jews in traditional eastern European garb do occasionally appear on German klezmer CDs, but romanticizing the shtetl life also meets with a harsh critique. One of few venues in Berlin where shtetl nostalgia is put on stage is the Bimah Jewish Theater. One of its musicals *Wenn der Rebbe tanzt, tanzt auch die Rabbinerin* [When the Rabbi dances, his wife dances too, (2006)] takes place in a generic shtetl to the background of klezmer music. Sometimes joyful, sometimes melancholy, this show is composed of loosely connected Jewish jokes and Yiddish songs, and belongs to one of the most popular productions of Bimah. In fact, the play has also been adapted into a special New Year's Eve program, which also features a raffle and a "traditional Jewish" buffet.

[43] Halkowski, *Żydowski Kraków*, 21–26.
[44] Chone Shmeruk, *Legenda o Esterce w literaturze jidysz i polskiej* (Warszawa: Oficyna Naukowa, 2000), 9–35.

Most German klezmer musicians, though, avoid sentimentalization. Karsten Troyke, with his *Forgotten Yiddish Songs* (1997) [*Jidische Vergessene Lieder*], presented the world of the Polish shtetl as filtered through the sufferings and hardships of a Jewish woman, not as a site of nostalgia. Similarly, Mark Aizikovitch, with his *In a Yiddish Word* (2000) [*in jiddischn wort*], demystified Jewish life in eastern Europe. Paying tribute to the Jewish poets murdered in the Soviet Union between 1933 and 1948, Aizikovitch's record denoted the shtetl as a space of persecution.

Many of the Germany-based klezmer musicians discard the clichés of the shtetl romance as inadequate. Henner Wolter, of the band Forszpil, finds the shtetl romanticization "quite wrong and deeply reactionary," stressing that the Jewish village was also "where pogroms were taking place and where people were falling ill, where they were constantly in danger."[45] Forszpil's website, like those of many

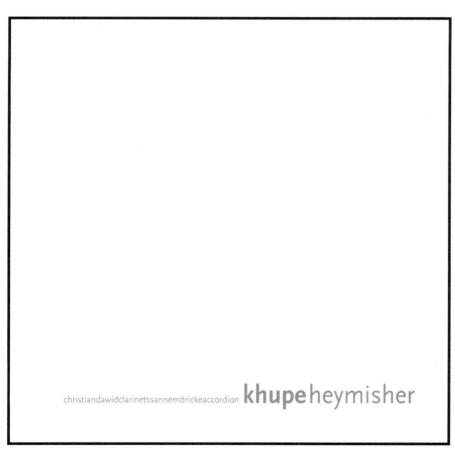

Fig. 4.8 Cover of Khupe's *Heymisher*, 2003. Courtesy of Christian Dawid.

[45] Henner Wolter, interview by the author, Berlin, December 1, 2006.

other German klezmer bands, has a modern design; the musicians smile in photos shot in front of a graffiti-covered wall. This minimalistic design is characteristic for the German klezmer scene on the whole. For most performers it is a conscious choice to avoid shtetl-related imagery and Jewish symbols of any kind. The Berlin-based klezmer duo Khupe, whose album *Heymisher* (2003) is wrapped in a blank, white cover and their *Eyns, tsvey, dray* (2005), sold in a plain cardboard envelope closed with a paper clip, is probably in the avant-garde of this trend.

Many of the non-Jewish musicians in Berlin believe that the use of Jewish symbols in their visual materials would turn them into impersonators. The Yiddish singer Fabian Schnedler states simply: "I don't want people to think that I'm Jewish; if I want to make it clear, I should avoid all Jewish icons."[46] Hardy Reich of Aufwind is likewise proud of the fact that his band is "the only klezmer band with a non-Jewish name."[47] The band's name and the neutral imagery are meant to testify to the musicians' non-Jewish identity: "We don't want to conceal our background. We are Germans," concludes Reich.[48] Simon Jakob Drees of the avant-garde band Ahava Raba declares that he would not want to use symbols such as the menorah on his CDs for a similar reason: "If I used the [Jewish] symbols, I would feel like I'm cannibalizing them . . . By cannibalizing I mean something not as drastic as abuse, but manifesting something that I am not."[49] It seems that many of the *klezmorim* in Berlin interpret Jewish symbols as signifiers of ethnic, religious, or national identity. As such, they are perceived as emblems that the musicians find inappropriate to reproduce.

By means of imagery that does not connote "Jewishness," the musicians turn their CD covers into a statement about their non-Jewish identity; at the same time they also conceptually separate Jewish music from Judaism, the state of Israel, and the Shoah. Karsten Troyke points out the fact that symbols such as the menorah can have multiple meanings: "A menorah can mean: 'I'm interested in Jewish things,' or 'our family maintains the traditions,' or 'we want to go to Israel' . . . I don't object to those symbols but why should I put them on my records? I don't want to say more than I want to say."[50] For Franka Lampe of Schikker-wi-Lot, using Jewish symbols while playing Jewish folk music would be equivalent to employing a Christian cross if she were dealing with German folklore, both of which she finds out of place.[51] There are also musicians who believe that Jewish symbols on their records could have a political meaning. Alexandra Dimitroff of Di Grine Kuzine argues: "If we used Jewish symbols I would feel like

[46] Fabian Schnedler, interview by the author, Berlin, February 8, 2006.

[47] Reich interview.

[48] Ibid.

[49] Drees interview.

[50] Troyke interview.

[51] Lampe interview.

I'm supporting the Israelis in the conflict, but not the Palestinians."[52] Finally, some artists, like Anna Schubert, are preoccupied that "when you use the Star of David, people associate it with the Holocaust only."[53]

Apart from symbols, certain stage behavior or even terminology used in promotional materials undergo a form of self-censorship. Detlef Pegelow of Tants in Gartn Eydn lists *"jiddeling,"* or parodying the Jewish manner of speaking, as unacceptable during his band's concerts.[54] Fabian Schnedler, in turn, makes a point of avoiding in his stage announcements even the very term *"jiddische Lieder"* (Yiddish songs), which corresponds, in his understanding, to a cliché of Yiddish culture as "romantic and tragic." Instead, he prefers to use what is in his view the more neutral *"jiddischer Gesang"* (Yiddish singing).[55]

While avoiding shtetl clichés, Berlin klezmer bands do not shun humor, irony, and puns. The first track of the album *Klezmer Schwof* by Tants in Gartn Eydn opens with a paraphrase of the opening of Genesis: "Now the earth was without shape and empty, and darkness was over the surface of the watery deep. People went to klezmer concerts, but no one danced."[56] The band also plays with the image of the biblical Garden of Eden on the cover. The photo on the inside of the liner notes pictures a typical German allotment garden adorned with a garden gnome and the protruding behind of a gardener who is weeding the flower beds. Carsten Wegener explains that the intention of Tants in Gartn Eydn was to

Fig. 4.9 Image from the liner notes of Tants in Gartn Eydn's *Klezmer Schwof*, 2001. Photo by Carsten Wegener.

[52] Alexandra Dimitroff, interview by the author, Berlin, January 5, 2006.

[53] Anna Schubert, interview by the author, Berlin, January 31, 2006.

[54] Pegelow interview.

[55] Schnedler interview.

[56] "Und die Erde war wüst und leer und es war finster auf der Tiefe. Die Menschen gingen zu Klezmerkonzerten und keiner tanzte." Track 1, Tants in Gartn Eydn, *Klezmer Schwof*, Rent a Poet, 2001, CD. "Schwof" in the Berlin dialect (Berlinerisch) means dance.

"break up the cliché"; he wants their CD to be taken as "something funny, not serious." "Of course, you could put there a picture from the ghetto, but it's not our thing,"[57] concludes the musician. Other bands attempt to add a touch of humor to their performances by means of a special scenic look. Thus Di Grine Kuzine, which in addition to klezmer plays a mix of world music, performs in slightly flamboyant retro outfits. The drummer, Snorre Schwarz, says that the band wants their audiences to perceive the music as contemporary. "I always try to present us as the boys in suits, and then we're cool, gangster-style, fresh, not like from the past, but very much from the present."[58] Clearly, klezmer in Berlin is hip, not heritage.

This wink toward the audience seems to also perform the role of comic relief. A gangster-image or visual jokes attempt to free klezmer from associations with the Holocaust and help to present it as what it has always been: entertainment music. Not every attempt at breaking clichés has the desired effect, though, and experimentation on the klezmer scene might quickly stir up controversy.

While working on their *Klezmer Schwof*, the musicians of Tants in Gartn Eydn decided to mix the opening of a rough melody of the *honga* with the puffing noise of a locomotive. The tuba-player Detlef Pegelow remembers that several years after the release of the CD, one of the band members confided in his colleagues that the train arrangement had always bothered him, because someone could associate it with the Holocaust transports. "I always have to watch what I am doing," commented Pegelow, "because we have to be aware that we're dealing with a culturally and historically difficult issue." "But if you do it too much," he warned, "you become much too consumed by the idea that you always have to be politically correct."[59]

The dilemma concerning how to retain political correctness without compromising artistic freedom seems to be quite serious for some German klezmer musicians. Especially since some oversensitive reactions from concertgoers surprise the musicians themselves. Carsten Wegener of Tants in Gartn Eydn recollects a concert in Hackesches Hoftheater, when he performed wearing a T-shirt of a Hamburg soccer team, F C St. Pauli. The logo of the club, derived from a pirate flag and featuring a skull and crossbones, is associated in Germany with the antifascist and working-class identity of St. Pauli's fans. What the bassist of Tants in Gartn Eydn considered a symbol of leftist nonconformity, however, was read quite differently by his audience:

> After several pieces, during the break, somebody came up and said: "Do you know what you're wearing?" "A St. Pauli T-shirt," I answered. "It's the same symbol as the Waffen-SS!".[60] I was like: "It's not true: they had a

[57] Wegener interview.

[58] S. Schwarz interview.

[59] Pegelow interview.

[60] *Totenkopf* was the emblem of the *SS-Totenkopfverbände*, tasked with guarding the concentration camps, which were later incorporated into Waffen-SS as *SS-Division Totenkopf*.

Totenkopf, but it is a different symbol!" This is how people react to it, they immediately create some connections. You can try to respect it and take it into consideration, but you cannot predict what associations people might have. If you want to pay attention to everything, you go crazy. That's why my idea is: try to respect it, but do it the way you think is right.[61]

Playing Jewish music in present-day Germany is no doubt a task requiring great sensitivity and diplomacy. Cautious not to reproduce shtetl clichés, German musicians, however, do not always find their diplomatic efforts met with appreciation. Stefan Kühne of the Bremen band Klezgoyim remembers how the band's name once inspired ridicule from his Jewish colleagues. "When I told them our name they only laughed. For the leader of the band the name *goyim* was a bad word, like for Germans the word *Kanake* maybe, which we use for the Turks and other southern Europeans. The band was Jewish, and they found it very amusing that someone would call himself this voluntarily."[62] But if avoiding the accusation of impersonation is one of the important motivations behind the ostensibly non-Jewish names of some klezmer bands, the restraint in using shtetl imagery in Germany can probably also be explained by the different status that the representations of eastern European Jews have had in recent German history.

The *Ostjuden* functioned in Germany as an important reference point for a long time. They annoyed the post-Haskalah assimilated Jews, inspired Jewish modernists looking for authenticity, and, finally, fell victim to the anti-Semitic propaganda of the National Socialists. In the period of the Jewish Enlightenment, eastern European Jews were viewed with disdain by their German co-religionists. Just as *Polacken* became the butt of German jokes, the Jews of the eastern shtetls became the inferior other to the assimilated German Jewry. The Jewish press at the turn of the nineteenth century portrayed the *Ostjuden* as a negative photographic image of the native German Jewry. As Wertheimer notes, it was a common opinion among German Jews that their eastern brethren were "backward and fanatical" and "mired in superstitious and unenlightened culture."[63] Their shtetl constituted the opposite pole to the urban values the German Jews cherished, and westernization was deemed the only means of improvement. This inner Jewish "clash of civilizations" reverberated in the public discourse, and even in the urban Jewish folk songs in Berlin and Vienna, which ruthlessly mocked the new Jewish immigrants from the East.[64]

---

[61] Wegener interview.

[62] Kühne interview.

[63] Jack Wertheimer, *Unwelcome Strangers: East European Jews in Imperial Germany* (New York: Oxford University Press, 1987), 148.

[64] Bohlman,"Die Volksmusik und die Verstädterung," 36–38.

Around the turn of the twentieth century, *Ostjuden* gradually won new appreciation. In a period of disillusionment caused by the new wave of anti-Semitism in Germany, the search for a new Jewish identity made native Jews rediscover the shtetl as the last bastion of Jewish authenticity. Writers such as Martin Buber, who introduced his German audience to the Hasidic heritage, were trying to "bridge the old gulf between German and East European Jews,"[65] and also attract young non-Jewish readers to the spirituality of "exotic" Jewish cultures. For many intellectuals of that period, such as Kurt Tucholsky, Alfred Döblin, Joseph Roth, and Else Lasker-Schüler, who grew increasingly critical of their German Jewish contemporaries, the eastern European Jew became "an external Jewish model."[66]

This idealized representation of the "true" Eastern Jew, which took shape in the period of modernism, was, however, permeated with new values and visualized with new means of expression. The *Ostjude,* as portrayed by Joseph Roth in *The Wandering Jews* (1927), for example, was a deeply spiritual figure. Roth clearly saw the eastern European Jews as intellectually superior to their surroundings. "While the other peasants only now begin to learn writing and reading, the Jew behind his plow struggles with the problems of the theory of relativity," he wrote.[67] Apart from literature, other forms of Jewish cultural activity of the early twentieth century were also inspired by the eastern European influence. As Michael Brenner notes, in that time "[c]omposers of liturgy . . . claimed to base their compositions on oriental Jewish music, artists depicted *Ostjuden* in book illustrations, and Jewish museums displayed Jewish folk art." Brenner is also quick to point out that "the rich cultural treasures of the Jewish past . . . were combined with *modernist art tendencies.*"[68] Thus the image of the shtetl in Germany's popular culture underwent a fundamental change because it came to be understood as the cradle of Jewish heritage, and because it was visualized in a fresh, daring, modernist way. Ephraim Lilien's expressionist illustrations and the performances of the Vilna Troupe, employing avant-garde stage design and direction, defined the new way in which the intellectuals of the Weimar Republic imagined eastern European Jewish life.[69]

The onset of the economic crisis in the 1920s brought about another change. The anti-Semitic discourse in Germany became more radical, and *Ostjuden* were turned into the scapegoats of the deteriorating economic situation. Jewish immigrants from the East were blamed for the lost war, economic depression, and growing unemployment. The police started raiding the poor Jewish neighborhoods in Berlin, looking for illegal immigrants, and it was not long before the

---

[65] Amos Elon, *The Pity of It All: A Portrait of the German-Jewish Epoch 1743–1933* (New York: Picador, 2003), 239.

[66] Brenner, *The Renaissance of Jewish Culture in Weimar Germany,* 142.

[67] Joseph Roth, cited in ibid., 146.

[68] Ibid., 156, italics mine.

[69] Ibid., 190.

Scheunenviertel district, inhabited by eastern European Jews, suffered a pogrom in 1923. The language of hate toward Jews from Poland and Russia became overtly racist. Expressions such as *"Ostjudenplage"* [the plague of eastern Jews] began to circulate in the public discourse.[70] Soon the propaganda of National Socialism instrumentalized images of eastern European Jews. The 1940 film *Der Ewige Jude* [The Eternal Jew], shot in the ghettos of Nazi-occupied Poland, presented an image of Polish Jews as "proof" of the "true racial character" of the seemingly assimilated Jews in Germany.[71] This film, with its ghetto footage, has become, in the words of Jeffrey Herf, one of the most "familiar icons of modern consciousness and memory of the Nazi era."[72]

These templates of eastern European Jews in German visual culture clearly differ from the images circulating in Poland. While in Poland the image of the caftan-clad shtetl Jew with sidelocks does not immediately connote an anti-Semitic intention, the approval for such a representation in Germany is limited. *Ostjuden* have for centuries been represented in Germany as part of the East/West dichotomy. This comparison, unfavorable for the eastern Jews, served to present the assimilationist model of German Jews as superior. The image of the shtetl was therefore explicitly negative. The period of the first "renaissance" of Yiddish culture in Germany brought a change to this representation, but the modernist vision of the *Ostjuden* it generated was still very different from the images prevalent in the Polish romantic school. Additionally, it was the spirituality and mysticism—not the physiognomy or external attributes of shtetl Jews—that played a dominant role in these representations. The focus on the Jewish body returned in the anti-Semitic campaigns of the 1920s and 1930s. In the propaganda of National Socialism, eastern European Jews had distinct facial features and characteristic attire. The often-reproduced poster of the 1937 anti-Semitic exhibition *Der Ewige Jude* in Munich, picturing an eastern European Jew grasping gold coins in his hand, was a quintessential image of this period, and influenced the way Germans might perceive folklorized images of *Ostjuden* today. Discredited in this way, images of Jews in traditional eastern European garb might carry a certain ambiguity for a German viewer, even if they are not meant as a caricature. The figure of the melancholy shtetl Jew that seems to be so omnipresent in Polish popular culture evokes too many specters from the past to be palatable in Germany.

[70] Ludger Heid, "Der Ostjude," in *Antisemitismus: Vorurteile und Mythen*, ed. Julius H. Schoeps and Joachim Schlör (München, Zürich: Piper, 1995), 245–49.

[71] *Der Ewige Jude*, directed by Fritz Hippler (Deutsche Filmherstellungs- und -Verwertungs- GmbH, 1940).

[72] Jeffrey Herf, *The Jewish Enemy: Nazi Propaganda during World War II and the Holocaust* (Cambridge, MA: Harvard University Press, 2006), 14.

The Incorporated Jew

The "Jewish romance" in Poland pictures a world of vivid contrasts and blissful coexistence. The Jew is the magical other but at the same time the inhabitant of a multicultural paradise lost. And where the Jewish other becomes a sign of longing for a pluralist society, the Jewish and non-Jewish realms become superimposed; the "Jewish" becomes subsumed into the "Polish."

The multi-ethnic Poland of the interwar period is a common point of reference for many musicians dealing with Jewish heritage. This is conditioned, on the one hand, by the very idea of a revival, which idealizes the past as something worth returning to. On the other hand, however, the klezmer revival is part of a more all-embracing wave of nostalgia for pre-1939 Poland, which surfaced with particular force after 1989. For many klezmer artists, this Poland, which regained its independence in the aftermath of World War I and ceased to exist in 1939, is more than a historical and geographical entity; it is an emotionally charged, nearly utopian place, associated with certain values. The Warsaw-based band Cukunft, for example, promotes their CD of Mordechai Gebirtig's songs as a "record for everyone who cherishes the idea of Poland of many cultures."[73] This multicultural Poland emerges also in personal interviews with klezmer musicians. Irena Urbańska, a singer of Yiddish songs from Kraków, remembering Przemyśl, her hometown, before the war, speaks of an idyllic place where "Jewish women would bring their homebaked cakes to their Christian neighbors and Christians, in turn, would share their famous *kutia*—a dish made from wheat and poppy seeds—with the Jews."[74] This image, she says, has accompanied her in her work, especially as she started noticing the similarities between Yiddish and Polish folk songs.

The mutual borrowings between Polish and Jewish folk music that the musicians trace testify to cultural commonalities, which seem to confirm the narrative of peaceful coexistence. "I treat Jewish culture, if you can isolate it as such at all, as an element of Polish culture," says Jasha Lieberman, a violinist from Kraków. "In Europe," he adds, "Jewish culture was so multinational and multicultural that it absorbed everything."[75] The affinities between eastern European folk music and klezmer seem to be indeed of great importance to Polish klezmer musicians, and become addressed by virtually every interviewee. For some, they mean that klezmer is ultimately Polish. For others, merely that Poles have a certain privileged access to this music. Jerzy Bawół of Kroke sees it in these terms. In his eyes, many Poles "instinctively understand" Jewish music and identify with it because it is mentally so close to them.[76] Jarosław Bester of the former Cracow Klezmer

---

[73] Ireneusz Socha, a review of *Lider fun Mordechaj Gebirtig* (2005), accessed November 27, 2007, http://www.serpent.pl/recenzje/c.html.

[74] Urbańska interview.

[75] Lieberman interview.

[76] Bawół [Kroke] interview, April 18, 2004.

Band takes the argument a step further, saying that the mystical beauty of Hasidic music *derives* from the "Slavic softness" of the nations among whom the Hasidim lived.[77] In the liner notes of Sława Przybylska's compilation of Yiddish songs we also read that Jewish music is a "synthesis of biblical depth and Slavic nostalgia."[78] Klezmer emerges not only as a product of the bygone multicultural Poland but also an art form defying ethnic boundaries. Some of the klezmer productions from Kraków challenge the musical boundary between what can be defined as Polish or Jewish in very unexpected ways. A case in point is Di Galitzyaner Klezmorim's "Chopin's Freilach," which, playfully transposing Chopin into the klezmer style, won first prize at the Kraków "Chopin Open" competition in 1999.

This process of incorporation of klezmer into the body of Poland's heritage can have many interpretations. On the one hand, it indicates a new tendency to frame Jewish culture as no longer alien and external but instead part of the multicultural heritage of prewar Poland. On the other hand, it is clear that the emphasis on the commonalities between Jewishness and Polishness also serves to legitimize the appropriation of Jewish heritage by non-Jewish artists. However instrumental the "incorporating" mode might be, there is no doubt that it subverts a long sequence of historic representations of the Jew as the "threatening other."[79]

The oldest among these is the image of the Jew as a deicide. The concept of guilt ascribed to Jews, and sustained for centuries by the official teaching of the Catholic Church, served Christians to define their Christian identity in opposition to Jews. The image of the Jew as a deicide is therefore one of the most deeply rooted representations of Jews in Polish folklore. Some folk customs, especially related to Lent and Easter, still circulate the cliché. The most vivid "reminders" of Jewish "guilt" are the performances of the Way of the Cross, or the "hanging of Judas," a folk custom surviving in certain rural areas of southern Poland until the 1980s, which originally consisted in hanging an effigy of Judas in front of Jewish houses and burning it.[80]

The myth of ritual murder, related to the image of the Jew as a deicide, has left traces on the Polish perception of Jews. The accusations of Jews for alleged ritual murders were relatively numerous in Poland between the sixteenth and eighteenth centuries; in the city of Sandomierz, where three infamous blood libel trials took place, two local churches still host nineteenth-century paintings depicting ritual murders.[81] Despite the controversies that they provoke, anthropological research indicates that some of the local inhabitants still consider the

---

[77] Bester interview.

[78] Liner notes of Sława Przybylska's *Alef-Bejs: Pieśni i piosenki żydowskie*, Tonpress, 2005, CD.

[79] See Michlic, *Poland's Threatening Other*, 24ff.

[80] See Cała, *Wizerunek Żyda w polskiej kulturze ludowej*, 177–78; and Joanna Tokarska-Bakir, *Rzeczy mgliste* (Sejny: Pogranicze, 2004), 73–94.

[81] In that period there were at least eighty-two trials of Jews accused of alleged ritual murder. Stanisław Musiał, *Czarne jest czarne* (Kraków: Wydawnictwo Literackie, 2003), 44–45.

myth of ritual murder plausible.[82] The latest case concerning an accusation for ritual murder does not lie in the very distant past: in 1946 it provoked a pogrom in Kielce, during which the mob, aroused by false allegations that local Jews had kidnapped a Polish child, murdered sixty to seventy Holocaust survivors.[83]

If blood libel lies at the roots of Polish religious anti-Semitism, the stereotype of the Jew as the economic other defines "secular" anti-Semitism and still circulates widely in present-day Polish society. The demonization of the Jewish usurer, middleman, or banker derived from the medieval belief that there was a connection between Jews and the devil. It was an evil force that supposedly helped Jews in their business affairs, and since Jews were among the few who used money in the preindustrial economy it added to the popular conviction that Jews dealt with an unearthly matter. The idea of Jewish financial power resurged in Poland in a particularly vivid way after the collapse of Communism.[84] As the regime ceased to exist, many Poles resorted to the traditional scapegoat—the Jew—thus recycling old myths of the Jewish conspiracy. And indeed, the early 1990s witnessed a collective paranoia about the hidden Jewish identities of prominent politicians and a Jewish scheme to take over power in Poland.[85]

Although traditional, religiously motivated anti-Semitism has become more marginal and, according to current surveys, Poles list more positive than negative features of Jews, old stereotypes of the Jew as antithetical to the category of "Pole" are still latent.[86] It is all the more remarkable that these traditional devices coexist in contemporary Poland with the ever more pronounced "incorporative" tendencies. In 1991, for example, more than 40 percent of Poles declared in a survey that "Jews are an integral part of our nation."[87] And although this level of incorporation was lower than in other East European countries, it should also be considered in relation to the widespread post–World War II practice of

---

[82] Joanna Tokarska-Bakir, *Legendy o krwi: Antropologia przesądu*, (Warszawa: WAB, 2008); Joanna Tokarska-Bakir, "Obrazy sandomierskie," *ResPublica Nowa* 1 (2007): 18–63.

[83] The number of victims varies in different sources, because the killings took place not only in the town of Kielce but also in the surrounding area. The estimate comes from Stefan Krakowski "Kielce," *Encyclopaedia Judaica*, 2nd ed., vol. 12, 147. See also Jan T. Gross, *Fear: Anti-Semitism in Poland after Auschwitz. An Essay in Historical Interpretation* (Princeton: Princeton University Press, 2006); Joanna Tokarska-Bakir, "Cries of the Mob in the Pogroms in Rzeszów (June 1945), Cracow (August 1945), and Kielce (July 1946) as a Source for the State of Mind of the Participants," *East European Politics and Societies* 25, no. 3 (2011): 553–74.

[84] Cała, *Wizerunek Żyda w polskiej kulturze ludowej*, 98.

[85] Michlic, *Poland's Threatening Other*, 263ff.

[86] Cała, "Autostereotyp i stereotypy narodowe," 206–18; Ireneusz Krzemiński and Ewa Koźmińska Frejlak, "Stosunek społeczeństwa polskiego do zagłady Żydów," in *Czy Polacy są antysemitami? Wyniki badania sondażowego*, ed. Ireneusz Krzemiński (Warszawa: Oficyna Naukowa, 1996), 132.

[87] Zvi Gitelman, "Collective Memory and Contemporary Polish-Jewish Relations," in *Contested Memories: Poles and Jews during the Holocaust and its Aftermath*, ed. Joshua D. Zimmerman (New Brunswick, NJ: Rutgers University Press, 2003), 283.

subsuming Jewish victims into the category of Polish war losses. In fact, Polish popular culture and public discourse often appropriated Jewish suffering during the Holocaust into the Polish martyrological narrative. Many postwar officials and intellectuals presumed a Polish–Jewish "commonality of experience" during the German occupation, or inscribed the Warsaw ghetto uprising within the tradition of "Polish" patriotism. This view of history is also often taught in Polish schools. As Steinlauf observes, "[t]he majority of textbooks subsume the fate of the Jews during World War II under the fate of the Polish population."[88] Even the Auschwitz-Birkenau Museum for a long time "Polonized" Jews who perished in the camp, classifying, counting, and commemorating victims until the late 1980s according to their nationality.[89] Outstanding Jewish personages, such as the teacher and pediatrician Janusz Korczak (Henryk Goldszmit), have also repeatedly been represented in Polish popular culture within the framework of Christian martyrdom.[90] Stanisław Krajewski referred to such practices as "Christianization," and Henryk Grynberg as nothing less than a "theft" of the Holocaust.[91]

This practice of Polonizing the Jews and painting an image of peaceful Polish–Jewish coexistence has, furthermore, played its role in the debate on anti-Semitism and anti-Jewish violence in Poland. Particularly after the groundbreaking publications of Jan T. Gross's *Neighbors* (2001) and *Fear* (2006), which triggered an intensive and at times embittered discussion in Poland, the vision of Polish-Jewish harmonious coexistence became a counter-pole to the narrative of Polish–Jewish relations as dominated by an ethnic conflict. Gross's *Neighbors*, originally published in Polish in 2000, brought the infamous pogrom in Jedwabne into the public consciousness for the first time.[92] Gross, a US-based historian who left Poland in the aftermath of 1968, was not the first one to write about Jedwabne, but his voice of an external observer provoked an unprecedented outcry. His book reconstructed the events that unfolded in a small Polish town, northeast of Warsaw, on July 10, 1941, when a group of local inhabitants—Catholics—drove their Jewish neighbors out of their houses, beat them, robbed them, humiliated them, and then locked them in a barn and burned them alive. The account provoked an avalanche of defensive responses, including those relativizing, or even denying, the Polish complicity in the crime. Polish historians, social scientists, and journalists became divided into two camps, either welcoming Gross's publication and acknowledging

---

[88] Michael C. Steinlauf, "Teaching about the Holocaust in Poland," in Zimmerman, *Contested Memories*, 266.

[89] Marek Kucia, *Auschwitz jako fakt społeczny* (Kraków: Universitas, 2005), 172ff; see also Janine P. Holc, "Memory Contested: Jewish and Catholic Views of Auschwitz in Present-Day Poland," in *Antisemitism and its Opponents in Modern Poland*, ed. Robert Blobaum (Ithaca, NY: Cornell University Press, 2005), 301–25.

[90] Terri Ginsberg, "St. Korczak of Warsaw," in Glowacka and Zylinska, *Imaginary Neighbors*, 110–34.

[91] Stanisław Krajewski, *Żydzi, Judaizm, Polska* (Warszawa: Vocatio, 1997), 243.

[92] Jan T. Gross, *Sąsiedzi: Historia zagłady żydowskiego miasteczka* (Sejny: Pogranicze, 2000).

the need for Poles to confront their shameful history, or criticizing his research methods and sources, and decidedly refuting his theses.[93] As Gross's interpretations of the pogrom in Jedwabne and, later, the one in Kielce, met with this vehement rejection from many sections of Polish society, the romantic vision of Polish–Jewish neighborly relations gained an additional appeal. The belief in the commonality of the Polish and Jewish wartime experiences performed at this point an "anesthetic function," testifying to the need of "autotherapy" in the aftermath of the Jedwabne debate.[94]

Although the incorporation of Jews into the narrative of a peaceful and multiethnic society is to an extent correlated to the specifically Polish topos of the shtetl romance, it can function in other contexts, too. Thus, in Germany, the incorporative mechanism is usually based on the linguistic commonalities between Yiddish and German. And despite the fact that the German Jewish history provides a whole new set of implications to the idea of "incorporation," some arguments used by Polish and German klezmer musicians are astoundingly similar.

"The Jewish tradition and the German tradition are so closely connected with one another that you don't really have the impression that it is something alien," says Simon Jakob Drees of Ahava Raba. He also adds that he has always had the feeling that Yiddish heritage was a part of his culture.[95] Snorre Schwarz of Di Grine Kuzine is, likewise, convinced that klezmer music is "special for Germans . . . because it touches something in our souls."[96] Clearly, German klezmer musicians recognize Yiddish music as part of the German tradition because both languages stem from the same root, and German performers and audiences can easily understand many of the Yiddish lyrics.

Such a strategy of incorporation has a tradition in Germany. The period of emancipation turned Jews of the German-speaking countries into participants of a shared German-language culture. The immense contribution of Jews to German arts was obvious even to the National Socialists, who thought it necessary to cleanse German museums of "degenerate art," burn books by Jewish authors, and ban concerts of "suspicious" music. This expulsion of the Jewish element from German culture is seen today as self-mutilation (*Selbstamputation*),

---

[93] Tokarska-Bakir, *Rzeczy mgliste*, 95–115; Michał Bilewicz, "Wyjaśnianie Jedwabnego: Antysemityzm i postrzeganie trudnej przeszłości," in *Antysemityzm w Polsce i na Ukrainie*, ed. Ireneusz Krzemiński (Warszawa: Scholar, 2004), 248–69. For an overview of the debate after the publication of Gross's *Fear*, see Monica Rice, "Resisting a Phantom Book: A Critical Assessment of the Initial Polish Discussion of Jan Gross's *Fear*," in *Polin: Studies in Polish Jewry*, vol. 22, *Social and Cultural Boundaries in Pre-Modern Poland*, ed. Adam Teller, Magda Teter, and Antony Polonsky (Oxford: Littman Library of Jewish Civilization, 2010) 427–53.

[94] Henryk Szlajfer, *Polacy Żydzi: Zderzenie stereotypów. Esej dla przyjaciół i innych* (Warszawa: Scholar, 2003), 25 and 67.

[95] Drees interview.

[96] S. Schwarz interview.

and many Germans think along the lines of historian Nicolaus Sombart, who once poignantly exclaimed: "What are the Germans without the Jews? Nothing."[97] Jewish artists are celebrated in the German cultural pantheon, and the myth of the "German Jewish symbiosis" is still as much cherished as it is contested by historians.[98]

This "incorporative" mode gains a particular dimension in the klezmer revival. There is no denying that the Ashkenazi Jews and their language come from Germany, but framing Yiddish-language culture as an integral part of "German" culture obscures the tension between the contribution of assimilated Jews to German high culture and the dissimilationist character of the Yiddish-language cultural production in in the advent of World War II.

The presence of the "incorporative" discourse on the Polish and German klezmer scene also indicates a more general development in the realm of culture and in contemporary Jewish Studies. The increasing non-Jewish fascination with Jewish heritage, and the participation of non-Jews in its revival, calls for a new, broader definition of "Jewish culture." As the historian David Biale advocated, the boundaries of what constitutes "Jewish culture" and even "the very notion of an autonomous Judaism" need to be critically investigated. In his view, Jewish culture should be conceptualized as part of a greater organism, where the boundaries between the Jewish and the non-Jewish are inherently unstable, dynamic, and permeable.[99] From this perspective, Jewish culture emerges as an organic part of a larger cultural sphere and is not endemic.

This same idea reverberates also in the field of Jewish cultural studies. Barbara Kirshenblatt-Gimblett and Jonathan Karp, in their inspiring discussion of the boundaries of "Jewish art," define Jewishness as contextual and contingent, especially in the framework of artistic creation. "Jewish becomes subjunctive," they argue; it becomes "a consideration, a lens, a frame of reference, a contingency for what is shown."[100] Simon Bronner, in trying to delineate the field of Jewish Cultural Studies, built on an open definition of Jewish culture too. To Bronner, it should comprise not only "what Jews do," but also "what is thought about Jews."[101] Clearly, including the non-Jewish contribution to Jewish culture into the lens of Jewish Studies not only answers to the exigencies of documenting new cultural

---

[97] Nicolaus Sombart, "Der Beitrag der Juden zur deutschen Kultur," in *Juden als Träger bürgerlicher Kultur in Deutschland*, ed. Julius H. Schoeps (Stuttgart: Burg Verlag, 1989), 17–40.

[98] For the contribution of Jews to German culture see, Schoeps, ed., *Juden als Träger*; and for a critical analysis of the historical discourse concerning German Jewish symbiosis, see Leslie Morris and Jack Zipes, eds., *Unlikely History. The Changing German-Jewish Symbiosis 1945–2000* (New York: Palgrave, 2002).

[99] David Biale, "Confessions of a Historian of Jewish Culture," *Jewish Social Studies* 1 (1994): 44.

[100] Kirshenblatt-Gimblett and Karp, introduction to *The Art of Being Jewish*, 5.

[101] Simon J. Bronner, "The *Chutzpah* of Jewish Cultural Studies," in *Jewish Cultural Studies*, vol. 1, *Jewishness: Expression, Identity and Representation*, ed. Simon J. Bronner (Oxford: Littman Library of Jewish Civilization, 2008), 1.

phenomena, such as the contemporary Jewish heritage revival in Europe, but it also allows a better insight into the dynamics of Jewish/non-Jewish relations.

The Syncretic Jew: Klezmer Meets "Balkan Surfspeedpunkfolk"

A stage in the middle of a forest is pulsating with music and light. The audience is cheering and swaying. A young man is crowd-surfing as a black-hatted violinist, a double-bassist, and an accordionist are rocking the young audience. This might not be how one imagines a typical klezmer concert. Yet, the video of ecstatic crowds from the 2004 world music festival Urkult in Sweden features the Cracovian band Kroke, which started out playing klezmer in the Jewish restaurants of Kazimierz. Kroke, who swayed the crowds in the picturesque Swedish countryside, feel they are modern *klezmorim*, although they long ago dropped the label "klezmer" from their records and now compose their own music, only loosely inspired by Jewish folk melodies. Tomasz Lato states, "We are doing the same that the original *klezmorim* were once doing: traveling, emigrating, and drawing on other cultures. Today, we are doing the same, only a bit quicker: we are not emigrating, but we travel the world, meet various musicians at different festivals, listen to many kinds of ethnic music, draw on them and join everything together—this is what *klezmerstwo* is."[102]

Klezmerstwo, this Hebrew compound with a Polish suffix, stands for both a way of making music and a lifestyle. For an increasing number of young musicians, *klezmerstwo* does not imply just the traditional klezmer repertoire or even playing Jewish music. And, indeed, CDs marketed under the label of "klezmer" in Poland contain a heterogeneous mix of music, coming from very different Jewish traditions or beyond. The group Sholem, for example, lists on their CD *Mazl Tov* (2005) a song by Mordechai Gebirtig, an Israeli evergreen, and an instrumental Balkan folk piece. The term "klezmer" has become not only a generic label for all kinds of Jewish music but also embraces musical experimentation in which traditional klezmer is only the starting point, or at least one of the ingredients.

New trends on the world music scene bring fusion, sampling, and deconstruction into Jewish heritage music. On the international Jewish music scene, experimental impulses have been there for a while. John Zorn's manifesto "What is Radical Jewish Culture" dates back to 1992, when this American avant-garde musician turned to Jewish tradition for inspiration. Within the Radical Jewish Culture series, Zorn's label Tzadik issued many recordings whose Jewish character has been contested. Among others, Zorn produced six records of the non-Jewish Cracow Klezmer Band. In promoting what he called "adventurous recordings" and "Jewish music beyond klezmer," Zorn clearly challenged the definition of Jewish music as made by Jews and for Jews.[103] The new Jewish music was to be "radical"

---

[102] Lato [Kroke] interview, April 17, 2004.

[103] See "Tzadik Website," accessed May 24, 2009, http://www.tzadik.com/.

both in its experimental approach and innovation, and because of its close relation to the "roots" of the Jewish tradition. Many other artists after Zorn have tried to create a foundation for this "new Jewish music." The Canadian DJ Socalled, the British group Oi Va Voi, and the Israeli band Boom Pam, among others, have made such an attempt by compiling the first CD of the Nu Juwish Music series, which includes such diverse styles as hip-hop, Gypsy, and Middle Eastern music.[104]

It is therefore not surprising that the hybridizing trend in Jewish heritage music has also reached Poland. With their 1999 record *The Sounds of the Vanishing World*, Kroke abandoned the traditional klezmer sound, reaching out to a new audience beyond the klezmer scene.[105] The Cracow Klezmer Band has likewise drifted away from klezmer themes toward their own avant-garde compositions, eventually shedding the last trace of their klezmer past by changing the band's name to Bester Quartet in 2007. New impulses are also coming from other directions: the Warsaw-based band Cukunft produced a record of Gebirtig's songs with an electric guitar replacing the vocals. Soon afterwards, Cukunft's leader, Raphael Rogiński, founded Shofar, and in 2007 produced a CD combining Hasidic music with free jazz. Meanwhile, Wrocław-based Nina Stiller issued in 2006 her first record, containing Yiddish songs in disco arrangements. *New Polish Klezmer Music* (2011) by Jarek Adamów, in turn, announces hybridity and the search for a common denominator of Polish and Jewish folk music as the defining feature of "Polish klezmer," which draws on "multicultural Polish folk music" and has a contemporary beat.[106] It was not long before critics started writing about the new "dybbuk" speaking through Polish musicians.[107]

The local klezmer scene in Kazimierz has also changed over recent years. Many bands have adopted a modern, neutral stage image, and although many still perform a traditional klezmer repertoire, they avoid shtetl romance in their CD design. The Klezzmates, who have evolved from the more traditional band Yahrema, were the first to risk a performance of what they call "modern klezmer" in front of their tourist audiences in the restaurants of Szeroka Street. The Klezzmates perform in black, wearing funky orange sunglasses. Their music joins classical and jazz elements with swing, rock, and a touch of the oriental. Although not all audience members accept the change of style, and the artists speak of disappointed German tourists shouting, "*Klezmer, bitte!*" during their restaurant gigs, the band is happy to have abandoned the "klezmer corner." One of the Klezzmates, Jarosław Wilkosz, who believes that he would never be able to play Jewish music in an authentic "Jewish way," says that the new neutral image of the band and the repertoire, which the musicians can relate to as their own, liberates the group. Writing their own pieces, which are only inspired by klezmer music, is rewarding; it also allows

[104] *JuMu Nu Juwish Music*, JuMu V$_2$ Music, 2007, CD.
[105] Kroke, April 17, 2004.
[106] Jarek Adamów, *Etnomalia Projekt: New Polish Klezmer Music*, Folken Music, 2011, CD.
[107] Dorota Szwarcman, "Muzyka od dybuka," *Polityka*, September 1, 2007, 63–64.

Fig. 4.10 The Klezzmates. Photo by Przemysław Stachyra.

the band to address a younger audience and perform in new locations. But the metamorphosis of the Klezzmates, along with opening new career possibilities, also protects the band from the usual accusations of heritage appropriation.[108]

In this process of making sense of klezmer music and adapting it for their own purposes, non-Jewish klezmer musicians in Kraków now produce music that not only carries the musical imprint of their other musical interests but also frame the genre of klezmer in universalist terms. To Maciej Inglot, leader of Sholem, klezmer embodies the universal values of brotherhood. "The lyrics [of Yiddish songs] speak of love and respect toward others, of a nation that had no country of its own and was everywhere, but in which everyone loves and respects the other,"[109] he says. The Cracow Klezmer Band (now Bester Quartet) relates their music to universal values in a different way. Their third record, *Bereshit*, named after the first book of the Torah and dedicated to *tzadik* Nachman of Bratslav, represents to the musicians a voyage back to the beginnings of humankind. To Jarosław Bester, this Torah-inspired music is supposed to be a "form of prayer" but is really "non-denominational" and "uncontaminated" by ideology or politics.[110] Even while making a very clear reference to the Judaic tradition, The Bester Quarter locates their work on a higher plane of universal meaning. The Jewish heritage is here a metonymy of a greater spiritual realm: it is the ecumenical, not the particular, that comes to the fore.

[108] Wilkosz and Wiercioch [Klezzmates] interview.
[109] Inglot [Sholem] interview.
[110] Bester interview.

This universalization seems to be an integral part of the very phenomenon of a music revival. As Abigail Wood argues, klezmer musicians need to "maintain a self-conscious sense of difference from the past." This distance from the past can be achieved by means of "a dislocation from particularity." According to Wood, "[m]usical traditions become universalized as representations of an abstracted 'folk' and in turn re-appropriated by revivalists via their expressions of commitment to this or that particular musical culture."[111] This "dislocation from particularity" has a special dimension for the klezmer revival in places like Poland and Germany, where most of the artists are non-Jewish. Abstracting klezmer from Jewishness makes it easier for musicians to consider it as "their own."

* * *

A club concert like many others in Berlin. A postindustrial location in the hip district of Prenzlauer Berg, a small stage, dim lights. The popular band RotFront, representing the "emigrantski raggamuffin style," plays with a supporting band that has "klezmer" in the name but is all but traditional. Advertising itself as a *VerfremdungsklezmerBund*, this Berlin-based ensemble acknowledges both the heritage of Brechtian theater and the Jewish *Bund*. Performing under the name of The Painted Bird, this unorthodox band is clearly seeking dissonance and shock. Daniel Kahn, songwriter and frontman of the band, sports a white *commedia dell'arte* Venetian mask of the Plague Doctor with its protruding beak. He chants the lyrics of his Yiddish, German, and English songs through the megaphone, accompanied by his band playing klezmer tunes in rhythmic punk-rock arrangements. When he begins "Six Million Germans," a quick-paced ballad about the Jewish partisan Abba Kovner, the audience of young clubgoers seems perplexed. Kovner, a Jew from Vilnius who, during World War II, commanded the United Partisan Organization, founded in 1945 an underground Jewish cell called *Nakam* (Heb: vengeance) to carry out a terrorist attack to avenge Holocaust victims.[112] The song about the *Nakam* members, who conspire to poison water sources in Hamburg and Nuremberg in order to kill six million Germans, seems to make a bewildering impression on some of the party-goers, and a few leave the room as Kahn chants the disturbing refrain:

> Six million Germans
> You might say it was insane
> Six million Germans
> That it was misdirected pain

---

[111] Abigail Wood, "(De)constructing Yiddishland, Solomon and SoCalled's *HipHopKhasene*," *Ethnomusicology Forum* 16, no. 2 (2007): 245.

[112] For the story of Abba Kovner, see Tom Segev, *The Seventh Million: The Israelis and the Holocaust* (New York: Henry Holt, 2000).

Six million Germans
They didn't want the war to end
Six million Germans
They wanted one thing—*Nakam*: Revenge

For every Jew the Nazis gassed
For every racist law they passed
For every wrong that wasn't right
For all the dead *Nakam* would fight.[113]

Daniel Kahn is a Jewish American musician who came to Berlin in 2005 from Detroit in order to found his unusual klezmer band. The music The Painted Bird plays combines the political content of socialist Yiddish songs, the dark style of Tom Waits, and the subversive humor of Brechtian theater. "I could try to rationalize it and say that it's to counteract all of the sentimentality and kitsch, not only within the German Jewish music scene," says Kahn, "but on the other hand, I think there is room for this music, there is room for something heavy, dark, punk-rock, gothic folk, negative, and political. I think there is room for that in Jewish music . . . this music had teeth, too."[114] In Kahn's opinion, innovation should be the crucial feature of the klezmer revival: "Any modern music movement, if it's gonna be interesting, it has to be innovative, imaginative. The thing about Yiddish music that draws me to it is that it has to be an innovative and imaginative project because the culture was murdered, so we have to do a kind of Frankenstein thing."[115] Bringing klezmer back to life means for Kahn not only resurrecting the genre but crossbreeding it together with other musical impulses.

And so the Berlin klezmer scene buzzes with new ideas. There are klezmer dancing events, mockingly called by some musicians "klez-robic,"[116] new Yiddish songs being written, and a lot of fusion and experimentation in instrumental music. The music of Fayvish, marketed as "Yiddpop," could well belong to the pop mainstream, if not for the fact that all their lyrics are in Yiddish and speak of the Jewish sweatshop laborers in the United States, or the Russian revolution. The leader of Fayvish, Fabian Schnedler, who refers to his arrangements as "Yiddish campfire music," uses both old Yiddish songs and poems, and writes new texts in Yiddish himself. Performing in several klezmer bands, Schnedler hopes to demonstrate with his work that the shtetl world contained all kinds of Yiddish music. "In the Yiddish world there were Socialists, Zionists, Communists," lists Schnedler, "and they all made music." It is important for him, he declares, to break people's

[113] Daniel Kahn and The Painted Bird, "Six Million Germans," *Partisans and Parasites*, Oriente, 2009, CD.

[114] Daniel Kahn, interview by the author, Berlin, January 17, 2006.

[115] Daniel Kahn, cited in Stührmann, "Six million Germans!"

[116] Wegener interview.

cliché of Yiddish culture as "a museum that is nice to look at." Yiddish is a language that is still spoken, and there are artists creating Yiddish culture in many places of the world, he points out. With his Fayvish project, Schnedler wants to locate himself as part of the "global shtetl." "Neither fish (not even *gefilte*) nor meat, rather a fish-burger with horseradish," Schnedler defines his musical mixture on his website.[117]

Ahava Raba, although named after a Jewish prayer, is not a very traditional klezmer band, either. Simon Jacob Drees, the man behind the project, takes Jewish heritage music as the warp around which to weave his own antiformalist and antistructuralist music. Yiddish songs were the departure point for him, but with time he moved on to developing what he calls a "free, imagined language."[118] Drees rejects on principle preexisting formats, choosing improvisation and spontaneous free speech as a means of musical expression. The Jewish tradition, however, in particular the Hasidic *nigun*, is important to him. Considering the collective vocal chants of the Hasidim as a prototype of spontaneous musical expression, the Ahava Raba musicians see themselves as innovative but rooted in the heritage of Jewish traditional music.

One of the most popular ways of giving klezmer a new edge is, however, mixing it with other styles of ethnic music, or with jazz. And thus in 2008, klezmer concerts staged in Berlin included, for example, "traditional Berlin Balkan Klezmer Surfspeedpunkfolk" by the Berlin-based Miserlou, and a hybrid of house music and Greek, Israeli, and Yiddish folk by a band whose very name (JewDyssee) promised a musical journey.[119] Hybridization of klezmer has, in fact, many enthusiasts. When the Berlin-based VonGinzburgBand launched their KlezmerJazzFusion project, a music journalist wrote that they "catapulted klezmer music into the new millennium."[120] Another critic applauded the JewDyssee project for making the old music "really groove."[121] Other Berlin bands, such as Paul Brody's Sadawi, who produce their records on the Radical Jewish Culture label, are also very successful in serving what they call a "healthy mix of traditional klezmer and fantasyful improvisations."[122] Sadawi's Jewish American trumpet-player, Paul Brody, defines their sound on the band's website in a truly onomatopoeic way: "A bass clarinet jamming with a banjo on a blues hora, a growling Ellingtonish trumpet battling through tribal bulgar beats, a Hasidic folk

[117] "Fayvish's website," accessed June 14, 2009, http://www.myspace.com/fayvish.

[118] Drees interview.

[119] "Miserlou's website," accessed June 1, 2009, www.myspace.com/miserloumusik; *Zitty. Illustrierte Stadtzeitung*, no. 20, 2008.

[120] Shelly Kupferberg, cited on "Von Ginzburg Band website," accessed February 15, 2008, http://www.vonginzburgband.de/band_de/band/index.htm.

[121] Jonathan Scheiner, "Wenn Jiddisch richtig groovt," *Jüdische Allgemeine*, no. 11/09, March 12, 2009, 9.

[122] "Paul Brody's website," accessed February 15, 2008, http://www.paulbrody.net/projects/index.php.

song woven around impressionistic trance beats and prayer loops squeezed though the soundboard of a guitar."[123] Surely, eclectic klezmer is at home in Berlin.

But while fusing klezmer with pop, rock or jazz redefines the boundaries of the genre, experimentation on the German klezmer scene goes farther than that. *Alpen Klezmer* (2012) by the Munich-based vocalist Andrea Pancur and accordionist Ilya Shneyveys from Riga brings together the most emblematically German folk music—Bavarian—with Yiddish songs and klezmer. The seemingly impossible—and perhaps improper—fusion turns out neither oxymoronic nor redemptive; instead it pointedly reveals the deep links of German and Yiddish musical traditions. Pancur and Shneyveys, alongside with an ensemble featuring some of the most distinguished klezmer musicians worldwide, explore forgotten parallels and cultural transfers, and enable a unique musical dialogue, in which German and Jewish musicians not only speak to each other in their respective idioms, but also borrow one another's voice, and counterpoint each other. Blending Yiddish and yodeling stands here for more than postmodern hybridity—it is a deeply informed and emotional attempt at investigating one's own heritage through the lens of the music of the other.[124]

Conclusion

Projects like *Alpen Klezmer* point to a social need that seems to underlie the klezmer revival both in Germany and in Poland—namely that to incorporate Jewish heritage into the vision of a (lost) multi-ethnic society. This happens along slightly different lines in Kraków and Berlin. While Jewish heritage in Poland is inscribed into the romantic tableau of the prewar pluralist universe of the shtetl, in Germany it forms part of the contemporary cosmopolitan urban spirit, incarnated by the world music scene.

The klezmer revival is not really about evoking selected elements from some defined reservoir of "Jewish culture." More importantly, it is about redefining the category of "Jewish heritage" anew—also by means of bringing it in a dialogue with the German or the Polish element. According to Oswald de Andrade, the result of cultural anthropophagy is a new language of expression (see Introduction). This end product takes shape in the process of appropriation and is, naturally, marked by a confrontation with the culture it draws on, but it is also novel, unprecedented, and autonomous. It is neither a copy of what underwent borrowing nor is it something emerging exclusively from the target culture. Instead, it constitutes a "third space," and is characterized by something we could call the

---

[123] Ibid.
[124] Pancur Andrea and Ilya Shneyveys, *Alpen Klezmer*, Globalistas Records, 2012, CD.

"third quality." The new language of klezmer is indeed born of a fusion of two (or more) other tongues, but it becomes a medium of communication in its own right, possibly even a "native language" to its new users.

If we want to extend this linguistic metaphor, we could compare the revived klezmer to a creole. Creolization is the emergence of a new language, generated in the process of fusion and amalgamation. Coined in the colonial context, the term illustrates the process of new language formation in places where European languages, imposed by colonizers, merged with local idioms. A new variety emerging from this encounter of languages is a pidgin, which in time expands its functions and becomes a mother tongue of the new generation: a creole.[125] The new vernacular klezmer resembles a creole: it emerged in a process of mixing, simplifying, and making compromises and also because it is often received negatively as contamination or distortion. Creoles were long understood as bastardized, corrupted, and inferior languages.

Indeed, the language metaphor seems to be valid for the klezmer scene in Germany and Poland. The name of a Berlin klezmer band Tants in Gartn Eydn for example, is spelled in a "creolized" Yiddish. "Garden" is *gortn* in Yiddish, but in this particular collocation it is pronounced *gan-eydn*. The musicians of Tants in Gartn Eydn realize that the band's name is not in correct Yiddish, but they spell it this way so that their German audience can understand the name more easily. Thus, in the process of appropriation, the language of klezmer transforms.

This process is, of course, conditioned by the needs of the new klezmer audiences who do not know Yiddish. Carsten Wegener of Tants in Gartn Eydn admits that his manner of singing is also modified by the fact that the addressees of his music speak a different language: "When I sing . . . I'm surely making mistakes, and mixing some dialects together, but when I sing, it's not at the center of my attention. . . . In the text there are some words that the Germans can understand, and when I'm singing, I'm probably pronouncing them in such a way, consciously or unconsciously, so that the Germans can understand them."[126] It is the new role of the music that determines the performance here, not linguistic accuracy.

The creolization of Yiddish, the language of klezmer, has one more dimension. A number of klezmer ensembles, particularly in Germany, use derogative Yiddish terms for a non-Jew (*goy*), or a non-Jewish girl (*shickse*) in their band names. Names such as Klezgoyim or Klezmerschicksen serve to manifest the identity of the musicians, but they also have a subversive function. They translate a negative term into a positive identity marker, or even express a new approach to Jewish music, such as in the case of the Neue Goyische Musik. The non-Jewish musicians using such names are usually aware of the emotional charge of these Yiddish

---

[125] Suzanne Romaine, "Pidgins and Creoles: Overview," in *Encyclopaedia of Language and Linguistics*, ed. Keith Brown (Amsterdam: Elseviere, 2006), 600–606.

[126] Wegener interview.

words and use them deliberately. At times, however, their choices result in unintended puns for Yiddish speakers. Thus, a Dutch all-female band who named themselves Di Kalles (*kale* means bride in Yiddish) was surprised to find out from a Yiddish-English translator that the plural *kales* might also translate as "The Silly Sluts."[127]

These language games are less common in Poland, where the musicians and their audiences are also less conversant with Yiddish. It is much more common that klezmer with a Polish inflection amounts to translating traditional Yiddish songs into Polish. But, as we have seen in the example of "Chopin's Freilach" by Di Galitzyaner Klezmorim and *New Polish Klezmer Music* by Jarek Adamów it is also Polish heritage that can become inflected the Jewish way. Just as in Germany, klezmer is also deconstructed in Poland and reassembled according to a cultural grammar familiar to Poles. This transformation might often entail simplification, but it can also evolve into a full-fledged idiom, which then becomes a mother tongue to the initial appropriators.

Adapting Jewish culture to the needs of a different community of consumers naturally involves an entirely new set of tools different than those in the case of a heritage revival enfolding within the limits of one ethnic group. The most fundamental difference concerns here the concept of "authenticity." Authenticity belongs to the main preoccupations of revivalists who "rediscover" their own heritage. This is so because the very function of such a revival is to draw on one's own past to look for a "true" and "genuine" model of collective identity. It is the postulated authenticity of heritage that makes it attractive. And it is its preservation that motivates the revivalists, who might also, in their fervor, become purists. In the context of cultural appropriation, the notion of authenticity loses its significance. The borrowed product must be, first of all, readable to its new users. Communicability and functionality, not authenticity, become of supreme importance.

And while this search for authentic Jewish music inspired the fascination with Eastern European Jewish folk music within the Zionist movement, or the beginnings of the klezmer revival in the United States, it is futile to consider non-Jewish klezmer in Europe in terms of authenticity. The stake is different here and the role of klezmer music has diametrically changed. The new klezmer is no more the idiom of the shtetl but a creole of postmodern popular culture. And in contemporary Poland and Germany, where the genre became the soundtrack to collective rituals of remembering, it becomes harnessed to fulfill new social functions and is given new political significance.

---

[127] Michael Wex, *Born to Kvetch: Yiddish Language and Culture in All of Its Moods* (New York: Harper, 2005), 240.

5

Performing Memory

Klezmer and the Politics of Remembering

Tova Reich, in her controversial novel *My Holocaust* (2007), stigmatizes the instrumentalization of the Shoah in uncompromising, satirical language and does not spare the klezmer revivalists. In one of the central episodes of the novel, set in the Birkenau concentration camp, Reich presents today's klezmer: grotesque Reb Tikkun from the Shtetls. Reb Tikkun (Heb: the mending of the world), who is "dressed like a Polish peasant except for a fringed garment over his white shirt and black vest, . . . the beard and curled sidelocks," comes to the camp to commemorate Holocaust victims by jamming on his "klezmer fiddle." His performance soon turns into an absurd musical duel against another character, who tries to hijack the commemorative event by listing the victims of the "African American Holocaust." In response, Reb Tikkun starts rhythmically chanting, to the melody of a Yiddish dirge, camp numbers of gassed Jews.[1]

Is such "mending of the world" really the concern of klezmer revivalists? Most klezmer bands and Yiddish singers both in Poland and in Germany have indeed performed at various celebrations commemorating the Holocaust, such as Yom Hashoah, or anniversaries of Kristallnacht and liberation of concentration camps. Some musicians produce records that could even be considered as commemorative projects in themselves. Brave Old World issued *Song of the Lodz Ghetto* (2005), which featured, alongside new arrangements, ethnographic recordings of survivors from Lódź singing songs they remembered from the ghetto. The Wrocław-based singer Bente Kahan has in her repertoire several programs that refer to the Holocaust, such as the musical drama *Voices from Theresienstadt*. And the "king of klezmer," Giora Feidman, created a Holocaust commemoration program: Wenn du singst, wie kannst du hassen? [When you sing, how can you hate?], which was later made into a film featuring Feidman playing klezmer in Birkenau.[2]

---

[1] Tova Reich, *My Holocaust* (New York: Harper Collins Publishers, 2007), 172.

[2] *Wenn du singst, wie kannst du hassen?* directed by Jens Scheffler (NDR, 1995) VHS.

Holocaust commemoration has important implications, especially for the klezmer scene in Kraków. With Kazimierz being a transit point for Holocaust tourists heading to Auschwitz and a stage for many commemorative initiatives, the musicians performing in the Jewish-style restaurants of the district find themselves, willingly or not, at the center of this commemorative process. It is not surprising that this junction of commemoration and entertainment seems to many an uncomfortable place. "It is often the case that they [the concert audience] have come here right after a trip to Auschwitz," recounts Maciej Inglot, who performs in one of the restaurants in Kazimierz. "They are often in a state of heavy shock, wondering how this could have happened, how a man could have become such a beast. And then, at once, these people, in this state of shock, are facing us. They don't know what to think, how to behave, and we are supposed to play Jewish music for them."[3] The apparent contradiction between concerts of Jewish wedding music staged in Kazimierz and Auschwitz-bound Holocaust tourism might be difficult to handle, but it can also offer a unique chance to address those who come to Poland to visit sites of Jewish death.

The late Chris Schwarz, founder of the Galicia Jewish Museum in Kraków, believed that by staging concerts of klezmer for Holocaust tourists, he could offer the traumatized Auschwitz visitors a lively counterrepresentation of Jewishness. "We have here a lot of groups from America and Israel, doing their tour of Auschwitz," he said.

> Auschwitz tells you nothing about Jewish culture. Auschwitz is, in fact, a monument to Nazi ideology. So what I say is: after you have been to Auschwitz, come, look around this museum, and then we put on a really nice, good klezmer band for you. And it works! We had one school group here, they were from a socially deprived area of London, there were a lot of black kids, they had never heard music like that. . . . And here, I thought, this is going to bore them, they are going to hate it. But it was the opposite, and I was amazed. They were all punching the air, saying "This is cool man," "This is fantastic," "This is the best we have ever had."[4]

The concerts at the Galicia Museum are supposed to complement the somber visit at the concentration camp and be a tool of education. Here klezmer becomes a medium to tell the visitors about the flourishing Jewish life in prewar Kraków, but also about the survival of Jewish heritage in post-Holocaust Poland, even if not always in Jewish hands. In this way, klezmer concerts provide a counterpoint

---

[3] Inglot interview.
[4] C. Schwarz interview.

to the visit at the concentration camp; they also function as a site of abreaction, a space where Holocaust tourists can reflect on their fresh experiences. This creates a great challenge for the local klezmer musicians.

Urszula Makosz, a Yiddish singer from Kraków, is convinced that her work is also a form of commemoration. The emotional response of some of her specta-tors, who cry during her concerts and share their memories with her, has made her aware of the responsibility she has as an artist. For one of the programs she performs at the Galicia Jewish Museum in Kraków, she selected songs of the Jewish resistance movement in order to pay tribute to the artistic production of Jews during the Holocaust. The CD that resulted from this program, *Dos lid funem khurbn* [The Song of the Holocaust], was released in 2005.[5]

For some klezmer performers all Jewish music relates to the Shoah. The mel-ancholy and sadness of some prewar Yiddish songs are thus interpreted by many as a prefiguration of the catastrophe to come. Katarzyna Jamróz, who performs in Leopold Kozłowski's ensemble, states that "the way you can cry out songs in Yiddish, you cannot sing in any other language."[6] The musicians of Kroke, in turn, believe that klezmer music expresses an invitation to "meditation and nostalgia."[7]

The idea of framing Jewish music, and Jewish heritage more generally, ex-clusively through the lens of the Holocaust, is not uncontroversial, though. The late Cracovian writer, Henryk Halkowski, argued that creating a narra-tive of Jewish Kraków that focused only on the Holocaust and what he termed "Schindler's myth" was incorrect. Picturing the Jews of Kraków solely as victims of the Holocaust reduces Jewish *Polin*—the place that, according to legend, was indicated to Jewish settlers by God—to "Auschwitzland." This, to Halkowski, has made not only the Jewish identity but also the Polish identity "handicapped."[8]

This critique notwithstanding, klezmer concerts in Kraków will continue being part of the Holocaust tourist experience in Poland. Also, because of the vicinity of Kraków to Auschwitz, Kazimierz will remain a crucial node of what William Miles calls "darker tourism."[9] The Holocaust might be just one of the frames through which Polish klezmer musicians approach the music they play, but it is one which is impossible to escape, at least in Kazimierz. Although many klezmer artists see their work rather as a counterrepresentation to the death and destruction that the Holocaust stands for, all the *klezmorim* performing in Kraków have to face

---

[5] Makosz interview.

[6] Katarzyna Jamróz, interview by the author, Kraków, April 19, 2004.

[7] Kroke interview, April 18, 2004.

[8] Henryk Halkowski, "A World Before a Catastrophe?" in *A World Before a Catastrophe: Kraków's Jews between the Wars* (Kraków: International Cultural Centre, 2007), 25ff.

[9] William, F. S. Miles , "Auschwitz: Museum Interpretation and Darker Tourism," *Annals of Tourism Research* 29, no. 4 (2002): 1175–78.

the ongoing process of Holocaust commemoration and respond to the particular needs of their audiences who are doing "memory work."

It is not much different in Germany. Although Berlin might not lie directly on the route to a death camp, the city is an important destination for anybody interested in the history of National Socialism; it has become the central location for the German *lieux de memoire*—sites of memory—related to the Holocaust. Klezmer music has also been, since its early days in Germany, part of ritualized commemorations of the Holocaust. The Berlin Days of Yiddish Culture, first organized in 1987 in East Berlin, understood its mission distinctly as *Trauerarbeit*—the "work of mourning."[10] For this reason the festival, which became one of the most important stages for Jewish folk music in Germany, was annually scheduled around January 27, the anniversary of the liberation of Auschwitz-Birkenau. With time, klezmer music has also become the standard musical accompaniment to Holocaust commemoration events. While the anniversaries of the Kristallnacht pogrom, annually observed in Berlin on November 9, would until the 1980s usually include a concert of either classical or synagogal music, the events have now begun to feature klezmer music.[11] Currently, klezmer musicians are invited to many official Holocaust commemorations, including those on a state level. Thus, Giora Feidman, celebrated as Germany's "king of klezmer," performed in front of the German Bundestag for the Holocaust Commemoration Day in 2000. Dozens of other similar events, organized by local municipalities, Jewish communities, church congregations, cultural institutions, and even political parties, likewise hire klezmer musicians. Klezmer and Yiddish songs accompany celebrations at sites of persecution or deportation of Jews, in synagogues and churches, and even at antifascist demonstrations.

Jan Hermerschmidt of Aufwind, whose band usually gives such concerts on the anniversary of Kristallnacht, describes the formula of such events in the following way: "On the ninth of November we almost always play in a church. . . . Usually, the pastor is reading from some relevant psalm, and says a little bit about how it was for Jews in that particular place, where they were deported to, etc."[12] Not all commemoration scenarios follow this pattern. Some musicians bring Holocaust commemoration into a completely new context. The singer and songwriter Daniel Kahn, who writes new Holocaust-inspired songs, performs them in Berlin's clubs and bars. One of his songs, "Birkenau," evokes the central visual

---

[10] Hans-Dieter Dyroff, "Die jiddische Kultur—wichtiger Teil unserer schöpferischen Vielfalt," in *Doss lid is geblibn: Tage der Jiddischen Kultur 1987–1996*, ed. Andrej Jendrusch (Bonn: Deutsche UNESCO-Kommission, 1995), 3.

[11] On the basis of materials of the *Archiv der Stiftung Neue Synagoge Berlin Centrum Judaicum*, signatures: (5B1 217 68), (5B1 228 106), (5B1 218 162).

[12] Hermerschmidt interview.

icons of the Holocaust: a watchtower, the gate to the concentration camp in Auschwitz, the "pit full of lye":

> The day it is done and the twilight is nigh,
> The sun is replaced with a watchtower eye
> And the clouds have been stained with an ominous dye,
> Like the butcher has wiped off his knife on the sky.
> The cold iron letters read "ARBEIT MACHT FREI"
> And it may seem a lie but it's hard to deny,
> If your work is to try to forget how to cry
> And your *freiheit* is found in a pit full of lye.[13]

Kahn does not create music for the purpose of Holocaust commemoration; he confronts his German audience with texts relating to the Holocaust in order to trigger an ongoing process of *Vergangenheitsbewältigung*—"handling the past." Kahn, who admits to be "haunted by the Holocaust," believes that the German "national process of shame" should become extended also into what he calls *Heuteverarbeitung* and *Zukunftsbearbeitung*.[14] In other words, Germans should learn how to deal not only with their dark past but also work on their present and the future.

Despite the fact that using Jewish folk music for Holocaust commemoration events is a very common practice in Germany, many musicians have second thoughts about it and are reluctant to perform for such occasions. Max Hacker of Di Grine Kuzine remembers one such performance, which left him with many reflections on the role of German musicians in Holocaust commemoration. The commemorative event took place at the Grunewald *S-Bahn* station in Berlin, which had served as a deportation point for local Jews:

> It was very cold and very early. It was in the winter at 7 a.m. in the morning. It was freezing cold, below zero. . . . It was weird, because we were playing Jewish music and we were not Jewish. But they hired us, so they must have had a reason to ask us. The playing was pretty intense, because people were really listening. First, there was a speech by Claudia Roth,[15] I think she was part of the group who initiated a monument there; when she finished, she said: "And now, there will be some music," and everybody was looking at us—just two people standing there with all the press and cameras around. . . . It was a little weird and a little moving, too. You try to figure out how it must have been at this station fifty years ago, and you can't understand how it really was.[16]

---

[13] Daniel Kahn, "Birkenau," *The Broken Tongue*, Chamsa Records, 2006, CD.
[14] Kahn, cited in Stührmann, "Six Million Germans!"
[15] The chair of the Green Party in Germany.
[16] Hacker interview.

Detlef Pegelow of Tants in Gartn Eydn also reports having a "very odd feeling" about practices that connect klezmer music to the Holocaust.[17] Alexandra Dimitroff of Di Grine Kuzine goes as far as to say that playing klezmer music for such occasions is "a bad exorcism" because German folk, classical, or even rock music could also convey a message of empathy with Holocaust victims.[18] To Ulrike Kloock of the Klezmer-Orchester, performing klezmer for a Holocaust-related event is "almost macabre"; she would find it more appropriate to invite, instead of a klezmer band, "a modern ensemble with a rough sound which really hurts when you listen to it."[19] Heiko Lehmann, who belongs to the pioneers of the klezmer revival in Berlin, also has some reservations toward Holocaust commemorations that use klezmer as their soundtrack:

> I respect these events. But I don't want to be on stage there playing the music, for two reasons. The first is that this music is not a museum for me, it's alive. . . . The second reason is that it is a meeting of people who suffered, you can't name it. They were in the Holocaust on the victims' side and they meet because they can't forget it. Why should *I* stand there and play music? Why should I stand there and play *Yiddish songs*?[20]

The preoccupations of the German musicians concern two different issues. One of them, as Hacker and Lehmann suggest, is the fact that non-Jewish musicians might feel inadequate in a situation where they represent what is understood as the music of the Jewish victims in a commemorative context. The other is the dissonance between the original function of the genre (klezmer as wedding music) and its postulated use (honoring the dead). The unfortunate and, from the perspective of many German klezmer musicians, unwanted connection between klezmer and the Holocaust does not correspond to how they approach the genre they play. In their eyes, klezmer stands for the vitality of Jewish life and is, therefore, antithetical to the representations of Jews merely as victims of the Holocaust. Martin Borbonus, who plays klezmer for dancing, states: "We like this music and we want to have fun with it. Our intention is to show that this culture is not only the Holocaust, dying and suffering, but that Jews also had nice parties—they had fun and made happy music, too."[21] Jan Hermerschmidt adds that, even when invited to a Holocaust commemoration event, his band "always plays a happy program, anyway." He also concludes, "We don't want people to think: 'Oh no, I'm going to this ninth of November thing, everything will be so sad there.'"[22] Clearly, klezmer as the soundtrack to Holocaust commemorations embodies a morbid oxymoron.

---

[17] Pegelow interview.

[18] Dimitroff interview.

[19] Kloock interview.

[20] Heiko Lehmann, interview, Berlin, June 16, 2005.

[21] Borbonus interview.

[22] Hermerschmidt interview.

The relation of the klezmer revival to the process of coming to terms with the Holocaust in Germany is crucial, though. But should we perceive the klezmer boom as an offshoot of the German process of coming to grips with the Holocaust? Or rather, is the revival of "happy Jewish music" a counterreaction to the saturation of Holocaust imagery in Germany?

"The New Desire for Life—Klezmer," reads a headline in *Tip*, a Berlin cultural magazine, in 1996.[23] The smiling faces of klezmer musicians on the cover testify to the vitality of the booming scene. "Life" is the key word here. Nothing is a more powerful celebration of life than a wedding. And it is wedding music that is the embodiment of what is the most vigorous in folk culture. Snorre Schwarz of Di Grine Kuzine, when asked about what attracted him to klezmer, states that the genre was simply strikingly different from the usual associations that a German might have with Jews: "When you read about Jews in Germany, they are always in the victim position, of course," says Schwarz. "But this was a totally different approach: fantastic, lively, strong, sometimes mean, funny music. It was something very alive. That's why I was so fascinated."[24] Fabian Schnedler believes that this vital and joyful element that klezmer incarnates stands in sharp contrast to the imagery associated with Yiddish songs. "Both in the GDR and in West Germany," says Schnedler, "Yiddish songs had the flavor of ghetto songs, and sad songs. It changed with the klezmer revival, as it expressed the idea of happy Jewish music."[25] Till Schumann of the Berlin-based label Oriente, which has issued records by several of the local klezmer bands, is even inclined to say that klezmer is just like any other kind of world music and "became a musical genre just like tango and flamenco, which can serve for Saturday-night entertainment."[26] But does klezmer really function as an appealing representation of Jewish culture minus the Holocaust?

One of the consequences of the intensive *Erinnerungsarbeit*, or "memory work," of the 1980s was that Jewish culture in Germany was mostly presented in the context of the Holocaust. However important it was to bring the Holocaust into the collective consciousness of Germans, framing Jews in the first place as victims of genocide at times eclipsed the narrative of their life before the catastrophe. The klezmer boom emerging in the aftermath of this debate might indicate a social demand for this other, alternative frame, focused on Jewish life, not death. On the other hand, however, this yearning for an image of Jewishness untainted by the German history of atrocity might be also read, and indeed has already been read, as a tendency to historicize the Holocaust.[27] But we can certainly ask if klezmer

---

[23] "Die neue Lust am Leben: Klezmer!" *Tip Berlin*, November 27, 1996, 26–31.

[24] S. Schwarz interview.

[25] Schnedler interview.

[26] Schumann interview.

[27] See Joel Rubin, "Ambivalente Identitäten: Die Amerikanische Klezmer-Bewegung als Reaktion auf Krise und Trauma," in *Berichte aus dem ICTM-Nationalkomitee Deutschland*, vol. 13, ed. Marianne Bröcker (Bamberg, 2004), 95ff.

really is dissociable from the Holocaust, and if the klezmer scene is indeed a cultural enclave comfortably protected from Germany's dark history. The role that klezmer music plays in the rituals of commemoration suggests the opposite, and so does the way klezmer becomes politicized. Just as klezmer is inscribed into the public practice of collective remembering of the Holocaust, the Holocaust is inescapably inscribed into klezmer. The genre might lure audiences in Poland and Germany with escapism, but it is unlikely ever to become mere "Saturday-night entertainment."

Politicization of Klezmer

One of the reasons why klezmer will always be a charged genre is the music's political potential, which has manifested itself in the revival from its very inception. Indeed, Ottens and Rubin note that in the 1970s klezmer played an important role for the young generation of Jewish Americans who protested against the right-wing political attitude of the Jewish American establishment toward Israel.[28] The klezmer revival was in this respect a "counterculture phenomenon," as Strom puts it—a movement searching for a spatial and cultural reference point alternative to Israel.[29] Even today, messages of social or political critique are not uncommon on the international klezmer scene. The American all-female klezmer band Mikveh has been engaged in a feminist campaign to stop violence against women, and the celebrated Klezmatics advocated progressive gender politics in their songs and also commented on 9/11 in their cover of Holly Near's famous "I Ain't Afraid." Socialist and Communist songs, including the Yiddish "Internationale," are also in the repertoire of the American klezmorim, reminding us that the political involvement of Yiddish-speaking Jews originated in the Old World. But the political potential of klezmer has also become apparent in Germany and Poland, where the music itself has become a political statement.

The early wave of interest in Yiddish songs in West Germany dates back to the 1960s and the German student movement. Peter Rohland, with his 1963 program "Der Rebbe singt" [The rabbi sings], is considered the first German singer to have broken the postwar silence over the Nazi persecution of Jews and made a gesture of reconciliation.[30] His manifesto concerning the treatment of Yiddish songs as part of German folk music was received as programmatic.[31] Yiddish songs thus came to be employed by left-wing artists as a means of protest against the generation compromised by its participation in the Nazi regime. However, despite the

---

[28] Ottens and Rubin, *Klezmer-Musik*, 296.

[29] Michael Alpert cited in Strom, *The Book of Klezmer*, 224.

[30] Eckhard Holler, "The Burg Waldeck Festivals, 1964–1969," in *Protest Song in East and West Germany since the 1960s*, ed. David Robb (Rochester, NY: Camden House, 2007), 102–3.

[31] Holger Böning, "Die Anfänge musikalischen Protests in der Bundesrepublik und der DDR: Ausländische Einflüsse im politischen Lied," in *Rebellische Musik: Gesellschaftliche Protest und kulturel- ler Wandel um 1968*, ed. Arnold Jacobshagen and Markus Leniger (Köln: Dohr, 2007), 183.

success of some of the bands, which included Yiddish songs in their repertoire, the music was never really used for political purposes on a mass scale. What ultimately prevented such an instrumentalization of Yiddish songs was the anti-Zionist sentiment on the leftist scene that resented the possible association of Jewish music with the state of Israel.[32]

The beginnings of the klezmer revival in the 1980s coincided with intensive historical debates in West Germany and with a very particular political momentum in the GDR. Jewish music in East Germany had a specific political significance. Musicians who performed it in the GDR and who, in 1987, organized the first festival of Yiddish culture in East Berlin, report that their activities always met with suspicion from the authorities. Jalda Rebling, daughter of Lin Jaldati, the "First Lady" of Yiddish song in the GDR, recalls that after the Six Days War, her mother received an informal work ban and was hardly allowed to perform.[33] According to Jan Hermerschmidt, the band Aufwind, founded in 1984, also came to the attention of the Stasi (secret police of the GDR), whose officers would occasionally attend the concerts to see if Aufwind's songs did not have a Zionist content.[34] Hermerschmidt remembers that there was a lot of debate concerning the lyrics of their songs and that the band had a hard time issuing their first recording. Only once the authorities made sure that Aufwind's music "had nothing to do with Israel, but with Eastern Europe," did they lose interest in the band.[35]

Musicians dealing with Jewish heritage music in the GDR saw their concerts as politically significant. Hermerschmidt emphasizes that Aufwind's performances were a form of political protest, because the musicians were "saying on stage things that were not taught in a socialist school."[36] Jalda Rebling remembers, in turn, that the anniversary of the Kristallnacht (November 9) was a good date for a dissident event, which would be safe to attend. "The particular thing with Yiddish music," says Rebling, "was that they did not dare to act against it."[37] She remembers that concerts of Yiddish music in the 1980s attracted people critical of the Communist regime. A vast majority of people would attend the Kristallnacht gatherings "because it was an alternative event, outside of the official cultural schedule of East Germany."[38] Since Yiddish concerts concerned the "Jewish question," one could take part in them "without having to fear awful consequences," recounts Rebling.[39] Yiddish, which, as she puts it, "has never been the language of violence, [but rather] the language of those who had no power," gained a new

---

[32] Eckstaedt, "*Klaus mit der Fiedel, Heike mit dem Bass*," 29.

[33] Rebling interview, February 6, 2006.

[34] Research in the *Archiv der Stasi-Unterlagen-Behörde*, Berlin, did not bring confirmation that Aufwind was under the observation of Stasi.

[35] Hermerschmidt interview.

[36] Ibid.

[37] Rebling interview, February 6, 2006.

[38] Ibid.

[39] Ibid.

symbolic meaning. Thereafter, Yiddish culture came to be understood as "the culture of resistance . . . of fighting against a major power."[40]

The Communist authorities also realized the importance of Yiddish songs and
made use of them for their own purposes. Yiddish songs, especially those with
revolutionary content, were performed during flagship commemoration events.
Kristallnacht anniversaries over the entire period from 1948 to 1988 were used as
a vehicle for Communist propaganda. Political speeches emphasized on such occasions that anti-Semitism was a problem of German monopolistic capitalism, and
that the GDR guaranteed its Jewish citizens the security that the Western states
were unable to offer.[41] Beyond such official statements, though, Jewish culture
was not necessarily welcome in the public domain of the GDR.

Yiddish songs were also a way for the Communist authorities to convey Soviet
propaganda. Particularly the new Yiddish songs, written in the Jewish Autonomous Oblast of Birobidzhan, were used to praise the Soviet system. An anthology
of Yiddish songs titled Es brennt, Brüder, es brennt [It's burning, brothers, it's burn-
ing], first published in 1966 in East Berlin, makes this evident. The introduction to
the collection, edited by Lin Jaldati and Eberhard Rebling, unmistakably captures
the mood of the political correctness of the day. "Despite the injustice related to
the emergence of Stalin's personality cult," comment the editors, "[a] song from
Birobidzhan celebrates the new life of Jews under Socialism, free from misery
and existential fear. The melancholy, which suppressed joy in the past, has disappeared here, and bright optimism emanates from this and many other songs from
Birobidzhan."[42] The "brightly optimistic" song "Dos Lid fun Birobidshan," cited in
the anthology, celebrates industrial progress in Birobidzhan's wilderness under
Soviet rule, emphasizing the Jewish bliss in the new province:

Zwischn gdichte welder	Through dense woods
Jogt mit frajt a ban,	Merrily speeds a train
Naje jidn kumen	New Jews are coming
In Birobidshan.	to Birobidzhan
Un ojf frische felder	And on fresh fields
Schtroj ojf najen dach:	Straw for the new roof
's hobn asoj jidn	And Jews have never
Kejnmol nischt gelacht![43]	laughed like that before!

---

[40] Ibid.

[41] Bodemann, Gedächtnistheater, 103.

[42] Lin Jaldati and Eberhard Rebling, eds., Es brennt, Brüder, es brennt: Jiddische Lieder (Berlin:
Rütten & Loening, 1985), 22.

[43] Lin Jaldati and Eberhard Rebling, eds., Es brennt, Brüder, es brennt: Jiddische Lieder (Berlin:
Rütten & Loening, 1969), 186. Translated into English by the author.

Despite the fact that Yiddish songs were often the paragon of political correctness, the first festival of Yiddish culture in Berlin in 1987 did not take place without some obstacles created by the authorities. Jalda Rebling, one of the organizers, had to seek political support for the idea of the festival, and only after the *Komitee für Unterhaltungskunst* [Committee for Entertainment] approved the project could she proceed with the preparations. Despite the backing received from the committee, the organizers faced the threat of the festival being called off a few days before it was scheduled. According to Rebling, the responsible authorities panicked at the last moment when West German media sent their reporters to East Berlin to document the festival. Finally, however, the authorities gave it a green light, after making sure that the festival would center on Soviet artists.[44]

Although it was officially part of East German state policy to support the dwindling Jewish community, it was only under Erich Honecker that the limitations put on Jewish life were noticeably reduced. In 1981 Klaus Gysi, East German State Minister for Religious Affairs, declared in an interview to *Reform Judaism* magazine that although the Communist authorities were not interested in supporting religious life, they took measures to sustain the GDR's Jewish community, whose existence was crucial to the legitimacy of the antifascist state.[45] An example of such "measures" was the state-funded Synagogal Choir of Leipzig (since 1962), or the highly popular productions of *Fiddler on the Roof* in *Komische Oper* in Berlin, staged repeatedly between 1971 and 1988. Concerts of Jewish music were a convenient way of making Jewish heritage visible to the public, even in the absence of a vibrant Jewish life. Ironically, Jewish music provided accompaniment to the GDR's very demise. The 1989 celebrations of the fortieth anniversary of East Germany included, among other events, a televised concert of Yiddish and Hebrew folk music.

Jewish heritage music was hence doubly politicized in East Germany. On the one hand, concerts of Yiddish music were used as pretexts for informal gatherings and a vehicle for a subtle antitotalitarian opposition in the late 1980s. On the other hand, the Communist regime itself made use of Jewish culture, presenting the GDR as an antifascist state and hoping for the approval of the western world.

After the reunification of Germany, the politicization of Jewish heritage music intensified. Klezmer bands performed at political rallies, for example, against racism, or in support of the Israeli-Palestinian peace process. *Yiddish Songs against the Nazis* [*Jiddische Lieder gegen die Nazis*] was a songbook issued in 1996 as a template for school teachers, who were thereby urged to use Yiddish music to campaign against anti-Semitism.[46] The interest of politicians in the klezmer scene probably reached its peak in 2001, when "the king of klezmer," Giora Feidman, was honored by the president of the German Bundestag, Wolfgang Thierse, and

---

[44] Rebling interview, October 18, 2006.

[45] Aron Hirt-Manheimer, "Ten Days in East Germany," *Reform Judaism* 9, no. 3 (February 1981): 1.

[46] Benjamin Ortmeyer, ed., *Jiddische Lieder gegen die Nazis* (Witterschlick/Bonn: Verlag M. Wehle, 1996).

awarded the Great Order of Merit of the Federal Republic of Germany. During the ceremony in the Reichstag building, Thierse addressed Feidman as the "great ambassador of reconciliation" who, by means of his music, "creates friendship between people and overcomes divisions."[47] This symbolic gesture of political appreciation toward one of the initiators of the klezmer revival in Germany only confirmed that Jewish heritage music had been endowed with political meaning. But attempts to instrumentalize klezmer for political purposes also came from within the Jewish community.

At the time of the Second Intifada in 2001, the head of the cultural department of the Jewish Community in Berlin, Moishe Waks, stated that the edition of the festival Jüdische Kulturtage, devoted that year to Tel Aviv, was to be a manifestation of solidarity with Israel.[48] Franka Lampe of Klezmer Techter recollects that at the beginning of the war in Iraq in 2003 her band performed at a Holocaust commemoration event where Paul Spiegel, the former leader of the Central Council of Jews, gave a prowar speech, demanding the involvement of Germany in Iraq. Lampe reports that the statement perplexed the band:

> The audience was standing there, thinking: "Oh, God, how do we react to this now? If we boo him, it's anti-Semitic." That was really strange. . . . We behaved as if nothing had happened, we were hired there to play and not to comment on any political statements. So we just played, and then people criticized us for not having commented on that. Some people were angry that we played at all.[49]

Many other musicians admit that the politicization of their performances bothers them. Carsten Wegener of Tants in Gartn Eydn, who is occasionally asked to play at rallies of left-wing parties, says that he is not keen on such gigs: "Although I am leftist myself . . . you're always afraid that you're going to be used."[50]

On the other hand, many artists consciously choose to make a political statement with Jewish music. In 2005 Konstantin Wecker, a popular German singer, together with Avitall Gerstetter, the first German female cantor, recorded a CD titled Say No to Anti-Semitism [Sage Nein zu Antisemitismus]. Wecker's title song, originally written in 1985, denounced not only the radical Right in Germany but also Holocaust deniers, giving the record a clearly political edge.[51] The income from the CD was aimed at supporting a Jewish online magazine, but the recording itself was meant to be distributed in schools, as part of a campaign against racism.

---

[47] Wolfgang Thierse, cited in Pressemeldung des Deutschen Bundestages, March 27, 2001, accessed March 4, 2008, http://webarchiv.bundestag.de/archive/2007/0814/aktuell/presse/2001/pz_0103271.html.

[48] "15. Jüdische Kulturtage," Der Tagesspiegel, October 25, 2001, 3.

[49] Lampe interview.

[50] Wegener interview.

[51] Avitall and Konstantin Wecker, Sage Nein zu Antisemitismus, Amazonas Musik, 2005, CD.

Jewish music also made it into headlines in the context of the protest against the NPD (*Nationaldemokratische Partei Deutschlands*/National Democratic Party) and the radical German Right. When in July 2007 the NPD announced a mass rally in Heiligenstadt, in Thuringia, the local Social Democrats hired the Klezmer-Orchester, the biggest klezmer ensemble in Germany, to play at the counter-demonstration. This local political showdown had an unexpected denouement, as Thuringia's local authorities banned the klezmer group from performing, fearing that klezmer would provoke the right-wing extremists to a violent confrontation. After the Social Democrats protested against the ban, a compromise was reached, and instead of the whole orchestra, only a klezmer trio played at the demonstration.[52]

Clearly, the political potential of klezmer does not escape the attention of politicians, cultural organizers, and even the musicians themselves. Although some of them resent using klezmer at political events, others engage themselves in campaigns against the NPD and anti-Semitism. The most prominent political issue that reverberates on the klezmer scene, however, is the Israeli-Palestinian conflict. The ongoing terrorist attacks and military clashes in Israel are given a lot of attention in Germany, and the klezmer scene often becomes associated with the events in Israel.

"What do you think about the Israeli-Palestinian conflict?" According to Stefan Kühne of Klezgoyim, this is one of the most common questions after his concerts. "It's bad, but what does it have to do with klezmer?" he usually answers, but his audiences are not always convinced that klezmer concerts are not meant as statements on the political situation in Israel. Sometimes what happens in Israel can influence the atmosphere of klezmer concerts in Germany. Harry Timmermann believes that the peak of the klezmer boom, which coincided with the term of Yitzhak Rabin and the hopes for peace in the Middle East, was for many klezmer fans "a way of participating in the peace process" in Israel. Timmermann recollects that after Yitzhak Rabin was assassinated in 1995, his concert on the following day "almost automatically became a memorial concert."[53]

Also, the political situation in Israel can directly influence concert schedules. During the Israeli intervention in Lebanon in 2006, a cultural institution in Trier called off the concerts of Avitall, and an Israeli jazz band, arguing that in view of the ongoing fights in Israel and Lebanon, "synagogal singing does not fit the political situation." Although the organizers withdrew their objections later on, the incident was noticed by the press and interpreted as an echo of the war in Lebanon.[54]

---

[52] "NPD-Aufmarsch: Ordnungsamt wollte jüdische Protestmusik gegen Nazis verhindern," *Spiegel Online*, June 8, 2007, accessed June 11, 2007, http://www.spiegel.de/kultur/musik/0,1518,487443,00.html.

[53] Timmermann interview.

[54] Philipp Gessler, "Jüdische Lieder unerwünscht," *Die Tageszeitung*, August 5, 2006, accessed April 6, 2008, http://www.taz.de/index.php?id=archivseite&dig=2006/08/05/a0100.

Some artists, however, consciously make a connection between klezmer and the political situation in Israel. In 2008 Daniel Kahn, in a joint project with the Russian songwriter and performer Psoy Korolenko and the Israeli klezmer band Oy Division, issued *The Unternationale*, a CD with political Yiddish songs. The lyrics of one of them, adapted from the Hasidic nigun "Dumay!" was printed in the CD booklet against the background of the Israeli Wall, and can be clearly read as a commentary on the Israeli-Palestinian conflict:

Hob ikh mir in harts a kholem	I carry in my heart a dream
heyb ikh oyf a fon fun sholem	A flag of peace and a land redeemed
Ober in mayn kholem shteyt a moyer	But in my dream is a wall of wire
ful mit payn un ful mit troyer . . .	Stone and iron, forged in fire . . .
Vos far a folk on a medine?	The land is holy, but for whom?
Say yisroel, say palestine	God of the star, or the crescent moon?[55]

Daniel Kahn also comments on the situation in Israel in "Six Million Germans." The story of Abba Kovner that the song narrates ends in Israel, with his failed attempt at vengeance as a prefiguration of the future predicament of Israelis and Palestinians.

And so Nakam was all disbanded
On Palestina's shore they landed
And Abba Kovner and his crew
Became like many other Jews

They put aside their rage and hate
And worked to build a Jewish state
With Jewish towns and Jewish farms,
Jewish guns and nuclear arms

Can vengeance put upon a shelf
Be taken out later on someone else?
Well, be careful how you read this tale
'Lest your own prejudice prevail

For look around the world today
And consider the role vengeance plays
'Cause history has its unpaid debts
And is it better if we forget?[56]

[55] Daniel Kahn, "Dumay!" *The Unternationale*, Auris Media, 2008, CD.
[56] Daniel Kahn, "Six Million Germans," *Partisans and Parasites*, Oriente, 2009, CD.

Kahn believes that his German audiences enjoy the song because it raises important questions about the status of Jews as innocent victims and also about the relationship between the Holocaust and the founding of the state of Israel.[57] Picking up on these themes, though, Kahn is not interested in providing easy or straightforward answers.

Other klezmer musicians based in Germany see klezmer and Yiddish music as unrelated, even antithetical, to the conflict in the Middle East. The Yiddish singer Karsten Troyke, for example, emphasizes that his music has "nothing to do with Israel today" because Yiddish culture symbolizes "people who never had power as a state."[58] Jan Hermerschmidt of Aufwind stresses that his band makes an active effort to "differentiate between what is Jewish and what is Israeli." Hermerschmidt looks at the state of Israel "the way it is today" very critically and confesses that his band avoids playing Israeli folk songs such as "Hava Nagila," even if requested by the audience, because they are "too nationalist."[59] Thomas Römer, a dance instructor who cooperates with Tants in Gartn Eydn in their klezmer dancing program, also feels obliged to draw a line between the Israeli folklore that he performs and the political situation in the Middle East. He says that dancing Israeli folk dances does not have a political meaning for him: "There is a dance called 'Look at the Golan Hills,' but I don't dance it because I'm in favor of occupying the hills, or because I want to give them back. The dance is not a political symbol for me . . . I dance it because it's beautiful."[60]

It is noteworthy that artists based in Germany ponder the political implications of Israeli folklore or occasionally take a stance against Israel, even if only by avoiding a certain repertoire. On the one hand, it might be related to the fact that criticism of the politics of the state of Israel is quite prominent in German public discourse. On the other hand, it also seems that the German klezmer scene is, on the whole, much more politically engaged than its counterpart in Poland. Indeed, many performers on the German klezmer scene and its peripheries do not hesitate to formulate a "message," which their music is supposed to put across.

One such artist is, clearly, Daniel Kahn. Speaking of his motivation to start dealing with Yiddish music, Kahn does not conceal that there is an ideological dimension to his revivalist work. Yiddish-language culture, he notes, has had a "long history of radical political action, and revolutionary culture."[61] Exploring this half-forgotten heritage also means for him "to go against the conservative, nationalistic, victim-based version of what it means to be a Jew in the twentieth century."[62] He is interested in providing a critique of the conservative discourse

[57] Daniel Kahn, cited in Stührmann, "Six Million Germans!"
[58] Troyke interview.
[59] Hermerschmidt interview.
[60] Thomas Römer, interview by the author, Berlin, February 28, 2006.
[61] Kahn interview.
[62] Ibid.

within the Jewish community, but also in something more than that. For Kahn, Yiddish songs belong to the universal "legacy of fighting against injustice," and address social problems that are still burning today. History repeats itself constantly, he believes, and old songs of social protest are, sadly, still relevant.

If Daniel Kahn is the voice of the revolutionary klezmer in Germany, Giora Feidman can be called the klezmer missionary par excellence. Feidman, who has been a towering figure of the German klezmer scene since the 1980s, was born in 1936 to Jewish immigrants in Argentina, and he turned to klezmer after having received an education in classical music. He moved to Israel, where he had an eighteen-year career in the Israel Philharmonic Orchestra, but it was only his overwhelming success in Germany that turned him into a celebrity and bestowed him with the titles of "King of Klezmer" and "wonder clarinetist." In the past two decades, Feidman has appeared in German feature films and documentaries, performed in front of Pope Benedict XVI, and received a selection of awards, including one for his "contribution to international understanding."[63]

Giora Feidman is most widely known, however, for his unorthodox musical projects, which aim at bringing various nations, ethnicities, and religions together via the medium of klezmer music. Feidman, whose teachings Barbara Kirshenblatt-Gimblett has compared to "romantic mysticism reminiscent of the fin-de-siècle Orientalism of Martin Buber,"[64] believes that the message he is putting across in his music has played a role in the "healing process between Jews and Germans" and that this mission has been given to him by God.[65]

Some of the German klezmer musicians admit that Giora Feidman, with his philosophy of forgiveness, played a crucial role in the klezmer revival. Ulrike Kloock from the Klezmer Orchester believes that Feidman "found a way for the people to deal with their past through music, and gave them a liberating message":

> He said that all is klezmer, and we are all the same and we want peace. . . .
> I think this is what the people want: a bit of esotericism in the concert,
> on the one hand, and, on the other, a harmonization with their past. . . .
> It does something for the conscience [when] you go to a concert and confront something that the Germans destroyed."[66]

Harry Timmermann also gives Giora Feidman credit for "addressing something universal and all-human" with his music. Although he is aware of the criticism directed at Feidman, he believes that healing through klezmer is actually taking place and can have universal dimensions. "People speak of sham forgiveness and

[63] Giora Feidman's website, accessed March 7, 2008, http://www.giorafeidman-online.com/index. html.

[64] Kirshenblatt-Gimblett, "Sounds of Sensibility," *Judaism* 47, no. 1 (1998): 54.

[65] Feidman interview.

[66] Kloock interview.

charlatanism, because this is only music," says Timmermann, "but I think that the power of music can go quite far. . . . The core of what [Feidman] is doing are very simple melodies, which are accessible to all. This reconciles not only Germans and Jews, but the world in general."[67] Feidman's music makes a strong impression on concertgoers, critics, and musicians alike, but his conviction that klezmer can perform a healing function in Germany also has followers.

Alex Jacobowitz, an American klezmer street performer who often tours in Germany, is also persuaded that "music can be therapeutic." In his view, many klezmer musicians in Germany are "afraid of this very strong emotional connection" with their audiences. Jacobowitz himself senses a strong need among his German spectators for sharing the emotions that Jewish music triggers in them and considers the situation of a klezmer concert to be a potential site of therapy via music. This process, he admits, can be very challenging for a musician:

> If people start thinking about how their relatives either shot somebody, or were shot by somebody . . . how are you going to get them back and hear the concert here? . . . What happens when, after a concert, people come and say: "Oh, we loved you, we cried the whole time," or the people are so touched that they bring the stories of why they're sad, and they want you to listen carefully, as if you were their father, or rabbi, as if you were going to give them advice about what to do? It's all very difficult, very touchy, because the music is not just about the sound, it's about the human experience. . . . The music is not about saying who is good and who is bad . . . it's looking for advancing, it's looking for progressing, it's saying: "Yes, we take the past with us, but we're taking it into the future."[68]

Although some musicians performing in Germany see klezmer as a medium that can help Germans progress into a future less haunted by the specters of the past, many are skeptical about what they read as a philosophy of easy forgiveness. Rabbi Joshua Spinner from the Lauder Foundation in Berlin, who attended one of Feidman's concerts, found the experience deeply troubling. In his words, Feidman took his audience on "a little emotional roller-coaster ride" in which the spectators could take part in a "cathartic experience of crying with the Jew and feeling better with the Jew."[69] The accordionist Franka Lampe is likewise mistrustful toward the outcomes of Feidman's teaching in Germany. Lampe, who is also a performing artist, declares she does not want her audience to "behave as if they were going to confession, or doing penance." She believes it is "superficial" if a

---

[67] Timmermann interview.

[68] Jacobowitz interview.

[69] Spinner interview.

musician creates a mood for the audience, which allows them to "live all their pity in the music."[70] Her stance is that klezmer should not be a shortcut for coming to terms with Germany's difficult past.

This warning repeatedly appears on the German klezmer scene, even making its way onto klezmer records. In 1998, the already nonexistent group La'om accompanied their CD *Riffkele* with a statement that could also be read as a sort of manifesto of the German klezmer revival:

> We absolutely don't see it as a sign of "the new normality" that many Germans play klezmer today and that klezmer concerts throughout the country are so well attended. Likewise, by no means do we see our music making in terms of a contribution to the German *Vergangenheitsbewäl-tigung*. We make instrumental music and follow primarily our ears; we find the music simply not suitable as a means for coming to terms with German history.[71]

La'om's text is a statement of intention addressed at critics, but it is also a warning aimed toward their audience. Klezmer in Germany should not be treated as a "cheap form of *Wiedergutmachung* [reparation]."[72] Not by those who consume it, and not by those who interpret the motivations of the klezmer scene.

Daniel Kahn made a similar admonishment into a song. "The Broken Tongue," which to an extent echoes Michael Alpert's "Berlin 1990," is directed at klezmer audiences and is an exhortation against using Jewish music as self-therapy:

> Now you who gather joyfully beneath the festive lights
> And warm each other soulfully with all of your delight
> Take not too much comfort in this song . . .
> For in the dying embers of a century of blood
> Is all we must remember to avoid the coming flood
> Of prophesies we all refuse to hear
> For singing broken melodies in broken tongues
> Cannot erase the memory of bells already rung
> Nor can it unring the bells we hear[73]

Kahn is convinced that "you can't *wiedergutmachen*. . . . [and] you can't fix history."[74] Klezmer is not redemptive. As the song warns, reconstructing the

---

[70] Ibid.

[71] "La'om's statement," accessed January 7, 2006, http://www.pickolino.de/lm_klezd.html, translated by the author.

[72] Ibid.

[73] Daniel Kahn, "The Broken Tongue," *The Broken Tongue, Chamsa Records*, 2006, CD.

[74] Kahn interview.

forgotten language "cannot erase the memory." "Music does heal," argues Kahn, "but not in this way that it should give too much comfort in relation to gruesome events from the past."[75] "The Broken Tongue" is a manifesto against forgetting, but it is also against treating klezmer as catharsis, which can cleanse Germans of Holocaust trauma. And if klezmer does have a function in contemporary society, it is not that of giving solace but rather alerting us that "history repeats its bloody tune."[76]

The exhortations of La'om and Daniel Kahn that klezmer should not become a sonic metaphor for overcoming the difficult past are probably too late. Both in Germany and in Poland a whole set of meanings have grown around the term "klezmer," turning the music into a symbol for Jewish/non-Jewish reconciliation, multi-ethnic coexistence, and ecumenism. Whether klezmer musicians themselves endorse it or not, klezmer music has turned into a signifier that many avail themselves of at will.

Also in Poland, klezmer music appears as accompaniment to a range of political events, which may or may not be connected with Jewish history. Thus, klezmer bands from Kraków have performed at a celebration honoring the Righteous among the Nations, at the Polish Days in London, at meetings devoted to inter-religious dialogue, and even during the anniversary of 9/11. Some klezmer bands have also received invitations to play at political rallies of Social Democrats (SLD) and the centrist Freedom Party [*Unia Wolności*]. Jewish heritage music has clearly become a "politically correct" genre, which is being successfully employed not only in the context of Holocaust-related events but also as a soundtrack to occasions where the accompaniment of Jewish music does not seem obvious.

Not unlike their German colleagues, many Cracovian musicians disapprove of such an instrumentalization of their work. Maciej Inglot of Sholem is skeptical of the officials who make use of Jewish culture for their purposes: "Politicians love to appear in the aura of tolerance and dialog; they make some wonderful promotion for themselves in this way, but no one speaks of the fact that we have a neo-Nazi political party."[77] The musicians of Kroke also oppose attempts at manipulating them for political goals. They report that during a radio interview in Berlin, they were suddenly asked about their opinion on the high level of anti-Semitism in Poland; they refused to answer the question, feeling instrumentalized. In fact, the musicians of Kroke, who often tour in Germany, feel that the media sometimes frames their concerts in a way that makes them feel uncomfortable. On one occasion a German TV station, which covered one of their concerts,

---

[75] Ibid.

[76] Kahn, "Son of Plenty," *The Broken Tongue*, Chamsa Records, 2006, CD.

[77] The speaker is referring to the League of Polish Families, whose representatives co-created the government from 2005 to 2007, and whose youth organization, Młodzież Wszechpolska, is notorious for anti-Semitic and xenophobic manifestations and support for neo-Nazi ideology.

arrived at the concert venue with two policemen who took up positions outside of the artists' dressing room. Tomasz Lato recollects:

> As soon as the interview was over, the policemen departed. It was an evident show! In the interview they asked us whether we feel safe in Germany. When Jerzy [Bawół] answered, "Yes," they said, "Camera stop. I'm not sure you understood the question." . . . Because the point was to shoot those bodyguards and then us saying that yes, we do feel safe, because there are security forces here. . . . When I came out into the foyer to arrange our CD stand, the TV crew was still shooting some interviews with people who had come to the concert. As soon as they saw me, the journalist shouted, "Camera stop, get out, get out, you are not supposed to be here!" And why? Because I was not supposed to go around without the bodyguards![78]

Even though the musicians generally try to evade situations in which their music can be used for political purposes, they cannot always avoid it, since the klezmer revival receives a lot of attention from the media and the local authorities.

Already the first edition of the Jewish Culture Festival in Kraków in 1988 caught the attention of the media and was acclaimed as "a cultural event of great importance."[79] Journalists, then unaware of the East Berlin Days of Yiddish Culture, extolled the festival as "unprecedented not only in Poland but also in the socialist bloc,"[80] and a groundbreaking event "marking a new path and new direction of action in a field which had been exceptionally neglected and belied."[81] The organizers of the festival do not remember having encountered any problems on the part of the Communist authorities, although, in retrospect, they see their festival as "amateur overthrowing of Communism."[82] And indeed, a lot has already been inscribed into the history of the Cracovian Jewish festival.

As it grew in size and importance, the political significance ascribed to the festival by the media increased accordingly. Reporting on the festival's final concert in 1995, the daily *Gazeta Wyborcza* wrote that Polish Jewish dialogue is easier to carry out by "means of culture" than by "listing the wrongs suffered."[83] Similarly, the weekly *Polityka* interpreted the festival's final concert in 2004 as a "symbol of reconciliation, forgiveness, and victory of life over death, recognizable both in

---

[78] Lato interview, April 18, 2004.

[79] Oskar Sobański, "Więcej niż fascynacja," *Film*, no. 27, July 3, 1988, repr. in *Powiększenie*, nos. 1–4, 1990, 250.

[80] Janusz Michalczak, "Swoi i obcy," *Dziennik Polski*, May 20, 1988, repr., 251.

[81] Sobański, "Więcej niż fascynacja," 250.

[82] Krzysztof Gierat cited in R. Radłowska, "Dybuk nim trzęsie niemiłosiernie," *Gazeta Wyborcza*, June 27, 2008, 23; Makuch interview, May 3, 2007.

[83] Grażyna Lubińska, "W blasku synagogi Tempel," *Gazeta Wyborcza Kraków*, June 19, 1995, 3.

Poland and in the world."[84] Clearly, the impact ascribed to the revival of Jewish heritage in Poland, epitomized by Kraków's Jewish Culture Festival, has come to be measured in universal values.

No wonder that many politicians and local authorities noticed the revival of Jewish music as a useful exemplar of a successful multicultural policy. Poland's former president, Aleksander Kwaśniewski, spoke of the Jewish festival in Kazimierz as a platform of dialogue, a source of hope for European integration, and part of "a common heritage."[85] Similarly, the mayor of Warsaw, Kazimierz Marcinkiewicz, expressed his belief that the Jewish festival in Warsaw "is serving the present Polish-Jewish dialogue and . . . propagating the idea of tolerance."[86] To the previous mayor of Kraków, Józef Lassota, the Jewish Culture Festival in his city constituted nothing less than a counterimage of the Holocaust. He opened the fourth edition of the festival with the words: "I hope that just like Auschwitz became the symbol of Extermination, Kraków will become the symbol of Preservation of what can be preserved—the memory of the Polish Jews and their culture."[87]

Others interpret the successful revival of Jewish heritage in Poland as a proof of Poland's traditional openness and a counterargument against accusations of anti-Semitism. Kazimierz Marcinkiewicz spoke of the Jewish festival as an event that allows its visitors to "get to know and remember Warsaw as a city open to a variety of cultures and religions."[88] Jerzy Buzek, the former prime minister, wrote, addressing the participants of the Jewish Festival in Kraków, that the city "has always been open and hospitable."[89] And in one of the festival press reviews one can read that "[n]o one who attends the great feast of Jewish music in Kazimierz is ever going to believe that Poland is an anti-Semitic country."[90]

Not surprisingly, perhaps, the revival of Jewish heritage music has become a prime example of Polish–Jewish reconciliation, invoked in particular as a neutralizer to xenophobic and anti-Semitic acts of violence. Large-scale performances of Jewish heritage, such as the Jewish Culture Festival in Kraków, the final concert of which is broadcast on public television and watched by several hundred thousands of Poles, are particularly powerful symbols. As flagship cultural events, they

---

[84] Katarzyna Janowska, "Festiwal żydowski: Duch Kazimierza," *Polityka*, July 10, 2004, 58.

[85] Aleksander Kwaśniewski, in *11. Festiwal Kultury Żydowskiej w Krakowie* (Kraków: Jewish Festival, 2001), 3.

[86] Kazimierz Marcinkiewicz, in *Festiwal Kultury Żydowskiej Warszawa Singera* (Warszawa: Fundacja Szalom, 2006), 5.

[87] Józef Lassota cited in *4. Festiwal Kultury Żydowskiej w Krakowie. 19.–26. czerwca 1994* (Kraków: Graffiti, 1994), 2.

[88] Marcinkiewicz, cited in *Festiwal Kultury Żydowskiej Warszawa Singera*, 5.

[89] Jerzy Buzek cited in *11. Festiwal Kultury Żydowskiej w Krakowie* (Kraków: Jewish Festival, 2001), 4.

[90] Elżbieta Morawiec, "Polska leży w Europie," *Nowy Świat*, June 23, 1992, repr. in *4. Festiwal Kultury Żydowskiej w Krakowie. 19.–26. czerwca 1994* (Kraków: Graffiti, 1994), 55.

are repeatedly used as proof of a positive attitude toward Jews in Polish society and a panacea alleviating the pain of accusations of anti-Semitism.

On the other hand, Poland does not lack politicians who see the promotion of Jewish heritage as a process detrimental to the furthering of nationalist values. Shortly after being sworn in as the Polish prime minister, Jarosław Kaczyński put this point of view into words on the Catholic TV channel *Telewizja Trwam* in July 2006. After a viewer called the studio to complain about the partiality of public television, which had broadcast "some klezmer band" during the final concert of the Jewish festival, but had made no reference to a pilgrimage of the country's "best Poles, that is, Catholics and patriots," to the shrine of the Black Madonna in Częstochowa, Kaczyński responded:

> Here I fully agree with you, the example was terrific. Something impor-
> tant is taking place in Częstochowa, something which should be broad-
> cast, and at length, and nothing is said about it. Instead, there is an event
> of, frankly speaking, local, maybe municipal importance, and it is shown.
> I have nothing against it being shown, but there is a certain hierarchy.
> And it should be respected.[91]

The hierarchy to respect is, in this case, "Polish (Catholic) heritage first."

Although the nationalist-Catholic media, such as *Telewizja Trwam* and the daily *Nasz Dziennik*, use the symbolic force of initiatives such as festivals of Jewish culture to emphasize Polish benevolence to the Jews, they also resent the public visibility of such events.[92] As was illustrated by protests against the erection of a monument of David the Psalmist in Zamość in 2007, the defenders of "Polishness," who are concentrated around right-wing dailies such as *Nasz Dziennik*, consider any representation of Jewish heritage "alien to [Polish] culture and national identity."[93] In this battle for primacy of heritage, space dedicated to Jewish heritage is, from their perspective, lost space for Polish heritage. The same principle may be what motivates those who, with unwavering determination, year after year, paste large tags reading "cancelled" [*odwołane*] on the posters advertising the Jewish Culture Festival in Kraków. This symbolic act, be it marginal in respect to the wide-ranging publicity of the festival, exemplifies the persistent mood of rejection of Jewish heritage among some Poles.

The organizers of the Kraków festival complain less about such individual acts of vandalism than they lament the general lack of interest on the part of

---

[91] Jarosław Kaczyński cited in "Premier Kaczyński w Radiu Maryja, Rozmowy niedokończone, 23 lipca Radio Maryja i Telewizja Trwam," *Gazeta Wyborcza*, July 29–30, 2006, 16.

[92] See, for example, the letter of the Patriotic League of American Polonia [Patriotyczna Liga Polonii Amerykańskiej] published in "W obronie prawdy," *Nasz Dziennik*, August 3, 2007, accessed June 10, 2008, www.naszdziennik.pl/index.php?dat=20070803&typ=po&id=po51.txt.

[93] Mariusz Kamieniecki, "Niechciany pomnik," *Nasz Dziennik*, May 22, 2007, accessed June 10, 2008, http://www.naszdziennik.pl/index.php?dat=20070522&typ=po&id=po33.txt.

authorities in promoting other less spectacular local initiatives aimed at preserving Jewish heritage in Poland. Janusz Makuch, the director of the Jewish festival, believes that Polish politicians are losing an opportunity to change Poland's image abroad as far as Polish–Jewish relations are concerned. Although Kraków's Jewish Culture Festival is supported in part by the Ministry of Culture and National Heritage, and takes place under the honorary patronage of the president of Poland, Makuch fears that Polish authorities still do not fathom the festival's true significance: "I never cease to urge politicians to realize of what value this festival is," says Makuch, and he adds: "I believe that our politicians still treat this festival as just some event, not understanding the fact that it is an expression of certain hopes, expectations, and wishes originating from the fact that 3.5 million Jews once lived here, and now there is a void."[94]

Walter Zev Feldman, one of the pioneers of the American klezmer revival, notes the discrepancy between the positive image generated by the festival and the real problems of Polish–Jewish relations, which remain unresolved. Feldman, observing the political situation in Poland in the summer of 2007, when the leader of the extreme right-wing League of Polish Families [*Liga Polskich Rodzin*], Roman Giertych, was appointed minister of education and deputy prime minister, remarked:

> I can see that in this situation, anything that makes Poland seem like a fair, liberal, honest country would serve the interests of people representing Poland to the world. And it's the kind of thing that would look positive, even if all the underlying issues were never resolved at all. It's possible for a country to have a festival like this and still have an anti-Semitic party in charge of education.[95]

Makuch is also aware of the fact that the festival often serves as "a fig leaf to conceal the real problem." He wishes that the festival could cease being a mere "rhetorical device" in political speeches and become a vehicle to trigger "a program of mental changes" in Poland:

> People have to realize the dimensions of the enormous evil that has been done here and understand that it is important to cleanse oneself of it. The festival creates a confessional space, which should serve people to realize what happened here and what we have lost. We have to ask ourselves the question why we lost it, what our guilt is, what our Polish complicity is in the fact that this Jewish world is not only gone, but will never return.[96]

---

[94] Makuch interview, May 3, 2007.
[95] Walter Zev Feldman, interview by the author, KlezKanada Festival, August 23, 2007.
[96] Makuch interview, May 3, 2007.

It is, however, exactly the question of the Polish complicity in the "disappearance" of the Jewish world that provokes the most vehement opposition in the public debate. There is no doubt that events such as the Jewish Culture Festival are enormously important in making Poles sensitive to the loss Polish society suffered in the Holocaust and the malady of anti-Semitism. And yet, rather than serving as a starting point of painful therapy, the Jewish heritage boom is often flaunted as ultimate proof of perfect health.

Apart from being a rhetorical tool in Polish political discourse, the klezmer scene and the Jewish Culture Festival are also spaces in which political events resonate with a particular force. This is particularly true for the political upheavals originating in the Middle East. And so the Jewish festival has become a site of political declarations, a target of critique, and even a site of demonstrations.

In 2002, news of the standoff between Fatah militants and the Israeli Defense Forces at the Church of the Nativity in Bethlehem triggered a protest targeted at the Jewish festival. A group of Polish veterans, represented by their spokesman Jerzy Bukowski, composed an open letter to the Kraków municipal authorities and the organizers of the Jewish Culture Festival, urging them to cancel the event. The authors of the letter, who justified their appeal with "concern for the safety of the festival's participants, particularly the guests of Jewish origin as well as Arab restaurant owners in Kraków,"[97] requested that the financial means devoted to organizing the festival be redirected to rebuilding the damaged fragments of the Bethlehem church. Shortly thereafter, the signatories, together with activists from the Polish-Arab Cultural Association, organized a demonstration against the Israeli occupation and again demanded that the Jewish Culture Festival be called off.[98]

The line of argument connecting the festival with the conflict in the Middle East was striking in that it reflected domestic partisan considerations more than any true concern for Israelis or Palestinians. Although protest organizers declared they feared that the festival might become a scene of violence, they were particularly outraged by the "merciless attack of the Israeli army on one of the holiest sites of Christianity."[99] The Jewish Culture Festival was thus turned into a screen onto which to project a critique of Israeli politics and, at the same time, recall the stereotypes of Jews as enemies of Christianity.

Although the Jewish Culture Festival in Kraków concentrates primarily on the heritage of Eastern European Jews, it has also fostered good relations with Israel and includes Israeli culture in its program. The embassy of Israel in Warsaw is among the festival's sponsors, Israeli artists are frequent guests, and the 2008 edition of the festival included many special events to celebrate the sixtieth

---

[97] "List otwarty do władz miasta Krakowa i organizatorów Festiwalu Kultury Żydowskiej," *Gazeta Wyborcza Kraków*, April 10, 2002, 2.

[98] "Przeciw okupacji i festiwalowi," *Gazeta Wyborcza Kraków*, April 13, 2002, 4.

[99] "List otwarty," 2.

anniversary of the State of Israel. The festival director makes it clear that he has no intention of disowning Israel, and in moments of military or political tension in the Middle East, he does not hesitate to express his open support for Israel. In 2006, for example, when the festival coincided with the conflict in Lebanon, Makuch introduced the open-air concert of the Israeli drummer Shlomo Bar by saying: "Shlomo Bar is the voice of the desert, the voice of Israel, with which we all share solidarity."[100] Consequently, the final concert of the festival was also presented as a gesture of support for the Jewish state at war.

With the special focus on Israel, it was all but inevitable that the 2008 festival would also turn into a political event. The festival organizers themselves created some distance from the political dimension of the 1948 anniversary by declaring that the festival does not aim to "celebrate a political act," but rather to "present the great melting pot of cultures in Israel."[101] Their statement, however, did not prevent a neo-Nazi group from demonstrating against Israel in front of one of the synagogues during the address of the Israeli ambassador David Peleg. The organization behind the protest, the *Narodowe Odrodzenie Polski* [National Renaissance of Poland], which is notorious for its anti-Semitic publications and fascist inclinations, framed its manifestation in terms of a human rights protest, accusing Israel of committing genocide against the Palestinians. The organizers of the festival reacted to the protest by forming a human chain to keep the banners out of sight. The showdown, ultimately, did not turn out to be violent, but it showed that the Jewish festival, on the one hand, is a litmus test measuring the attitudes of Poles toward Jews, more generally, and Israel, more specifically. On the other hand, it also indicated that events like the festival are vulnerable targets for politically motivated extremists.

Even though the Jewish festivals in Poland are events that carry a certain political potential, the klezmer scene itself does not resonate with political messages of any kind. Indeed, the utter lack of any kind of political content on the Polish klezmer scene makes this absence conspicuous. Given that socially engaged and socialist songs make up a significant part of the Yiddish-language musical legacy, the apparent disinterest of Polish musicians in the more politically explicit material constitutes an omission that says something about the selective approach to Jewish heritage in Poland. Socialist and Communist Yiddish songs remain taboo, and the klezmer scene does not produce any kind of commentary to the current social debates. It is all the more astonishing if we consider that the klezmer revival in Poland was developing exactly at the time when Poles were starting, in a particularly intensive way, to come to terms with their implication in the Holocaust. The publication of Gross's *Neighbors* in 2000/1 led to an outpour of polemical and also supportive responses in all kinds of media. But while the heated

---

[100] Makuch June 8, 2006.

[101] Makuch cited in Ryszard Kozik, "W izraelskim tyglu kultur," *Gazeta Wyborcza*, June 27, 2008, 18.

debates about Polish anti-Semitism and post-Holocaust pogroms were sending shock waves through Polish society, not a single song or concert was dedicated as a comment, voice of empathy toward the victims, or sign of protest against all the anti-Semitic sentiments unleashed by the debate. Although there is no doubt that the Polish Jewish past is a subject of deep political significance in Poland, the klezmer revivalists divorce their work from politics entirely.

The explanation for this phenomenon lies in the great resentment of the klezmer musicians toward politicizing their work. It is a common stance of many of the Cracovian artists that they do not want their music to be "contaminated" by politics,[102] or that they do not play klezmer music "for ideological reasons."[103] But do Polish musicians avoid political overtones because they fear a further instrumentalization of the klezmer revival in the public discourse? Or do they distrust the combination of "Jewish" and "political," as often employed in anti-Semitic propaganda?

The most poisonous conflation of this kind is without doubt that of "Jews" and "Communism." Right-wing nationalist politicians and publicists had already begun to link "Jewishness" with Communism back in the 1920s, when the term "Judeo-Communism" [Żydokomuna] was coined. Inspired by the French for "Judeo-Masonry" [judéo-maçonnerie], the term was the Polish expression of the commonplace nineteenth-century European perception of Jews as conspiring to seize control of the world. The myth of Judeo-Communism postulated that all Jews were Communists, and all Communists were Jews.[104]

After 1945, this stereotype was based on two assumptions. First, that the Jews had supported Communism before World War II and had made up a majority within the Communist Party of Poland. Second, that they had imposed the Communist regime on the Poles after the war, enjoying a privileged position within the regime.[105] Historians have dismantled this stereotype, pointing out that Jews were no more supportive of Communism than were Poles, even though the percentage of high-ranking party officials of Jewish descent was greater than the percentage of Jews in Polish society. This, however, was due to a higher literacy rate among Jews as well as the fact that many in Poland's postwar Jewish community survived the Holocaust in the Soviet Union and perceived in the Communists—first in the Polish Workers' Party, then the Polish United Workers' Party—the only force that could protect them after the war. Moreover, Jews did not necessarily profit from their leftist inclinations, given that the Polish United Workers' Party grew increasingly anti-Semitic over time and orchestrated anti-Jewish campaigns, such as in 1968, which ultimately forced most Jews to leave Poland.[106]

---

[102] Bester interview.

[103] Wiercioch interview.

[104] Paweł Śpiewak, Żydokomuna: Interpretacje historyczne (Warszawa: Czerwone i Czarne, 2012).

[105] Gross, Fear, 192.

[106] Ibid., 199; Michael Steinlauf, Pamięć nieprzyswojona, polska pamięć Zagłady (Warszawa: Cyklady, 2001), 65–66.

At the peak of hostility toward Jews in 1968, official anti-Semitic discourse revolved around political issues. After the Six Days War in 1967, when Poland's Communists sided with the Arabs, Polish Jews were depicted as a "fifth column," collaborating with "ex-Nazis," denigrating the Polish nation's martyrdom, and blaming Poles for the Holocaust.[107] The key features ascribed to the "anti-Polish Zionists" in 1968 were linked to their supposed political engagement with the "wrong" side. Jews were depicted as members of the "political, financial, or cultural establishment" and even assigned mutually exclusive identities, for example, both "Stalinists" and "agents of American imperialism."[108]

Polish musicians may indeed be wary of the echoes of 1968 in their reluctance to make political statements in Jewish music. Would songs of the *Bund* on a Polish stage invoke the specter of Judeo-Communism? Daniel Kahn and his band The Painted Bird[109]—whose very name prompted a Polish journalist to remark: "They came to provoke"—explore complicated elements of Polish Jewish history, but they do so in Berlin.[110] Polish klezmer musicians prefer, in general, to avoid political connotations and controversy. But can Poles speak of an honest revival of Poland's Jewish heritage without addressing the Jewish revolutionary legacy and confronting anti-Semitic depictions of Jews as Communists?

Conclusion

The historian Michael Meng, in his book *Shattered Spaces*, puts forward a claim that the interest in preserving Jewish heritage in Poland and Germany takes the form of "redemptive cosmopolitanism," which, in celebrating the (past) multi-ethnicity, offers Poles and Germans a closure, preventing them to critically engage with the past and the present failures of liberal democracies to foster a truly tolerant society.[111] Harnessed into a narrative of successful "return" of Jewish culture to Poland and Germany, klezmer music often seems to play the same redemptive role. And yet, as we have seen in hostile reactions to klezmer music, what can be a soothing medicine for some is still an irritant for others. While klezmer might have escapist qualities, the associations with the Holocaust that it often evokes and the political instrumentalization that it is exposed to turn the klezmer revival

---

[107] Ibid., 102; Michlic, *Poland's Threatening Other*, 230–61.

[108] Dariusz Stola, "Fighting against the Shadows: The Anti-Zionist Campaign of 1968," in *Antisemitism and its Opponents in Modern Poland*, ed. Robert Blobaum (Ithaca, NY: Cornell University Press, 2005), 284–300.

[109] *The Painted Bird* is the title of one of Jerzy Kosiński's novels, accused by some critics of being anti-Polish. Kosiński's book was banned in Poland until 1989.

[110] Mariusz Wiatrak, "Kabaret makabryczny," *Gazeta Wyborcza Kraków*, June 29, 2007, 7.

[111] Michael Meng, *Shattered Spaces: Encountering Jewish Ruins in Postwar Germany and Poland* (Cambridge, MA: Harvard University Press, 2011), 10.

into a site where Poles and Germans are confronted with their past and where they also negotiate their collective self-image as pluralist societies.

This negotiation is unavoidably marked by selectiveness. In the context of cultural appropriation, the choice of what to put in the foreground and what to omit reveals thresholds of acceptance toward the heritage of the other, but it also uncovers a value system, which guides this process of cultural anthropophagy. The noninclusion of Socialist Yiddish repertoire in Poland, or the resentment toward Israeli folk songs in Germany, thus tells us of the limits of appropriation and the social needs that spurn the klezmer revival. We choose what we value, transform it to fit our needs, and reject what we cannot identify with. If the culture of the other serves a reflection on the collective self, it is not the factual that matters but the functional. Even if the new klezmer might be applied to self-serving needs, as we will see in chapters 6 and 7, the identity debates that the non-Jewish participation in the klezmer revival triggers often cause acute tension, ambivalence, and crisis, rather than having a soothing effect.

6

People In Between

The Consequences of Standing In

In his prize-winning novel *Reservation Blues*, Sherman Alexie tells the story of a Native American Indian blues band, which sets out on a promising career but eventually loses a record contract against their former non-Indian groupies dressed up as Indians. Pondering the enthusiasm of young Americans to appropriate Indian identity, Chess Warm Water, member of the "authentic" Indian band, poignantly states, "You ain't really an Indian unless there was some point in your life that you didn't want to be."[1] Non-Indians fascinated with Native culture might play their music in a more commercially successful way than the Indians themselves, but they will always remain in the realm of the simulacrum and never partake in the community of those touched by the trauma of reservation life. Chess Warm Water's criterion of "real" Indianness provokes the question of what kind of bonding to and through music *is* possible in a situation of cultural appropriation such as that described in Alexie's novel. If wannabe Indians can never be "real" Indians, what else do they become? In more general terms, if we deny the possibility of "authentic" identification via ethnic music to those who do not belong to the ethnic group that "owns" the music, does it mean that their engagement in the culture of the other bears no significance whatsoever for their identity?

Much of the critical writing about the non-Jewish klezmer revival in Europe follows Chess Warm Water's skeptical stance, discarding the phenomenon as profit-oriented "poplore," which is not "the real thing" and can be at best irrelevant for the Jewish community.[2] Non-Jewish klezmer musicians appear as envoys of hyperreality, disconnected from the tradition they perform, usurping musical landscapes where they do not belong. Because it takes place in the context of appropriation, many suggest that the act of music making is not as meaningful to

---

[1] Sherman Alexie, *Reservation Blues* (New York: Grove Press, 1995), 98.
[2] Ottens, "Die wüste Stadt Berlin"; Birnbaum, "Jewish Music, German Musicians."

non-Jewish performers as it is to Jews, and that the motivations of non-Jewish musicians are of a merely economic nature.[3] Other critics, if they see a deeper significance in non-Jewish klezmer music, interpret it as an attempt of the musicians and audiences to lessen their feelings of guilt connected to the Holocaust.[4] Thus, according to Henryk Broder, the klezmer revival is part of the strategy of people from the "perpetrator milieu" to identify with Holocaust victims.[5] But others also have claimed that non-Jewish klezmer musicians suffer from "strong guilty feelings"[6] which they relieve by performing Jewish music or taking part in "therapeutic events," such as Jewish culture festivals.[7]

Ethnic music performed by outsiders has often been portrayed as "out of place" and therefore without meaning.[8] There is also nothing new about the claim that heritage appropriation can have a self-serving dimension and that our need for the culture of the other is motivated by specific desires and political agendas.[9] But one may ask if the hypothesis is tenable that klezmer, in places such as Germany and Poland, is a purely exploitative enterprise, which involves appropriation of not only Jewish heritage but also identity? But what happens to Poles and Germans exposed to Jewish culture on a daily basis, and how do non-Jewish klezmer musicians identify with Jewishness?

Many observers of the klezmer phenomenon have claimed that non-Jewish actors in the Jewish heritage revival aspire toward a Jewish identity. Michal Bodemann labels the revival of Jewish culture in Germany as a "judaising milieu," placing revivalists among "professional almost-Jews" [Berufs-fast-Juden].[10] Ruth Gruber denotes "outsiders" who take the place of "real Jewish protagonists" as "virtual Jews."[11] Diana Pinto uses the term "Jewish Space" to name the platforms of interaction where Europeans channel their interest in Jewish culture.[12] And even though these authors are well aware of the complexities of Jewish identity in post–Holocaust Europe and the voices of those who, like Erica Lehrer, distance themselves from essentialist categories of "Jewish" versus "non-Jewish" become increasingly heard, most of the terminology used in this debate implies that

---

[3] Broder, "Die Konjunktur des Jüdischen"; Weiss, "Jewish Disneyland."

[4] For example: Birnbaum, "Jewish Music, German Musicians"; Broder, "Die Konjunktur des Jüdischen"; Ottens "Der Klezmer als ideologischer Arbeiter."

[5] Broder, "Die Konjunktur des Jüdischen," 362–63.

[6] Ottens and Rubin, "The Sounds of the Vanishing World."

[7] Tempel, "Alan Bern lehrt die Deutschen das mollige Kuscheln mit Klezmer."

[8] Martin Stokes, "Place, Exchange, and Meaning: Black Sea Musicians in the West of Ireland," in Firth, Popular Music, vol. 4, Music and Identity, 101–3; Iain Chambers, Urban Rhythms: Pop Music and Popular Culture (New York: St. Martin's Press, 1985), 199.

[9] Lowenthal, Heritage Crusade, 81–84.

[10] Bodemann, Gedächtnistheater, 50–51.

[11] Gruber, Virtually Jewish, 43.

[12] Pinto, "The Third Pillar?"

people dealing with Jewish culture are, at the very least, somehow represented by the adjective "Jewish."[13]

Although many authors have used the example of klezmer to comment on the non-Jewish appropriation of a Jewish identity, there have been, so far, no studies of how non-Jewish klezmer musicians define themselves vis-à-vis Jewish culture. Aaron Eckstaedt's *Klaus mit der Fiedel, Heike mit dem Bass* presents biographical interviews with klezmer musicians in Germany and in so doing attempts such a study of the German case. However, it offers no analytical framework to evaluate the interviews from the perspective of identity theory. Although Eckstaedt confronts his interviewees with the question of whether "playing Yiddish music in Germany has a special meaning" to them, he does not follow up from there to the more difficult question of what it means to his speakers to play klezmer "as Germans."[14]

This and the following chapter address the two popular theses that are often articulated in relation to the klezmer revival: that the involvement with Jewish culture implies for klezmer musicians the desire to become Jewish, and that non-Jews become attracted to Jewish heritage because they feel guilty on account of their parents or grandparents who participated in or witnessed the Holocaust.

The people who narrate their experience here are klezmer musicians and cultural organizers from Kraków and Berlin, who either identify themselves as non-Jewish, or whose relationship to Jewishness escapes a straightforward definition—for example, they might have Jewish ancestors but were not raised Jewish. Unlike in the previous sections of this book, where interviewees spoke mainly about their work and artistic decisions, and were quoted with their full names, the interviews in this chapter often concern their private lives and are, therefore, coded (see appendix).

The Importance of Being Jewish

Social psychology tells us that we can speak of an individual's "group identity" on two conditions. First, the individual must be aware of membership in a given group, or must have chosen to belong to it. Second, she must be recognized as a member thereof by the outside world. In the case of some groups, there might also be the necessity of meeting some objective criteria.[15] Judaism, for example,

---

[13] Lehrer, "Bearing False Witness?," 91–97. See also: Erica Lehrer, "Virtual, Virtuous, Vicarious, Vacuous? Towards a Vigilant use of Labels," in *Jewish Cultural Studies*, vol. 4, *Framing Jewish Culture: Boundaries and Representations*, ed. Simon J. Bronner, 383–95 (Oxford: Littman Library of Jewish Civilization, forthcoming 2013).

[14] Eckstaedt, *"Klaus mit der Fiedel, Heike mit dem Bass,"* 74.

[15] See G. Breakwell, "Some Effects of Marginal Social Identity," in *Differentiation between Social Groups: Studies in the Social Psychology of Intergroup Relations*, ed. Henri Tajfel (London: Academic Press, 1978), 301–36.

prescribes objective criteria for membership, which are regulated by the rabbinical law, or, so far as Israel's recognition of new immigrants is concerned, by the
Law of Return.[16] Although censuses and surveys measuring the Jewish population usually are based on subjective criteria (self-identification), recognizing that
the patterns of Jewish identity have become more complex and fluid, such a definition is not a normatively binding one.[17] According to rabbinical law, only matri-
lineal descent or a halachic conversion determine the person's status as a Jew.
Reform and Liberal Judaism accept bilinear descent, and the Law of Return embraces also children, grandchildren, and spouses of Jews, but does not, of itself,
define the *status* of a person as a Jew.

If we want to consider the way non-Jews who are deeply involved with Jewish
culture might potentially relate as members of a Jewish collective, we also have to
take into consideration these "subjective" and "objective" criteria of membership.
In other words, we need to examine the way these individuals define themselves
and the way they are perceived by their surroundings.

When asked if they felt somehow between the non-Jewish and the Jewish
world, many of my interviewees answered in the negative. "We are Poles and musicians,"[18] responds the leader of one of the klezmer ensembles from Kazimierz.
"We treat it purely professionally," reacts his colleague from another band. "The
fact that this is Jewish music, and not some other kind is cool, but we are interested in it only from the musical point of view."[19] This distanced approach, in fact,
seems to be relatively widespread among the klezmer bands in Kazimierz.

Similar positions are also represented among German klezmer musicians.
A young male artist who performed for many years in the Hackesches Hoftheater
explains that he never wanted to take over the role of a representative of Jewish
culture, although the venue where his concerts took place was marketed as an "authentically Jewish" site. Asked if he feels caught between the Jewish and German
worlds, he replies in the negative: "I don't see myself as Jewish. I see myself as a
person who is able to know about Jewish culture to a certain extent, [and] who has
a lot of respect toward every religion." Although familiar with Jewish traditions,
he stresses that he always shunned the role of instructor about Jewish culture:

> I had always the difficulty to think what I was actually doing there. Am
> I actually trying to pretend that I'm Jewish? I never did that. . . . If people

---

[16] The Law of Return regulates the acceptance and absorption of new immigrants. The Israeli law
of 1950 states "every Jew has the right to immigrate to the State of Israel." According to the 1970
amendment, a Jew is defined as "a person who was born of a Jewish mother or has become converted
to Judaism and who is not a member of another religion". See Sergio Della Pergola, "Demography," in
The Oxford Handbook of Jewish Studies, ed. Martin Goodman (Oxford: Oxford University Press, 2002),
797–823.

[17] Della Pergola, "Demography," 807–9.

[18] K13. Please see appendix for codes.

[19] K01.

asked me about Judaism, or if they had any questions, I'd be pleased to answer as good as I can and as much as I am informed but I would not try to stay in front of the audience and tell them how Judaism works, because I'm not anything like a teacher . . . Jews are there for this purpose. . . . If the people are interested, they should go to them and not to me.[20]

Although whenever he answers questions from the audience, the musician finds himself de facto in a situation of mediating Jewish culture he makes a clear distinction between his artistic performance and his self-identification.

Some of the musicians go farther and say and that their interest in music does not have to entail any particular bond to Jewish culture at all. "I hear a lot of interesting music and I adapt it for myself, I play it for myself, and it is my music then, and I don't have to, I don't want to, propagate Jewish culture. This is not my aim,"[21] says a young male semi-professional klezmer performer from Berlin. A singer from another local band adds that if the feeling of in-betweenness accompanies her work, it is between many more worlds than a Jewish and non-Jewish one.

I feel between many more [worlds] than just two. It's hard to say clearly what German culture is and what Jewish culture is. It might also have a lot to do with the place that we're living in. We are in Berlin and the place is always developing. . . . We have rehearsals in Wedding, [where] there is a huge Turkish community, and a lot of Africans, in Pankow, in turn, it's completely different. You can choose what you want every day. So I'm in the middle of all of that, but Jewish culture? I have never been to Israel, I don't celebrate Jewish holidays, I have nothing to do with Jewish culture. German culture is drinking very bad coffee, I like going to Italy to have good coffee.[22]

The possibility of "choosing what you want" on the multicultural, globalized, and constantly changing world-music scene extends in this case to Jewish culture, which becomes listed as just another source of inspiration and an integral part of Berlin's mix of cultures. What seems to be at work here is what Zygmunt Bauman, in his study on postmodernity, labeled the "tourist" mentality. The contemporary klezmer musician might, like Bauman's tourist, delve into an alien element in search of new experiences but only temporarily, and with escape routes available.[23]

---

[20] B04.

[21] B05.

[22] B06.

[23] Zygmunt Bauman, "From Pilgrim to Tourist—or a Short History of Identity," in *Questions of Cultural Identity*, ed. Stuart Hall and Paul DuGay (London: Sage, 1996), 18–36.

For those to whom Jewish music becomes a more long-lived experience, however, informing non-Jews about Jewish traditions might become a daily mission. "I answer a lot of questions about Jewish culture," says a Berlin-based musician who has been playing Jewish music for roughly two decades. "I count as an authority," he adds, "and I start discussions and also react when people say bullshit. There was a time recently when people started saying again: 'It's enough with this Jewish subject all the time, let's finish it, we don't want to hear it anymore.' This is what I consciously act against."[24] Recognizing his own responsibility to retort in such situations, the musician makes it clear that it has nothing to do with any sort of subjective affiliation with Jewishness on his part: "We have no pretense to say: 'Oh we are a little bit Jewish after all,'" he states about his band. "Our identity is clearly East German." Interestingly, in denying the aspiration toward a Jewish identity, the musician is also distancing himself from existent national categories, pointing to his marked identity as "East German."

It is indeed often the case that dealing with the culture of the other makes klezmer musicians in the first place more aware of their own group identity. An instrumentalist from Berlin, who has been performing klezmer for more than ten years, confides that playing in front of an audience of Jews makes his own identity even more salient. This clear awareness precludes for him any feeling of being "between" cultures. "I have never tried to perform in a concert as a Jew," he explains, and adds that he also has never aspired to be "a cultural ambassador who wants to represent Jewishness in front of the audience."[25] An interest in klezmer and Judaism animated him, instead, to rediscover his own Christian heritage. The musician, who also used to teach at a university, recounts having had at one point a strong interest in Judaism, especially the Kabbalah, and giving a seminar about Jewish mysticism. This interest in rabbinical literature was transitory, though. "It remained an episode in the end, I didn't have the need to understand it better," he admits. "I've also never had the idea of converting to Judaism. These remained for me just texts, which were difficult and which one could only carefully approach and try to identify certain structures in them," he adds. It was only through getting involved with the Judaic tradition, that made him aware of the fact that his scholarly interest in his own religion was infinitely smaller: "I realized that I had three hundred books about Judaism and maybe thirty about Christianity," he said. This observation marked a turning point for him:

Now, I'm much more interested in the writings of Ratzinger. My way was therefore one of understanding Christianity vis-à-vis Judaism, and now I've arrived at the question of what a German pope understands under

---

[24] B08.
[25] B07.

Christianity. This interests me more now than doing research on the Kabbalah only because I incidentally play klezmer.[26]

Although the musician admits that it was also the election of the German pope that gave him an impulse to become more interested in Catholic writings, he clearly relates his "rediscovery" of Christianity to his previous interest in Judaism. It was the fascination with the religion of the other that sparked the need to study his own.

Another implication of knowing more about another culture is that it allows a more critical distance toward one's own group, opening up a perspective from the outside. "Working on the other side, the Jewish side," says a musician who started his klezmer career in the GDR, "I had the chance to look at Germany and to look at Germans . . . from the outside, through the eyes of the people you're working with." And Germany as seen "from the Jewish side" was, admittedly, a challenge:

> I remember being in New York in 1992, and there were riots against foreigners in Germany, in East Germany. And this was a big topic in the US. . . . They knew that I was from East Germany so they were [asking me], "Hey, what is going on there?" And suddenly you have to explain a world you thought you knew to another culture, but in a way that they understand it. . . . They didn't know anything about East Germany apart from Billy Wilder movies . . . what was known was the clichés.[27]

Accounting to his Jewish American friends for the xenophobic violence in Germany makes him realize the uniqueness of his position. He is a translator of his own culture. Yet, despite his position as an intermediary between the two groups, the contact with the other makes the musician's German identity only more reinforced: "I don't think I'm in the position of mediating, or even being an interpreter, between the two worlds," he concludes. "I'm *definitely* a non-Jew and I won't belong to this world because this world, the Jewish world, identifies itself in a different way. And this is where I would not fit."[28] The (subjective) self-ascription of the speaker as "definitely" non-Jewish matches here the (objective) standards of the group.

Acknowledging familiarity with the other culture, or having a special access to it, for example, by means of the language, does not mean that non-Jewish klezmer musicians forget about the boundary that divides them from Jews. A German musician who performed with his ensemble in the United States recounts how an encounter with New York Orthodox Jews made the band vividly aware of their

[26] B07.
[27] B01.
[28] Ibid.

outsider status. The band, whose concert was reported in a local Yiddish newspaper, went to the Jewish neighborhood to buy the paper and read the review of the concert:

> They noticed immediately that we didn't belong there and were stunned that we were buying a newspaper in Yiddish and then browsing through it in the street. When they realized we were German, they were amazed: here the enemy comes into the shop, can read Yiddish and even gave a concert here! . . . We noticed that it was strange for them, like, "What was that?"[29]

Even though the German musicians shared a part of the cultural code of the Jewish neighborhood because they could speak Yiddish, they were plagued by a feeling of not only being outsiders but also "enemies." Here, again, the external criteria of belonging (acceptance of the group, objective criteria of membership) played a crucial role. The awareness of the rules guiding group membership in Judaism and of the fact that German nationality might be particularly charged for Jews determines the feeling of estrangement.

To be sure, self-ascription among klezmer musicians does not follow only one pattern. While some do not feel any inclination toward identifying with Jewishness and point out situations in which their non-Jewish identity becomes salient, others feel that their involvement with Jewish culture occupies such a considerable part of their lives that it becomes a part of who they are. One such person is a female Polish musician I met in Kraków, who, apart from performing classical music by Jewish composers, teaches at the Music Academy. "I think that I am quite an interesting case," she states. "I am Polish, without any [Jewish] roots, and I represent this culture to the outside world. This means I accept it as mine, as something good, and I represent it. It seems to me that in this sense I am definitely an ambassador of this culture, although this may be saying too much, but in part this is how I feel." Performing Jewish music and teaching it to students, she feels Jewish culture has a central place in her life. "I cannot identify with this group as far as descent is concerned," she says, "but I can identify with it in terms of spiritual affinity."[30] Positioning herself as an "ambassador of Jewishness," the musician finds an alternative identification with Jewishness beyond the category of ethnicity.

Recognizing their position as between Jews and non-Jews, some klezmer musicians understand their identity as one progressing toward Jewishness. A young male German musician from Berlin muses, "Maybe I'm on the way between this Christian German world and the Jewish Ashkenazi world. My roots are in the German world, but maybe I'm moving toward this Jewish world." Having

[29] B08.
[30] K14.

dedicated more than fifteen years of his life to Yiddish music, and having studied Yiddish at university, he is convinced that being a Yiddish singer constitutes an important part of his identity. But traveling toward Jewishness means for him also the impossibility of ever arriving at the destination:

> This is a part of how I live. But I don't think of myself as one of these people who live in two worlds and have double identities. . . . When I stepped more intensively into this Yiddish world, and the academic Yiddish world is quite a small world, there was one period when I felt it was important to feel accepted there, and then all of these [questions], "Where are you from?" "What's your family background?" were not so easy for me at that time. . . . They felt like one community, or seemed to be one community, and I wondered, do I still belong there if I'm not Jewish? . . . But today I can just say: "no, I'm not Jewish, and this is just my interest." At a certain point you don't think that you have to prove anything.[31]

Entering a Yiddish-speaking community and expanding his language competences, that musician feels as if he is entering into a Jewish realm. But the process of actually crossing the boundary and becoming an insider is also inescapably connected to a feeling of non-belonging and estrangement because, as a non-Jewish Yiddish-speaker, the musician is an atypical member of the group.

Non-Jewish artists who express a particular affinity toward Jews often use the metaphor of traveling, which suggests a process rather than a state. One German klezmer musician describes himself as a "wanderer between two worlds,"[32] and a young Polish singer admits that she sometimes feels "suspended" between cultures.[33] Rather than being bound toward any concrete destination, though, these in-between people choose a "to and fro" movement. Asked if he feels in-between Jews and Germans, a young musician from Berlin answers:

> Maybe. Yeah. I would say I feel not so much German, I feel somehow closer to Jewish culture. At the same time, though, I have the feeling that I should be more interested in it, the Jewish holidays, and so on. I would like to learn more. But there is already a connection that I have to Jewish culture and to Jewish people.[34]

Only very few venture to arrive at the final destination, converting to Judaism. For the only interviewee who took this radical step, the decision did not come as

---

[31] B13.
[32] B09.
[33] K16.
[34] B10.

a result of playing klezmer, but rather klezmer became important to her as an expression of her new group affiliation. Performing Jewish music has a spiritual meaning to this speaker, and she places it in a clearly religious context. "I want to connect and I want to mediate. Connect to my Creator," is the way in which she describes her personal motivation to play Jewish music. "But I also hope that the people feel that it's not only me standing there on stage," she adds, "it's a gift from my Creator and I can give it to other people. And I hope something reaches [them]."[35] Klezmer thus becomes a medium for flagging a religious Jewish identity: a statement not only of artistic preferences but also of beliefs.

In their professional lives, non-Jewish klezmer musicians permanently find themselves in the situation of presenting Jewish culture to non-Jews, or responding to Jewish queries on behalf of Germans or Poles. But, although they often realize that they occupy a particular position of stand-ins, and have unique access to Jewish culture, this by no means results in their self-ascription as Jews.

Group membership, however, relies not only on the internal criteria, but also on the recognition of the individual as a group member by the outside world and, in particular, by the group concerned.[36] In theory, both aspects should be compatible. In practice they not always are, and it is perhaps not surprising that it is so in the case of non-Jewish klezmer musicians. While they mostly distance themselves from the category of Jewishness, their audiences often believe or expect them to be Jewish.

Both Polish and German musicians report manifold situations in which they were taken for Jews. A young female musician from Berlin recounts that after nearly every concert some members of the audience come over and ask who in the band is Jewish. "What people usually think is that at least one of us, usually me, must be Jewish":

> And then I say: "No, since the eighteenth century our ancestors have been German peasants, and we have researched as far back as it goes and we can prove it." And they say: "No, that's not possible, some grandfather of yours must have had an adventure."[37]

The incredulity and insistence that klezmer musicians must have at least a drop of Jewish blood is a reaction that Polish musicians also encounter. An older Polish artist, who sings in Yiddish, reports situations in which her audiences repeatedly asked her whether she was Jewish and then refused to believe she was not: "Very many Jews, and also non-Jews who come here, treat me as if I was Jewish. They

[35] B11.
[36] Breakwell, "Some Effects of Marginal Social Identity," 301.
[37] B12.

say, 'Don't deny it,' or 'Why don't you want to admit you're Jewish?' They often also ask me where I was hiding [during the Holocaust]."[38]

Sometimes the audience's demand for alterity is satisfied with information about the artist's not necessarily Jewish, but at least foreign, background. A female musician from Berlin recounts:

> They would come up after the concert and ask "Are you Jewish?" They're always satisfied when I say that my father is Bulgarian. When we say, "We're from Berlin," it's not a satisfactory answer, so then I wait a little bit and say, "My father is Bulgarian," and then they say, "OK. There must be some foreign blood in it!"[39]

Performing the music of the other, the klezmer musician becomes a screen on which the audience projects the imagined and desired other. This performance persona sometimes overshadows the individual behind it. And the cliché that "only a Jew can play klezmer like that" demands that the artist be categorized as a Jew.

The projection of otherness onto klezmer musicians leads in extreme cases to acts of anti-Semitic hostility. Anti-Semitic incidents against klezmer musicians might not be frequent, but one out of three interviewed non-Jewish musicians in Poland and in Germany reported a situation in which they experienced anti-Semitism directed at them. These incidents are consequential, as they create for the musicians an ultimate experience of being in the other's shoes. Facing anti-Semitism, more than any other situation, makes them realize what it is like to be classified as the "other" in their home societies.

A young Polish artist, who toured Poland with her ensemble, recounts one of the most striking stories of this kind. After a successful concert in Częstochowa— seat of a famous Catholic sanctuary in southern Poland—the musician was shocked to see an anti-Semitic picket in front of the concert venue. "We had trouble leaving that place," she says. "City guards had to be called, because some skinheads were standing there outside, holding white and red flags and banners saying: 'Poland for Poles.' It was very unpleasant."[40] Although such acts of open hostility toward musicians happen relatively rarely, the possibility that they *might* take place deeply affects the musicians. A female performer of Yiddish songs from Kraków remembers having to perform under police protection in Bytom, in southern Poland. "In Silesia they don't love Jews especially much, and some incidents do happen there," she recounts. "I had a concert there . . . It was organized by the Bytom Opera. It was the first time that I performed there and police were guarding the building. . . . Apparently, they were afraid of some incidents."[41]

[38] K17.
[39] B06.
[40] K02.
[41] K17.

Another artist from Kraków reports having had difficulties finding a venue for her concert, once the host institution found out what genre of music was going to be played. The concert, which was, ironically, part of a festival called Multicultural Myślenice, organized just south of Kraków, was scheduled to take place in a local cultural center. "But one day before the concert," the singer recalls, "the managers of the center found out that it was going to be a concert of Jewish music, and they made a scene, saying, 'Why didn't we know it was going to be *such* music?' They refused to host the concert there, and we had to move it to another venue."[42] The incident made it clear to the artist that Jewish music can provoke resentment, even in contexts where one would not necessarily expect it. Similarly, Father Naliwajko who invited a klezmer ensemble to play in a church also recollects that the first reaction of his superiors was skeptical. "When it turned out that we were going to have a klezmer concert in our church, I quickly heard voices of complaint in our convent, asking 'But how?' 'Why?' 'What?' 'Why should we have this café-music, wedding music, in the temple?'" he recounted.[43] The concert, which finally took place despite these primary reservations, was, in the eyes of its organizer, a catalyst revealing deeply embedded anti-Semitic attitudes, and helping, ultimately, to overcome them.

The organizers of the Jewish Culture Festival in Kraków have, likewise, witnessed small-scale acts of anti-Semitism directed against the event. One of the employees of the festival office recollects that some minor incidents during the festival are recurrent. Nevertheless, she is at the same time convinced that the festival organizers must simply take them in stride. Asked whether she has ever faced anti-Semitism firsthand, she replies in the negative. Later, she mentions somewhat reluctantly small acts of vandalism, which have accompanied the festival from its beginning:

> During the festival they tear off our posters, but I don't know if this is connected to the fact that it is a Jewish festival. . . . For many years now, as soon as our posters appear on the poster pillars someone sticks on them a strip saying "canceled." It is done in a very elegant way, without damaging the posters. It is a kind of unpleasant gesture. It wasn't nice at the beginning, but after some time we began laughing about it.[44]

According to Janusz Makuch, head of the festival, the only serious anti-Semitic incidents accompanied the early festival editions in the 1990s. He reports two such events, which were met with an immediate reaction from both festival guests and the local police forces:

---

[42] K15.
[43] Naliwajko interview.
[44] K18.

In 1990, when we installed such huge Stars of David on the Main Market Square and other places, someone wrote "Jews get out of here!" on one of them. . . . That year Miłosz,[45] who was the festival's special guest, said, "Nazis are among us." It was a very powerful statement. Another attempt took place in 1992 during the final concert in Szeroka Street, when a group of skinheads turned up. They were, however, somehow indecisive. . . . The police surrounded them [the skinheads] and gently pushed them out into Miodowa Street.[46]

Open manifestations of hostility toward Jewish culture events are definitely marginal in the context of the Jewish Culture Festival in Kraków, but they are experiences crucial for the self-definition of non-Jews who deal with Jewish heritage. Facing anti-Semitism not only gives them a taste of how it might feel for Jews to encounter prejudice, but it also forces them to revise the image of their own community.

Klezmer concerts occasionally become pretexts for anti-Semitic episodes in Poland and also in Germany. Several bands from Berlin state that they encountered some hostility when they played in the eastern parts of the country, where support for the extreme right-wing party, NPD, is more considerable than in the rest of Germany. Some klezmer groups performing there had their posters smeared with swastikas,[47] faced anti-Semitic comments from the audience,[48] or had the air removed from the tires on the band's van.[49] Most of the musicians blame such anti-Semitic or xenophobic incidents on alcohol and consider them as overall marginal. Others note that they encounter people of extreme right-wing convictions on a regular basis. "It happened in East Germany before the Wall came down," recollects a musician with a long touring experience, "and sometimes you can get weird reactions even now when you tell people what you're playing. I mean, there are Nazis, they are in Berlin, you meet them in bars and you meet them everywhere. If they're not sure, they will ask if you're Jewish. And once they hear you're not Jewish, they ask you, 'Why do you play this shit?' And you tell them."[50] Performing Jewish music in different locations and for a wide range of audiences, klezmer musicians do become targets of potential resentment and thus first-points-of-contact who counterreact to verbal violence.

Apart from these incidents in the professional context, some musicians experience anti-Jewish resentment also in their private lives. One of the Berlin-based

---

[45] Czesław Miłosz (1911–2004), Polish poet, prose-writer, and diplomat; Nobel Laureate in Literature in 1980.

[46] Makuch interview, May 3, 2007.

[47] B02.

[48] B04.

[49] B08.

[50] B01.

musicians, after receiving some anti-Semitic phone calls and having a Star of David drawn on his mailbox, decided to take precautions by withdrawing his address from the phone directory.[51] Several Polish klezmer musicians confessed, in turn, that some of their colleagues from the music academy, taking them for Jews, ascribed the success of their musical careers to Jewish in-group solidarity, saying "They've made it because they're Jewish."[52]

In some cases, non-Jewish musicians come across anti-Semitism even in their own families. One young Polish singer, on telling her family what kind of music she was performing, reports sensing dissatisfaction and surprise.[53] A German musician recalls a similar situation: "We played once at a family party of our flute-player and her great-aunt said, 'Such nice and pretty young girls and they play this Jewish music!' And then I thought, 'Damn, it's still there.' And that was a relative!"[54] Encountering such prejudiced reactions from the people in their immediate surroundings makes a particularly sobering impression on the musicians.

Yet, interestingly, some of the interviewees who relate such incidents at first deny that they have ever experienced anti-Semitism. A Polish female musician recounts a story by pointing out that anti-Semitism in Poland is not a real problem:

> No, I do not experience [anti-Semitism] myself. A couple of years ago someone tore off the posters of the Jewish festival in the entire city. But I think it was more hooliganism than anti-Semitism. These young boys who do it have not even seen Jews with their own eyes! . . . To my mind, this is more foolishness, doing something for laughs. I have never met with it. Well, that is, once. When I began to sing [in Yiddish] I got two anonymous letters. The editor in chief of *Echo Krakowa* . . . received an anonymous letter after he published a beautiful review of my concert, which said, "*Jude raus*. Hitler didn't kill enough of you." You know, it was filth of this kind. . . . Apart from that, my son received another letter saying, "Leave Polish girls alone, or else we'll do to you what your mum didn't do when you were born." I never tried to find out who that was; an anonymous letter is an anonymous letter.[55]

The calm and composure with which the musician narrates and categorizes her experiences is in dissonance with the gravity of the facts she quotes. Despite having witnessed explicit anti-Semitism, the speaker is reluctant to draw conclusions about the general mood in the country. This pattern reverberates in other, similar, statements from klezmer musicians in Kraków and Berlin alike.

[51] B20.
[52] K06.
[53] K25.
[54] B12.
[55] K17.

Asked whether they have ever experienced anti-Semitism themselves, some of them deny it at first, even though they later report concrete anti-Semitic incidents aimed at them. What is more, their personal experience does not always correspond to their opinion about whether anti-Semitism is a problem in Poland or Germany. While many of those who have never faced anti-Semitism themselves are convinced that the phenomenon has frightening dimensions in their country, some of those who fall victim to it deny it. These seemingly contradictory messages result, on the one hand, from the fact that the different speakers might define anti-Semitism in different terms. While for some, anti-Semitism subsumes all manifestations of prejudice against Jews, others speak of it only in reference to violent acts. On the other hand, the ambiguity in these narratives might also simply testify to the challenge that encountering anti-Semitism firsthand poses for non-Jewish klezmer musicians. For one, it gives them a taste of what it can feel like to belong to a discriminated minority. At the same time, it can seriously question their positive identification as Germans or Poles.

But if encountering anti-Semitism opens for non-Jewish *klezmorim* additional opportunity for expressing solidarity with Jews or realizing a commonality of experience with them, being taken for a Jew does not make a non-Jewish person feel Jewish. Social psychologists envisage that where internal and external criteria of membership are not compatible (i.e., if a non-Jewish person is considered by the outside world to be Jewish, or if a person considering himself or herself to be Jewish is not recognized as such), the individuals in question will suffer ambivalence.[56] We have seen in the example of the controversy between the Polish band Kroke and the authors Rita Ottens and Joel Rubin (see chap. 2) that such "non-recognition" can have direct consequences for the way those concerned come to position themselves as group members. The dissonance between the internal and external criteria of membership also causes a state of stress and tension, which individuals strive to find a solution for.

Indeed, the anxieties of our self-image have much to do with how others perceive us but also how we perceive ourselves in relation to others. In the social environment, each social group is ascribed a status, and other groups serve as a frame of reference for this status system. What follows is that a positive or negative value attributed to a given membership has great significance for the way an individual defines his allegiances.[57] And there is no question that group status weighs heavily on the intergroup relations of Poles, Germans, and Jews.

Historical events play a crucial part in how groups conceive of their own status among other groups. Since, in order to be able to imagine ourselves as members of a community, we must be aware of a common history that binds us as a collective, harm carried out by one's group is a particular challenge. It has an impact on the way we think of our own nation, for example, and also on how members of

---

[56] Breakwell, "Some Effects of Marginal Social Identity," 302.

[57] John Turner and Rupert Brown, "Social Status, Cognitive Alternatives, and Intergroup Relations," in Tajfel, *Differentiation between Social Groups*, 201–34.

the harmed group will categorize us.[58] Psychologists confirm that the Holocaust continues to be of considerable relevance for collective identities of both Germans and Jews, and that contemporary Germans are likely to be perceived as a perpetrator group by Jews.[59] Although the historical position of Poles toward Jews as simultaneously co-victims, bystanders, and perpetrators is more nuanced in this respect, Jews may still categorize Poles as perpetrators on the intergroup level.[60]

Since the very idea of the klezmer *revival* implies invoking the past, the history of Polish/Jewish and German/Jewish relations is likely to become salient on the klezmer scene. The legacy of genocide, anti-Jewish violence, and anti-Semitism might in this situation contribute to the low self-esteem of non-Jewish klezmer musicians vis-à-vis Jews. But we must ask if the memory of past harm inflicted upon Jews by Germans and Poles really affects the way klezmer musicians identify themselves with the music they make.

Germany: "It makes you think twice about your grandfather"

"The sense of guilt," recounts one middle-aged German musician, "constitutes a small bit of the respect toward Jewish culture that I have":

> I don't want to destroy this culture again that was already destroyed by my people. It doesn't mean that I'm ridden with a sense of guilt, but a small part remains . . . I cannot distance myself from the fact that Germany is responsible for the Holocaust, for the end of klezmer and this culture![61]

A similar reflection on Germany's Nazi past also accompanies the work of many other klezmer revivalists in Berlin. A vocalist recalls that his interest in klezmer back in the 1980s was a result of his interest in German history: "I was quite young still, and I was thinking about the fascist past in Germany and then listening to klezmer music came together with that." Discovering klezmer through the prism of the Holocaust he needed a long time to, as he puts it, "come to terms with the fact . . . that as a German I'm doing Jewish music."[62]

---

[58] Michael J. A. Wohl and Nyla R. Branscombe, "Forgiveness and Collective Guilt Assignment to Historical Perpetrator Groups Depend on Level of Social Category Inclusiveness," *Journal of Personality and Social Psychology* 88, no. 2 (2005): 288–303; Michael J. A. Wohl, Nyla R. Branscombe, Yechiel Klar, "Collective Guilt: Emotional Reactions When One's Group Has Done Wrong or Been Wronged," *European Review of Social Psychology* 17, no. 37 (2006): 1–37.

[59] Wohl and Branscombe, "Forgiveness and Collective Guilt," 288.

[60] Michał Bilewicz, "History as an Obstacle: Impact of Temporal-Based Social Categorizations on Polish-Jewish Intergroup Contact," *Intergroup Processes and Intergroup Relations* 10, no. 4 (2007): 553.

[61] B03.

[62] B13.

Reflection on German history might therefore be an incentive to become interested in Jewish music, but it is also the experience of performing klezmer that invites a contemplation of the past. One young musician, who started playing in a klezmer band quite by chance, explains that touring with his ensemble made him reflect more on the German Jewish history:

> We've played in synagogues, we've played with some real klezmer musicians, we toured Eastern Europe, where there definitely were more Jewish people in the audience. That makes you think about it more. But I'm German and I have a grandmother and grandfather who lived at the time of the Holocaust, so, other than music, I also have a connection with Jewish history and it has nothing to do with [the band]. But maybe when you're on tour with [the band], it makes you think twice about your grandfather and how Germany used to be.[63]

It is the contact with the other—the Jewish audiences and also the "real," presumably Jewish, klezmer musicians—that makes the musician reflect on his own family history, too. The encounter brings with it a challenge to the self-image. The context of meeting actual Jews is important in that it inspires critical questions, but it can also actually serve as a counterbalance to the representations of German/Jewish relations in history textbooks. As some musicians point out, the knowledge of Germany's heritage of atrocity has accompanied them since their childhoods. The way in which they were exposed to the question of German guilt, however, provokes in them a feeling of overdose. "I never really wanted to deal with history," confesses a young female musician from Berlin. "That is a horrible past for me and when I had to go to the concentration camps as a child with school groups, I found it just disgusting," she adds.[64] Another male musician in his thirties reports how the Holocaust education he received in school conditioned in him a paralyzing anxiety vis-à-vis Jews:

> I was so trained in my childhood about this historical context and I was so careful that I didn't even dare to breathe when I was next to a Jew, because it was so important, because there was so much history on me. I've learned to relax now. I have a cool relationship with my [Jewish] friends. . . . It's also a chance to grow, . . . It's good to live it with a person, and to argue and to drink, then it's easier. You know that not everything you do is connected with the Holocaust.[65]

[63] B14.
[64] B12.
[65] B15.

The wish "to be able to breathe" makes many klezmer musicians distance their work from the process of the national "memory work." One young male musician from Berlin makes a clear distinction between the historical responsibility resting on Germany and his own responsibility as a klezmer musician: "This is bullshit, all this dwelling on history stuff. Sure, Germans have to carry the burden of what happened between 1933 and 1945, but to refer to that and to say that it is very ambivalent now to play klezmer music is stupid," he argues.[66] Another young musician, who plays klezmer in addition to his other musical interests, notes that he does not ponder the "Jewish-German question" while he is working. "I'm too involved with the music to think about it." At the same time, he has the impression that his German identity weighs on the professional contact that he has with Jewish colleagues. "When I meet some Jewish musicians, for example, I have the impression that they can't look me straight in the eye, as if there was a deep mistrust there," he says, but then relativizes the remark immediately: "I don't know, this is my impression, maybe it's complete bullshit."[67]

While some musicians wish to emancipate the realm of their musical creativity from the obligation to reflect on the past, others believe they should take a stance toward "what happened between 1933 and 1945" within the context of their work. The former Berlin ensemble La'om, in the liner notes of their 1998 album *Riffkele*, verbalized it poignantly. "Dealing with Jewish culture as a matter of course is certainly not possible here in Germany," reads the statement, "because the culture, which klezmer music also originates from, was annihilated in a mass murder which began in Germany."[68]

The reason why this "matter-of-courseness" is hardly attainable on the German klezmer scene is, among others, the expectations of klezmer audiences. Paraphrasing the American term "Borscht Belt,"[69] denoting profitable tour destinations for klezmer musicians in the summer resorts of the Catskill Mountains in New York State, many insiders of the German klezmer scene speak of playing in a "Guilt Belt."[70] Satisfying the needs of audiences, purportedly attracted to klezmer concerts by political correctness, involves a particular kind of pressure. One young German musician, whose band eventually dropped the label "klezmer," claims that audiences in Germany had specific motivations that brought them to klezmer concerts: "They always came with such high expectations, philosophical and aesthetic: historical responsibility, the Holocaust and Hitler and everything."

---

[66] B16.

[67] B10.

[68] "La'om's statement," accessed January 7, 2006, http://www.pickolino.de/lm_klezd.html, translated by the author.

[69] See Sapoznik, *Klezmer!*, 169–75.

[70] I was introduced to the term "Guilt Belt" by Till Schumann, the head of the Oriente label in Berlin.

The suspicion that people were coming to concerts to heal their own low self-esteem as Germans disheartened him:

> They are sitting there and they want to see it all on stage in Berlin Mitte. And I go on stage and play *umpa, umpa,* and it's a really great pressure. You can ignore it and just sell your CDs and smile, but, in a way, I know that this culture was killed by Germans and so it's . . . I don't want to make money on that. . . . All of the musicians have, I hope, decent feelings about making this music and everybody who comes has certain reasons to come, but all together, when you put all the parts together, something is wrong. It's not a naturally grown stuff; it's about German psycho problems.[71]

Expecting "Holocaust and Hitler" on stage is, according to this musician, accompanied by a need for catharsis. And selling this catharsis is something that he deeply resents. Interestingly, the speaker ascribes "therapeutic" motivations only to the klezmer audiences, who long to see on stage more than the musicians are comfortable with giving them.

The audience's desire for a mystic encounter with the other, embodied by the klezmer performer, becomes a burden not only because German musicians cannot satisfy it but also because they do not want to become actors in such a psychological process. For one middle-aged male musician from Berlin, making music and dealing with the past belong to two different realms of experience, which should not be conflated. "Making music is something different from handling the past," he states. "You have to be aware of it all, but you mustn't forget that you're making music." This proves particularly difficult when audiences understand klezmer as an incarnation of the Jewish return to Germany:

> Since the focus on history and the Holocaust responsibility is so great, sometimes I think that also the audience, they don't come because of the music, but they come because of the Holocaust and they want to see something which is lost in Germany. They want to find something again. Then I have to admit that I am not a Jew. They ask me, "Are you?" And then I say I am not. They want to touch my aura and then I'm not. . . . People sometimes expect so much of this music and the musicians.[72]

The difficulty of facing German klezmer audiences lies in the fact that they might expect to see *real Jews* on stage and also because of their particular mind-set. A few musicians describe this attitude with the German concept of *Betroffenheit:*

[71] B15.
[72] Ibid.

moral mourning and empathy triggered, for example, by a historic event. Some klezmer artists who believe that their audiences too overtly manifest a studied pose of contriteness resent it. A middle-aged musician from Berlin does not mince words, criticizing public displays of *Betroffenheit* as philo-Semitism, which in his view "is exactly like anti-Semitism, a kind of racism—both of them are criminal to me."[73] The suspicion that some German audiences treat klezmer concerts self-servingly, as spaces where they can publicly demonstrate political correctness, bothers the musicians, as some of them believe that such behavior only reinforces clichés.

Interestingly, despite ascribing to their audiences the attempt at instrumentalizing klezmer for private acts of reparation, *Wiedergutmachung*, most of my interviewees deny that they themselves are motivated by similar sentiments. A young male musician from Berlin states:

> There was a lot of discussion about the involvement of German musicians in the klezmer movement and why it is so successful here. Many said that a lot of the people in the audience come to the concerts to relieve their bad conscience. That was never a factor for me. I did it because I liked the music and also later developed an interest in Jewish culture, but not the other way around . . . I have personally no feelings of guilt about the Holocaust, I have never experienced it, I find it also a bit abstract. I have seen those pictures and the Holocaust films. I am a German and I have to deal with it somehow, especially when I meet Jews. I know that it's out there, but not that I feel really guilty.[74]

The owner of one of the Berlin klezmer labels also denies being motivated by a feeling of guilt: "If we're publishing Jewish music, we're doing it because of the music, and not because we think we have an obligation toward the Jewish nation, because our forefathers tried to annihilate them."[75] One of the issues klezmer musicians and producers raise here is the fact of temporal distance. While klezmer audiences might also include elderly people, the key figures of the klezmer revival today belong to the second and, more often, third generation, born after World War II. Their memory of the Holocaust is a "postmemory," fueled by photographs and film. This distance makes the Holocaust "abstract" for them and so removed in time that they do not feel directly morally responsible for it.

"I don't feel guilty," states another middle-aged musician, indignant at the proposition that Germans of the postwar generation should suffer pangs of conscience in relation to Germany's Nazi past. "It's impossible that I should feel guilty for another generation," he punctuates. "If one thinks like this, one can just as

[73] B09.
[74] B10.
[75] B18.

well hang himself."[76] A young female musician, asked to comment on the common proposition that German klezmer musicians become attracted by the genre to relieve their feelings of guilt, responds in a similar vein:

> Whether this gives me a good conscience? I wouldn't say so. I think I don't feel guilty enough for that. I am already the next generation, sometimes I feel a certain tension, for example in Poland or in the Czech Republic. When I was speaking in German with my friend on the tram, I could see that there were some tensions there. The thought comes back: do I say now that I'm German? Should I be happy that somebody considers me Swedish, in Poland, for example? It's definitely there. But in general terms I have understood that I am not guilty.[77]

Another male musician speaks not only of the impossibility to feel guilty for a crime committed by another generation but also of the difficulty to emotionally identify with any of the actors of the Holocaust. Recollecting his first trip to the concentration camps and the feelings that the visit evoked in him, he states:

> I was a teenager at that time [in the 1980s] and I went to Poland with a group to see the concentration camps. There was a lot of feeling about who these victims were. I won't say that I didn't have these feelings, to identify myself more with the victims, even if you can't really . . . you can't really . . . for me there is always the feeling that the Shoah, the Holocaust, you can't really understand and imagine, you can't really take part in it, either as a victim, or as the perpetrator.[78]

Many German klezmer musicians speak of a "perpetrator stigma" that they have had to confront, often as early as in middle school. Their awareness of the "German guilt," consequently, shapes the way they approach klezmer. Even though some of them insist on separating their music making from "memory work," many point out how difficult it is in Germany, where klezmer audiences seem to expect of the genre more than just entertainment. Thus the history of National Socialism remains a constant shadow over the klezmer scene, where the group belonging of its protagonists falls under the special scrutiny of critics and audiences alike. And the "perpetrator status" accompanies German klezmer musicians wherever they go, as the following statement makes vividly clear. "It happened to me several times in Arab countries," reports a male German musician in his forties, "that people congratulated me on being German, because the Germans killed the Jews. So this is what you have," he continues bitterly. "Whether you're blamed for having killed

[76] B02.
[77] B19.
[78] B13.

the Jews, or you're praised for having killed the Jews, the problem is just that you never killed a Jew."[79]

Poland: "Jedwabne was like a cold shower for us."

The fact that ethnic Poles did take part in crimes against Jews before, during, and immediately after World War II belonged for decades to the unexplored dark chapters of Polish history. The popular narrative of the war, which concentrated on the Polish losses and celebrated the martyrology of a nation invaded by two enemies and abandoned by its allies, did not leave much space for the suffering of the Polish Jews. But even if it did, the perpetrators of the hideous killings orchestrated on Polish soil were invaders and common enemies of both ethnic Poles and Jews: the Germans. It was only Jan T. Gross's book *Neighbors* that finally unleashed a massive debate about the Polish complicity in anti-Jewish violence and triggered a discussion of "Polish guilt." At the time of my field research, a few years after the publication of *Sąsiedzi* (*Neighbors*), which appeared in Poland in 2000, this freshly opened "Pandora's box" was still engaging the attention of large parts of society, many wishing that it had never been opened. Many Polish klezmer musicians referred to Gross's revelations about the pogrom in Jedwabne as a landmark in Poland's coming to terms with her difficult past and as an event that was of crucial importance for them personally.

A young male musician from Kraków states:

> Jedwabne was like a cold shower for us. Many people had not known about it at all. And then, suddenly, this feeling of being a poor and suffering Pole, who would never hurt anybody, was challenged. We thought: everybody was always against us—Germans, Austrians, Russians, and others. We were always the miserable ones, victimized by all the others. And now it suddenly turned out that Poles are murderers too! The reaction of many people was, "Wait a second! What do you mean: *us*? *Killing*? *There*? No way, it can't have been us! It must have been the Germans or Russians, or they forced us to do it!"[80]

The incredulity of many Poles and their refusal to accept the facts published by Gross originated, according to this speaker, in the Polish myth of innocence. The idea of Polish victimhood, which developed in the course of the nineteenth century when the country was partitioned among Russia, Prussia, and Austria, denoted Poland as the "Christ of nations" bleeding at the hands of and heroically resisting the occupying forces. In this romantic vision, Poland—redeeming the

[79] B01.
[80] K05.

entire continent through her suffering—was pictured as innocent and virtuous. The story of Jedwabne was probably the single most resonant narrative that challenged this myth of innocence, making way also for the question of how Poles have treated other minorities. The same Cracovian musician who recounted the initial shock at the publication of *Neighbors* added that the debate over anti-Jewish violence served for him personally as a catalyst to reflect on Poland's other ethnic minorities.

> Through all the years of Communism, Poles became used to the fact that it was only us who always got the beating, and we are so absolutely holy that we have never harmed anyone. The example of the cemetery of the Eaglets of Lvov (*Cmentarz Obrońców Lwowa*) is related to this problem. For years the media has been addressing the problem of Ukrainians opposing the cemetery. OK, they oppose it. But it was only recently mentioned, and only on the side, that there is this problem that we happened to have killed a couple of Ukrainians too![81]

The Polish-Ukrainian conflict over the cemetery of Polish defenders of Lvov serves the speaker as a parallel to the case of Jedwabne. After 1989, when the Polish authorities started lobbying for renovation of the cemetery, negotiations with the Ukrainian side led to a standoff over how to commemorate Polish soldiers and civilians who fought against Ukrainians for hegemony over the multiethnic Eastern Galicia region during the Polish-Ukrainian war (1918–19). The discussion over the cemetery opened old wounds concerning mutual atrocities against civilians in the aftermath of the two world wars, and it became a pretext for voicing mistrust and demonstrating self-defensive postures on both sides.

Rethinking the status of Poles as not just victims but also as perpetrators in World War II, induces some Polish musicians to make comparisons between the status of Poles and Germans. A young male musician, performing in a Jewish-style restaurant in Kazimierz, states that the silence which for decades surrounded anti-Semitic violence in Poland is unacceptable:

> Not to the same extent as Germans, but Poles should also feel ashamed of their ancestors who participated in the killing, in the tragedy of this nation [Jews]. Poles were also murdering them, and if they were sincere and willing to openly confront their history, many other things could be openly discussed. Unfortunately, we have the Communist mentality here, Poles tend to close themselves up in their own little worlds and prefer not to talk about anything.[82]

---

[81] K05.
[82] K13.

In a similar vein, one female performing musician speaks of a sense of guilt that, she believes, should be shared by Poles of various generations:

> From the perspective of my generation I can say that one can feel a sense of guilt, in as much as there is always a sense of guilt for something which could have been done, but wasn't. I'm talking here about the Holocaust and the responsibility of the Poles who collaborated with the Germans and handed Jews over to them. On the other hand, I identify myself more with the people who helped Jews. Nevertheless, it's impossible to claim, the way that we were taught in school in history class, that Poles were only helping Jews. It turned out that it was not all so rosy.[83]

An honest confrontation with Polish history, however, should not result in a direct comparison of Polish and German responsibility. Reacting to the controversy that arose around the term "Polish death camps," used in Western media and criticized by the Polish foreign minister Adam Daniel Rotfeld in 2005 as an attempt to shift responsibility for the construction of the camps onto Poles, this speaker warns against conflating Polish guilt with that of Germans:

> From a human point of view, there is this sense of guilt . . . definitely not a feeling of responsibility for the fact that Auschwitz and other extermination camps were located in Poland—this is what we have to cut ourselves off from. It was the fascists who opened the camps here and they knew what they were doing: they knew they were going to be associated with Poland. However, the feeling of guilt for every person who could have helped and didn't is there. Having met some people in Israel and seen how they retain their national identity and collective memory about the Holocaust, I think that young Poles should also know more about it and carry in themselves a feeling of sorrow, maybe not remorse, but sorrow for the great crime that took place here.[84]

Notably, the musician, again, makes a distinction between the degrees of responsibility that Poles and Germans carry.

As many of my interviewees from Kraków emphasize, remembering Jedwabne is important for the sake of commemorating the past. But it is also necessary to deal with anti-Semitic attitudes still latent in contemporary Poland. A number of musicians working in Kazimierz quote daily instances of anti-Semitism they encounter. At the same time, not all interviewees interpret them in the same way.

[83] K14.
[84] Ibid.

When a young musician remarks that anti-Semitism in Poland is still apparent on the language level, his colleague tries to argue that the instances quoted have a historic explanation:

> MUSICIAN 1: The word "Jew" has a negative connotation in Poland.
> MUSICIAN 2: But this has a historical background.
> MUSICIAN 1: It doesn't matter what background it has, there is anti-Semitism in Poland! If you go to a football match, you'll hear "fucking Jews." And . . . where I live, there is a shop open every day of the week and elderly people who go there to shop always say that they go to "the Jew."
> MUSICIAN 2: Because they used to own most shops once.[85]

The word *Żyd* [Jew] in Polish has, especially regionally, an impressive range of significances, often with a negative or derisory tinge. As the two musicians note, one of the contexts in which the word has been perverted is the language of Polish football hooligans, who use it as a slur against adversary teams. Interestingly, in Kraków, the "Cracovia" football club, disparagingly called "*Żydzi*" [Jews] by their opponent teams, adopted the epithet as a self-assertive tag.[86] In most cases, however, the word *Żyd* circulates in colloquial speech as a noun denoting annoying occurrences, such as, for example, an ink spot, an obstacle you trip on, or the spatter of water that enters the cockpit of a boat.[87] The exchange of the two musicians testifies, on the one hand, to the new sensitivity toward this "banal" anti-Semitism encoded in language and, on the other, to the popular tendency of overlooking or justifying it.

Debates on anti-Semitism or the implication of Poles in anti-Jewish violence do indeed reverberate on the klezmer scene, but for many cultural activists, Jewish music becomes a medium through which their message can be better heard in the society at large. According to Father Naliwajko, klezmer "brings with it a challenge to the core of one's identity." He holds that introducing Catholics to Jewish music can provide a salutary shock, which can make believers more sensitive also to anti-Semitism within the church and eventually "face them with the question of the responsibility for the Shoah."[88] Acknowledging the responsibility of the church for historic violence against Jews, such as religiously motivated pogroms, is for the young priest a prerequisite for any honest dialogue between Christians and Jews. And his belief is strong that this dialogue can also begin in the realm of music.

---

[85] K20 and K21.

[86] See Agata Dutkowska, "Visual Semiotics of 'Jewishness' in Kazimierz," in *Cultural Representations of Jewishness at the Turn of the Twenty-first Century: EUI Working Papers*, ed. Magdalena Waligórska and Sophie Wagenhofer (Florence: European University Press, 2010), 27–41.

[87] See Tokarska-Bakir, *Legendy o krwi*, 42–44.

[88] Naliwajko interview.

The klezmer scene, offering one of few public spaces where Poles can come into congress with Jews, provides particular conditions for encounter. "We have a greater awareness of what Poles did to Jews thanks to the conversations that we have with the Jews who were thrown out of Poland,"[89] reports a young Cracovian musician who tours Europe extensively with his band. But instances of difficult "truth-telling" take place also in Poland, when klezmer musicians meet their, often foreign, Jewish audiences. Although for many musicians the confrontation with the point of view of their Jewish interlocutors can be an eye-opening experience, for others, it also comes as a shock. "Recently a woman came to us after a concert," recalls a young musician performing in a Jewish-style restaurant, "and asked with this peevish tone of voice why we play Jewish music, given that Poles were killing Jews. She stupefied us with this question. Such a simpleton she was!"[90] Clearly, many attempts at communication between Jews and non-Jews in the context of the klezmer revival are painful, and not all of them are successful.

Conclusion

The particular microclimate for Jewish/non-Jewish dialogue in the klezmer scene depends not only on the mere possibility of encounter but also on the position of the non-Jewish musicians as mediators of Jewish culture and, sometimes, as stand-ins for Jews. Klezmer musicians who are considered to be Jewish by their surroundings, or who become targets of anti-Semitism, have a unique vantage point of people in between. This does not mean that they assume a vicarious Jewish identity nor that the experience of being "in between" necessarily has a therapeutic or soothing effect. Stepping into the other's shoes is a trying experience, especially when individuals are being directly confronted with one's group's historic harm-doing. Feeling empathy with Jews coincides here therefore with a feeling of shame for the dark past of Germany or Poland.

This ambivalent situation of the "people in between" is not without influence on how they come to define their collective identity. And it is not surprising that in a state of tension that the Jewish/non-Jewish encounter generates, defensive mechanisms come to play a role. We have seen, for example, that some of the interviewees referred to the "years of Communism" or "Communist mentality" in Poland, suggesting that the past regime is to blame for the rise of the Polish myth of victimhood and the blank spots in Polish historiography. The reference to the Communist rule, imposed on Poles by the Soviets, is a way of delegating at least part of the responsibility for the shameful episodes in Poland's past to an external

[89] K07.
[90] K19.

agent. Another defensive strategy, most vividly manifest in the last interview excerpt, is to delegitimize a critical interlocutor as unjustifiably aggressive and thus disregard their query entirely.

The critical encounter with the other in the context of cultural appropriation triggers anxiety that calls for a counterreaction. It is indeed hurtful to confront a difficult German Jewish or Polish Jewish past and intergroup "truth-telling." This crisis situation thus releases mechanisms, which allow individuals to reinterpret their position. The dynamics of this identity-reshuffle is the focus of the next chapter.

Triangles of Relief

Klezmer and the Negotiation of Identities

Henri Tajfel, a Polish-born social psychologist who survived the Holocaust in various POW camps, after finding that his family back in Poland had perished in the Shoah, devoted his entire academic life to researching the dynamics of intergroup relations and mechanisms of prejudice. The Social Identity Theory, which he developed together with his followers, aimed to answer the question of how our interaction with members of other groups contributes to our self-image. The basic premise of Tajfel's work is that group membership is crucial for our individual self-esteem. For this reason, groups constantly compare themselves to other groups in a way that favors the in-group.[1] And since a positive group identity belongs to our basic needs, once the image of the group becomes endangered, we will take measures to save it, or—should that be impossible—we will waive our group identity for another. This means that individuals belonging to a group stigmatized with the "perpetrator" status will see their basic psychological demand for a positive social identity unfulfilled. And this fact will inescapably trigger a counterreaction in the form of an identity-saving strategy.[2] In chapter 6 we read that the klezmer revivalists in Poland and Germany face a similar situation of tension. The present chapter, using Tajfel's theory as a framework of analysis, shows how they try to resolve it.

One of Tajfel's basic premises was that we always construct our collective "we" in reference to some collective "them." This mechanism of comparison also plays a role in maintaining our positive group image. Thus, when comparing our group to other out-groups, we follow the principle of in-group favoritism, trying to find a relevant field of competition that would allow us to celebrate the advantages of our group over others. The strategy of direct competition, though, will usually be used by groups of a relatively high status, for whom it is easier to affirm an existing

---

[1] Michael A. Hogg, "Intragroup Processes, Group Structure and Social Identity," in *Social Groups and Identities: Developing the Legacy of Henri Tajfel*, ed. W. Peter Robinson (Oxford: Butterworth-Heinemann, 1996), 67.

[2] John C. Turner, "Toward a Cognitive Redefinition of the Social Group," in *Social Identity and Intergroup Relations*, ed. Henri Tajfel (Cambridge: Cambridge University Press, 1982), 34–36.

superiority.[3] Comparing our own group to others has also one more downside. Implying direct competition, the strategy might breed conflict between the two groups involved.[4] Despite this, many individuals might resort to competitive comparisons if they see that the outcome will be of advantage for their in-group status.

Poles have a long tradition of comparing themselves to and competing against Jews. Stanisław Krajewski identifies two crucial fields of competition, which have defined recent Polish/Jewish relations. One of them is what he terms a "competition for the glory of suffering," which consists, on the part of Poles, in undermining the Jewish sufferings during World War II due to the fear of Polish wartime misery passing unnoticed. The other field of comparison concerns the myth of Poland as a promised land for medieval Jews expelled from Western Europe. In this case, emphasizing Poland's historical benevolence toward Jews allows Poles to see themselves in a positive light vis-à-vis other European nations.[5]

The conviction that Poles suffered just as much as Jews during World War II is, actually, quite popular in Poland and has become more widespread over the last years. A 2002 survey showed that 47 percent of Poles believed that Jews and Poles suffered to the same extent in World War II, while only 38 percent agreed that Jews suffered more. It is also interesting that in comparison to a survey conducted one decade earlier, more Poles insisted on the parity of suffering, while fewer pointed to Jews as having suffered more.[6]

The belief in the singular and redeeming suffering of the Polish nation dates back to long before World War II. It was the rising Polish nationalism of the nineteenth century that generated the myth of the historical innocence of Poland.[7] The partitioned nation, in danger of assimilation, was in particular need of protecting the positive collective identity. This was maintained by means of establishing a negative opposition to the image of a Pole. The Jew and the German served this role particularly well.[8] The Polish/Jewish competition, however, had an additional dimension. Since Poles were increasingly fascinated with messianic philosophy, borrowing the Jewish notion of the "chosen people" to explain their own position as purportedly the most victimized nation of Europe, the two forms of messianism were becoming mutually exclusive. The Polish claim to "chosenness," existing side by side with the Jewish one, required a monopolization of

---

[3] Rupert J. Brown, and Gordon F. Ross, "The Battle of Acceptance: An Investigation into the Dynamics of Intergroup Behaviour," in Tajfel, *Social Identity and Intergroup Relations*, 157.

[4] Turner and Brown, "Social Status, Cognitive Alternatives, and Intergroup Relations," in Tajfel, *Differentiation between Social Groups*, 205.

[5] Krajewski, *Żydzi, Judaizm, Polska*, 172.

[6] Ireneusz Krzemiński, "O Żydach i antysemityzmie po 10 latach," in *Antysemityzm w Polsce i na Ukrainie*, ed. Ireneusz Krzemiński (Warszawa: Scholar, 2004), 120.

[7] Andrzej Friszke in "Dzielić cudzy ból," *Znak*, no. 541, 2000, accessed October 1, 2008, http://www.miesiecznik.znak.com.pl/polowanie.html.

[8] Krzemiński, "O Żydach i antysemityzmie po 10 latach," 108–9.

suffering, along the lines of the Polish maxim that "two chosen peoples cannot live in one country."

Yet another field for comparison between Poles and Jews has opened up around the notions of Polish anti-Semitism and the so-called Jewish anti-Polonism. Statistics show that many Poles tend to downplay the problem of anti-Semitism. In 2002, only one in every five Poles considered anti-Semitism a serious problem, while almost two-thirds believed it was a marginal issue. One in ten Poles claimed that the problem did not exist at all. At the same time, 30 percent of Poles manifested views that sociologists classify as anti-Semitic. Interestingly, what Poles thought about the magnitude of Polish anti-Semitism was correlated with their convictions about the equal suffering of both nations during the war, which suggested a defensive character of both of the responses.[9] The concept of anti-Polonism, likewise, fulfills this self-protective function and is a direct counterreaction to the charges of anti-Semitism. Thus, the narrative of anti-Polonism frames accusations of xenophobia as part of the Jewish defamation campaign against Poland, and relativizes anti-Semitsm as an equivalent to anti-Polonism. Not surprisingly, both Jerzy Kosiński and Jan T. Gross, popularly considered the greatest anti-Polonists, have earned this status for their drastic representations of anti-Jewish violence at the hands of Poles.[10]

Stanisław Krajewski, one of the founders of the Polish Council of Christians and Jews and of the Polish/Israeli Friendship Society, does not deny that animosity between Poles and Jews might be mutual but points to their asymmetrical character. While anti-Polonism is a belief that Poles are particularly morbid anti-Semites—a generalization based on the Jewish predicament in Poland in the twentieth century—anti-Semitism is a much older and more comprehensive phenomenon, which, unlike anti-Polonism, had actual deadly consequences for Jews.[11] The distinction between the two matters is often lost on the participants of the Polish public discourse, where the "problem of anti-Polonism" has gained prominence. The Polish episcopate, for example, stated in 2000 that anti-Polonism should be combated with the same determination as anti-Semitism,[12] and the parliamentary committee responsible for relations with Poles abroad included a campaign against anti-Polonism in its 2005 agenda.[13]

Juxtaposing anti-Semitism with anti-Polonism, and negating the singularity of Jewish suffering during World War II, is a manner of direct intergroup

[9] Ibid., 128.

[10] In fact, Kosiński's novel, *The Painted Bird* (1965), which was first published in Poland only in 1989, never explicitly named the location of the action or the ethnicity of its protagonists.

[11] Krajewski, *Żydzi, Judaizm, Polska*, 155–56.

[12] "List Rady Episkopatu Polski do spraw Dialogu Religijnego z okazji Wielkiego Jubileuszu Roku 2000, August 25, 2000," accessed May 20, 2009, http://www.episkopat.pl/?a=dokumentyKEP&doc=dialog.

[13] "Komisja walczy z antypolonizmem," accessed May 20, 2009, http://wiadomosci.wp.pl/kat,1342,title,Komisja-walczy-z-antypolonizmem,wid,8114347,wiadomosc.html.

competition. By drawing attention to one's group suffering caused by an external enemy—the Nazis, or anti-Polonism—Poland's status as a victim-country is re-inforced. Pointing a spotlight at the hatred directed *at* the in-group obscures the hatred executed *by* the in-group. Thus the ordeals suffered are used to neutralize, perhaps even justify, the harm-doing inflicted by the in-group.

These relativizing comparisons can have a different scope and do not always have to be revisionist. For example, some klezmer musicians in Kraków point out the similarities in the predicament of Poles and Jews during the war, although they are far from negating the Jewish suffering. One Polish male musician makes a parallel between the fate of Poles and Jews, even though he is aware that Jews have suffered "incomparably" more than ethnic Poles.

> Let us not forget that Poland was invaded, and that people were being murdered here. It is a fact that the losses suffered by the Jewish nation are incomparably greater, which was because the Nazis had a different policy toward Poles. Poles were just occupying a different position on the list of victims. . . . It's hard to find a family in which someone did not die during World War II. No matter if it was a Jewish, or a Christian, Polish family. Practically in every household there was someone who was deported, imprisoned in a camp, died in battle, or was sent to a gulag.[14]

Although the interviewee admits here that the scale of atrocities suffered was different in the case of Christian Poles, he also raises the argument that Poles could have been next in the Nazi extermination plans. Thus, the Polish and Jewish suffering is directly compared, and both groups are identified as victims. What this comparison eclipses, though, is the fact that although Poles and Jews suffered side by side and at the hands of a common enemy, the probability of survival they faced was drastically different.

The external enemy (Nazi Germany) features in some interviews not only as the harm-doing agent but also as the evil force inspiring Polish anti-Semitism. One female interviewee presents the following explanation of brutal Polish prewar nationalism:

> This nationalism, the persecution of Jews, and anti-Semitism appeared in the 1930s under the influence of Nazi propaganda. But for one thousand years Jews had been living on Polish lands in a great friendship [with Poles]. Poland was a tolerant country, and these cultures were thoroughly mixed with one another, especially in Galicia, or the area surrounding Vilnius.[15]

---

[14] K12. Please see appendix for codes.
[15] K17.

The German occupation is portrayed here as a counterpoint to a long history of harmonious Polish/Jewish relations. The peaceful coexistence and intermingling of Poles and Jews before World War II is an image that becomes a frequent point of reference. The klezmer revival itself seems to feed on and support this idealized vision. Framed as part of the rich traditions of the once multiethnic Poland, klezmer becomes evidence of the beauty of a lost world.

The idealized perspective on past Polish/Jewish relations fulfills one more function. The past idyll offers a counterimage to the vision of Poland as a cemetery of the Holocaust. A young female musician feels that what happened before the Holocaust should have more prominence for those who come and visit spaces such as Kazimierz.

> I have this small objective to remind people that, in fact, Jewish and Polish people coexisted in Kazimierz for over seven hundred years. Together. Always together. Of course, God forbid, I do not want to forget about the Holocaust and everything that happened during World War II and later, but I am irritated by the fact that Poland, and particularly Kraków and Oświęcim, are viewed only as a great cemetery. One forgets about the centuries of common culture, the life together, and the intertwining of these cultures. Here Poles lived with Jews and Jews with Poles. Here everything was mixed, particularly in this district. And it is extremely important to remember it—the fact that Poland is not only a cemetery.[16]

Kazimierz appears in this passage as a space of good neighborly relations, characterized by very close contact: "intertwining," "mixing," and "togetherness." By means of a reference to a distant past, the interviewee contrasts the narrative of Poland as a site of extermination of Jews with the story of a long-term coexistence, where Polish benevolence toward Jews comes to the foreground. Overlooking the fact that Kazimierz became a Jewish town as a result of Jews being expelled from Kraków in 1495, and that life in the district was dominated by a constant religious and social boundary between Jews and Christians, the speaker presents Kazimierz as a symbolic counterpoint to Auschwitz, the site of a *positive* Polish/Jewish narrative.

If the topoi of the historic benevolence of Polish rulers toward Jews, who settled on Polish lands in the Middle Ages, features large in identity-saving techniques, the question of anti-Semitism in Poland constitutes another core issue that enables many comparisons. Although my interviewees did not usually negate the existence of the phenomenon in Polish society at large, they at times denied that anti-Semitism took place in their immediate surroundings. "Where I live, I have never had any contact with Jews, anti-Semitism, or racial prejudices," states a young female musician. "I was brought up in a Catholic family and I must say

---

[16] K16.

that I have never noticed anti-Semitism in the Catholic Church, either."[17] Interestingly, the speaker enumerates "Jews" in the same sentence as "anti-Semitism" and "racial prejudices," as if the presence of Jews was a prerequisite for anti-Semitism. The modifier "where I live" limits the force of the statement, though. In this way, the speaker does not exclude the possibility that anti-Semitic acts can be happening elsewhere, but she delegates them to the periphery of her immediate social context. A similar device is used by another young Cracovian musician who, when asked if she has ever come across anti-Semitism in Kraków, responded, "No, in Kraków surely not. Kraków, thanks to its Jewish district, is a city exceptionally tolerant toward Jews."[18] Here, Kazimierz comes to play yet another role: a space that breeds tolerance, and a legacy that is visible proof of good Polish/Jewish relations.

Other musicians, who did acknowledge anti-Semitism around them, often ascribed it only to the margin of Polish society. One musician, commenting on the fact that someone was damaging posters promoting the Jewish festival, called it "more of a hooligan, than an anti-Semitic action."[19] Another musician used a similar argument, also suggesting that Poland's reputation as an anti-Semitic country is a projection of the West:

> Perhaps we are viewed this way in the West? But anti-Semitism occurs when some national minority is directly and physically attacked. If it's some hooligan writing some stuff on a wall, it's just a proof of their stupidity, nothing else. Let's take into consideration one more thing: 80 percent of those people who shout anti-Semitic slogans don't know anything about Jewish culture. In Poland a Jew is still imagined like in Nazi propaganda: an old Jew swinging in prayer, dressed in a long traditional coat and with sidelocks.[20]

The speaker is both downplaying the existence of anti-Semitism in Poland and acknowledging that the image of Jews in Poland is still shaped by Nazi propaganda. These contradictory claims form part of the same argument thanks to the definition of anti-Semitism that the musician offers. Describing anti-Semitism as targeted physical violence, which directly involves a Jewish minority, prejudice, or acts of hostility such as anti-Jewish graffiti, but existing in the absence of Jews, can be interpreted as a less urgent problem.

That anti-Semitic graffiti does not equal anti-Semitism is also the opinion of another musician who states that the press "exaggerates with these stories" and, advocating freedom of speech, asks provocatively: "Someone writes '*Jude raus,*'

[17] K08.
[18] K19.
[19] K17.
[20] K06.

and so what?"[21] The trivialization of manifestations of anti-Semitism, such as graffiti, testifies here to the use of identity-saving techniques. It also indicates what one could call "banal anti-Semitism," which, flagged daily in urban spaces, becomes almost invisible because of its ubiquity. Like "banal nationalism" documented by Michael Billig, this banal anti-Semitism in Poland makes up part of the urban landscape, but its daily manifestations often remain for local Poles below the threshold of their perception.[22]

But even the more spectacular events, such as the Auschwitz cross controversy, are not necessarily read as having an anti-Semitic undertone. The conflict in Auschwitz, which concerned the presence of various Christian religious symbols on the grounds of the concentration camp, dates back to 1985, when a Carmelite convent was located in a building adjacent to the camp. The conflict escalated in the late 1990s, when a group of Catholics launched a campaign in defense of a large wooden cross, which was first used for the visit of Pope John Paul II to Auschwitz in 1979 and then, in 1989, erected permanently next to the contested convent. Attempts to remove the cross caused an outcry among the local inhabitants and church officials, and inspired Catholic activists to plant more than three hundred smaller crosses around it. In 1999 the "protest" crosses were finally removed, but the "papal" cross remained.[23] Commenting on the controversy, one of the musicians performing in Kazimierz says, "It was all staged. They were paying people to do it, to make a scandal out of it."[24] Interpreting the incident as media manipulation, the speaker dismisses the question of anti-Semitism as not worthy of real attention.

While some of the Polish interviewees attempted to counter the image of Poland as an anti-Semitic country by presenting anti-Semitism as a harmless or marginal phenomenon, others used a direct comparison with other European countries. A young male musician, who tours extensively with his band, pointed out that what is shameful in Poland is not so much the existence of anti-Semitic incidents but rather the common indifference toward them:

> In Poland anti-Semitism is manifested by seventeen-year-olds painting swastikas on walls and Stars of David hanging from gallows. . . . There is greater anti-Semitism in Germany, but they paint it [anti-Semitic graffiti] over. Fifteen minutes, and it's gone. In Poland it stays there on the wall. And tourists come in order to see these walls. It's our own fault.[25]

---

[21] K24.

[22] Michael Billig, *Banal Nationalism* (London: Sage, 1995).

[23] For the controversy in Auschwitz, see Genevieve Zubrzycki, *The Crosses of Auschwitz: Nationalism and Religion in Post-Communist Poland* (Chicago: University of Chicago Press, 2006); Kucia, *Auschwitz jako fakt społeczny*, 52–56, 241–44; Krajewski, *Żydzi, Judaizm, Polska*, 221–59; Holc, "Memory Contested: Jewish and Catholic Views of Auschwitz."

[24] K09.

[25] K07.

This diagnosis of the Polish problem uses a comparison, which has a relieving function, because it indicates Germany as a more anti-Semitic country, but at the same time it acknowledges the Polish responsibility for the high level of acceptance toward anti-Semitic graffiti.

The argument of anti-Polonism among Jews does not directly appear in the interviews but is occasionally implied. Often, several different areas of competitive comparison surface in a single utterance. A young female musician, for example, expressing her grievance toward Israeli tourists in Kraków, refers to Jedwabne:

> When a tourist group from Israel comes to Kraków, and they go through the Main Market Square, they all ostentatiously carry their backpacks on their stomachs. It's like a slap in the face for Poles. I know that Poles are not holy and that we have a reputation as thieves, but why exaggerate so much? Why so ostentatiously? And all of these debates about who did something in Jedwabne, or in Katyń,[26] or somewhere else! Many Jews were killed during the war, but also a lot of Poles. And many Poles were helping Jews but nobody talks about it.[27]

Here, the speaker accuses Israelis of manifesting their exaggerated mistrust toward Poles and cultivating stereotypes. At the same time she juxtaposes the crime in Jedwabne, committed *by* Poles, with the crime of Katyń, committed *on* Poles, switching the emphasis from Poles as perpetrators to Poles as victims. The contrast relativizes the weight of the Jedwabne crime, especially since a suggestion is made that the provenance of the perpetrators is dubious. Finally, the interviewee points out the suffering of Poles during World War II and their assistance to Jews. All of these devices help her present Poles in a better light than the group of reference, in this case, Israelis, who appear as prejudiced against Poles and unappreciative toward their engagement in saving Jews during the Holocaust.

While the superior scale of Jewish suffering in World War II is usually not questioned, the relativization of anti-Semitism in Poland is much more frequent. Although Polish klezmer musicians agree that Jews have indeed suffered prejudice and violence in Poland, with some even ready to acknowledge a Polish collective responsibility for crimes committed by Poles on Jews, the anti-Semitism of today remains a highly contested issue. This pattern in the responses corresponds to Krzemiński's 2004 survey on anti-Semitism in Poland. His team observed that the respondents negating the existence of anti-Semitism in Poland were also the most likely to say that Jews suffered more than Poles in the war. Krzemiński and his team interpreted this apparently inconsistent behavior as the principle of "fair play," that is, giving equal recognition to both nations.[28] The same rule might also

---

[26] A site of mass execution of Polish prisoners of war by the Soviet Red Army in 1940.

[27] K02.

[28] Krzemiński, "O Żydach i antysemityzmie po 10 latach," 129.

be at work in the case of klezmer musicians who, even if defensive about their in-group, still have a fair attitude about the proportions of Polish and Jewish suffering.

Apart from competitive comparisons, individuals suffering from a negative group identity might also adopt more creative techniques of comparison. According to Turner and Brown, we can do this by comparing the in-group to the out-group in a new way, which can bring a more favorable result.[29] Such a tactic, indeed, proved popular among the Kraków interviewees.

In June 2005 the European Commission against Racism and Intolerance issued a report pointing out the "persistence of anti-Semitism" in Poland and urging Polish authorities to take more decisive measures against it.[30] The report reverberated in the Polish media, interpreted by many as an ungrounded accusation. The publication also inspired a defensive reaction from one of the klezmer musicians, who found out about the report from the radio:

> [When] they said that on the radio, a real avalanche of commentaries started. Many people called into the studio, luckily smart people, and they said very basic things. Someone also immediately said what I was thinking at that moment: "Please, come to Kraków for the Jewish Culture Festival . . . come and have a look at what is going on there around the synagogue!"[31]

The report on racism, read as a direct accusation against Poland, is countered here with another image: that of the successful festival in Kraków. In this way, the basis for comparison between Poland and, in this case, other EU countries is changed from the issue of anti-Semitism to the Jewish heritage boom. And maintaining Jewish culture in Poland is what many klezmer musicians take pride in.

The redundancy of security measures, be it at the Jewish festival or in Kraków's synagogues, is another related argument, which allows the musicians to draw conclusions about whether Poland is a dangerous place for Jews or not. Especially the artists who tour abroad realize that this situation is an exception. Two of them remark in a conversation:

> MUSICIAN 1: A German journalist once asked us whether we feel safe if we go around without bodyguards. If they could see our festivals and concerts, with basically no security measures! Last year the ambassador of Israel and a couple of other ambassadors were here [at the festival] and

---

[29] Turner and Brown, "Social Status, Cognitive Alternatives, and Intergroup Relations," in Tajfel, *Differentiation between Social Groups*, 201–34.

[30] European Commission against Racism and Intolerance, "The Third Report on Poland," June 14, 2005, accessed October 16, 2008, http://www.coe.int/t/e/human_rights/ecri/1-ECRI/2-Country-by-country_approach/Poland/Poland_CBC_3.asp#TopOfPage.

[31] K07.

there were perhaps just a handful of policemen. Shevach Weiss[32] was dancing here, in Szeroka Street, without any security!

MUSICIAN 2: I don't know if something like that would be possible anywhere else in Europe![33]

Pointing out that strict security measures are a daily routine at similar events elsewhere in Europe, the musicians consider their absence in Kraków an advantage. The fact that no security measures are applied is interpreted as meaning that no security measures are needed, an argument that seems to contradict the claims of anti-Semitism in Poland.

The everyday experience of observing Jews visiting Kraków gives the musicians another unique opportunity to make comparisons. Of course, the routines in the backstage of Jewish heritage tourism do not always invite favorable comments. One performing artist, working in a Jewish-style restaurant in Szeroka Street, recounts a story reported to him by a colleague hired to play Polish folk music for a large group of tourists:

The Jews are served their food, you cannot hear the music at all because they yell so much, and three-quarters of the food ends up on the floor. After the group leaves, a team with shovels comes in [to clean]. Excuse me, but maybe I should be proud of being a Pole? It doesn't matter what nationality one is, but let's be normal and well-mannered.[34]

The misbehavior of the tourist group whose nationality is not clear, but which is denoted here as "Jewish," is implicitly compared to Polish audiences listening to klezmer concerts and comes out poorly. As we can see, comparisons between Poles and Jews are drawn constantly and in many different contexts, including those, like table manners, which might not be directly relevant to the problem areas of Polish/Jewish dialogue.

Most of these alternative intergroup comparisons, however, relate to the present. Today's Jewish heritage boom and heritage tourism are central issues, which is not surprising given that they belong to the daily experience of klezmer musicians. The choice to switch the focus from the potentially shameful past to the present might also be indicative of a more general trend. The focus on contemporary issues, as Bilewicz concludes in his study of Polish/Jewish encounters during the annual March of the Living in Auschwitz, creates positive attitudes and allows people to see similarities between the in-group and the out-group.[35] In

[32] The Israeli ambassador to Poland 2000–3.

[33] K05 and K12.

[34] K13.

[35] Bilewicz, "History as an Obstacle," 560. The March of the Living is an annual Holocaust commemoration event, during which thousands of Jewish teenagers and adults, along with survivors and representatives of other faiths, march in silence from Auschwitz to Birkenau.

other words, a change of topic might not only be salutary to social identity, but it can also potentially open new perspectives on the commonalities between the self and the other.

The Polish Triangle of Relief

Creativity in negotiating a positive identity might go farther. Apart from changing the grounds of comparison, we might also change the group we are contrasting with our own. In this case, we would usually juxtapose our group with one relatively similar to ours but inferior in status.[36] In Poland, the role of the third significant other is invariably played by the Germans.

The resulting Polish-Jewish-German triangle is determined here by the Polish collective memory of World War II and reinforced by national mythology and stereotypes of Jews and Germans. From the Polish perspective, Poles and Jews function in it as fellow victims, with Germans as the perpetrators. The fact that Jews and also Germans might imagine these roles differently is rarely pondered. And thus the unquestionable status of the Germans as the aggressors in World War II and the perpetrators of the Holocaust gives relief to Poles, anxious about their own harm-doing toward Jews.

Germans have played the role of villains in the Polish imagination for quite a long time, and this accumulated cliché owes its persistence in many ways to the history of World War II. The stereotype of the evil German, the eternal foe of the Pole, dates back to the Middle Ages. The idea of "hereditary enmity" between Poles and Germans appeared only after World War I. In the atmosphere of the postwar Polish/German tensions and ascendant nationalism, Poles began to view Germans as threatening. This image of Germans as violent, megalomaniac, and contemptuous was fueled also by the expansionist *Drang nach Osten* (thrust toward the East) and the politics of Bismarck and then Hitler.[37] The vision of the German threat still prevails in the current Polish public discourse, for example in regards to the issue of German restitution claims.[38] And since the image of the malevolent German has been so crucial for the Polish collective identity as a

---

[36] Turner and Brown, "Social Status, Cognitive Alternatives, and Intergroup Relations," in Tajfel, *Differentiation between Social Groups*, 201–34.

[37] Frank Golczewski, *Das Deutschlandbild der Polen 1918–1939: Eine Untersuchung der Historiographie und der Publizistik* (Düsseldorf: Droste, 1974), 64–102 and 139–42.

[38] The threat that the German expellees from the so-called recovered lands might claim reparations from the Polish government has been a recurrent motif defining the public discourse about Germany in Poland and Polish/German relations in recent decades. The concept of an aggressive and revisionist German enemy, represented in particular by the German Federation of Expellees (*Bund der Vertriebenen*) and its head Erika Steinbach, has been frequently instrumentalized in Polish political discourse. See Peter O. Loew, "Feinde, überall Feinde. Psychogramm eines Problems in Polen," *Osteuropa* 56, no. 11–12 (2006): 33–51.

counterimage of the virtuous Pole, parallels drawn between German and Polish anti-Semitism or culpability vis-à-vis Jews meet with a particularly vehement rejection.

The event that deeply shook the foundations of this Polish-Jewish-German triangle was, of course, the public debate on the pogrom in Jedwabne, which followed Jan T. Gross's publication of *Neighbors*. The public exposure of the Jedwabne pogrom made many Poles realize for the first time that their unambiguous victim status in the Polish-Jewish-German triangle might not be tenable, and that they must face their share of complicity in anti-Jewish violence. The Jedwabne debate revealed, as well, the difficulty of many Poles to accept the perpetrator status, expressed in the tendency to blame the killings on the Germans.[39]

"With Jews and Germans the situation is more transparent," said one cultural activist from Kazimierz, commenting on the discussions which followed the publication of *Neighbors*:

> Germans are the aggressors, Jews: the victims. The situation with Poles and Jews is much more complicated. Polish mythology speaks about tolerance and how good it was for Jews in Poland. [But] the year 1968, the second rejection of Jews after the war, is almost as traumatic as the Holocaust itself. Dialogue is difficult because we don't know who is who. In the case of Jedwabne, Poles are looking for other explanations because they can't come to terms with it.[40]

In the eyes of some, however, the redefinition of "who is who" in the Polish-Jewish-German triangle can also go too far, until Poles *replace* the Germans as the main perpetrators against the Jews. Many of my Polish interviewees emphasized the necessity of putting a sharp dividing line between Polish and German culpability. Asked whether he sees the klezmer revival in Poland as controversial, one young male musician responds:

> It must be remembered that Germans carry the burden of the genocide of Jews. So playing this music in Germany will always be controversial, there will always be questions of whether this is being done sincerely. In our case, in Poland, it's completely different. Why should Poland be a place where this music is controversial? It was here and not anywhere else that there was the biggest Jewish community in Europe.[41]

---

[39] For an analysis of the defensive arguments used in the Jedwabne debate, see Joanna B. Michlic, "The Dark Past: Polish-Jewish Relations in the Shadow of the Holocaust," in Glowacka and Zylinska, *Imaginary Neighbors*, 21–39; Joanna Tokarska-Bakir, "Jedwabne: History as Fetish," in Glowacka and Zylinska, *Imaginary Neighbors*, 40–63; Bilewicz, "Wyjaśnianie Jedwabnego," 248–69.

[40] K04.

[41] K06.

Another klezmer performer, when confronted with Henryk Broder's thesis that non-Jewish producers and fans of klezmer want to identify themselves with the victims of the Holocaust, protests:

> I would say this opinion makes sense to me, if spoken in reference to Germany and addressed at the German nation. If you were to say that Jewishness is fashionable in Germany because Germans identify with the victims, I would agree. I could sign my name under that statement. But in Poland, why? For what reason?[42]

It is, to a certain extent, striking that these Polish klezmer musicians so easily classify the involvement of their German colleagues as controversial or even therapeutic, while they vehemently deny having such motivations themselves. It seems that they perceive the German klezmer scene as an outlet for feelings of guilt because they regard Germans as a collective defined by a perpetrator identity. And if many Polish musicians are ready to speak of Polish responsibility for anti-Jewish violence, considerations of Polish guilt are particularly difficult if they entail drawing parallels between Poland and Germany.

Germans appear as important figures in the narratives of my interviewees, and their image is usually filtered through the (post)memory of World War II. On the other hand, Polish klezmer musicians, who often play in front of German audiences, also draw on their firsthand experiences. For this reason, while the image of the German is generally negative, one positive trait that makes its way into this stereotypical image is the German love of music. As many Polish musicians emphasize, Germans make better consumers of music than Poles, because of their superior musical education and respect for musicians. "Even in some backwater town you get a full house at a concert," states one Polish touring musician. "It's not because they're rich, but because they just like music."[43] Even this positive feature is still often framed in language that brings to mind martial associations. "The German audience is excellent," states the same musician, "well-disciplined, giving positive feedback. They sit quietly, and clap their hands when they're supposed to clap."[44] Despite the fact that the interviewee is genuinely impressed with the turnouts during the band's tour across Germany, a tone of mockery is evident. Even after face-to-face contact, stereotypes of the German militarist spirit might still guide the perception of Polish klezmer musicians.

And, indeed, despite positive comments about performing in Germany, many Polish musicians see their German audiences, particularly elderly ones, as possible perpetrators in World War II. One of the musicians performing in Kazimierz,

[42] K05.
[43] K20.
[44] Ibid.

who remembers World War II from her childhood, reports that she cannot help wondering about what the elderly Germans in her audience did during the war:

> When I see Germans aged between seventy and eighty, I wonder, "What did he do during the war?" And there is this certain characteristic ethnic type of German. It's in the facial features. Sometimes you see this German posture. Some of them remind me of German soldiers. Actually, my family and I did not suffer any persecution from the Germans. A part of my family was sent to a gulag. . . . But I lived through that time as a Pole and I was brought up in an incredibly patriotic family. So all of that is in me.[45]

The image of the German this speaker evokes is heavily laden with war-related imagery and draws on the racist language of biological essentialism. Even though she decides to counterbalance her observation with the caveat that it was not the Germans that her family suffered from, the German physiognomy embodies a trauma.

Another young musician, performing mostly in Kazimierz, believes that younger Germans visiting Kraków suffer from feelings of guilt when they are confronted with Jewish culture. Recalling one of her most memorable concerts, she mentions a young German who was on his first visit to Poland:

> He was sitting here and was shocked. I will never forget his face when he was listening to this music. He said that, listening to this music and getting to know this culture, he feels ashamed that he is German, ashamed for his ancestors and everything that happened. Most Germans do not have any idea about it all, and when they come here, they get a shock.[46]

Although firsthand encounters in Kazimierz bring some klezmer musicians to the conclusion that Germans relate to Jewish music in a special way because of the burden of historical responsibility that rests on their shoulders, others, particularly those touring abroad, note that the young generation of Germans does not identify itself through the prism of the Holocaust and that its reception of Jewish music does not involve coming to terms with the past. What, in the eyes of these musicians, frees klezmer from being associated with the Holocaust is not just the temporal distance from the Holocaust but the fact that klezmer concerts in Germany have had a long tradition, and have lost something of their initial liturgical aura. One touring musician, who often performs in Germany,

[45] K17.
[46] K25.

believes therefore that klezmer concerts are no longer a therapeutic space for Germans:

> When we were going there [to Germany] in the beginning, some ten years ago, we could distinctly feel a certain concentration during the concerts in places like churches. . . . People would come to us and tell us that they felt as if they were going to confession. In the past ten years everything has changed diametrically . . . I guess now it has lost the charm of novelty, a fashion [for klezmer] appeared and made people become accustomed to it.[47]

It is notable that German audiences, interacting with Polish musicians, communicate their response to the music by using the Roman Catholic concept of confession. Non-Jewish musicians from Poland, raised Catholic, can relate well here to the sensation described by the German concertgoers. They also believe to have intuited how, with time, the reception of klezmer in Germany has changed. Just as Germans seem to have become used to klezmer concerts, Polish musicians have accustomed themselves to performing for Germans. A young musician, reporting on her latest tour in Germany, notes:

> A couple of days ago we came back from Saarbrücken . . . where we played at a festival of klezmer and world music. . . . There were German and Dutch bands, us, even a group from Madagascar—an absolute mix. And you did not feel like anyone was burdened with anything. We also did not feel like we were in Germany, and therefore did not feel strange because we're Polish. If we put it all in the historical context, it would be completely absurd! We, Poles, playing Jewish music to Germans. You could make quite a horror story out of it. Only what for? If we are to brood over it and rummage through it in such a negative way, it is not going to be constructive. It's not going to bring about anything good.[48]

But while some Polish musicians hope that the klezmer scene can liberate itself from the weight of history, others are worried that Germany will forget its dark past too soon. Observing the rising popularity of right-wing extremist movements, the upsurge of new historical discourse centered on German victimhood, and the attention given to commemorating events such as the Allied bombing of Dresden, one male Polish klezmer musician speaks of a "new reality" in Germany. Wondering about the associations that German audiences might have when listening to one of his band's recordings, he states:

---

[47] K05.
[48] K16.

I was listening to our recording from Fürth, a piece emulating flying planes and falling bombs. We were not doing that on purpose, but we always had the impression that Germans were particularly moved by it. There are things that sound like a wailing siren [in that piece]. And every time someone was sobbing in the first row, or came to us after the concert to tell us that that piece overwhelmed them completely. And I was listening to it and asked my wife, "What do you think Germans associate with it when we play it?" And she said, "The bombing of Dresden." This was some gallows humor from my wife, but a lot of things are changing in Germany: these neo-fascist movements and the whole thing about Dresden. We are in a new reality now.[49]

The "new reality" stands not only for the decreasing importance of World War II for the young generation but also a shift of emphasis in contemporary historiography and the ascendance of victim-discourse in Germany. The space recently given to the commemoration of the civilian population bombed by the Allied Forces, the victims of mass rape, and the *Vertriebene*, German exiles from the territories that became Poland and Czechoslovakia after 1945, together with the celebration of the German anti-Nazi resistance, mark a change in the representation of World War II in the German media and popular culture. Polish klezmer artists touring Germany are becoming aware of this shift and find it problematic.

Placing Germans in the Polish-Jewish-German triangle, Polish klezmer musicians rely both on stereotypes and firsthand experience. On the one hand, they interpret their elderly German audiences' interest in Jewish music as motivated by feelings of guilt. On the other hand, although they often view Germans in the first place as villains of World War II, they also make more nuanced observations about the younger generation of Germans whom they directly encounter. But although the positive characteristics counterbalance, to a certain extent, the image of Germans as perpetrators, the group status of Germans remains decidedly negative. In the Polish-German-Jewish "triangle of relief," the status of each group results from the specific wartime situation. Poland was both the site of anti-Jewish atrocities, committed not only by Germans but also by Poles, and a land brutalized by the experience of aggression and occupation by two external powers. Owing to this particular constellation of forces, Poles tend to delegate part of their responsibility for anti-Semitism, or anti-Jewish violence, to the group they perceive as the main villain in World War II—the Germans. The status of each group in this triangle, however, is not necessarily stable, nor is it unanimously recognized by all the parties concerned.

[49] K05.

Longing for Galicia

"If somewhere in the world somebody asks me where I'm from," said one cultural organizer working in Kazimierz, "I say I'm from Kraków. I have a stronger spiritual affinity with Galicia than with Poland, because I actually don't know Poland very well. OK, I'm a Pole from the *official* point of view, but from the cultural one—absolutely not."[50] This declaration, although it sounds quite radical, is actually relatively common among Polish klezmer revivalists from Kazimierz.

Creative devices applied in negotiating a positive group identity might be based on a comparison to a third party but may not be limited solely to this. Alternatively, by seeking a more favorable comparison with the out-group, we might also shift the level of identification onto a higher, more universal plane ("we are all human"), or to a more personal one ("I am just me"), thus avoiding identification as a member of the perpetrator group.[51] An interesting variation on this strategy in Kraków is the salience given to the local "Galician" identity.

The choice of "Galician" as a substitute for Polish identity is striking, though, because it is not really tantamount to regional identity. Galicia, a southern province of Poland annexed by Austro-Hungary during the partitions of Poland at the end of the eighteenth century, is a historical region that ceased to exist in its original form. The kingdom of Galicia and Lodomeria was part of the Austro-Hungarian Empire until 1918. Later, it was incorporated into the independent Polish Republic. Today its territory is divided between Poland and Ukraine. Despite this, the relative freedom and prosperity of the Austro-Hungarian partition of Poland still inspires many myths, and Galicia functions as a successful trademark in Kraków, featuring in the names of restaurants, hotels, and klezmer bands. Connoting a multi-ethnic society and cultural ferment, Galicia has become a superordinate category, which subsumes both Jews and non-Jews.

"My grandmother knew Yiddish very well," recounts one musician from Kraków, "it was the Galician tradition. . . . All the old people in Lvov used to know [Yiddish] . . . the two communities were intertwined."[52] Galicia appears here as a pre-Holocaust melting pot, which enabled an exchange among the different ethnic groups inhabiting it and also a common identity. According to this musician, "all" Lvovians spoke Yiddish—a hugely exaggerated statement about a place, which was afflicted with serious ethnic conflicts and was also a site of pogroms in the aftermath of the Polish-Ukrainian war (1918–19).[53] Invoking idealized images

---

[50] K11.

[51] Bilewicz, "History as an Obstacle," 552.

[52] K17.

[53] Around seventy Jews lost their lives in the pogroms that accompanied the Polish/Ukrainian fights in November 1918. See Avraham Rubinstein, "Lvov: From 1914 to 1939," *Encyclopaedia Judaica*, 2nd ed., vol. 13, 290.

of the past coexistence of Poles and Jews serves here to create an inclusive per-spective. The speaker de-emphasizes boundaries between Jews and non-Jews, and stresses what the two groups have in common. Galicia becomes the locus of a superordinate mythic identity, accessible to both Jews and non-Jews.

Apart from common geographical coordinates, there are also religious inter-sections that offer the possibility to stress the shared heritage of Judaism and Christianity. The idea of Judeo-Christianity, referring to common canonic texts and standards of ethics, has been used, perhaps most prominently, by Pope John Paul II, who spoke of Jews as the "elder brethren" of Catholics. This superordinate category inspired one middle-aged male musician to identify himself with this common spiritual realm, which, in his view, transcends other boundaries:

> I have learned very much about Jewish culture . . . but I've gained some-thing also as a Catholic. Delving into the religious experience, learning about Jewish culture, old texts, customs, and the philosophy connected to Judaism, I have understood what it means that Christians are [Jews'] younger brothers in faith. . . . Through understanding Jewish culture I came to know the basis of what I believe in. . . . The world of Judaism and Christianity is one to me. What can separate these two worlds are earthly interests, but they belong to *this* world, not to *that* one. The spiritual world can only unite, the material world separates.[54]

Emphasizing the Jewish roots of Christianity, the speaker generates a vision of spiritual unity between Jews and Christians, and relegates the historical antago-nisms into the sphere of the profane. Similarities between the two groups thus become central, and the positive value ascribed to the common features of both religions permits the musician a positive identification as a Catholic.

But apart from the purely rhetorical techniques of negotiating a positive group identity, individuals might also apply more decisive means to improve their group's image. One of the ways to do this is to undertake social action, which can lead to a desirable change in the situation and in the group's ratings.[55] The daily work of klezmer revivalists can be seen in terms of social activism, too. By performing Jewish music and informing their audiences about Jewish culture, klezmer musi-cians become social agents who educate, mediate, and warn against stereotypes. And indeed, many of them see their work as a form of social action, which can eventually contribute to better Polish/Jewish relations. "We get great satisfaction from events such as the Jewish Festival," says a young Cracovian musician, "be-cause, thanks to them, people . . . start domesticating this [Jewish] culture and have less prejudice."[56] With this goal in mind, some klezmer revivalists take an

[54] K03.
[55] Brown and Ross, "The Battle of Acceptance," 157.
[56] K05.

active part in events advancing Polish/Jewish dialogue and occasionally even participate in political demonstrations. "I hate any signs of racism and anti-Semitism. Intolerance simply hurts me,"[57] says a young female musician involved in a Polish/German youth initiative and supporting projects against anti-Semitism, racism, and homophobia. Whenever asked to perform for an event campaigning tolerance, this musician does not hesitate to give her consent, regardless of whether the organizers can pay the band or not.

The Cracovian "klezmer chaplain," Jarosław Naliwajko, also sees his involvement as a form of social activism. He considers the first klezmer concert he organized as a breakthrough. Although the klezmer concert in a Jesuit church was just "a small step," it was one "which before World War II would not have been possible at all."[58] In his opinion, the Second Vatican Council (1962–65) provoked some changes in the way that the Catholic Church perceives Judaism, but only the adoption of its tenets in practice can further contribute to a complete change in mentality. Introducing Jewish music into the sacral space is for him the embodiment of the Church's vocation.

> Organizing a klezmer concert in a church means to a Catholic giving everything we have. It is a signal that we're open-minded and that, if the Gospel calls for openness and welcoming everyone, this is what really happens. Everyone was present at the concert, even the head of the Jewish community, and people are still talking about it. This is a realization of what the Church should be.[59]

Thanks to social activism, individuals involved can see their group in motion, in a process of change. Even though they might still be dissatisfied with the status quo, or the "bad" past, the unsatisfactory group identity weighs less when one is able to present a personal record of opposition.

"Situational" and "Marginal Jews"

Although the revival of Jewish heritage in Kraków is often seen as a non-Jewish effort, many of those involved in it do relate to Jewishness in a very personal way. The owner of one of the restaurants in Szeroka Street says that his engagement in Jewish culture has been for him a way to explore his Jewishness. "I am not a halachic Jew, but I obviously have some Jewish 'motifs' in my family, which somehow define who I am," he states. The project of opening the first Jewish restaurant in Kazimierz, which became a meeting point for many local Jews and "marginal

---

[57] K16.

[58] Naliwajko interview.

[59] Ibid.

Jews," was an attempt to recover a tradition he himself could not experience at home:

> It was all new to me because I was raised in a, you can say, Catholic family. Besides, Jewish families were mostly non-existent here. The majority of Polish Jews were not brought up in Jewish families. There were Catholic and atheist families, but no Jewish ones. There are people who are Jewish now, but they have arrived at that somehow. This is a common situation. I don't know if there is at least one person who could say that they had a Jewish home. This is the situation characteristic of Poland: everything has emerged from ashes.[60]

Lacking a benchmark for their quest for Jewish traditions, Jewish heritage revivalists eventually created spaces that substituted for the missing institution of a "Jewish home." For many of them, the Jewish district in Kraków became such a space, which they also feel they are responsible for co-creating. One Cracovian musician who, although Judaism is not his religion, has a Jewish background, describes his involvement with Jewish heritage as a "necessity":

> My interest in Jewish culture is obvious, because I am a descendant of the people saved by Schindler. My dad, who lives in Kazimierz, is a walking legend. He was shot by Amon Goeth in the Płaszów camp. The bullet entered his neck and went out the other side. It was a one in a million chance that he survived. My mother and grandmother, in turn, were saved by Schindler. This culture is not a question of interest for me, but of necessity.[61]

The klezmer revival appears, therefore, as a cultural space, which plays a crucial role for the local Jews and "marginal Jews." It gives them an opportunity to engage with Jewish culture without the need of practicing Judaism and provides them with many alternative ways of expressing their Jewish identity on a daily basis.

Henri Tajfel understood social identity as "the individual's subjective location in the network of social relationships."[62] Living in a web of social connections, however, we not only seek acceptance, compare ourselves to other groups, and compete against them, but we have at our disposal a degree of mobility, which also allows us in a crisis situation to move from one group to another. And hence, disappointed with the low status of our own group, we might seek membership in other, more attractive collectives, unless leaving the in-group is impossible for

---

[60] K22.

[61] K28.

[62] Henri Tajfel, "Instrumentality, Identity, and Social Comparisons," in Tajfel, *Social Identity and Intergroup Relations*, 503.

"objective" reasons, or it would conflict with values that we consider important to our self-image.[63] If leaving the group is feasible, we will aspire to join a group with a higher status. If not, we can still dissociate ourselves psychologically from the group. The most common way to do so is to consider oneself as an atypical group member and blame the vices ascribed to one's in-group on its other members.[64] Leaving the group is, no doubt, the most drastic among identity-saving strategies. There are, however, different degrees of "leaving," and a wide range of "exit options," which do not have to imply abandoning one's group entirely.

One possible path of dissociation is enabled by "situational" and "marginal Jewishness." Situational identification, as Jonathan Okamura defines it, takes place when an individual claims membership in "any one of a generally limited number of ethnic categories that they belong to, *or perhaps do not belong to*, in accordance with their belief that such a selection of ethnic identity will be to their advantage."[65] What I refer to as "situational Jewishness" embraces, then, the various ways in which non-Jews relate themselves to Jewishness in the context of cultural appropriation. "Situational Jewishness" is by definition a transient condition, emerging in response to a particular situation. It is also instrumental, since it is motivated by the wish to dissociate oneself from one's group and aspire toward some alternative "situational ethnicity."

Stanisław Krajewski's category of "marginal Jews" also denotes individuals who have at their disposal multiple ethnic identities with which they can potentially identify. It is, however, relating to a more specific group of people in contemporary Poland, some of whom, owing to a historical constellation of forces, were not even aware of their Jewish roots. Krajewski identifies as "marginal Jews" people of Jewish origin who do not practice Judaism, people born in mixed families and those of non-Jewish descent who identify themselves as Jewish. This last category of people may not formally belong to any Jewish community but feel a strong affinity with Jewishness because Judaism, or Jewish culture, plays a central role in their lives.

The adjective "marginal" that Krajewski uses is accurate in several ways. First of all, "marginal Jews" are Jews who discover their Jewishness or make the choice to become Jewish, but their being Jewish is not necessarily central to their identities. Second, the term reflects the peripheral position of these people in relation to the formally organized Jewish communities, as they usually do not feature as their members. Third, in quite a paradoxical and subversive way, the marginal Jew relates to Robert E. Park's early twentieth-century notion of the Jew as the "marginal man." Park, who set out to investigate people positioned between different

---

[63] Henri Tajfel, "Social Categorization, Social Identity, and Social Comparison," in Tajfel, *Differentiation between Social Groups*, 64.

[64] Turner, "Toward a Cognitive Redefinition of the Social Group," 34–35.

[65] Jonathan Y. Okamura, "Situational Ethnicity," *Ethnic and Racial Studies* 4, no. 4 (1981): 454; italics mine.

cultures, considered an emancipated Jew to be the paradigmatic marginal man: "a cultural hybrid, a man living and sharing intimately in the cultural life and traditions of two distinct peoples; never quite willing to break, even if he were permitted to do so, with his past and his traditions, and not quite accepted, because of racial prejudice, in the new society in which he now sought to find a place."[66] According to Park, this marginal man lives in a state of acute anxiety. Aspiring to shed his subaltern identity, he is nonetheless tormented by ambivalence and estrangement. Krajewski's marginal Jew, in contrast to the classic figure of the marginal man, may be likewise characterized by in-betweenness and ambivalence, but is in the process of dissimilation, not assimilation, seeking "to find a place" in Judaism.

Perhaps not surprisingly, there are a number of marginal Jews among Polish klezmer musicians. The story of the band Kroke and how they discovered the Jewish roots of two of their members might actually be representative of the predicament of many other Poles who learn, sometimes late in their lives, that some of their ancestors were Jewish. Tomasz Lato recounts how the band's interest in Jewish music made their families mention for the first time that two of them have Jewish roots:

> When we were beginning to play klezmer, we didn't know anything about our origins. The fact that we have Jewish roots emerged only when we were already playing this music. Our violinist was the first one to find out, and it was a big shock for him, raised in the Catholic tradition, that he had Jewish ancestors. The families started to talk to us about it only once we had been playing for a couple of years. . . . His grandfather never said a word and is already dead now. . . . It was only his uncle who came over and said: "Tomek, do you know why you play this music?" "Because I like it," he answered. And he said, "So I'll explain to you why you like it." And they got down to documents and genealogical trees and this is how it all came out. But in any case, it doesn't change anything for us. It's very important for us to know, to solve this riddle of why we were so fascinated by it, why this music was so attractive to us.[67]

Having found out about their Jewish background, the musicians start relating their interest in Jewish music to their discovery but, at the same time, declare that it did not change anything in their everyday lives. "Nothing changed in my life when I found out about my origins," says Tomasz Kurkuba. "I was just happy that I can play this music."[68] The "Jewish connection" is, therefore, important for the musician in as much as it helps him to frame his interest in klezmer as legitimate. Discovering Jewish roots does not automatically mean identifying oneself

---

[66] Robert E. Park, *Race and Culture* (Glencoe, IL: The Free Press, 1950), 354.

[67] Lato interview, April 17, 2004.

[68] Kurkuba, April 17, 2004.

as Jewish, but it can potentially serve as a means of gaining distance from the Polish identity, when necessary.

One of the most fascinating narratives of marginal Jewishness in Kazimierz is, undoubtedly, the story of Janusz Makuch, the head of Kraków's Jewish Culture Festival. To Makuch, who for more than two decades has been organizing one of the largest Jewish festivals in Europe, Jewishness is a life choice, and Israel a country he identifies as "the cultural and spiritual center of this world."[69] Journalists describe him as being possessed by a dybbuk.[70] He himself defines his life vocation as that of a *shabes goy*[71] or a *shames*[72], a catalyst who facilitates the revival of Jewish culture in Poland. "My role consists in traveling the world, like a *shames* . . . , knocking on Jews' window shutters in the morning, waking them for the prayers and inviting them to the greatest and most beautiful synagogue in the world— Kazimierz," says Makuch in an interview.[73] His story is that of one of the main instigators behind the Jewish heritage revival in Poland and, at the same time, that of a Pole who is exploring Jewishness and Judaism also on a personal level.

As many other participants of the klezmer revival, Makuch is often taken for a Jew:

> If someone looks at a guy like me, or goes to the festival's website and sees: "Janusz Makuch, Director," they think, "that must be a Jew, it's not possible that a non-Jew organizes the biggest Jewish festival in the world!" And it turns out that he can! But this is inconceivable. "OK, you're not Jewish," I've heard already millions of times, "but your grandmother was Jewish, right?" Not only was my grandmother not Jewish, but she would take me to church in Lublin and teach me prayers.[74]

Makuch's desk in the festival's office is adorned by a menorah, and he serves his guests Israeli coffee. He goes to synagogue on Jewish holidays, and "not only the important ones," as he told the Israeli newspaper *Haaretz*.[75] Conversion to Judaism has been an option for him, but one that he has never realized. "A couple of years ago I had a serious conversation with the famous cantor Benzion Miller," he recalls. "We were walking around Szeroka Street almost till dawn. He said:

[69] Makuch interview, May 3, 2007.

[70] Radłowska, "Dybuk nim trzęsie niemiłosiernie."

[71] A non-Jewish helper in a Jewish household, performing the work forbidden to Jews on the *shabes*.

[72] A sexton in a synagogue, also responsible for summoning Jews to prayer.

[73] Janusz Makuch cited in Anna Dobranowska, "Jestem jak szames. I jestem z tego dumny," Forum Żydzi, Chrześcijanie, Muzułmanie, June 25, 2003, accessed October 15, 2008, http://www.znak.org. pl/index.php?t=ludzie&id=34.

[74] Makuch interview, May 3, 2007.

[75] Janusz Makuch cited in Goel Pinto, "My Personal Atlantis," *Haaretz*, August 27, 2007, accessed October 15, 2008, http://www.haaretz.com/hasen/spages/897586.html.

'We need you the way you are, we have enough religious Jews.'" Makuch took the advice of the cantor seriously. He believes it is not enough to "want to be Jewish," but that there needs to be a response to this wish from God. "I am not too pushy toward G-d," Makuch says in an interview, "Perhaps I find myself in a very strange state of mind, but it doesn't bother me. I do not belong to any religion, but I know that if I need one in my life, it's Judaism."[76]

Asked about his identity as a Pole, Makuch gives a pluralist definition of Polishness. Inspired by the Polish romantic poet Cyprian Kamil Norwid (1821–83), he says "it is more important to be a human being in the Pole than a Pole in the human being." The conviction that it is possible to be a Polish patriot without "Polish egocentricity" helped him, as he said, "to embrace the Jewish world" as his own.[77] Defining national identity not in ethnic but in humanist terms allows Janusz Makuch to delve into Jewishness without leaving the category of Polishness. At the same time he realizes that his Polish Jewish identity is self-ascribed and not necessarily recognized by Polish society at large or by the Jewish community. "I have difficulty with my Polish identity, because I don't think that I am considered Polish by Poles," he acknowledges, "and from the point of view of the criteria existing in the Jewish world, I am certainly not a Jew." He pleads to both sides, though, for acceptance of such a hybrid identification, one that he believes is shared by a number of Poles involved with Jewish culture and Judaism: "A lot of our friends, those who have already passed away, or are still alive, have been defining themselves as Polish Jews. Couldn't it be possible for some of us, or at least for me, to say, with all of my spiritual and intellectual responsibility, that in as much as they are Polish Jews, I am a Jewish Pole?"[78]

Invalidating the dichotomy of "Polish" and "Jewish," Makuch draws attention to the model of multiple identities declared by many assimilated, patriotic Polish Jews in the past. His choice not to become a Jew through conversion but to remain a Jewish Pole is a way of asserting the Polish Jewish identity as legitimate, even though it is not likely to be recognized by the conservative norms of membership of either of the groups.

The ways of exploring this in-between space and expressing affinity with Jews can take different forms, however. The narratives of Polish "Jews by profession" include stories of genealogical research and also declarations of sympathy and solidarity with Jews, which do not have to be connected to any claims to Jewish identity whatsoever. A few klezmer musicians from Kazimierz have discovered, or speculate, that they have a Jewish ancestor. "I am not Jewish, and I'm rather not planning to convert," states a young female musician, "but thanks to all this,

---

[76] Janusz Makuch cited in Marek Bartosik, "Jestem tylko szabesgojem," *Gazeta Krakowska*, June 27, 2008, accessed June 22, 2009, http://www.jewishfestival.pl/plikiprasa/1215954686.pdf. I retained the original spelling of the word "G-d" as in the Polish version of the article.

[77] Makuch interview, May 3, 2007.

[78] Ibid.

I found my roots. Some generations back I had Jews in my family. This discovery was the result of my individual family quest, a pretty difficult one, unfortunately."[79] Opening with a seemingly straightforward declaration that she is not Jewish, the musician's statement becomes increasingly ambiguous, especially as she subsequently adds that she is no longer Catholic. As in many other cases, the personal quest for family roots began with music. It is klezmer that became the pretext, the motivation to ask "difficult" questions and dig into her family's past. This personal investigation is also crucial for the musician's self-identification. Pointing out her Jewish ancestors, she does not claim a Jewish identity but signals that she does not consider herself a typical group member, and that she has at her disposal the possibility to claim an identity alternative to that of "Polish" or "Catholic."

This "Jewish option" might, indeed, remain only in the sphere of speculation. A male musician in his forties narrates the following story:

> I went once to the parish of Corpus Christi, where I was the best man at my friend's wedding. When the priest was registering me as a witness, he told me that my surname appeared in the parish documents in the sixteenth century in the book of baptisms. This intrigued me that it was in Kazimierz of all places, and in the sixteenth century. It is indifferent to me whether I have something Jewish in me, or not. I like the music, and its emotionality, so I was never wondering whether I am Jewish, or not. But when I found out about it, a thought crossed my mind that maybe a Jew from Kazimierz got baptized and gave the beginning to my family.[80]

The mere contingency that his forefathers might have been Jewish opens up a field of eventuality that shakes the set assumptions about his Polish identity and allows for a way of expressing proximity to Jews.

This feeling of affinity toward Jews accompanies many Polish klezmer musicians. Some of them relate it to concrete events in their lives, which they interpret as also crucial for their artistic work. A singer performing Yiddish songs in Kraków recounts a particular story of how a traumatic episode during World War II made her develop a deep sympathy toward Jews. She reports that when she saw the movie *Schindler's List* for the first time she was deeply shocked by the scene of a train transport heading to a concentration camp, with the people inside the cattle cars calling out desperately for water:

> I came back home and managed to fall asleep only at 6 a.m. I had the feeling that my past had come back to me all of a sudden. That was an authentic scene that I saw myself. I was nine years old then and it was a hot summer day. It's an incredible story. This is why, when I started singing

[79] K16.
[80] K03.

these songs, I was singing as if from personal experience. I remembered that, I lived through that. . . . It was 1943, and I was crossing a stone bridge over the railway tracks leading to the other side of the town where the ghetto was located. After the ghetto had been liquidated, we had classes in the ruined houses. And one day I was coming back from school and I stopped on the bridge when a transport of Jews was passing beneath. And you were not supposed to stop on that bridge, which I didn't know about. Suddenly a Gestapo man came running at me and hit me with his truncheon. You know, this Gestapo rubber truncheon. And then I ran away. Back at home, by night, I got a high fever. My mom didn't know what I had and then I showed her these two blue marks on my back. So this is the experience that I had. . . . I am not Jewish, but I think that every Polish child could have experienced something like this.[81]

The experience that the musician relived after having seen *Schindler's List* is essentially one of a witness. The interviewee claims that having "seen" the Holocaust inspired in her a feeling of affinity to Jews and helped her perform Yiddish songs with a particular authenticity. What is more, she believes that the experience of witnessing deportations or suffering at the hands of the German occupiers is common to "every Polish child" from that period, thus claiming that Poles, having suffered together with the Jews, should have a special sympathy and a special understanding for the Jewish sufferings. The trauma remaining after a childhood episode, however, is here more than merely a source of compassion. It becomes also a means to legitimize the speaker's involvement with Jewish culture and to define her role as a musician and also that of a witness.

Recollecting wartime is also an opportunity for this interviewee to point out that she comes from a family of Poles who helped Jews during the war:

My father issued baptismal certificates for Jewish children on the original forms of the Roman Catholic Curia in Przemyśl. . . . There was a woman who came to me after one of the concerts, asking: "Do you know how many children your father saved?" I said that I had no idea. He never talked about it.[82]

The musician's witnessing of the deportations, her father's active helping of Jews, and her subsequent involvement with Jewish heritage all become interrelated in this biographical narrative. They mark key events for her personal identity, offering potential means to identify herself with Jews and distance herself from those Poles who lacked compassion for Jews during the war. The wartime narrative is, therefore, also a medium for constructing a positive group identity.

[81] K17.
[82] Ibid.

But thinking of Poles expressing an affinity with Jews only in terms of group dissociation is problematic. Undoubtedly there is a difference between declarations of sympathy toward Jews resulting merely from anxiety about the negative aspects of one's group identity, or Okamura's "situational ethnicity," and more permanent identifications with Jewishness. In contrast to situational Jews, marginal Jews might not be officially recognized as Jewish, but their identification with Jewishness is not merely instrumental and might have a more definite and permanent impact on their everyday lives. Naturally, it is not inconceivable that an unsatisfactory group identity can also trigger a more permanent identification with Jewishness, such as conversion. Erica Lehrer quotes a young Polish woman converting to Judaism who declares that she does not want to be "on the side that was bad."[83] I have not come across any similar cases of anxiety-driven change of group ascription, but there is no doubt that in the context of the recent historical debates and the Jewish heritage boom in Poland, Jewish identity has come to be evaluated, in certain circles, as positive. At the same time, the choices of "Jewish-identified" people cannot be reduced merely to identity-saving strategies. The marginal Jew, identifying *as* Jewish, and the situational Jew, identifying *with* Jews, are not two absolutely separate categories. Rather, they should be understood as two points in the continuum of possible identifications vis-à-vis Jewishness, which include both more transitory and permanent modes of referring to the other.

The narratives of "marginal Jews" demonstrate that identity processes taking place on the klezmer scene are more complex and nuanced than they might seem at first glance. Acts of dissociation from the Polish/Catholic identity and the workings of situational ethnicity challenge the neat bipolar categories of "non-Jewish" and "Jewish." They point, instead, to niches and gray zones that escape easy categorization. The notions of "Polishness" and "Jewishness" have become overlapped and interrelated, rather than mutually exclusive. And the particular space of the klezmer revival has emerged as a locus of identity negotiations that follow, as Erica Lehrer put it, a "different logic of Jewishness and of identification than either mainstream Jewish or Polish notions of Jewishness."[84] In other words, the identity processes within the klezmer contact zone mirror the new grammars of self-expression enabled by cultural appropriation.

The German Triangle of Relief

Not surprisingly, these grammars of self-identification are different in Poland and in Germany. The competitive comparisons, creating an analogy between the wartime sufferings of Poles and those of Jews, do not really find an equivalent on

---

[83] Lehrer, "Bearing False Witness?" 101–2.
[84] Ibid., 93.

the German klezmer scene. On the other hand, comparisons involving Poland are relatively frequent.

"'Why are Germans playing this kind of music?' is always the question," complains a male German musician in his thirties. "'Why are Poles playing this music?' Why does nobody ask that?!" he adds provocatively.[85] Although Poland might have emerged in the interviews as a natural point of reference (due to my own nationality), speakers who compared Germany to Poland mostly referred to their firsthand experiences and seemed to have already reflected on the issues they addressed. In the parallels they built, anti-Semitism played a central role:

> I mean, the Poles were as anti-Semitic as . . . Of course, they were very, very, very good to Jewish people during a certain time, no question about that. This was when West European Jews were moving to the east. But, in the countryside, there was as much anti-Semitism, and pogroms, as in Russia or anywhere else. Of course, the most difficult thing is, and I am aware of it: the mechanized killing. This is the most precise and the most crazy thing that has ever happened on earth. Built by human beings. And it is very tragic that the Germans were especially open to this.[86]

The Polish complicity in anti-Semitism, according to the speaker, has a significant bearing on the contemporary Jewish-heritage boom. If the intentions behind the German klezmer revival are being so thoroughly scrutinized, he argues, the same benchmark should also be used for Poland.

Some German klezmer musicians, bringing up the Polish case, refer to their own experience of traveling through Poland. A middle-aged musician who grew up in East Germany recounts his trip to Szczecin and the sobering impression that manifestations of anti-Semitism made on him there:

> I have memories of Poland during the Cold War; it was in Szczecin, a punk concert in 1988. . . . There was a band playing, a Polish band playing, and these were fucking Nazi songs that they were playing. . . . And on the walls of buildings, I saw this twice in Szczecin, there was written . . . "*Żydzi do Madagaskaru*" [Jews to Madagascar]. I saw this twice, and I thought, "What?" So there was an obvious anti-Semitic atmosphere in Poland, at least in the parts of the country where I have been.[87]

Encountering anti-Semitic content in song lyrics and spotting anti-Jewish graffiti shocks this musician, who is convinced that such an open display of anti-Semitism would never have been allowed in East Germany.

[85] B04.
[86] Ibid.
[87] B01.

It is not always the existence of a neo-Nazi scene that becomes the basis for a comparison between Poland and Germany. Another important aspect is Germany's progress in the field of *Vergangenheitsbewältigung* (coming to terms with the past). Some musicians, drawing attention to the comprehensive and thorough nature of this process in Germany, conclude that Poles might not have examined the dark chapters in their history honestly enough:

> I don't place a collective guilt on Poland, as a collective guilt was put on Germany . . . [but] I think it is necessary to research the national history of the Holocaust, the role the country played during the Holocaust. . . . Jewish people told me that they would rather spend money in Germany than in Poland, since Germans, whether it was of their own free will or because of the pressure from the outside, have researched their role in the Holocaust. I think that the Jewish people I was talking to missed that commitment of the Poles, the self-researching on history, their role in the Holocaust.[88]

Advocating a critical approach to Poland's past, the speaker distances himself from, as he suggests, the notion of collective guilt imposed on Germany by external agents. He is also cautious not to pass a direct judgment on Poles, and supports his argument with opinions that he has heard among Jews. Despite such an indirect form of critique, Poland appears in the statement as suffering a worse image among Jews than Germany. Switching the focus of comparison from responsibility for the Holocaust to critical self-analysis, the German musician points to an aspect where Germany is considered to have a leading role. And this is by no means an isolated point of view.

As Jefferey Olick notes, the German experiences in commemorating the Holocaust have become "the obvious reference point" in the international debates on collective memory or postconflict reconciliation, but they are also a model for creating institutional mechanisms of dealing with the past and generating a specific language and rituals of commemoration.[89] In the eyes of many, with all of the historical responsibility resting on Germany, the country has fully faced its past.

Yet, there is also a history of relativizing discourse in Germany. And if Poland features in the German "triangle of relief" today, historically an inner-German configuration played a similar role. The strategy of the GDR authorities to blame Nazism exclusively on West Germany determined the way East Germans conceived of their past. Celebrating the socialist state as antifascist, the East German state considered itself exempted from expiating the Nazi past, or paying reparations to its victims. This particular constellation of guilt-ascription, in which only

---

[88] B01.

[89] Jeffrey K. Olick, *In the House of the Hangman: The Agonies of German Defeat, 1943–1949* (Chicago: University of Chicago Press, 2005), 338.

West Germans featured as the moral heirs of the Third Reich, also influenced the way early East German klezmer revivalists pictured themselves vis-à-vis Jewish music. "We all learned in school that we were antifascist and this inhumane machinery belonged to the other Germans," recollects a middle-aged musician who started playing Jewish music in East Berlin. The collapse of the distinction between "good" and "bad" Germans forced him to revisit his identity:

> Only later did I realize, with my travels around the world, what it means for me as a non-Jew and German to make this music. Or what I had to face then. This became clear to me only later. Then I also studied Hebrew and Israel Studies. In Israel, I was constantly confronted with this subject in various interviews, or private conversations, and I didn't even know so much about it back then. I was just making this music.[90]

East Germans who started dealing with Jewish heritage approached Jewish music, at least at first, without necessarily picturing themselves as members of a perpetrator group dealing with the heritage of its victims. The end of Communism, however, also brought about the end of the relief-mechanism that helped East Germans delegate the responsibility for the Holocaust to an external group. Since then, they have had to look for new ways of coming to terms with the dark German past that suddenly became their own.

The strategy of the "triangle of relief" is present in both the Polish and the German interviews, although references to Germans are more frequent in the Polish narratives than vice versa. While the Polish interviewees draw attention to German military aggression and responsibility for the Holocaust, Germans bring up anti-Semitism in Poland, stressing the German commitment to coming to terms with the past. But that Poland surfaces in the German intergroup comparisons signifies not just that the speakers are critical of Polish myths of historical innocence, but that they are curious about their eastern neighbor, visit the country, and at least partially, follow the historical debates that are currently taking place in Poland.

"Ich bin ein Berliner"

Examining the out-group is not the only way to relieve one's negative group identity. Like many musicians in Kraków, klezmer artists in Berlin refer to a local sense of belonging that has become an alternative to the national identity. "I have never been proud of being German," says a male musician in his thirties, "I feel, rather, . . . I feel connected to Berlin, I'm a Berliner. My national pride is reduced

---

[90] B08.

to watching football."[91] Another young musician, when asked how his band reacts when audiences inquire whether the band is Jewish, answers, "When people ask us, we always say that we're not Jewish, but Berliner."[92] Surely, with all of the positive implications of Kennedy's famous proclamation of "Ich bin ein Berliner," identifying oneself as being "from Berlin" is a statement of belonging, which is less negatively charged in this context than being "German." Connoting freedom and resistance to the postwar division of Germany, the Berliner identity is also cosmopolitan. Indeed, categories that transcend national divides seems to be attractive to some of my interviewees.

Alternatively to this attempt at identifying on a more superordinate level, other musicians opted for a more personal level of identification. A male middle-aged musician states:

> I don't care if I'm German, Spanish, Jewish, or American. . . . The thing which makes it easier for me is the fact that I am not an average, normal German person anyway. . . . I'm a musician, I am an artist, I am me.[93]

Having the particular experience of being a musician, the speaker portrays himself as an atypical group member. The "artist," just as the "cosmopolitan" identity, not only supplants but also implies a critique of nationality as a supreme category of belonging.

Those who still think of their identity in national terms might seek an umbrella category that allows formulating a special affinity toward Jewish culture. Not surprisingly, many German klezmer musicians point out the common roots of German and Yiddish, identifying this shared heritage as a superordinate category to which both Germans and Jews may relate. "I feel much more connected to the Ashkenazi culture, the Sephardic culture seems to me quite alien," said one middle-aged musician who, in the course of his engagement with klezmer, also decided to study Yiddish:

> Today when you come across this old language, you find something familiar in it. It's this feeling when you come across a different culture, and then discover that it is German. In the language you notice it the most. When you learn the Hebrew alphabet and read Yiddish, then you understand almost everything.[94]

By subsuming Ashkenazi culture into the wider category of Germanic heritage, the speaker is able to relate himself to Jewishness on a more universal level. The

[91] B10.
[92] B08.
[93] B04.
[94] B17.

accessibility of the language offers here a means to connect to the culture of the other in a way that complements the purely musical experience.

Another platform that, next to language, embodies for the interviewees the cultural proximity of Germans and Jews is German-language high culture. In the 1920s, argues a middle-aged musician, as the assimilation of German Jews proceeded, "you couldn't say that somebody was Jewish, maybe by the name or the passport, but not in terms of culture. They were as German, or even more German, than the Germans were."[95] If Jews, with their exemplary participation in German cultural life, are presented as model Germans, the cement binding different ethnic groups into "Germanness"—German culture—becomes a common denominator for German Jews and non-Jews, and, as such, a positive value to identify with. Thus, defining German-language culture as co-created, the interviewee pictures his national heritage as heterogeneous and inclusive.

The ways in which Polish and German klezmer musicians shift the level of identification to avoid defining themselves in national terms reveal some similarities. Both groups make use of regional identity (Berliner, Galician), and they incorporate Jews into a more universal category of a Galician or Germanic heritage, which allows them to stress the proximity of both groups and common values. This emphasis on points of intersection and overlap suggests not just a wish to highlight a Polish Jewish or German Jewish harmony but also a more fundamental recognition that Jews have been an organic part of their host nations.

Exit Options

But despite the fact that some German klezmer musicians seek ways of framing their group identity beyond the nation, for most of them their national identity is a valid category, which guides their considerations of group identity, even if they decide to distance themselves from "Germanness." And, indeed, dissociation is by far the most popular identity-saving technique among the German interviewees. Their "exit options" differ, and are in each case conditioned by a personal life story, but all of them testify to the need of leaving the group that does not satisfy their need of a positive identity.

Dissociation is, of course, the easiest for those who can claim an alternative national identity. A young female musician from Berlin does precisely that:

> I have always felt special here in Germany because I'm only half-German.
> I'm different. My name is Bulgarian, my look is not typically German. . . .
> I'm not Bulgarian, I'm not German, I'm a mixture and the music I do is a
> mixture too, it's perfect.[96]

[95] B04.
[96] B06.

Pointing out that she is half-German, the artist concludes that she has a "different mentality" and is hence an atypical group member. Having a multiple identity does not in itself imply dissociation, but it supplies a possibility of choice. Having at one's disposal more than one group identity opens up space for maneuvering, particularly when we suffer because of the low status of one of the groups. Many of the interviewees choose this strategy to indicate that they do not identify themselves (exclusively) with the category of "German."

References to family history are quite frequent in the German interviews and play perhaps an even more central role than in the Polish case. One of the reasons for this is because many of my interviewees felt the need to investigate what their own ancestors did during World War II, especially whether they supported the Nazi regime. Several of them communicated the positive outcomes of this research with a certain emphasis. "I was very lucky that none of my family were Nazis. That was a very lucky part. I would have to suffer much more with my identity, if [it were otherwise],"[97] states one musician, adding that it had been very difficult for him to approach his own grandmother with inquisitive questions about the past. The noninvolvement of one's ancestors with Nazism allows the speaker here to picture himself, again, as an atypical German.

Similarly, another interviewee narrates the wartime story of her grandparents, who sheltered Jews. But although she points out that members of her family were victims of the Nazi regime, she makes sure not to conflate the German and the Jewish fate at the time of National Socialism. The speaker, a female musician who, at the time of the interview, was in the process of converting to Judaism, opens her account with a reflection on the different implications that the Holocaust has for herself and her Jewish friends:

> For me it's a different story, I haven't lost any members of my family. I almost did, when my grandparents sheltered Jews in the most difficult conditions. That was quite, quite dangerous and they all could have died if they had found out about it. . . . It was very difficult. It lasted one year. It was one year before the liberation. It's very important for me, but it's not my story. I have never met this [sheltered] man; I know it only as a story. But it's not like I have lost my grandparents because they were in a concentration camp, like many of my Jewish friends.[98]

The decision of the interviewee's grandparents not to join the NSDAP and to shelter a Jewish person is crucial in the narrative. The speaker repeatedly stresses the peril that it entailed. Nonetheless, the weight of the story is soon juxtaposed with a typical Jewish wartime narrative. The German suffering is contrasted with the incomparably harsher Jewish predicament—the German choice with the Jewish

[97] B04.
[98] B11.

impossibility of choice. The comparison captures a major challenge in the speaker's experience of becoming Jewish: If the Holocaust belongs to the cornerstones of the Jewish identity, the war experience of her family will always remain atypically Jewish (even if also atypically German). The heroic grandparents are, on the one hand, a reference point for the musician, but, on the other hand, they also represent values that she dissociates herself from:

> Maybe I would feel guilty if they had made another choice. It's possible that this plays a role. Maybe it would be more difficult for me, if I knew that they were Nazis. But I would take this step anyway to become a Jew. I'm an independent person. I don't have to follow the tradition of my grandparents. They would actually be appalled, if they had known it. They were very strict Christians.[99]

The family's clean record under Nazism is a way to dissociate herself from the category of "bad Germans" but not a founding myth for her new Jewish identity.

Bringing up family history can also be a way to present one's identity as a singular concatenation of individual destinies rather than a product of any national template. For some interviewees, narrating the family story is a way of opening up alternatives and presenting the identity project itself as tentative, contingent, and subject to selective interpretation. One middle-aged male musician sets out to summarize his family chronicle to speculate about its possible Jewish origin. As his narrative unfolds, the musician draws attention to the atypical episodes that mark his family's history over two generations:

> My grandfather's name was Levot. . . . [And] a friend of mine said that it's strange that this Levot is almost written like Levit, only that instead of an "i" there is an "o" there. And he said, "Are you sure you have nothing to do with the Jewish people?". . . . And then, somehow I felt like, "Let's check it out." It was a bit odd, because when my mom was a girl, after the war, people in her neighborhood, some of those old-style Germans, said she was a *Balg*, one of these impure kids, one of these mix-breeds. They often called her a little Jew. . . . Her father was a lawyer, and his father and so on, from generation to generation. So it was one of these typical professions, and that name. And it really happened [that] he had an office in Friedrichstrasse and the Nazis put the Jewish star there during the war. He was very upset and very afraid and he escaped to London, to disappear. He wrote a letter that he wasn't a Jew and was Catholic and that he could prove it . . . he returned, but he never went into the military service.[100]

[99] Ibid.
[100] B04.

The clues that the speaker lists here—a Jewish-sounding name, abuse from the neighbors and, finally, persecution by the National Socialists—have a crucial function, as they build up a scenario that could conceivably have happened to an assimilated German Jewish family of the period. They also give the narrative the structure of a typical secret family story. The resolution of the mystery is, ultimately, possible with the help of some genealogical research. The grandfather's family turns out to have come from the Saarland region, with no traces of Jewish descent evident. No traces, but an open possibility. "If that family had anything to do with Jews," concludes the musician, "then it must have been a very long time ago, in the ninth or tenth century, because it was the Western Ashkenazi tradition—the Jews who came to the East were first located in the German area, where they had moved with the Romans."[101] Although his suspicion is not confirmed, this quest to verify whether his ancestors were Jewish or not is very significant for his personal identity. On the one hand, it makes clear that group identities encase complex individual histories, which do not lend themselves so easily to straightforward classifications. However, it also opens up for the interviewee an alternative space of identification with Jewishness and allows distance from the category of Germanness.

Having an actual Jew in the family is a fact that the interviewees might invest with particular meaning, or not. And while some choose to bring it to the foreground, others are reluctant to relate Jewish ancestors to their personal identity at all. "I went very deeply into the culture, but it has nothing to do with the definitions [of Jewishness] today,"[102] explains a middle-aged male musician, who has been dealing with Jewish music for more than two decades. Jewish culture, he admits, is central in his life; he actually has a Jewish background, but he does not consider himself Jewish. "I would never go to the synagogue and feel like a Jew now, not even on high holidays," he states. He also finds it difficult to speak of his Jewish ancestry, since he does not feel that it is right to play the ethnic card. Asked whether he feels Jewish, he hesitates:

> People ask me this a lot, and my father's side *is* Jewish, but maybe three generations back there was the last who *davened*[103] and then it's gone, they became evangelic. So then it was his father and mother. But when I explain it like this it also sounds racist, because it's all about blood, blood, blood.[104]

The skepticism toward a biological definition of Jewishness, associated by the speaker with racial laws, makes him opt for a cultural definition, with religious

[101] Ibid.
[102] B20.
[103] Yid: *davnen*, to pray.
[104] B20.

observance as the decisive criterion. The conversion of his ancestors and his own distance from Judaism does not, in his view, qualify him as Jewish, yet his deep involvement in Jewish culture remains, unquestionably, an important part of his life.

Some klezmer musicians speak openly about the temptation to refer to a Jewish family member, especially when they face queries from their audiences or critics:

> But it's so tempting, you know, I have a relative in my family, an aunt, who is Jewish and she's only related to me by marriage, not by blood, but I feel sometimes so tempted to say, "Yes, I have Jewish people in my family too." Just to say that and have it over with once and for all. But I've managed never to use that argument. It is cheap, and too easy.[105]

Even though the musician has refrained from ever claiming a Jewish lineage for herself, she does ascribe to it an unequivocally positive value. Jewishness appears here as a desirable identity marker, even if only in the context of legitimizing her involvement in klezmer.

German klezmer musicians, in general, do indeed explore the possibilities of expressing an affinity with Jewishness, but the proximity they seek to articulate is often a fact of their lives. Participating in Jewishness as a cultural practice is, after all, a daily experience for klezmer performers. They play at Jewish weddings, have Jewish friends, travel to Israel, and speak Yiddish. No wonder that the special access to Jewish culture that they gain affects not only their professional but also their private lives. A middle-aged male musician who had a long relationship with a Jewish woman recalls how contact with a Jewish family allowed him to have a vicarious experience of Jewish life in its many facets. One of the formative moments for him was a period spent in Israel, where he lived among Orthodox Jews and participated in religious practices:

> I went every day to the synagogue and prayed with all the Jews. The rabbi was always taking me by the hand and showing me around. My girlfriend had to stay behind the carpet [curtain], because it was a traditional synagogue, so all the women had to go through a different entrance and stay behind the carpet, but I was totally introduced to the whole thing. And it was a great experience. Then we had shabbes with an orthodox family. And I never said I was Jewish. I never said I wasn't Jewish, either.[106]

Living the daily life of a Jew is an adventure and a unique learning opportunity. Presumably taken as a nonreligious Jew, the musician receives an introduction to Judaism, which would be less accessible to an outsider. The friendly relationship

[105] B12.
[106] B04.

he develops with the local rabbi is clearly a source of pride for him; being taken by the hand and allowed into a synagogue, he feels privileged. Since he is never asked whether he is Jewish or not, he does not feel the need to make any declarations and enjoys his status as a welcomed visitor. But when his identity is revealed, his feeling of belonging becomes reconfirmed. As his host family prepares for a wine harvest, the musician offers his help:

> But she said, "This is kosher wine, and if you're not absolutely kosher people, you can't pick any." And I said, "I'm not even Jewish." And she said, "But you know what: you're Jewish in your heart." [pause] And I said, "OK, thanks." It was a very pleasing compliment. And her son was an Orthodox Jew, he didn't mind, he knew I was German, and he didn't mind at all.[107]

This scene is crucial for the musician's narrative, and he recounts it with great detail and emotion. Being accepted by Orthodox Jews and being labeled as "Jewish at heart" is the denouement of his Israel travel report and one of the key moments in the process of negotiating his identity as an "insider-outsider." The introduction to Jewish life he gains in Israel gives him the awareness that living a vicarious Jewishness can also be a legitimate and deep experience. A sense of belonging sanctioned by halachic law does not matter to him. Taking part in Jewish culture in his everyday life gives him a way to be Jewish, too:

> What I always found wonderful about it is that I like certain kinds of Jewish food. It makes the whole Jewish thing easier if you actually like the food. If I make my daughter latkes, I make them according to a Jewish recipe. I've always eaten them in this way. . . . As long as I am able to make matzo ball soup, and as long as I like matzo ball soup, and have the memory of eating it for ten years, and these people I can call every day, and feel like they're part of my family, I will feel the Jewishness in myself. Without being Jewish.[108]

Jewishness as a practice and as an open option stands here, first of all, for a deeply personal experience and is not necessarily related to a collective identity. The sense of belonging and solidarity that the interviewee expresses relates to his immediate circle of friends and his private life. Receiving Rosh Hashanah greetings, lighting the Hanukkah lights, or cooking in a Jewish way is part of situational Jewishness, the scope of which might be limited only to certain social relations and does not ever have to be articulated as a claim to being Jewish.

[107] Ibid.
[108] Ibid.

But even for the interviewee who decided to convert and live a fully Jewish life, the fact of not having been born Jewish is an aspect that contributes to a feeling of ambivalence. Being in between, not fully part of the culture, and "Aryan-looking," as she puts it, the musician is bent on becoming a religious *and* a cultural insider. Learning Hebrew, planning to study Yiddish, and displaying symbols of Judaism are all ways of living *toward* Jewishness, a process in which one yearns to be crowned with a full-fledged membership. "Some people say that people going through conversion should not wear Jewish symbols," says the artist, pointing to a small *chai*-pendant on her neck, a combination of two Hebrew letters meaning "living." "But I don't hurt anybody with this," she argues. "I identify myself with it. By that people can see that this is important for me."[109] Asked whether her audiences ever inquire whether she is Jewish, she answers, laughing:

> They don't ask. I look very Aryan [laughter]. If they asked, what would I say? I'm a little Jewish, I'm on the way. . . . The problem is that even if you take this step there are still a lot of Jews who say, "But you were not born Jewish!"[110]

Speaking of the resentment that converts to Judaism sometimes face from both Jews and non-Jews, the musician legitimizes her position with the argument that the act of dissociation she is undertaking (abandoning the religion of her parents) is analogous to the laicization of many contemporary Jews, who break with the traditions of their forefathers. The argument seems to be that if ethnic Jews themselves negotiate new ways of being Jewish beyond religion, why should it be inappropriate for those born non-Jewish to seek ways of being Jewish beyond ethnicity? Still, advocating Jewishness as a choice, the musician appears to have a clear conception of "canonical Jewishness," defined by ethnic background and specific looks. As her story poignantly illustrates, self-ascription into a group does not always guarantee recognition as a group member by the outside world.

Apart from the people who identify as "a little Jewish," or aspire toward Jewishness, defined either in religious or cultural terms, there are also German klezmer musicians who consider Jewish culture as relevant for them, without the need to claim a Jewish identity at all. Their unique position "in between" might make some of them inclined to identify themselves as non-Jewish Jews, while others will merely accentuate their Jewish roots, or only a familiarity with Judaism, as a means of distancing themselves from the category of "average Germans." The affinity with Jews that they express has often more to do with their private lives than with their professional involvement as klezmer revivalists, but it is usually their musical careers that first bring them in touch with Jewish culture and Jews.

---

[109] B11.
[110] Ibid.

We have seen that the strategy of dissociation is one of the most significant similarities between the way Polish and German musicians frame their group identity. Interestingly, both groups use the reference to the Polish-German-Jewish triangle. Since the manner in which the Polish and German musicians conceptualize this triangle differs, both groups are able to use it to relativize their negative image. Pointing an accusatory finger at other harm-doing groups, though much more prominent in the Polish interviews, turned out to be irresistible for Germans, too.

Despite many parallels between the Polish and the German case, the ways in which klezmer musicians from Kraków and Berlin negotiate their group identities differ in many respects. First, although Poles are more inclined to compare themselves directly to Jews by drawing attention to their status as victims, German musicians opt for dissociation from their national identity rather than a defensive comparison. Second, while some Polish musicians emphasize a feeling of being on a mission, or the importance of their work in Poland and expected gratitude from Jews for their revivalist efforts, their German colleagues refrain from framing their work as that of guardians of Jewish heritage in the absence of Jews. Although some German klezmer musicians do hold lectures on Jewish culture in schools or take part in commemorative events, they are well aware that Jewish communities and Jewish institutions offer a lot in terms of cultural and educational activities. There are also many Jewish musicians performing klezmer in Germany, and therefore non-Jews on the Berlin klezmer scene are not really in a position to see themselves as the sole continuators of Jewish traditions.

The most notable difference in the way Polish and German musicians negotiate their group identity lies in the fact that the latter virtually never resort to comparing their in-group directly to Jews. Even though some of the German interviewees chose to take a defensive line about their group, Poles primarily served as a group of comparison in this case. But why are Poles so much more willing to use direct competition while it is such a taboo for Germans?

Henri Tajfel differentiates between "secure" and "insecure" comparisons between groups. "Secure" comparisons take place when two groups, which are competing for a higher status, are in a relationship in which "a change in the texture of psychological distinctiveness between them" is not possible.[111] "Insecure" comparisons, in turn, take place when the participants are aware that the existing social reality might change and alternatives to it are conceivable. In other words, when the status quo between the in-group and the out-group is "objectified," and there are no cognitive alternatives available, the low-status group will be discouraged to use the high-status group as a frame of reference and will tend to compare itself instead with other, more similar, low-status groups. If the comparison situation is "insecure," however, it will invite direct competition between the groups.

---

[111] Henri Tajfel cited in Turner and Brown, "Social Status, Cognitive Alternatives, and Intergroup Relations," in Tajfel, *Differentiation between Social Groups*, 207.

The lack of direct comparisons in the German interviews suggests that the Germans' perpetrator status vis-à-vis Jews has been objectified. Conversely, it is hard to deny the ambiguous position of Poles both as victims of World War II and as witnesses to as well as co-perpetrators of crimes against Jews. Since relations between Poles and Jews are "insecure," more Polish interviewees will be inclined to compare their group directly to Jews. The lack of ambiguity in the German case, though, makes such competitive strategies less likely. While the more complicated status of Poles allows them far more leeway in conceptualizing their collective identity vis-à-vis Jews, Germans have at their disposal a more limited number of identity-saving techniques. Still, both groups apply them in creative ways, challenging the existing boundaries and seeking alternative categories that can better represent their particular position between two cultures.

Commenting on the popularity of the Jewish Culture Festival in Kraków among non-Jewish Poles, Konstanty Gebert, a Polish Jewish intellectual, wrote that "Poland cannot understand itself without factoring in the Jews, without attempting to reclaim its Jewish past."[112] One could argue that the Polish engagement with Jewish culture is essentially introspective. If we can understand ourselves fully only by examining our relation with Jews, perhaps our involvement with the other is, in the first place, a quest for the self. Looking at one aspect of the Polish fascination with Jewishness, klezmer, we have seen this assumption confirmed. The culture that klezmer artists deal with inevitably brings them to reflect on who they are, as Poles, as Germans, as Christians, or as Jews.

The musicians and cultural workers creating the klezmer scene in Kraków and Berlin find themselves at the junction of Polishness/Germanness and Jewishness. Since they are likely to be acquainted with Jewish culture and history to a greater extent than their average co-nationals and often have intensive contact with Jews, they belong to a small minority whose perception of Jews is not entirely based on stereotypes or mediated knowledge. Even though the stories of "Jews by profession" presented here might not be representative of Poles or Germans as a whole, the reactions and strategies employed by this small group undoubtedly reflect the attitudes, clichés, and mental frameworks of the society that shaped them. The participants of the klezmer revival can be seen as atypical Poles and Germans, and can also be treated as a test group in the experimental condition of daily contact with Jewish culture.

To speak of Poles/Germans and Jews as bipolar categories is a fundamental simplification. The categories of "Polish," "German," and "Jewish" often overlap, and even the dichotomy of "Jewish" vs. "non-Jewish" hardly reflects the multiplicities, continuities, and ambiguities of the liminal identity spaces in between. "Jews by profession," in fact, often define Jewishness in ways that challenge ethnic or religious definitions. Their bond to Jewishness might consist in a shared

---

[112] Konstanty Gebert cited in Igal Avidan, "Jewish Spirit in Kraków," *Jerusalem Report*, August 20, 2007, 28.

cultural practice, familiarity with certain traditions, or sympathy toward a victimized minority. But this wish to seek proximity is very rarely accompanied by the desire to actually *become* Jewish through conversion. Affiliations with Jewishness are rather transient and situational, called forth by particular circumstances. Contrary to what many observers of the klezmer scene imagine, non-Jewish klezmer musicians do not aspire to become Jewish, but rather, being at the fault line of intergroup relations, turn introspective, trying to examine their group identities as Poles or Germans.

In this position, non-Jewish people involved in the klezmer revival have to confront many uncomfortable truths. Not immune to national myths and prejudice themselves, they often have to mediate between Jews and non-Jews and their varying perspectives on the common past. Anxiety about one's own national or religious identity is an inescapable side effect of opening oneself up to the narrative of the other. To what extent, however, can we consider this anxiety as equivalent to feelings of guilt?

Klezmer: a Therapy for Collective Guilt?

Given that a great majority of klezmer musicians both in Poland and Germany belong to the third postwar generation, the claim that the klezmer revival redeems any collective feelings of guilt begs the question of whether we can speak of a transgenerational collective guilt at all. In his *Guilt about the Past*, Bernhard Schlink calculates the temporal limits of guilt in quite precise terms: "In 2025 there will be no single German alive anymore, who could be guilty, in the legal sense, of what took place before 9 May 1945," he writes.[113] What kind of "inheritable" guilt are we talking about when we speak of the third postwar generation of Germans? What kind of guilt do we mean when we speak of Poles? And finally, does guilt, however defined, naturally entail *feelings* of guilt?

Karl Jaspers, who in the immediate postwar years called upon Germans to collectively contemplate their guilt in order to undergo a moral renewal, wrote in 1945 that "[t]o pronounce a group criminally, morally, or metaphysically guilty is an error akin to the laziness and arrogance of average, uncritical thinking."[114] Acknowledging individual guilt was an urgent necessity for Jaspers, but translating Germany's political responsibility for World War II into a collective moral guilt was unacceptable for him. On the other hand, his famous taxonomy of guilt included—next to criminal and moral guilt, which had an individual dimension—also political and metaphysical guilt, which were collective in nature. Political guilt for the Holocaust extended, in Jaspers's view, to all Germans and their

---

[113] Bernhard Schlink, *Vergangenheitsschuld* (Zürich: Diogenes, 2007), 11.
[114] Karl Jaspers in Olick, *In the House of the Hangman*, 289.

descendants, even if they opposed the Nazi regime and were personally innocent of any crime. But Jaspers's notion of metaphysical guilt referred to an even
wider circle of people and, in fact, could be read as universal. To Jaspers, the
mere act of survival while evil takes its toll among others makes us metaphysically guilty.[115]

Carl Jung's perspective on collective guilt was similar. The irresistible fascination of evil, in his view, contaminated space and caused a "magical impurity"
to spread over the whole of Europe after the Holocaust.[116] But, if collective guilt
extends not only to the perpetrators but also the bystanders and witnesses of the
Holocaust in Europe, does it also extend across generations? One crucial question that arises is that of the temporal distance from the Holocaust: Does a collective metaphysical or psychological guilt apply to those who have not directly
experienced the Holocaust, and who might even have very limited contact with
witnesses of that time?

Bernhard Schlink discusses the possibility of a transgenerational transfer of
guilt in some detail. Considering the notion of collective guilt from the perspective of the philosophy of law, Schlink lists as guilty those who bear the criminal
guilt for wartime atrocities and those who refrained from resistance and opposition, but also those who, belonging to the *Solidargemeinschaft* (community of
solidarity) together with the perpetrators, failed to dissociate themselves from,
or disown, them. Given these premises, the entanglement in guilt ends with the
third generation, as they no longer face the alternative to expel the wartime perpetrators or retain them in their community.[117]

Philosophical considerations on whether people *should* perceive a sense of guilt
do not necessarily correspond to whether in reality they feel guilty. Social psychologists define collective guilt as an emotional reaction based on group membership, which is determined by self-judgment rather than external accusations. The
necessary conditions for collective guilt are thus identifying oneself as a group
member, perceiving one's group as responsible for the harm it has inflicted, and
considering the group's actions as illegitimate.[118] Social psychologists observe
that the actual perception of collective guilt is by no means frequent. "[C]ollective
guilt should *not* be considered an automatic consequence of perceived in-group
harm-doing. . . . In fact, collective guilt might be a rather rare phenomenon precisely because people have a variety of strategies that allow them to legitimize
their group's harmful actions."[119]

---

[115] Karl Jaspers, *Die Schuldfrage: Für Völkermord gibt es keine Verjährung* (München: Piper Verlag,
1979), 52.

[116] Carl Jung, "Nach der Katastrophe," in *Gesammelte Werke: Zivilisation im Übergang*, vol. 10 (Olten:
Walter Verlag, 1986), 223–24.

[117] Schlink, *Vergangenheitsschuld*, 89.

[118] Wohl, Branscombe, and Klar, "Collective Guilt," 2.

[119] Ibid., 4.

What does Tajfel's notion of anxiety, present among klezmer musicians, tell us about their feelings of guilt, then? Even though anxiety is an emotional reaction based on membership, the whole range of strategies used by the musicians to gain a positive identity helps them to bypass self-ascription as a member of the harm-doing group. Undoubtedly, due to the nature of their profession, klezmer musicians encounter Holocaust-related narratives more often than others. The feeling of anxiety that they express about belonging to a perpetrator group is also fueled by the low status of the group in the eyes of others, and not necessarily the individual's subjective feeling that the low status is deserved. Although none of the German interviewees question the perpetrator status of Germans as a collective, virtually none of them declare that they suffer any sense of guilt on an individual level. Similarly, Polish klezmer musicians delegate the sense of guilt rather to their German colleagues. An awareness of one's in-group's low status is not necessarily tantamount to actually experiencing feelings of guilt. The argument that guilty feelings motivate the musicians to deal with Jewish music is therefore problematic. If, indeed, a sense of guilt is involved in the work of klezmer musicians, it is more likely the *result* of, rather than the *cause* of, their interest in klezmer. Often it is only the rejection that non-Jewish klezmer musicians sometimes suffer from, for example, Jewish audiences that leads them to reflect on the questions of collective guilt and their own identity. The klezmer adventure, rather than offering relief, poses a challenge and creates the conditions for the crisis.

Born and Hesmondhalgh, discussing various forms of "musically imagined communities," enumerate "psychic tourism" through music as one of the ways that people can relate themselves to the culture of the other.[120] This psychic tourism, by definition not a permanent state, can be motivated by curiosity or a search for pleasure rather than a definite wish to partake in the culture of the other. Nonetheless, musical tourism can also ultimately lead to a "real" identification with what they call an "ontologically prior" collectivity.[121] The Polish and German klezmer revival might be construed as a kind of "psychic tourism" through music and one that could have serious consequences for the "travelers." Born and Hesmondhalgh, in fact, do not view it as contradictory that music can be simultaneously a medium of "imaginary" and "real" identification. "It is precisely music's extraordinary powers of imaginary evocation of identity and of cross-cultural and intersubjective empathy . . . that render it a primary means of both marking and transforming individual and collective identities."[122] In other words, being able to imagine the self in the shoes of the other has the power to change the way we perceive ourselves.

[120] Born and Hesmondhalgh, introduction to *Western Music and Its Others*, 35.
[121] Ibid., 36.
[122] Ibid., 32.

The klezmer revival in Poland and Germany is a kind of musical journey, which leaves a deep impression on the psychic tourists, even though the destination might be different from what one might expect. Wandering between the Jewish and the non-Jewish world, the klezmer-travelers do not necessarily reach Jewishness as their point of arrival. More often than not, the adventure with Jewishness brings klezmer musicians back to their own identity, national myths, and family genealogies. Klezmer functions here as a lens that "magnifies otherness"[123] but also sharpens our perception of the self.

---

[123] Bohlman, "Composing the Cantorate," 189.

Conclusion

On March 8, 1969, a Polish playwright in Parisian exile, Sławomir Mrożek, records in his diary a meeting, which haunts him for the rest of the day. An inquisitive gold trader from the Rue des Rosiers, a commercial street in the heart of the Jewish district, insists on knowing whether Mrożek, a relatively fresh immigrant from Poland, is Polish or Jewish. For the playwright, who is growing increasingly disenchanted with Poland and critically investigates the very construct of a collective identity, the question opens up an abyss of ambivalence. "[I]n the course of my uprooting myself . . . " notes Mrożek, "a new, excellent opportunity to complement, accelerate, and perfect this process presented itself to me." Mrożek's new strategy is to "wholly weaken the Pole in myself through the potentiality of being a Jew—by no means becoming Jewish."[1]

It is easy to understand why Mrożek writes about questioning his Polishness at that particular time. The exiled playwright has difficulty relating to his home country, which has just staged a massive anti-Semitic campaign. But his project of "weakening the Pole with the (prospective) Jew"[2] is more than an expression of solidarity with expelled Polish Jews. It is, instead, an attempt to name the feeling of otherness that has accompanied Mrożek since his childhood. "The Jew" is here a metaphor for difference, ambivalence, and self-questioning.

Chapter 7 has shown that an encounter with Jewish culture can seriously affect the way non-Jewish Poles and Germans think of themselves as individuals and as group members. For Mrożek, such challenges to the self have a salutary effect. They trigger self-reflection and open a space of ambiguity. Putting the self in the position of the other makes us aware of how much our national identity is a construct, which is constantly in the process of being formed. If this experiment can have such far-reaching consequences for the individual, it might be equally transformative for whole societies. If this is so, the resurgence of Jewish heritage, epitomized by the klezmer revival, is part of a collective identity project.

---

[1] Sławomir Mrożek, *Dziennik: Tom 1 1962–1969* (Kraków: Wydawnictwo Literackie, 2010), 587.
[2] Ibid.

Klezmer contributes to Jewish/non-Jewish dialogue, offering a new mode of encounter, which enables non-Jews, via music making, listening, dancing, and the like, to participate in Jewish culture. Encounters through klezmer reveal disagreements and conflicts of interest, but they also provide the conditions for stepping into the other's shoes and developing empathy. The klezmer scene is therefore more than a space of inspiration cultivated by the art of the ethnic other. It is a space of introspection. "The New Goyish Music" from Bremen or Chopin à la klezmer from Kraków testify to a musical fusion and to a search for the self through the art of someone else. Enabling what Freedman called an "antinormative model of cultural reproduction,"[3] the klezmer scene attracts artists who want to venture beyond the boundaries of their own heritage along with those who only feel at home in the space in between. Klezmer opens up new non-normative ways of being Jewish, giving musicians and audiences the possibility to express their affinity with Jewishness without becoming Jewish.

But the klezmer scene owes its participatory character to the fact that klezmer music is a product, one that can be bought and enjoyed by anybody. The klezmer revival has, in fact, developed unprecedented patterns of consuming Jewishness. Klezmer as part of the Jewish heritage package offered by Jewish restaurants in Kazimierz is probably the most emblematic case of commodifying Jewish heritage, but klezmer's commercial success also has implications beyond the market of Jewish heritage travel. Klezmer has made Jewish culture more visible (and audible), bringing it to new places and new consumers who have begun to view Jewish heritage as fashionable. Thus the rising popularity of klezmer has coincided with and perhaps contributed to the salability of historic Jewish spaces, and products marketed as "Jewish," especially food and alcohol, souvenirs, guidebooks, collections of Jewish jokes, and the like. While a Polish daily newspaper recently reported that kosher vodka importers wish to "conquer Poland,"[4] Joanna Tokarska-Bakir noted that portraits of Jews holding golden coins have already done this, giving rise to a whole new set of rituals, which use the image of the Jew to secure the prosperity of the household.[5] In other words, Jewishness has never sold in Poland as well as now.

Having said this, it is important to point out that the Jewish heritage undergoing commercialization in Poland is not simply "ingested" in its entirety, but it certainly is adapted in a very selective way. And the manner in which Jewishness becomes domesticated on the klezmer scene tells us a lot about the desires and taboos that accrete around Polish/Jewish relations. We have seen that klezmer productions in Poland often rely on elements of the magical and the romantic, painting an image of a colorful prewar shtetl, where various ethnic groups dwelled in harmony. At the same time, certain elements of Jewish heritage, such

---

[3] Freedman, *Klezmer America*, 93.

[4] "Koszerna wódka chce podbić Polskę," *Rzeczpospolita*, February 14, 2011, accessed March 12, 2012, http://www.rp.pl/artykul/612226.html.

[5] Tokarska-Bakir, "Żyd z pieniążkiem podbija Polskę."

as the legacy of Communist and Socialist Yiddish songs, are expunged. The focus on peaceful coexistence and the avoidance of political overtones has a certain logic. Klezmer becomes incorporated into the narrative of Poland's past multi-ethnicity and is granted the status of a heritage that is not extraneous but our own and familiar. Such absorption of the other is a means of abolishing distance, and a way to venerate the similarities between the two cultures. Jewish music is presented here as belonging to a common superordinate category of Poland's folklore, and as such it feeds into the myth of prewar Poland as a multicultural arcadia.

In this way, klezmer becomes the soundtrack to an idealized image of pre-1939 Poland, which, after 1989, became the new founding myth of the post-Communist state. In the popular imagination, Poland of the interwar period (1918–39) appears as a home to many national and religious minorities, and connotes independence, victory, and rebirth. In reality, however, the so-called Second Polish Republic was a state that after more than a century of Russian, Prussian, and Austrian domination witnessed bitter ethnic conflicts, authoritarian rule, and the rise of xenophobic right-wing ideology. With ethnic animosities following the Polish-Ukrainian war over Eastern Galicia and the Polish-Lithuanian conflict over Vilnius, and plagued by growing anti-Semitism, interwar Poland was anything but a site of harmonious cohabitation. Still, the nostalgia for a territorially greater Poland with its own colonial ambitions in the East lingered in post-1945 Communist Poland to resurge with particular force after the systemic change of 1989. Prewar Poland became a symbol of a "better" place and time. It embodied the world before the catastrophe—before the Holocaust and before the loss of the eastern borderlands annexed in 1945 by the Soviet Union and before the Communist takeover.

The myth of prewar multiethnic Poland serves the function of assuaging the collective conscience. Especially after the Jedwabne debate in 2000, the myth of the harmonious Polish Jewish coexistence in the multiethnic Second Republic serves as a counternarrative to the accounts of Polish complicity in the Holocaust. Thereafter, visions of a colorful shtetl, inhabited by Poles, Jews, Ukrainians, and Roma fulfill an escapist function. Beautifying the prewar shtetl life by purging it of misery, conflict, and persecution, some klezmer productions provide an anesthetic for the Polish conscience and, at least indirectly, contribute to the self-serving mythology of innocence.

But if the Polish klezmer scene at times sustains stereotypes, which actually preclude coming to terms with the dark chapters in Polish history, it likewise has the potential of challenging them. We have seen that playing Jewish music in today's Poland can be a political statement. Klezmer, as a manifestation of Jewish culture, also has its opponents, as anti-Semitic incidents aimed even at non-Jewish klezmer musicians clearly demonstrate. In a country where anti-Semitic language is still widely accepted and banal anti-Semitism is prevalent on graffiti-covered urban walls, attending a klezmer concert can be a way of manifesting anti-anti-Semitism. In Poland, as in the rest of Europe, where gen⸍ al knowledge about Jewish culture is limited and often dominated by clichés, any nuanced presentation of Jewish heritage has the potential to decrease prejudice.

But Jewish heritage in Poland is significant not just because it can potentially be a medium of counteracting anti-Semitism. Ethnically homogenous Poland is becoming an increasingly attractive destination for refugees and labor migrants. Attention given to the heritage of the other can therefore be instrumental in bringing home the fact that ethnic diversity is a value and that minorities enrich the host society. But if in Poland today Jews have come to represent the ultimate in ethnic otherness, they also provide a universal metaphor for alterity. The feminist activist Agnieszka Graff points to the ways in which the figure of the Jew becomes conflated with the figure of the gay, both in homophobic and liberal discourse. She argues that sexual minorities become "Jewified" in ultraconservative language and that the support for gay and lesbian rights is often motivated by the will to protest against anti-Semitism.[6] Given the analogies drawn and the coalitions of solidarity they activate, those elements of Jewish heritage, like klezmer, that enter the mainstream culture have a highly symbolic potential in Poland.

Yet klezmer is a double-edged sword. It can be politicized to combat stereotypes, but it can also be instrumentalized by local authorities and the media to divert attention from anti-Semitism and thus present contemporary Poland as a tolerant country, devoted to the preservation of the heritage of its minorities. Furthermore, Polish klezmer artists themselves are usually reluctant to make political use of the music's subversive potential, but this might only be a question of time. Jewish music in Poland has a strong resonance. It can anaesthetize national anxieties; it can also open old wounds. It can accompany national myths, but it can also challenge them, forcing Poles to reflect on the painful aspects of Polish/Jewish relations.

* * *

If klezmer in Poland is the music of a generation, which for the first time since World War II, is collectively coming to terms with the Polish complicity in anti-Jewish violence, klezmer in Germany resounds in a very different memoryscape. Germany's coming to terms with the Holocaust started long before the advent of the klezmer revival. The critical investigation of the Nazi past began with the second postwar generation. In fact, given that the majority of klezmer musicians in Germany belong to the third generation, one can say that the greatest indictment of the country's history came from their parents. The year 1970, when

---

[6] Agnieszka Graff, "Gej czyli Żyd . . . I co dalej?" *Rykoszetem: Rzecz o płci, seksualności i narodzie* (Warszawa: WAB, 2008), 110–42.

Chancellor Willi Brandt kneeled down in front of the monument of the Warsaw Ghetto Uprising, honoring the victims of the Nazi genocide, was a symbolic turning point. The late 1970s and 1980s witnessed an unprecedented wave of Holocaust commemoration projects in West Germany. Germans seemed to be regaining their memory about the dark chapters of their history and owning up to their moral responsibility.

And although the early klezmer revival, especially in the GDR, might also have been fuelled by the impetus to remind Germans of their loss and save Jewish heritage from oblivion, the klezmer boom that took shape in the already reunited Germany of the 1990s marked the beginning of the new post-memorialization period. Klezmer offered a way to engage with Jewish culture beyond the rigid corset of politically correct formulae and somber commemoration rituals. It reminded Germans that there is more to Jewish heritage than the Holocaust and allowed for the simple enjoyment of Jewish culture. For the generation wary of investigating the past, klezmer offered a medium through which they could relate to Jewish heritage in a manner that enabled participation.

And so, from the very beginning, klezmer in Berlin has been framed as part of the local multicultural urban landscape. Identifying Yiddish music as part of a superordinate category of the German language tradition, German revivalists found a way of relating to klezmer and proudly presenting it as a legacy both familiar and meaningful. Jewish dancing music constituted an alternative to the rituals of memorialization, meeting the needs of the third generation of Germans who did not want to *forget* but wanted to *remember in their own way*, bringing living Jewish culture back into the public image of Jewishness, which was previously dominated by death.

And although critics warned that the German klezmer revival "diminishes the shock of the Holocaust and distances the country from its victims"[7] or even that "by abolishing the boundaries between Jews and non-Jews . . . volatizes the Shoah,"[8] the German klezmer revival never ran the risk of losing sight of the Holocaust. The klezmer scene, more so than any other social context where Jews and non-Jews interact, has been a place where intergroup boundaries are particularly salient, and the memory of the Holocaust continues to be achingly present. Klezmer remains a cultural territory where taboos are respected and where non-Jewish musicians seek to avoid any suspicion that they might be impersonating Jews. Bands like the Klezgoyim, or Klezmerschicksen make disambiguation their program. German klezmer bands avoid Jewish symbols on their records and, unlike some of their colleagues in Poland, consider dressing up as Jews absolutely taboo. Aware of the fact that they are on sensitive ground, German klezmer bands often address head-on the problematic issue of their legitimacy to play Jewish music. Their clarifications, statements of intent, and

---

[7] Birnbaum, "Jewish Music, German Musicians," 298.

[8] Ottens, "Der Klezmer als ideologischer Arbeiter," 29.

disclaimers sometimes make their way into the booklets accompanying klezmer records, as in the case of the 1998 album *Riffkele* by La'om. Musicians in Germany consciously reflect on what is acceptable on the klezmer scene and what is not, and they also raise the difficult questions of whether and to what extent they themselves bear the moral responsibility for the Holocaust and how that affects the way they should approach Jewish heritage.[9] Finally, many German klezmer bands regularly perform at Holocaust commemoration events and some of them, like Karsten Troyke with his CD *Forgotten Yiddish Songs* [*Jiddische Vergessene Lieder*], also record music written during the Holocaust. A close look at the German klezmer scene makes it clear that, even if the raison d'être of the revival was to give space to living Jewish culture, klezmer in Germany has always been overshadowed by the Holocaust.

After over two decades since the beginning of the klezmer revival, it is safe to conclude that contrary to the fears of some critics, klezmer has not lulled us into a self-satisfied amnesia. Klezmer in Poland and Germany has accompanied collective attempts to remember Jews and to factor Jewish culture into the vision of Polish and German national heritage, but this process has by no means been completed. The first decade of the twenty-first century witnessed the inauguration of many major commemorative projects in the German capital, such as the Jewish Museum Berlin (2001), the Memorial to the Murdered Jews of Europe (2005), and Topography of Terror (2010), which offered new spaces for remembering and new ways of integrating Germany's painful past into the urban texture. Although these projects grew out of the commemorative impulse of the 1970s and 1980s, the institutions have only begun to exert their true impact, attracting large numbers of visitors and launching their own educative programs. In Poland also, the last decade brought with it the opening of many institutions and memorial sites dedicated to Jewish culture and the Holocaust. The most important of them, the Museum of the History of the Polish Jews, built on the grounds of the former ghetto in Warsaw, will open in 2013. But apart from this monumental project, which has the chance of becoming one of the most significant Jewish museums in the world, we have also witnessed new, highly symbolic memorials being opened, for example, in Jedwabne (2001), and Bełżec (2004).

The klezmer revival, which has been developing against the background of this official memory work, complements these efforts in important ways. Bringing daily Jewish life and folk rituals into focus, it makes us remember Jews not only as victims but also as creative agents, expressing their emotions and concerns through an art form that still appeals to people today. Indeed, klezmer has the potential to breed empathy with victims of ethnic persecution, but it would be naïve

---

[9] See, for example, Heiko Lehmann, "Klezmer in Germany."

to think that it has exorcised anti-Semitism. New research reveals that almost every fifth German and every second Pole are of the opinion that Jews have too much influence, while a third of German and nearly half of Polish respondents maintain that Jews do not enrich their respective cultures.[10]

Klezmer cannot cure anti-Semites. By exposing Poles and Germans to Mrożek's "potential Jew" inside them, though, it can be a powerful catalyst of change. Jewishness is a vantage point, wrote Mrożek, that allows us to ponder the question of "to be or not to be, and what does it matter" in a way that is simultaneously "poignant" and "comfortable."[11] Klezmer, as a project of seeking answers about the self, of taking up the perspective of the other, can be an equally poignant experience. Even if it offers escapist visions, it simultaneously forces us to confront our greatest fears. Opening up the spaces of ambivalence, doubt, and hybridity, it teaches us how to communicate with the other, owning up to our past.

The afterlife of klezmer in Kraków and Berlin is, therefore, a digest of the past, in both of senses of the word. It is a compound of Jewish musical traditions, representing Jewishness as dreamed by others and serving today's exigencies, but it is also a result of "digesting" the other and one's own difficult past.

---

[10] Bundesministerium des Innern, "Antisemitismus in Deutschland, Erscheinungsformen, Bedingungen, Präventionsansätze: Bericht des unabhängigen Expertenkreises Antisemitismus," [Anti-Semitism in Germany, Its Forms, Conditions, and Prevention Projects: Report of the Independent Anti-Semitism Expert Group], 2012, 63, accessed March 12, 2012, http://www.bmi.bund.de/SharedDocs/Downloads/DE/Themen/Politik_Gesellschaft/EXpertenkreis_Antisemmitismus/bericht.pdf?__blob=publicationFile.

[11] Mrożek, Dziennik, 586.

GLOSSARY

Baʻal Shem Tov, Israel ben Eliezer (ca. 1700–1760). "Master of the Divine Name"; founder of Hasidism.

badkhn. A wedding jester who performed special humorous, and moralistic verses during an eastern European Ashkenazi wedding ceremony.

bar mitzvah. Literally, "son of the commandment"; ceremony at which a thirteen-year-old Jewish male becomes a member of the community.

bat mitzvah. Literally, "daughter of the commandment"; ceremony at which a twelve-year-old Jewish female becomes a member of the community.

bulgar. A dance popular among Romanian and Ukrainian Jews, originating from a Bessarabian line dance called *bulgareasca.*

chai. A combination of two Hebrew letters: het and yod (חי), denoting "living"; one of the most popular symbols of Judaism, often worn as a pendant.

cimbalom. Hammered dulcimer.

Cmentarz Obrońców Lwowa. (also Cmentarz Orląt Lwowskich). Pol: Cemetery of the Eaglets of Lvov; the necropolis of Polish soldiers and civilians who fought against Ukrainians during the Polish-Ukrainian war (1918–19), which became a bone of contention in the Polish-Ukrainian negotiations over the commemoration of war victims.

davnen. Yid: to pray.

dreydlekh. Musical ornamentations in klezmer music.

dybbuk/dibbuk. In Jewish folklore: an evil spirit which enters into a living person.

freylakh. Yid: lively, happy. One of the most popular klezmer dances.

froyen kapelyes. Women's ensembles; active, for example, in Lvov at the turn of the twentieth century, performing in restaurants and cafes.

honga. A line dance popular among Romanians and Jews from Bessarabia.

Jedwabne. A town in northeastern Poland and the site of a 1941 pogrom performed on the local Jewish community by the Polish inhabitants. The case became known after J. T. Gross's publication of *Neighbors* and became shorthand of Polish wartime atrocities against Jews.

jidancuta. A Moldavian folk dance inspired by klezmer music.

kale baveynen. Yid: "Crying with the bride"; part of a traditional Ashkenazi wedding ritual, accompanied by klezmorim and the badkhn.

kale bazetsn. Yid: "Seating of the bride"; part of a traditional Ashkenazi wedding ritual.

kale bazingen. Yid: "Singing for the bride"; part of a traditional Ashkenazi wedding ritual.

kapelye (pl. kapelyes). Ensemble.

khosidl. A Jewish dance in a 2/4 tempo originating in East Galicia and Bukovina.

khupe. The wedding canopy.

kiddush. Heb: sanctification; prayer recited over a cup of wine to consecrate the Shabbat.

klezmer loshn. Yid: klezmer language; an argot developed by klezmer musicians in eastern Europe.

klezmerzy. (**pl. of klezmer**). Pol: (1) Jewish musicians or (2) musicians playing in restaurants or
    night clubs; the term connotes in Polish low prestige and bad quality of music.

klezmorim. Yid: pl. of klezmer; musicians.

kneytshn. Yid: fold, wrinkle; a type of musical ornament used in klezmer music, which produces a
    short, swallowed sound.

krekhtsn. Yid: groans, moans; a type of musical ornament used in klezmer music which resembles
    a guttural stop.

Łowicz. A town in central Poland; the local folk costume is one of the most emblematic in Poland.

mikveh. Ritual bath.

nigun, (**pl. *nigunim*).** A wordless song, popular in particular in the Hasidic tradition, performed
    collectively *a cappella* as a form of prayer, often accompanied by dancing.

Ostjuden. Ger: Jews from regions east of Germany. The term was used as derogative in the Nazi
    propaganda.

peyes. Sidelocks.

Polacken. Ger: "Polacks"; a derogative term for Poles.

Purimspil. (also *Purim-shpil*) Purim plays commemorating the deliverance of Persian Jews (Esther,
    9:1–10:3), *Purimspiln* often play a carnivalesque role.

Scheunenviertel. (Ger: Barn District) a central quarter in Berlin, which before WWII hosted a
    large population of east European Jews.

shabes goy. A non-Jewish helper in a Jewish household, performing the work forbidden to Jews on
    the Shabbat (Heb: Sabbath).

shabes. Yid: Shabbat.

shames. A sexton or caretaker in a synagogue.

sher. Yid: scissors; a Jewish figure dance.

shtreimels. Fur hats worn especially by Hasidim.

simcha. Heb: gladness, or joy, used also to denote a festive occasion.

Solidargemeinschaft. Ger: Community of solidarity.

Solidarność. Pol: Solidarity; a Polish independent trade union founded 1980, which developed into
    a mass social movement demanding systemic change in Communist Poland.

tshoks (Yid: lavishness, splendor); a type of musical ornament used in klezmer music, which emu-
    lates laughter.

tzadik (**pl. *tzadikim*).** Hasidic spiritual leader.

Vergangenheitsbewältigung. A German compound of *Vergangenheit* = past and *Bewältigung* =
    coming to terms with, wrestling into submission, denoting a post WWII process of coming to
    terms with difficult past, in particular the Holocaust.

Vertriebene. Germans expelled from Czechoslovakia and Poland (and other areas in Eastern
    Europe) after WWII.

Yiddishkeit. Yiddishness.

BIBLIOGRAPHY

"15. Jüdische Kulturtage." *Der Tagesspiegel*, October 25, 2001, 3.

"Die antisemitischen Gebrüder Herrnfeld." *Jüdische Rundschau*, August 28, 1908. Accessed September 16, 2011, http://www.filmportal.de/material/die-juedische-rundschau-ueber-das-herrnfeld-theater.

"Die neue Lust am Leben: Klezmer!" *Tip Berlin*, November, 27, 1996, 26–31.

"Haushaltloch bei Jüdischer Gemeinde." *Der Tagesspiegel*, April 5, 2008, 11.

"James Bond und Le Parkour." Accessed May 6, 2009, http://www.reticon.de/nachrichten/james-bond-und-le-parkour_1529.html.

"Jiddische Kulturtage." *Neues Deutschland*, January 28, 1987, 4.

"Komisja walczy z antypolonizmem." Accessed May 20, 2009, http://wiadomosci.wp.pl/kat,1342,title,Komisja-walczy-z-antypolonizmem,wid,8114347,wiadomosc.html.

"Koszerna wódka chce podbić Polskę." *Rzeczpospolita*, February 14, 2011. Accessed March 12, 2012, http://www.rp.pl/artykul/612226.html.

"List otwarty do władz miasta Krakowa i organizatorów Festiwalu Kultury Żydowskiej." *Gazeta Wyborcza Kraków*, April 10, 2002, 2.

"List Rady Episkopatu Polski do spraw Dialogu Religijnego z okazji Wielkiego Jubileuszu Roku 2000, August 25, 2000." Accessed May 20, 2009, http://www.episkopat.pl/?a=dokumentyKEP&doc=dialog.

"NPD-Aufmarsch. Ordnungsamt wollte jüdische Protestmusik gegen Nazis verhindern." *Spiegel Online*, June 8, 2007. Accessed June 11, 2007, http://www.spiegel.de/kultur/musik/0,1518,487443,00.html.

"Premier Kaczyński w Radiu Maryja: Rozmowy niedokończone, 23 lipca Radio Maryja i Telewizja Trwam." *Gazeta Wyborcza*, July 29–30, 2006, 16.

"Przeciw okupacji i festiwalowi." *Gazeta Wyborcza Kraków*, April 13, 2002, 4.

"Report of the Workshop on the European Itinerary of Jewish Heritage 2008." Accessed May 20, 2009, http://www.jewishheritage.org/jh/upload/publications/JH_19.pdf.

"Tage der jiddischen Kultur wurden beendet." *Neues Deutschland*, January 29, 1987, 7.

"Tage jiddischer Kultur in Berlin." *Neues Deutschland*, January 27, 1987, 1.

"W obronie prawdy." *Nasz Dziennik*, August 3, 2007. Accessed June 10, 2008, www.naszdziennik.pl/index.php?dat=20070803&typ=po&id=po51.txt.

11. Festiwal Kultury Żydowskiej w Krakowie. Kraków: Jewish Festival, 2001.

3. Festiwal Kultury Żydowskiej w Krakowie. Kraków: Graffiti, 1992.

4. Festiwal Kultury Żydowskiej w Krakowie. 19.–26. czerwca 1994. Kraków: Graffiti, 1994.

Alejchem, Scholem. *Stempenju*. Leipzig: Reclam, 1989.

Alexie, Sherman. *Reservation Blues*. New York: Grove Press, 1995.

Anderson, Benedict. *Imagined Communities*. London: Verso, 1991.

de Andrade, Oswald. "Cannibalist Manifesto." Translated by Leslie Bary. *Latin American Literary Review* 19, no. 38 (1991): 38–47.

Apfeld, Wiltrud, ed. *Klezmer—hejmisch und hip: Musik als kulturelle Ausdrucksform im Wandel der Zeit: Dokumentation zur Ausstellung*. Essen: Klartext, 2004.

Aquino Correa, Alamir. "Immigration and Cultural Anthropophagy in Brazilian Literature." *Passages de Paris* 2 (2005): 273–80.

Attie, Shimon. *Sites Unseen*. Heidelberg: Umschau/Braus, 1998.

Avidan, Igal. "Jewish Spirit in Kraków." *Jerusalem Report*, August 20, 2007, 26–28.

Aylward, Michael. "Early Recordings of Jewish Music in Poland." In *Polin: Studies in Polish Jewry*. Vol. 16, *Focusing on Jewish Popular Culture in Poland and its Afterlife*, edited by Michael Steinlauf and Anthony Polonsky, 59–69. Oxford: Littman Library of Jewish Civilization, 2003.

Bałaban, Majer. *Historja Żydów w Krakowie i na Kazimierzu 1304–1868*. Kraków: Krajowa Agencja Wydawnicza, 1991 [1931].

Ball-Kaduri, Kurt Jakob, and Michael Berenbaum. "Berlin 1933–39" and "Berlin 1939–1945." In *Encyclopaedia Judaica*, vol. 3. Detroit: Thompson-Gale, 2007, 448–51.

Bartosik, Marek. "Jestem tylko szabesgojem," *Gazeta Krakowska*, June 27, 2008. Accessed June 22, 2009, http://www.jewishfestival.pl/plikiprasa/1215954686.pdf.

Bartoszewski, Władysław, ed. *Polin: Studies in Polish Jewry*. Vol. 4, *Poles and Jews: Perceptions and Misperceptions*, 129–42. Oxford: Littman Library of Jewish Civilization, 1990.

Baudrillard, Jean. *Simulacra and Simulation*. Ann Arbor: University of Michigan Press, 1999.

Bauer, Susan. *Von der Khupe zum Klezkamp: Klezmer-Musik in New York*. Berlin: Piranha, 1999.

Bauman, Zygmunt. "From Pilgrim to Tourist—or a Short History of Identity." In *Questions of Cultural Identity*, edited by Stuart Hall and Paul DuGay, 18–36. London: Sage, 1996.

Bax, Daniel. "Berliner Simulation." *Die Tageszeitung*, November 19, 1999, 15.

Benjamin, Walter. *Illuminations*. London: Pimlico, 1999.

Beregovski, Moshe. *Jewish Instrumental Folk Music: The Collections and Writings of Moshe Beregovski*. Translated and edited by Mark Slobin, Robert A. Rothstein, and Michael Alpert. Syracuse: Syracuse University Press, 2001.

Beregovski, Moshe. *Old Jewish Folk Music: The Collections and Writings of Moshe Beregovski*. Translated and edited by Mark Slobin. Philadelphia: University of Pennsylvania Press, 1982.

Bergmeier Horst, Eljal J. Eisler, and Rainer E. Lotz. *Vorbei/Beyond Recall: Dokumetion jüdischen Musiklebens in Berlin 1933–1938*. Hambergen: Bear Family Records, 2001.

Bertz, Inka. "Eine neue Kunst für ein altes Volk": Die jüdische Renaissance in Berlin 1900 bis 1924. Berlin: Jüdisches Museum, 1991.

Bhabha, Homi K. *The Location of Culture*. London: Routledge, 1995.

Biale, David. "Confessions of a Historian of Jewish Culture." *Jewish Social Studies* 1 (1994): 40–51.

Bilewicz, Michał. "History as an Obstacle: Impact of Temporal-Based Social Categorizations on Polish-Jewish Intergroup Contact." *Intergroup Processes and Intergroup Relations* 10, no. 4 (2007): 551–63.

Bilewicz, Michał. "Wyjaśnianie Jedwabnego: Antysemityzm i postrzeganie trudnej przeszłości." In *Antysemityzm w Polsce i na Ukrainie*, edited by Ireneusz Krzemiński, 248–69. Warszawa: Scholar, 2004.

Billig, Michael. *Banal Nationalism*. London: Sage, 1995.

Bilski, Emily D. *Berlin Metropolis: Jews and the New Culture 1890–1918*. Berkeley: University of California Press, 1999.

Birnbaum, Michael. "Jewish Music, German Musicians: Cultural Appropriation and the Representation of a Minority in the German Klezmer Scene." *Leo Beck Institute Year Book* 1 (2009): 297–320.

Blobaum, Robert, ed. *Antisemitism and its Opponents in Modern Poland*. Ithaca, NY: Cornell University Press, 2005.

Błoński, Jan. "Biedni Polacy patrzą na getto." *Tygodnik Powszechny*, no. 2, 1987, 1. In English: "Poor Poles Look at the Ghetto." In *My Brother's Keeper? Recent Polish Debates on the Holocaust*, edited by Antony Polonsky, 34–52. London: Routledge, 1990.

Bodemann, Y. Michal. *Gedächtnistheater: Die jüdische Gemeinschaft und ihre deutsche Erfindung*. Hamburg: Rotbuch Verlag, 1996.

Bohlman, Philip V. "Composing the Cantorate: Westernizing Europe's Other Within." In *Western Music and Its Others: Difference, Representation and Appropriation in Music*, edited by Georgina Born and David Hesmondhalgh, 187–211. Berkeley: University of California Press, 2000.

Bohlman, Philip V. "Die Volksmusik und die Verstädterung der deutsch-jüdischen Gemeinde in den Jahrzehnten vor dem Zweiten Weltkrieg." In *Jahrbuch für Volksliedforschung*, edited by Otto Holzapfel and Jürgen Dittmar, 25–40. Berlin: Erich Schmidt Verlag, 1989.

Bohlman, Philip V. "Historisierung als Ideologie: die 'Klesmerisierung' der jüdischen Musik." In *Jüdische Musik? Fremdbilder—Eigenbilder*, edited by Eckhard John and Heidy Zimmermann, 241–55. Köln: Böhlau, 2004.

Bohlman, Philip V. "Music, Modernity, and the Foreign in the New Germany." *Modernism/Modernity* 1, no. 1 (1994): 121–52.

Bohlman, Philip V. "Of *Yekkes* and Chamber Music in Israel: Ethnomusicological Meaning in Western Music History." In *Ethnomusicology and Modern Music History*, edited by Stephen Blum, Philip V. Bohlman, and Daniel M. Neuman, 254–67. Urbana: University of Illinois, 1991.

Bohlman, Philip V. *Jüdische Volksmusik—eine mitteleuropäische Geistesgeschichte*. Wien: Böhlau, 2005.

Böning, Holger. "Die Anfänge musikalischen Protests in der Bundesrepublik und der DDR: Ausländische Einflüsse im politischen Lied." In *Rebellische Musik: Gesellschaftliche Protest und kultureller Wandel um 1968*, edited by Arnold Jacobshagen and Markus Leniger, 181–91. Köln: Dohr, 2007.

Borkowski, Krzysztof. "Ruch turystyczny w Krakowie w 2011 roku." Kraków, Małopolska Organizacja Turystyczna, 2006. Accessed October 20, 2012, http://www.mot.krakow.pl/index, a,b,c,16.html.

Born, Georgina. "Modern Music Culture: on Shock, Pop and Synthesis." In *Popular Music: Critical Concepts in Media and Cultural Studies*. Vol. 4, *Music and Identity*, edited by Simon Frith, 293–319. London: Routledge, 2004.

Born, Georgina, and David Hesmondhalgh, eds. Introduction to *Western Music and Its Others*, 1–58.

Boym, Svetlana. *The Future of Nostalgia*. New York: Basic Books, 2001.

Breakwell, G. "Some Effects of Marginal Social Identity." In *Differentiation between Social Groups: Studies in the Social Psychology of Intergroup Relations*, edited by Henri Tajfel, 301–36. London: Academic Press, 1978.

Brenner, Michael. *The Renaissance of Jewish Culture in Weimar Germany*. New Haven, CT: Yale University Press, 1996.

Brenner, Michael. "The Transformation of the German-Jewish Community." In *Unlikely History. The Changing German-Jewish Symbiosis 1945–2000*, edited by Leslie Morris and Jack Zipes, 49–61. New York: Palgrave, 2002.

Broder, Henryk M., "Bildungsbürger als Bla-Bla-Blockwarte." *Spiegel*, January 19, 2008. Accessed January 13, 2009, http://www.spiegel.de/kultur/gesellschaft/0,1518,529487,00.html.

Broder, Henryk M. *Der Ewige Antisemit: Über Sinn und Funktion eines beständigen Gefühls*. Berlin: Berliner Taschenbuch Verlag, 2005.

Broder, Henryk M. "Der ewige Gute." *Spiegel*, January 19, 2006. Accessed January 14, 2009, http://www.spiegel.de/kultur/kino/0,1518,396116,00.html.

Broder, Henryk M. "Die Konjunktur des Jüdischen an der Schwelle zum 21. Jahrhundert." In John and Zimmermann, *Jüdische Musik? Fremdbilder—Eigenbilder*, 361–78. Köln: Böhlau, 2004.

Broder, Henryk M. "Die toten Juden von Kazimierz." *Themen der Zeit*, no. 21, 1990. Quoted in 3. *Festiwal Kultury Żydowskiej w Krakowie*. Kraków: Graffiti, 1992, 145.

Broder, Henryk M. "Wir sind alle traumatisiert." *tachles: Das jüdische Wochenmagazin*, July 14, 2006. Accessed January 13, 2009, http://www.hagalil.com/archiv/2006/07/selbsthass.htm.

Bronner, Simon, J. "The *Chutzpah* of Jewish Cultural Studies." In *Jewish Cultural Studies*. Vol. 1, *Jewishness: Expression, Identity and Representation*, edited by Simon J. Bronner, 1–26. Oxford: Littman Library of Jewish Civilization, 2008.

Brown, Michael F. *Who Owns Native Culture?* Cambridge, MA: Harvard University Press, 2004.

Brown, Rupert J., and Gordon F. Ross. "The Battle of Acceptance: An Investigation into the Dynamics of Intergroup Behavior." In *Social Identity and Intergroup Relations*, edited by Henri Tajfel, 155–78. Cambridge: Cambridge University Press, 1982.

Bułat, Mirosława M. *Krakowski teatr żydowski: między szundem a sztuką*. Kraków: Wydawnictwo Uniwersytetu Jagiellońskiego, 2006.

Bundesministerium des Innern. "Antisemitismus in Deutschland, Erscheinungsformen, Bedingungen, Präventionsansätze: Bericht des unabhängigen Expertenkreises Antisemitismus." [Anti-Semitism in Germany, Its Forms, Conditions, and Prevention Projects: Report of the Independent Anti-Semitism Expert Group] 2012. Accessed March 12, 2012, http://www.bmi.bund.de/SharedDocs/Downloads/DE/Themen/Politik_Gesellschaft/EXpertenkreis_Antisemmitismus/bericht.pdf?__blob=publicationFile.

Burns Coleman, Elizabeth, Rosemary J. Coombe, and Fiona MacArailt. "A Broken Record: Subjecting 'Music' to Cultural Rights." In *The Ethics of Cultural Appropriation*, edited by James O. Young and Conrad G. Brunk, 173–210. Chichester: Wiley-Blackwell, 2009.

Cała, Alina. "Autostereotyp i stereotypy narodowe." In *Czy Polacy są antysemitami? Wyniki badania sondażowego*, edited by Ireneusz Krzemiński, 199–229. Warszawa: Oficyna Naukowa, 1996.

Cała, Alina. *Wizerunek Żyda w polskiej kulturze ludowej*. Warszawa: Wydawnictwa Uniwersytetu Warszawskiego, 1992.

Cała, Alina, et al. "Koza ze styropianu, pejsy z pakuł." *Midrasz* 3 (2006): 9–13.

Cantwell, Robert. *Ethnomimesis: Folklife and the Representation of Culture*. Chapel Hill, NC: University of North Carolina Press, 1993.

Chambers, Iain. *Urban Rhythms: Pop Music and Popular Culture*. New York: St. Martin's Press, 1985.

Cichopek, Anna. *Pogrom Żydów w Krakowie: 11 sierpnia 1945*. Warszawa: Żydowski Instytut Historyczny, 2000.

Classen, Constance, and David Howes. "Epilogue: The Dynamics and Ethics of Cross-Cultural Consumption." In *Cross-Cultural Consumption: Global Markets, Local Realities*, edited by David Howes, 178–94. London: Routledge, 2000.

Cygan, Jacek. *Klezmer: Opowieść o życiu Leopolda Kozłowskiego-Kleinmana*. Kraków: Austeria, 2010.

Della Pergola, Sergio. "Demography." In *The Oxford Handbook of Jewish Studies*, edited by Martin Goodman, 797–823. Oxford: Oxford University Press, 2002.

Dobranowska, Anna. "Jestem jak szames. I jestem z tego dumny." Forum Żydzi, Chrześcijanie, Muzułmanie, June 25, 2003. Accessed October 15, 2008, http://www.znak.org.pl/index.php?t=ludzie&id=34.

Dodziuk, Anna. *Druga dusza: O dwudziestu Festiwalach Kultury Żydowskiej w Krakowie*. Warszawa: Czarna Owca, 2010.

Dorson, Richard. *Folklore and Fakelore: Essays toward a Discipline of Folk Studies*. Cambridge, MA: Harvard University Press, 1976.

Duda, Eugeniusz, and Marek Sosenko, eds. *Dawna pocztówka żydowska*. Kraków: Muzeum Historyczne Miasta Krakowa, 1997.

Dunin, Janusz. "Postać Żyda w polskiej kulturze popularnej do 1945 roku." In *Wszystek krąg ziemski—prace ofiarowane profesorowi Czesławowi Hernasowi*, edited by Piotr Kowalski, 316–23. Wrocław: Wydawnictwo Uniwersytetu Wrocławskiego, 1989.

Dutkowska, Agata. "The Visual Semiotics of 'Jewishness' in Kazimierz." In *Cultural Representations of Jewishness at the Turn of the Twenty-first Century*. EUI Working Papers, edited by Magdalena Waligórska and Sophie Wagenhofer, 27–41. Florence: European University Press, 2010.

Dyroff, Hans-Dieter. "Die jiddische Kultur—wichtiger Teil unserer schöpferischen Vielfalt." In *Doss lid is geblibn: Tage der Jiddischen Kultur 1987–1996*, edited by Andrej Jendrusch. Bonn: Deutsche UNESCO Komission, 1995, 3.

Eckhardt, Ulrich, and Andreas Nachama, eds. *Jüdische Orte in Berlin*. Berlin: nicolai, 2005.

Eckstaedt, Aaron. *"Klaus mit der Fiedel, Heike mit dem Bass": Jiddische Musik in Deutschland*. Berlin: Philo, 2003.

Eichler, Jeremy. "Klezmer's Final Frontier." *New York Times*, August 29, 2004, 1.

Elon, Amos. *The Pity of It All: A Portrait of the German-Jewish Epoch 1743–1933*. New York: Picador, 2003.

European Commission against Racism and Intolerance. "The Third Report on Poland." June 14, 2005. Accessed October 16, 2008, http://www.coe.int/t/e/human_rights/ecri/1-ECRI/2-Country-by-country_approach/Poland/Poland_CBC_3.asp#TopOfPage http://www.coe.int/t/e/human_rights/ecri/1-ECRI/2-Country-by-country_approach/Poland/Poland_CBC_3.asp - TopOfPage.

Fater, Isaschar, and Ewa Świderska. *Muzyka żydowska w Polsce w okresie międzywojennym*. Warszawa: Oficyna Wydawnicza, 1997.

Feld, Steven. "The Poetics and Politics of Pygmy Pop." In Born and Hesmondhalgh, *Western Music and Its Others*, 254–79.

Feldman, Walter Z. "Bulgareasca/Bulgarish/Bulgar: The Transformation of a Klezmer Dance Genre." *Ethnomusicology* 38, no. 1 (1994): 1–35.

Feldman, Walter Z. "Klezmer as 'Other Music' for American Jews, 1950–1980." Lecture held at the "Symposium Klezmer and other 'other' musics" at the Yiddish Summer Weimar, Weimar, July 14, 2007.

Feldman, Walter Z. "Klezmer Music: History, Memory, and Musical Structure, ca. 1750–1950." Manuscript.

Feldman, Walter Z. "Remembrance of Things Past: Klezmer Musicians of Galicia, 1870–1940." In Steinlauf and Polonsky, *Polin*, vol. 16, *Focusing on Jewish Popular Culture*, 29–57.

Festiwal Kultury Żydowskiej Warszawa Singera. Warszawa: Fundacja Shalom, 2007.

Festiwal Kultury Żydowskiej Waszawa Singera. Warszawa: Fundacja Shalom, 2006.

Freedman, Jonathan. *Klezmer America: Jewishness, Ethnicity, Modernity*. New York: Columbia University Press, 2008.

Friszke, Andrzej, et al. "Dzielić cudzy ból." *Znak*, no. 541, 2000. Accessed October 1, 2008, http://www.miesiecznik.znak.com.pl/polowanie.html.

Fuks, Marian. *Muzyka ocalona: Judaica polskie*. Warszawa: Wydawnictwa Radia i Telewizji, 1989.

Gebert, Konstanty. "Jewish Identities in Poland: New, Old, and Imaginary." In *Jewish Identities in the New Europe*, edited by Jonathan Webber, 161–67. London: Littman Library of Jewish Civilization, 1994.

Gebert, Konstanty. "Nieautentyczność?" Introduction to *Odrodzenie kultury żydowskiej w Europie*, by Ruth E. Gruber, 11–16. Sejny: Pogranicze, 2004.

Geisel, Eike, ed. *Im Scheunenviertel*. Berlin: Severin und Siedler, 1981.

Gessler, Philipp. "Jüdische Lieder unerwünscht." *Die Tageszeitung*, August 5, 2006. Accessed April 6, 2008, http://www.taz.de/index.php?id=archivseite&dig=2006/08/05/a0100.

Ginsberg, Terri. "St. Korczak of Warsaw." In *Imaginary Neighbors: Mediating Polish-Jewish Relations after the Holocaust*, edited by Dorota Glowacka and Joanna Zylinska, 110–34. Lincoln: University of Nebraska Press, 2007.

Gitelman, Zvi. "Collective Memory and Contemporary Polish-Jewish Relations." In *Contested Memories: Poles and Jews during the Holocaust and its Aftermath*, edited by Joshua D. Zimmerman, 271–90. New Brunswick, NJ: Rutgers University Press, 2003.

Glass, Judith. "Flowers on the Grave." *Jüdische Rundschau*, no. 22, 1990. Quoted in 3. *Festiwal Kultury Żydowskiej w Krakowie*. Kraków: Graffiti, 1992, 151.

Glowacka, Dorota, and Joanna Zylinska, eds. *Imaginary Neighbors: Mediating Polish-Jewish Relations after the Holocaust* (Lincoln: Nebraska University Press, 2007).

Główny Urząd Statystyczny. *Wyznania religijne, stowarzyszenia narodowościowe i etniczne w Polsce 2009–2011*. Warszawa: Zakład Wydawnictw Statystycznych, 2013.

Golczewski, Frank. *Das Deutschlandbild der Polen 1918–1939: Eine Untersuchung der Historiographie und der Publizistik*. Düsseldorf: Droste, 1974.

Gonet, Dorota. "Jesteśmy sentymentalni." *Gazeta Wyborcza Lublin*, April 23, 2001, 5.

Graff, Agnieszka. "Gej czyli Żyd . . . I co dalej?" *Rykoszetem. Rzecz o płci, seksualności i narodzie*. Warszawa: WAB, 2008, 110–42.

Greenberg, Clement. *Art and Culture: Critical Essays*. Boston: Beacon Press, 1961.

Greenblatt, Stephen. *Marvelous Possessions: The Wonder of the New World*. Oxford: Clarendon Press, 1992.

Gross, Jan T. *Fear: Anti-Semitism in Poland after Auschwitz. An Essay in Historical Interpretation*. Princeton: Princeton University Press, 2006.

Gross, Jan T. *Neighbors: The Destruction of the Jewish Community in Jedwabne, Poland*. Princeton: Princeton University Press, 2001.

Gross, Jan T. *Sąsiedzi: Historia zagłady żydowskiego miasteczka*. Sejny: Pogranicze, 2000.

Gross, Natan. "Mordechai Gebirtig: The Folk Song and the Cabaret Song." In Steinlauf and Polonsky, *Polin*, vol. 16, *Focusing on Jewish Popular Culture in Poland*, 107–17.

Groß, Thomas. "Der Auserwählte Folk." *Die Zeit*, June 24, 2003. Accessed June 21, 2009, http://www.zeit.de/2003/31/Klezmer.

Gruber, Ruth E. "Beyond Virtually Jewish . . . Balancing the Real, the Surreal and Real Imaginary Places." In *Reclaiming Memory: Urban Regeneration in the Historic Jewish Quarters of Central European Cities*, edited by Monika Murzyn-Kupisz and Jacek Purchla, 63–80. Kraków: International Cultural Centre.

Gruber, Ruth E. *Virtually Jewish: Reinventing Jewish Culture in Europe*. Berkeley: University of California Press, 2002.

Gruber, Ruth E. "Wierzchołek nieistniejącej góry." *Tygodnik Powszechny*, July 3, 2005. Accessed August 1, 2005, http://tygodnik.onet.pl/1548,1235372,0,354087,dzial.html.

Halkowski, Henryk. "Rodzinny dom w knajpę przemieniony, czyli o kiczu na Kazimierzu." *Midrasz* 3 (2006): 16–19.

Halkowski, Henryk. "A World Before a Catastrophe?" In *A World Before a Catastrophe: Kraków's Jews between the Wars*, 21–32. Kraków: International Cultural Centre, 2007.

Halkowski, Henryk. *Żydowski Kraków: Legendy i ludzie*. Kraków: Austeria, 2009.

Halkowski, Henryk. *Żydowskie życie*. Kraków, Austeria: 2003.

Handrock, Ariane. "Klischees als Verkaufsschlager: die jüdische Musikszene in Deutschland." In *Musik Netz Werke, Konturen der neuen Musikkultur*, edited by Lydia Grün and Frank Wiegand, 95–105. Bielefeld: Transcript, 2002.

Hart, Jonathan. "Translating and Resisting Empire: Cultural Appropriation and Postcolonial Studies." In *Borrowed Power: Essays on Cultural Appropriation*, edited by Bruce Ziff and Pratima V. Rao, 137–68, New Brunswick, NJ: Rutgers University Press, 1997.

Heid, Ludger. "Der Ostjude." In *Antisemitismus: Vorurteile und Mythen*, edited by Julius H. Schoeps and Joachim Schlör, 245–49. München: Piper, 1995.

Heid, Ludger. "Ostjüdische Kultur im Deutschland der Weimarer Republik." In *Juden als Träger bürgerlicher Kultur in Deutschland*, edited by Julius H. Schoeps, 329–55. Stuttgart: Burg Verlag, 1989.

Herf, Jeffrey. *The Jewish Enemy: Nazi Propaganda during World War II and the Holocaust*. Cambridge, MA: Harvard University Press, 2006.

Hertz, Aleksander. *The Jews in Polish Culture*. Evanston, IL: Northwestern University Press, 1988.

Heskes, Irene. "Miriam's Sisters: Jewish Women and Liturgical Music." *Notes* 48, no. 4 (1992): 1193–1202.

Hirsch, Lily E. *A Jewish Orchestra in Nazi Germany: Musical Politics and the Berlin Jewish Culture League*. Ann Arbor: University of Michigan Press, 2010.

Hirsch, Marianne. "The Generation of Postmemory." *Poetics Today* 29, no. 1 (2008): 103–28.

Hirsch, Marianne. "Surviving Images: Holocaust Photographs and the Work of Postmemory." *Yale Journal of Criticism* 14, no. 1 (2001): 5–37.

Hirt-Manheimer, Aron. "Ten Days in East Germany." *Reform Judaism* 9, no. 3 (Feb. 1981): 1.

Hoffman, Eva. *Shtetl: The Life and Death of a Small Town and the World of Polish Jews*. London: Secker and Warburg, 1998.

Hogg, Michael A. "Intragroup Processes, Group Structure and Social Identity." In *Social Groups and Identities: Developing the Legacy of Henri Tajfel*, edited by W. Peter Robinson, 65–93. Oxford: Butterworth -Heinemann, 1996.

Holc, Janine P. "Memory Contested: Jewish and Catholic Views of Auschwitz in Present-Day Poland." In *Antisemitism and its Opponents in Modern Poland*, edited by Robert Blobaum, 301–25. Ithaca, NY: Cornell University Press, 2005.

Holler, Eckhard. "The Burg Waldeck Festivals, 1964–1969." In *Protest Song in East and West Germany Since the 1960s*, edited by David Robb, 97–131, Rochester: Camden House, 2007.

hooks, bell. "Eating the Other: Desire and Resistance." In *Media and Cultural Studies: Key Works*, edited by Meenakshi G. Durham and Douglas M. Kellner, 366–80. Oxford: Blackwell, 2006.

Howes, David. "Cultural Appropriation and Resistance in the American Southwest: Decommodifying 'Indianness.'" In *Cross-Cultural Consumption: Global Markets, Local Realities*, edited by David Howes, 138–60. London: Routledge, 2000.

Idelsohn, Abraham Z. *Jewish Music in Its Historical Development*. New York: Schocken Boooks, 1967.

Ilie, Rodica. "Cultural Anthropophagy: A Poetic Counter-Ideology Pau Modernism—Futurism's Re-signification." *Caietele Echinox* 14 (2008): 68–78.

International Cultural Centre. *A World Before a Catastrophe: Kraków's Jews Between the Wars*. Kraków: International Cultural Centre, 2007.

Jaldati, Lin, and Eberhard Rebling, eds. *Es brennt, Brüder, es brennt: Jiddische Lieder*. Berlin: Rütten & Loening, 1985 and 1969.

Janion, Maria. *Bohater, spisek, śmierć*. Warszawa: WAB, 2009.

Janion, Maria. *Do Europy tak, ale razem z naszymi umarłymi*. Warszawa: Sic!, 2000.

Janion, Maria. *Niesamowita Słowiańszczyzna: fantazmaty literatury*. Kraków: Wydawnictwo Literackie, 2006.

Janowska, Katarzyna. "Festiwal Żydowski: duch Kazimierza." *Polityka*, no. 28 (July 10, 2004): 58.

Jaspers, Karl. *Die Schuldfrage: Für Völkermord gibt es keine Verjährung*. München: Piper Verlag, 1979.

Jendrusch, Andrej, ed. *Doss Lid is geblibn: Tage der jiddischen Kultur 1987 bis 1996*. Berlin: Projektgruppe Tage der Jiddischen Kultur, 1995.

John, Eckhard, and Heidy Zimmermann, eds. *Jüdische Musik? Fremdbilder—Eigenbilder*. Köln: Böhlau, 2004.

Jung, Carl. "Nach der Katastrophe." In *Gesammelte Werke: Zivilisation im Übergang*. Vol 10, 219–44. Olten: Walter Verlag, 1986.

Kafrissen, Rokhl. "A Jewish Cultural Manifesto." *Jewish Currents*, November 2005. Accessed May 19, 2008, http://www.jewishcurrents.org/2005-nov-kafrissen.htm.

Kamieniecki, Mariusz. "Niechciany pomnik." *Nasz Dziennik*, May 22, 2007. Accessed June 10, 2008, http://www.naszdziennik.pl/index.php?dat=20070522&typ=po&id=po33.txt.

Kessler, Judith. "Kultus- oder Kulturjuden?" hagalil.com, May 8, 2003. Accessed April 26, 2009, http://www.berlin-judentum.de/gemeinde/mitgliederbefragung-2.htm.

Kirshenblatt-Gimblett, Barbara. "Sounds of Sensibility." *Judaism* 47, no. 1 (1998): 49–78.

Kirshenblatt-Gimblett, Barbara, and J. Karp, eds. *The Art of Being Jewish in Modern Times*. Philadelphia: University of Pennsylvania Press, 2008.

Klugman, Aleksander. *Żyd—co to znaczy?* Warszawa: Wiedza Powszechna, 2003.

Kohl Bines, Rosana. "Samba and Shoah: Ethnic, Religious and Social Diversity in Brazil." *European Review of History* 18, no. 1 (2011): 101–09.

Kozik, Ryszard. "W izraelskim tyglu kultur." *Gazeta Wyborcza*, June 27, 2008, 18.

Krajewski, Stanisław. "The Impact of the Shoah on the Thinking of Contemporary Polish Jewry. A Personal Account." In Zimmerman, *Contested Memories*, 291–303.

Krajewski, Stanisław. *Żydzi, Judaizm, Polska*. Warszawa: Vocatio, 1997.

Krakowski, Stefan. "Kielce." *Encyclopaedia Judaica*, 2nd. ed., vol. 12, 146–47.

Krzemiński, Ireneusz, ed. *Antysemityzm w Polsce i na Ukrainie*. Warszawa: Scholar, 2004.

Krzemiński, Ireneusz, ed. *Czy Polacy są antysemitami? Wyniki badania sondażowego*. Warszawa: Oficyna Naukowa, 1996.

Krzemiński, Ireneusz. "O Żydach i antysemityzmie po 10 latach." In *Antysemityzm w Polsce i na Ukrainie*, edited by Ireneusz Krzemiński, 15–168. Warszawa: Scholar, 2004.

Krzemiński, Ireneusz, and Ewa Koźmińska Frejlak. "Stosunek społeczeństwa polskiego do zagłady Żydów." In *Czy Polacy są antysemitami? Wyniki badania sondażowego*, edited by Ireneusz Krzemiński, 96–145. Warszawa: Oficyna Naukowa, 1996.

Kucia, Marek. *Auschwitz jako fakt społeczny*. Kraków: Universitas, 2005.

Kueppers, Kirsten. "Marketing mit Davidstern." *Die Tageszeitung*, November 20, 2000, 19.

Lachmann, Renate. "Remarks on the Foreign (Strange) as a Figure of Cultural Ambivalence." In *The Translatability of Cultures: Figurations of the Space Between*, edited by Sanford Budick and Wolfgang Iser, 282–93. Stanford: Stanford University Press, 1996.

Laufer, Peter. *Exodus to Berlin: The Return of the Jews to Germany*. Chicago: Ivan R. Dee, 2003.

Lehmann, Heiko. "Klezmer in Germany, Germans and Klezmer: Reparation or Contribution." Accessed April 21, 2008, http://www.sukke.de/lecture.html.

Lehrer, Erica. "Bearing False Witness? 'Vicarious' Jewish Identity and the Politics of Affinity." In Glowacka and Zylinska, *Imaginary Neighbors*, 84–109.

Lehrer, Erica. "Can There Be a Reconciliatory Heritage?" *International Journal of Heritage Studies* 16, nos. 4–5 (2010): 269–88.

Lehrer, Erica T. *Jewish Poland Revisited: Heritage Tourism in Unquiet Places*. Bloomington: Indiana University Press, 2013.

Lehrer, Erica. "Repopulating Jewish Poland—in Wood." In Steinlauf and Polonsky, *Polin*, vol. 16, *Focusing on Jewish Popular Culture*, 335–55.

Lehrer, Erica. "Virtual, Virtuous, Vicarious, Vacuous? Towards a Vigilant use of Labels." In *Jewish Cultural Studies*. Vol. 4, *Framing Jewish Culture: Boundaries and Representations*, edited by Simon J. Bronner, 383–95. Oxford: Littman Library of Jewish Civilization, forthcoming 2013.

Leveson, Ian, and Sandra Lustig. "Caught between Civil Society and the Cultural Market: Jewry and the Jewish Space in Europe: A Response to Diana Pinto." In *Turning the Kaleidoscope: Perspectives on European Jewry*, edited by Sandra Lustig and Ian Leveson, 187–204. New York: Berghahn Books, 2006.

Lipsitz, George. "Cruising Around the Historical Bloc: Postmodernism and Popular Music in East Los Angeles." In Frith, *Popular Music*. Vol. 4, *Music and Identity*, 324–40. London: Routledge, 2004.

Loew, Peter Oliver. "Feinde, überall Feinde: Psychogramm eines Problems in Polen." *Osteuropa* 56, no. 11–12 (2006): 33–51.

Lott, Eric. *Love and Theft: Blackface Minstrelsy and the American Working Class*. New York: Oxford University Press, 1993.

Lotz, Rainer E. *Discographie der Judaica Aufnahmen*. Bonn: Brigit Lotz Verlag, 2006.

Lowenthal, David. *The Heritage Crusade and the Spoils of History*. Cambridge: Cambridge University Press 2005.

Lubińska, Grażyna. "W blasku synagogi Tempel." *Gazeta Wyborcza Kraków*, June 19, 1995, 3.

Lustig, Sandra, and Ian Leveson. "Introduction." In *Turning the Kaleidoscope: Perspectives on European Jewry*, edited by Sandra Lustig and Ian Leveson, 1–23. New York: Berghahn Books, 2006.

Lustiger-Thaler, Henri. "Remembering Forgetfully." In *Re-situating Identities: The Politics of Race Ethnicity and Culture*, edited by Vered Amit-Talai and Caroline Knowles, 190–217. Peterborough, ONT: Broadview Press, 1998.

Lynch, Kevin. *What Time Is This Place?* Cambridge, MA: MIT Press, 1993.

Meng, Michael. *Shattered Spaces: Encountering Jewish Ruins in Postwar Germany and Poland*. Cambridge, MA: Harvard University Press, 2011.

Meyer, Michael. "Klezmer und Bagel." *Berliner Zeitung*, June 18, 2001. Accessed January 13, 2009, http://www.berlinonline.de/berliner-zeitung/archiv/.bin/dump.fcgi/2001/0618/none/0056/index.html.

Michalczak, Janusz. "Swoi i obcy." *Dziennik Polski*, May 20, 1988. In *Powiększenie*, no. 1–4, Kraków, 1990, 251.

Michlic, Joanna B. "The Dark Past: Polish-Jewish Relations in the Shadow of the Holocaust." In Glowacka and Zylinska, *Imaginary Neighbors*, 21–39.

Michlic, Joanna B. *Poland's Threatening Other: The Image of the Jew from 1880 to the Present*. Lincoln: University of Nebraska Press, 2006.

Miles, William F. S. "Auschwitz: Museum Interpretation and Darker Tourism." *Annals of Tourism Research* 29, no. 4 (2002): 1175–78.

Morawiec, Elżbieta. "Polska leży w Europie." Nowy Świat, June 23, 1992. In *4. Festiwal Kultury Żydowskiej w Krakowie. 19.–26. czerwca 1994*. Kraków: Graffiti, 1994, 55.

Morris, Leslie. "The Sound of Memory." *German Quarterly* 74, no. 4 (2001): 38–62.

Morris, Leslie, and Jack Zipes. "German and Jewish Obsession." In Morris and Zipes, *Unlikely History*, xi–xvi. New York: Palgrave, 2002.

Morris, Leslie, and Jack Zipes, eds. *Unlikely History. The Changing German-Jewish Symbiosis 1945–2000*. New York: Palgrave, 2002.

Mrożek, Sławomir. *Dziennik: Tom 1 1962–1969*. Kraków: Wydawnictwo Literackie, 2010.

Mueller, Kerstin. "Normalizing the Abnormal: Joshua Sobol's *Ghetto* in West Germany." *Seminar: A Journal of Germanic Studies* 45, no. 1 (2009): 44–63.

Murzyn, Monika A. *Kazimierz: Środkowoeuropejskie doświadczenie rewitalizacji*. Kraków, Międzynarodowe Centrum Kultury, 2006.

Musiał, Stanisław. *Czarne jest czarne*. Kraków: Wydawnictwo Literackie, 2003.

Netzky, Hankus. "Three Twentieth-Century Jewish Musicians from Poland: Frydman, Rosner, and Bazyler." *Polish Music Journal* 6, no. 1 (2003). Accessed October 23, 2012, http://www.usc.edu/dept/polish_music/PMJ/issue/6.1.03/Netsky.html.

Nora, Pierre. "Between Memory and History: Les Lieux de Memoire." *Representations*: Special Issue: Memory and Counter-Memory 26 (1989): 7–24.

Okamura, Jonathan Y. "Situational Ethnicity." *Ethnic and Racial Studies* 4, no. 4 (1981): 452–65.

Olick, Jeffrey K. *In the House of the Hangman: The Agonies of German Defeat, 1943–1949*. Chicago: University of Chicago Press, 2005.

Orla-Bukowska, Annamaria. "Goje w żydowskim interesie: Wkład etnicznych Polaków w życie polskich Żydów." In *Polacy i Żydzi: Kwestia otwarta*, edited by Robert Cherry and Annamaria Orla-Bukowska, 223–41. Warszawa: Więź: 2008.

Orliński, Wojciech. "Szanuj Menela Swego." *Duży Format: Gazeta Wyborcza*, June 30, 2008, 2–4.

Ortmeyer, Benjamin, ed. *Jiddische Lieder gegen die Nazis*. Witterschlick/Bonn: Verlag M. Wehle, 1996.

Ottens, Rita. "Der Klezmer als ideologischer Arbeiter." *Neue Zeitschrift für Musik* 159, no. 3 (1998): 26–29.

Ottens, Rita. "Die wüste Stadt Berlin: ein Versuch zur Standortbestimmung jiddischer Musik unter den jüdischen Zuwanderern aus der ehemaligen Sowjetunion in Berlin." In *Jüdische Musik und Ihre Musiker im 20. Jahrhundert*, edited by Wolfgang Birtel, Joseph Dorfman, and Christoph-Hellmut Mahling, 73–132. Mainz: Arc Edition, 2006.

Ottens, Rita. "Ikonografie der Andersartigkeit: Rassismus und Antisemitismus in der deutschen Popularmusik." *Neue Zeitschrift für Musik* 163 (2002): 54–57.

Ottens, Rita, and Joel Rubin. *Klezmer-Musik*. München: Bärenreiter, 2003.

Ottens, Rita, and Joel Rubin. "'The Sounds of the Vanishing World.' The German Klezmer Movement as a Racial Discourse." Accessed January 4, 2009, http://mki.wisc.edu/Resources/Online_Papers/MusicConfPapers/Ottens-RubinPaper.pdf.

Park, Robert E. *Race and Culture*. Glencoe, IL: The Free Press, 1950.

Pinto, Diana. "The Challenges of Progressive Jews in Twenty-first-century Europe." Accessed September 28, 2011, http://www.eupj.org/paris-2010/69-dr-diana-pinto.html.

Pinto, Diana. "The Third Pillar? Toward a European Jewish Identity," 1999. Accessed June 2, 2006, http://www.ceu.hu/jewishstudies/pdf/01_pinto.pdf.

Pinto, Goel. "'My Personal Atlantis.'" Haaretz, August 27, 2007. Accessed October 15, 2008, available at http://www.haaretz.com/hasen/spages/897586.html.

Pordes, Anis D., and Irek Grin. *Ich miasto: Wspomnienia Izraelczyków, przedwojennych mieszkańców Krakowa*. Warszawa: Prószyński i Spółka, 2004.

Pratt, Mary Louise. "Arts of the Contact Zone." *Profession* 91 (1991): 33–40.

Prokopówna, Eugenia. "The Image of the Shtetl in Polish Literature." In Bartoszewski, *Polin: Studies in Polish Jewry*. Vol. 4, Poles and Jews, 129–42. Oxford: Littman Library of Jewish Civilization, 1990.

Radano, Ronald, and Philip Bohlman. "Introduction: Music and Race, Their Past, Their Presence." In *Music and the Racial Imagination*, edited by Ronald Radano and Philip Bohlman, 1–53. Chicago: University of Chicago Press, 2000.

Radłowska, Renata. "Dybuk nim trzęsie niemiłosiernie." *Gazeta Wyborcza*, June 27, 2008, 22–23.

Radłowska, Renata. "Kazimierz: Protesty przeciwko rewitalizacji. Woleli plac martwy." *Gazeta Wyborcza*, July 8, 2002, 3.

Radłowska, Renata. "Kazimierz: Reaktywacja. Dlaczego tu mieszkają, dlaczego odchodzą? Nasze ulice pustych domów." *Gazeta Wyborcza Kraków*, June 27, 2003, 7.

Radłowska, Renata, and Ewelina Niemczura. "Kazimierz. Reaktywacja." *Gazeta Wyborcza Kraków*, June 23, 2003, 1.

Reich, Tova. *My Holocaust*. New York: Harper Collins, 2007.

Reiss, Józef. "Dusza żydostwa w muzyce." *Muzyk Wojskowy*, July 1, 1928, no. 13, 2.

Remmler, Karen. "Encounters Across the Void: Rethinking Approaches to German-Jewish Symbioses." In Morris and Zipes, *Unlikely History*, 3–29.

Rice, Monika. "Resisting a Phantom Book: A Critical Assessment of the Initial Polish Discussion of Jan Gross's Fear." In *Polin: Studies in Polish Jewry*. Vol. 22, *Social and Cultural Boundaries in Pre-Modern Poland*, edited by Adam Teller, Magda Teter, and Antony Polonsky, 427–53. Oxford: Littman Library of Jewish Civilization, 2010.

Rogovoy, Seth. *The Essential Klezmer*. Chapel Hill, NC: Algonquin Books, 2000.

Romaine, Suzanne. "Pidgins and Creoles: Overview." In *Encyclopaedia of Language and Linguistics*, edited by Keith Brown, 600–606. Amsterdam: Elseviere, 2006.

Romanowski, Rafał, and Seweryn Blumsztajn. "Jak grać na Szerokiej: Najazd Hunów. Pod rozwagę." *Gazeta Wyborcza Kraków*, September 24, 2004, 1.

Rosenberg, Leibl. "Jüdische Kultur in Deutschland heute." In *Juden in Deutschland nach 1945. Bürger oder "Mit"-Bürger?*, edited by Otto R. Romberg and Susanne Urban-Fahr, 234–43. Frankfurt: Tribüne, 1999.

Rosenfelder, Ruth. "Whose Music? Ownership and Identity in Jewish Music." Paper presented at the conference "Jewish Culture in the Age of Globalisation," University of Manchester, July 22, 2008.

Rubin, Joel. "Ambivalente Identitäten: Die Amerikanische Klezmer-Bewegung als Reaktion auf Krise und Trauma." In *Berichte aus dem ICTM-Nationalkomitee Deutschland*, edited by Marianne Bröcker, 89–115. Bamberg: Universitätsbibliothek, 2004.

Rubin, Joel, and Rita Ottens. "Klezmer-Forschung in Osteuropa: damals und heute." In *Juden und Antisemitismus in östlichen Europa*, edited by Mariana Hausleitner and Monika Katz, 177–93. Berlin: Harassovitz Verlag, 1995.

Salmen, Walter. " . . . *denn die Fiedel macht das Fest."*: Jüdische Musikanten und Tänzer vom 13. bis 20. Jahrhundert*. Innsbruck: Helbling, 1991.

Salmen, Walter. "The Post-1945 Klezmer Revival." In *Yiddish in the Contemporary World: Papers of the First Mendel Friedman International Conference on Yiddish*, edited by Gennady Estraikh and Mikhail Krutikov, 107–17. Oxford: Legenda, 1999.

Sapoznik, Henry. *Klezmer!* New York: Schirmer Trade Books, 1999.

Sapoznik, Henry. "Klezmer Music: The First One Thousand Years." In *Musics of Multicultural America: A Study of Twelve Musical Communities*, edited by Kip Lornell and Anne K. Rasmussen, 49–71. New York: Schirmer Books, 1997.

Saß, Anne-Christin. *Berliner Luftmenschen: Osteuropäisch-jüdische Migranten in der Weimarer Republik*. Göttingen: Wallstein, 2012.

Sauerbaum, Peter. "Ich fordere die Zwänge heraus!" *Jüdische Zeitung*, no. 4, December, 2005, 22.

Scheiner, Jonathan. "Wenn Jiddisch richtig groovt." *Jüdische Allgemeine*, no. 11/09, March 12, 2009, 9.

Schlink, Bernhard. *Vergangenheitsschuld*. Zürich: Diogenes, 2007.

Schlör, Joachim. *Das Ich der Stadt—Debatten über Judentum und Urbanität 1822–1938*. Göttingen: Vandenhoeck & Ruprecht, 2005.

Schoeps, Julius H., ed. *Juden als Träger bürgerlicher Kultur in Deutschland*. Stuttgart: Burg Verlag, 1989.

Schomacker, Tim. "Zeichen der Zeit: Notizen vom 4. Klezmer Festival im Vegesacker Kito." *Die Tageszeitung*, May 2, 2000, 23.

Schumann, Coco, Max Christian Graeff, and Michaela Haas. *Der Ghetto-Swinger: Eine Jazzlegende erzählt*. München: Deutscher Taschenbuch Verlag, 2005.

Segev, Tom. *The Seventh Million: The Israelis and the Holocaust*. New York: Henry Holt, 2000.

Shmeruk, Chone. *Legenda o Esterce w literaturze jidysz i polskiej*. Warszawa: Oficyna Naukowa, 2000.

Sholem, Gershom. "Dibbuk." *Encyclopaedia Judaica*, vol 5, 2nd ed., 643–44.

Slobin, Mark. ed. *American Klezmer: Its Roots and Offshoots*. Berkeley: University of California Press, 2002.

Slobin, Mark. *Fiddler on the Move: Exploring the Klezmer World*. Oxford: Oxford University Press, 2000.

Slobin, Mark. "Klezmer." In *Enzyklopädie jüdischer Geschichte und Kultur*, ed. Dan Diner, 375–79. Stuttgart: J. B. Metzler, 2012.

Sobański, Oskar. "Więcej niż fascynacja." *Film*, no. 27, July 3, 1988. In *Powiększenie*, no. 1–4, 1990, 250.

Sobolewski, Tadeusz. "Festiwal z przyszłością." In *3. Festiwal Kultury Żydowskiej w Krakowie*, Kraków: Graffiti, 1992, 144.

Socha, Ireneusz. "Lider fun Mordechaj Gebirtig." Accessed November 27, 2007, http://www.serpent.pl/recenzje/c.html.

Sombart, Nicolaus. "Der Beitrag der Juden zur deutschen Kultur." In Schoeps, *Juden als Träger bürgerlicher Kultur in Deutschland*, 17–40.

Sommerfeld, Adolf. *Das Ghetto von Berlin*. Berlin: Verlag Neues Leben, 1992.

Śpiewak, Paweł. *Żydokomuna: Interpretacje historyczne*. Warszawa: Czerwone i Czarne, 2012.

Sprengel, Peter. *Populäres jüdisches Theater in Berlin von 1877 bis 1933*. Berlin: Haude & Spener, 1997.

Steinlauf, Michael, and Antony Polonsky, eds. *Polin: Studies in Polish Jewry*. Vol. 16, *Focusing on Jewish Popular Culture*. Oxford: Littman Library of Jewish Civilization, 2003.

Steinlauf, Michael C. "Teaching about the Holocaust in Poland." In Zimmerman, *Contested Memories*, 262–70.

Steinlauf, Michael C. *Pamięć nieprzyswojona: polska pamięć Zagłady*. Warszawa: Cyklady, 2001.

Steinlauf, Michael. "Something Lost that Seeks Its Name: Dybbuks in Post-Communist Poland." Paper presented at the conference "Modern Jewish Culture: Diversities and Unities," University of Wrocław, June 26, 2008.

Stokes, Martin. "Place, Exchange, and Meaning: Black Sea Musicians in the West of Ireland." In Frith., *Popular Music*. Vol. 4, *Music and Identity*, 101–16. London: Routledge, 2004.

Stola, Dariusz. "Fighting against the Shadows: The Anti-Zionist Campaign of 1968." In Blobaum, *Antisemitism and its Opponents in Modern Poland*, 284–300.

Strom, Yale. *The Book of Klezmer*. Chicago: A Cappella Books, 2002.

Strom, Yale, and Elisabeth Schwartz. *A Wandering Feast: A Journey Through the Jewish Culture of Eastern Europe*. San Francisco: Jossey-Bass, 2005.

Stührmann, Anette. "Six Million Germans!" *Exberliner*, June 2007. Accessed June 4, 2007, http://www.exberliner.net/verbatim.php?action=inthisissue.

Szlajfer, Henryk. *Polacy Żydzi: Zderzenie stereotypów. Esej dla przyjaciół i innych*. Warszawa: Scholar, 2003.

Szwarcman, Dorota. "Czy muzyka żydowska musi być kiczowata?" *Midrasz* 3 (2006): 20–21.

Szwarcman, Dorota. "Muzyka od dybuka." *Polityka*, September 1, 2007, 63–64.

Tajfel, Henri, ed. *Differentiation between Social Groups: Societies in the Social Psychology of Intergroup Relations*. London: Academic Press, 1978.

Tajfel, Henri. "Instrumentality, Identity, and Social Comparisons." In Tajfel, *Social Identity and Intergroup Relations*, 483–507.

Tajfel, Henri. "Social Categorization, Social Identity, and Social Comparison." In Tajfel, *Differentiation between Social Groups*, 61–76.

Tajfel, Henri, ed. *Social Identity and Intergroup Relations*. Cambridge: Cambridge University Press, 1982.

Taylor, Charles. *Multiculturalism: Examining the Politics of Recognition*. Princeton: Princeton University Press, 1994.

Teller, Adam, Magda Teter, and Antony Polonsky, eds. *Polin: Studies in Polish Jewry*. Vol. 22, *Social and Cultural Boundaries*. Oxford: Littman Library of Jewish Civilization, 2003.

Tempel, Sylke. "Alan Bern lehrt die Deutschen das mollige Kuscheln mit Klezmer." *Die Welt*, September 1, 2004. Accessed June 20, 2008, http://www.welt.de/print-welt/article337596/ Alan_Bern_lehrt_die_Deutschen_das_mollige_Kuscheln_mit_Klezmer.html.

Thierse, Wolfgang. "Pressemeldung des Deutschen Bundestages, March 27, 2001." Accessed Mach 4, 2008, http://webarchiv.bundestag.de/archive/2007/0814/aktuell/presse/2001/pz_ 0103271.html.

Tkaczyk, Viktoria. "'Wir sind die Indianer Europas.'" *Die Welt*, August 6, 2001. Accessed September 20, 2006, http://www.welt.de/data/2001/08/06/509284.html?prx=1.

Tokarska-Bakir, Joanna. "Cries of the Mob in the Pogroms in Rzeszów (June 1945), Cracow (August 1945), and Kielce (July 1946) as a Source for the State of Mind of the Participants." *East European Politics and Societies* 25, no. 3 (2011): 553–74.

Tokarska-Bakir, Joanna. "Jedwabne: History as Fetish." In Glowacka and Zylinska, *Imaginary Neighbors*, 40–63.

Tokarska-Bakir, Joanna. *Legendy o krwi: Antropologia przesądu*. Warszawa: WAB, 2008.

Tokarska-Bakir, Joanna. "Obrazy sandomierskie." *ResPublica Nowa*, no. 1, 2007, 18–63.

Tokarska-Bakir, Joanna. *Rzeczy mgliste: eseje i studia*. Sejny: Pogranicze, 2004.

Tokarska-Bakir, Joanna. "Żyd z pieniążkiem podbija Polskę." *Gazeta Wyborcza*, February 18, 2012. Accessed March 12, 2012, http://wyborcza.pl/1,76842,11172689,Zyd_z_pieniazkiem_ podbija_Polske.html.

Tunbridge, John E., and Gregory J. Ashworth. *Dissonant Heritage: The Management of the Past as a Resource in Conflict*. Chichester: Wiley, 1996.

Turner, John C. "Towards a Cognitive Redefinition of the Social Group." In Tajfel, *Social Identity and Intergroup Relations*, 15–40.

Turner John, and Rupert Brown. "Social Status, Cognitive Alternatives, and Intergroup Relations." In Tajfel, *Differentiation between Social Groups*, 201–34.

Urry, John. *Consuming Places*. London: Routledge, 1995.

Vasagar, Jeevan, and Julian Borger. "A Jewish Renaissance in Poland." *Guardian*, April 7, 2011. Accessed September 9, 2011, http://www.guardian.co.uk/world/2011/apr/07/jewish-renaissance-poland.

Waligórska, Magdalena. "*Kleznetworks*: The Transnational and the Local Dimension of Jewish Culture Festivals." In *Jewish Spaces: Die Kategorie Raum im Kontext kultureller Identitäten*, edited by Petra Ernst and Gerald Lamprecht, 137–56. Innsbruck: Studienverlag: 2010.

Weiss, Iris. "Jewish Disneyland—the Appropriation and Dispossession of 'Jewishness.'" *Golem*, no. 3, 2002. Accessed April 6, 2008, http://www.hagalil.com/golem/diaspora/disneyland-e. htm.

Weissberg, Liliane. "Reflecting on the Past, Envisioning the Future: New Perspectives in German-Jewish Studies." Lecture of the Leo Baeck Institute and the German Historical Institute, Washington, October 2003.

Werb, Bret. "Majufes." In *Enzyklopädie jüdischer Geschichte und Kultur*, Stuttgart: J. B. Metzler, forthcoming.

Werb, Bret. "Majufes: A Vestige of Jewish Traditional Song in Polish Popular Entertainment." *Polish Music Journal* 6, no. 1 (2003). Accessed September 9, 2011, http://www.usc.edu/dept/polish_ music/PMJ/issue/6.1.03/Werb.html#[4].

Wertheimer, Jack. *Unwelcome Strangers: East European Jews in Imperial Germany*. New York: Oxford University Press, 1987.

Wex, Michael. *Born to Kvetch: Yiddish Language and Culture in All of Its Moods*. New York: Harper, 2005.

Wiatrak, Mariusz. "Kabaret makabryczny." *Gazeta Wyborcza Kraków*, June 29, 2007, 7.

Wilson, Peter N. "Jazz und 'Jewish roots.'" In John and Zimmermann, *Jüdische Musik? Fremdbilder— Eigenbilder*, 257–68. Köln: Böhlau, 2004.

Winkler, Georg. *Klezmer: Merkmale, Strukturen und Tendenzen eines musikkulturellen Phänomens*. Bern: Peter Lang, 2003.

Wistrich, Robert S., ed. *Demonizing the Other: Antisemitism, Racism, and Xenophobia*. Jerusalem: Harwood Academic Publishers, 1999.

Wohl, Michael J. A., and Nyla R. Branscombe. "Forgiveness and Collective Guilt Assignment to Historical Perpetrator Groups Depend on Level of Social Category Inclusiveness." *Journal of Personality and Social Psychology* 88, no. 2 (2005): 288–303.

Wohl, Michael J. A., Nyla R. Branscombe, and Yechiel Klar. "Collective Guilt: Emotional Reactions When One's Group Has Done Wrong or Been Wronged." *European Review of Social Psychology* 17, no. 37 (2006): 1–37.

Wöhlert, Meike. "Der Hype um den Davidstern." *Zitty*, no. 16, 1998, 14–20.

Wood, Abigail. "Commemoration and Creativity: Remembering the Holocaust in Today's Yiddish Song." *European Judaism* 35, no. 2 (2002): 43–56.

Wood, Abigail. "(De)constructing Yiddishland: Solomon and SoCalled's *HipHopKhasene*." *Ethnomusicology Forum* 16, no. 2 (2007): 243–70.

Wood, Abigail. "The Multiple Voices of American Klezmer." *Journal of the Society for American Music* 1, no. 3 (2007): 367–92.

Wood, Abigail. "Stepping Across the Divide: Hasidic Music in Today's Yiddish Canon." *Ethnomusicology* 51, no. 2 (2007): 205–37.

Young, James E. *At Memory's Edge: After-Images of the Holocaust in the Contemporary Art and Architecture*. New Haven: Yale University Press, 2000.

Young, James O., and Conrad G. Brunk, eds. *The Ethics of Cultural Appropriation*. Oxford: Wiley-Blackwell, 2009.

Young, James O., and Susan Haley. "'Nothing Comes from Nowhere:' Reflections on Cultural Appropriation as the Representation of Other Cultures." In *The Ethics of Cultural Appropriation*, edited by J. O. Young and Conrad G. Brunk, 268–89. Oxford: Wiley-Blackwell, 2009.

Zacher, Peter. "Erfolgreicher Versuch der Wiederannäherung an Unaufgebbares: Drei Tage jiddischer Kultur in Berlin." *Nachrichtenblatt der Jüdischen Gemeinden in der Deutschen Demokratischen Republik*, June 1987, 10–12.

Zacher, Peter. "Erneute Wiederannäherung: Möglichkeiten und Grenzen der Darstellung jiddischer Kultur heute." *Nachrichtenblatt der Jüdischen Gemeinden in der Deutschen Demokratischen Republik*, June 1988, 12–14.

Ziegler, Susane. *Die Wachszylinder des Berliner Phonogramm-Archivs*. Berlin: Ethnologisches Museum, 2006.

Zielinski, Siegfried. "History as Entertainment and Provocation: The TV Series 'Holocaust' in West Germany." In *Germans and Jews Since the Holocaust: The Changing Situation in West Germany*, edited by Anson Rabinbach and Jack Zipes, 258–83. New York: Holmes and Meier, 1986.

Ziff, Bruce, and Pratima V. Rao. "Introduction to Cultural Appropriation: A Framework for Analysis." In *Borrowed Power: Essays on Cultural Appropriation*, edited by B. Ziff and P. V. Rao, 1–27. New Brunswick, NJ: Rutgers University Press, 1997.

Zimmerman, Joshua D., ed. *Contested Memories: Poles and Jews during the Holocaust and its Aftermath*. New Brunswick, NJ: Rutgers University Press, 2003.

Zubrzycki, Genevieve. *The Crosses of Auschwitz: Nationalism and Religion in Post-Communist Poland*. Chicago: University of Chicago Press, 2006.

Discography

Adamów Jarek. *Etnomalia Projekt. New Polish Klezmer Music*. © 2011 by Folken Music, CD.

Aizikovitch, Mark. *in jiddischn wort*. © 2000 by Raumer Records, CD.

Aufwind. *"Lomp noch nit farloschn."* © 1989 by AMIGA/VEB Deutsche Schallplatte, Berlin, DDR, LP.

Avitall, and Konstantin Wecker. *Sage Nein zu Antisemitismus*. © 2005 by Amazonas Musik, CD.

Brave Old World. *Beyond the Pale*. © 1994 by Rounder Select, CD.

Brave Old World. *Dus gezang fin Geto Lodzh: Song of the Lodz Ghetto*. © 2005 by Music Edition Winter & Winter, CD.

Cukunft. *Lider fun Mordechaj Gebirtig*. © 2004 by Rafael Rogiński, CD.

Eisel, Helmut. *Klezmer at the Cotton Club*. © 2006 by Indigo, CD.

Jaldati, Lin. *Jiddische Lieder*. © 1997 by Barbarossa, CD.

JuMu Nu Juwish Music. © 2007 by JuMu V2 Music, CD.

Kahn, Daniel, and The Painted Bird. *Partisans and Parasites*. © 2009 by Oriente, CD.

Kahn, Daniel, and The Painted Bird. *The Broken Tongue*. © 2006 by Chamsa Records, CD.

Kahn, Daniel, Psoy Korolenko, and Oy Division. *The Unternationale*. © 2008 by Auris Media, CD.

Khupe. *Heymisher*. © 2003 by Yellowjacket Music, CD.

Kroke. *The Sounds of the Vanishing World*. © 1999 by Oriente, CD.

Kroke. *Trio*. © 1996 by Oriente, CD.

Makosz, Urszula. *Dos lid funem khurbn: Songs from the Ghetos and Jewish Resistance*. © 2005 by Muzeum Galicja, CD.

Mazel. *Un brukhe*. © 2006 by tylkomuzyka, CD.

Pan Kazimierz. © 2007 by Poemat, CD.

Pancur Andrea and Ilya Shneyveys. *Alpen Klezmer*. © 2012 by Globalistas Records, CD.

Przybylska, Sława. *Ałef-Bejs: Pieśni i piosenki żydowskie*. © 2005 by Tonpress, CD.

Rettig, Samuel. *Z albumu pieśni żydowskich*. © 1964 by Polskie Nagrania Muza, LP.

Shofar. *Shofar*. © 2007 by Kilogram Records, CD.

Sholem. *Mazl Tov*. © 2005 by Inglot Klezmer Trio, CD.

Stiller, Nina. *Nina Stiller*. © 2006 by EMI Music Poland, CD.

Tants in Gartn Eydn. *Klezmer Schwof*. © 2001 by Rent a Poet, CD

Teatr Zwierciadło. *Piosenki Żydów z Odessy*. © 2000 by Andromeda, CD.

Tencer, Gołda. *Miasteczko Bełz*. © 1988 by Arston, LP.

The Upward Flight: The Musical World of S. An-sky. A CD accompanying G. Safran, S. J. Zipperstein, *The Worlds of S. An-sky: A Russian Jewish Intellectual at the Turn of the Century*. Stanford: Stanford University Press, 2006.

Troyke, Karsten. *Jiddische Vergessene Lieder*. © 1998 by Raumer Records, CD.

Troyke, Karsten. *Yiddish Anders*. © 1992 by Raumer Records, CD.

Urbańska Irena. *Kołysanki żydowskie*. © 2008 by Tylkomuzyka, CD.

Urbańska, Irena. *Pieśni żydowskie Mordechaja Gebirtiga*. © 2002 by Art CD, CD.

Żywiołak. *Nowa Ex-Tradycja*. © 2008 by AKW Karrot Kommando, CD.

Filmography

A Tickle in the Heart. Directed by Stefan Schwietert. IDEA, 1996, VHS.

Broken Sound. Directed by Wolfgang and Yvonne Andrä. 1 meter 60 Distribution, 2011, DVD.

Der Ewige Jude. Directed by Fritz Hippler. Deutsche Film Gesellschaft, 1940.

Die junge Fiedler auf dem Dach. Directed by Michael Goldman. N3 Channel, 1989, VHS.

Ein ganz gewöhnlicher Jude. Directed by Charles Lewinsky and Oliver Hirschbiegel. NFP Marketing and Distribution, 2005, DVD.

Eine Hochzeit ohne Klezmer ist wie ein Begräbnis ohne Tränen. Directed by Yale Strom. Saarlaendische Rundfunk, 1995, VHS.

Fiddler on the Hoof. Directed by Simon Broughton. BBC, 1992, VHS.

Ich komme spät nach Hause. Directed by Klaas Rusticus. ZDF/arte, 1996, VHS.

Klezmer in Germany. Directed by Caroline Goldie and Krzysztof Zanussi, BBC, 2007, DVD.

Klezmer Musicians Travel "Home" to Krakow. Directed by Curt Fissel. Jem/Glo, 2003, DVD.

Klezmer on Fish Street. Directed by Yale Strom. Castle Hill Productions, 2003, DVD.

Sabbath in Paradise. Directed by Claudia Heuermann. WDR, 1997, VHS.

Und wenn der Rebbe lacht. Directed by Christa Espey. DDR 2TV, 1988, VHS.

Wenn du singst, wie kennst du hassen? Directed by Jens Scheffler. NDR, 1995, VHS.

Appendix

LIST OF INTERVIEWS

Abaszidze, Wiaczesław. Interview recorded in Kraków, June 30, 2006.

Aizikovich, Mark. Interview recorded in Berlin, February 3, 2006.

Alpert, Michael. Interview recorded at the KlezKanada Festival near Montreal, August 25, 2007.

Backes, Gigi. Interview recorded in Berlin, December 12, 2006.

Bern, Alan. Interview recorded in Weimar, July 16, 2006.

Bester, Jarosław. Interview recorded in Kraków, April 17, 2004.

Borbonus, Martin. Interview recorded in Berlin, February 27, 2006.

Brody, Paul. Interview recorded in Berlin, March 8, 2005.

Brudzińska, Magdalena. Interview recorded in Kraków, June 30, 2006, and January 23, 2008.

Desatnik, Gennadij. Interview recorded in Berlin, November 30, 2006.

Di Galitzyaner Klezmorim [Mariola Śpiewak, Grzegorz Śpiewak, Rafał Seweryniak]. Interview recorded in Kraków. April 24, 2004.

Dimitroff, Alexandra. Interview recorded in Berlin, January 5, 2006.

Drees, Simon Jakob. Interview recorded in Berlin, February 10, 2006.

Feidman, Giora. Interview recorded in Berlin, December 4, 2006.

Feldman, Walter Zev. Interview recorded at the KlezKanada Festival near Montreal, August 23, 2007.

Ginzburg, Wlady. Interview recorded in Berlin, August 9, 2007.

Gofenberg, Jossif. Interview recorded in Berlin, January 23, 2006.

Hacker, Max. Interview recorded in Berlin, January 16, 2006.

Halkowski, Henryk. Interview recorded in Kraków, June 29, 2006.

Hermerschmidt, Jan. Interview recorded in Berlin, December 1, 2006.

Hildebrandt, Bert. Interview recorded in Berlin, January 12, 2006.

Jacobowitz, Alex. Interview recorded in Berlin, February 1, 2006.

Jamróz, Katarzyna. Interview recorded in Kraków, April 19, 2004.

Jasha Lieberman Trio [Jasha Lieberman, Jacek Hołubowski, Roman Ślazyk]. Interview recorded in Kraków, July 5, 2006.

Kahn, Daniel. Interview recorded in Berlin, January 17, 2006.

Khupe [Sanne Möricke and Christian Dawid]. Interview recorded in Berlin, May 9, 2005.

Klezzmates [Jarosław Wilkosz and Marcin Wiercioch]. Interview recorded in Kraków, June 30, 2006.

Kloock, Ulrike. Interview recorded in Berlin, January 19, 2006.

Komnatoff, Karel. Interview recorded in Berlin, January 9, 2006.

Kozłowski, Leopold. Interview recorded in Kraków, April 20, 2004.

Kroke [Jerzy Bawół, Tomasz Lato, and Tomasz Kurkuba]. Interview recorded in Kraków, April 17, 2004, April 18, 2004, and June 25, 2005.

Kühne, Stefan. Interview recorded in Berlin, March 12, 2005.

Kupferberg, Shelly. Interview recorded in Berlin, April 12, 2007.

Lampe, Franka. Interview recorded in Berlin, January 7, 2006.

Lehmann, Heiko. Interview recorded in Berlin, June 16, 2005, and October 6, 2007.

Leś Zdzisław. Interview recorded in Kraków, June 10, 2006.

Lic, Lesław. Interview recorded in Kraków, July 11, 2006.

Łypik-Sobaniec, Barbara. Interview recorded in Kraków, July 3, 2006.

Makosz, Urszula. Interview recorded in Kraków, July 8, 2006.

Makuch, Janusz. Interview recorded in Kraków, April 18, 2004, and May 3, 2007.

Mayer, Lisa. Interview recorded at the KlezKanada Festival near Montreal, August 23, 2007.

Miodunka, Maria. Interview recorded in Kraków, July 4, 2006.

Naliwajko, Jarosław. Interview recorded in Kraków, April 21, 2004.

Ornat, Wojciech. Interview recorded in Kraków, June 29, 2006.

Pash, Boaz. Interview recorded in Kraków, July 4, 2008.

Pegelow, Detlef. Interview recorded in Berlin, January 18, 2006.

Petranyuk, Vitaliy. Interview recorded in Kraków, January 21, 2008.

Piekarski, Przemysław. Interview recorded in Kraków, July 4, 2008.

Rebling, Jalda. Interview recorded in Berlin, February 6, 2006, and October 18, 2006.

Reich, Hardy. Interview recorded in Berlin, June 13, 2005.

Reiner, Roman. Interview recorded in Kraków, June 28, 2006.

Róg, Andrzej. Interview recorded in Kraków, April 19, 2004.

Römer, Thomas. Interview recorded in Berlin, February 28, 2006.

Runge, Irene. Interview recorded in Berlin, January 16, 2006.

Russek, Joachim. Interview recorded in Kraków, June 29, 2006.

Samech [Anna Ostachowska and Agata Krauze]. Interview recorded in Kraków, July 7, 2006.

Sapoznik, Henry. Interview recorded at the KlezKanada Festival near Montreal, August 23, 2007.

Schnedler, Fabian. Interview recorded in Berlin, February 8, 2006.

Schubert, Anna. Interview recorded in Berlin, January 31, 2006.

Schumann, Till. Interview recorded in Berlin, December 12, 2006.

Schwarz, Chris. Interview recorded in Kraków, July 5, 2006.

Schwarz, Snorre. Interview recorded in Berlin, January 23, 2006.

Seidemann, Burkhart. Interview recorded in Berlin, January 4, 2006.

Sholem [Maciej Inglot, Tomasz Michalik, and Ewelina Tomanek]. Interview recorded in Kraków, July 1, 2006.

Spinner, Joshua. Interview recorded in Berlin, January 13, 2006.

Symons, David. Interview recorded in Berlin, January 4, 2006.

Tencer, Gołda. Interview recorded in Warsaw, January 18, 2008.

The Saints [Grzegorz Lenart, Karol Pacholec]. Interview recorded in Kraków, April 23, 2004.

Timmermann, Harry. Interview recorded in Berlin, November 8, 2006.

Troyke, Karsten. Interview recorded in Berlin, January 12, 2006.

Urbańska, Irena. Interview recorded in Kraków, July 10, 2006.

Wegener, Carsten. Interview recorded in Berlin, February 27, 2006.

Wex, Michael. Interview recorded at the KlezKanada Festival near Montreal, August 22, 2007.

Wolter, Henner. Interview recorded in Berlin, December 1, 2006.

Wydra, Katarzyna. Interview recorded in Kraków, February 23, 2006.

List of Coded Interviews (see chapters 2, 4, 6, and 7)

Interviewee code	Date of the interview	Place of the interview	Sex	Occupation
B01	2005	Berlin	m	musician
B02	2005	Berlin	m	musician
B03	2005	Berlin	m	musician
B04	2006	Berlin	m	musician
B05	2006	Berlin	m	musician
B06	2006	Berlin	f	musician
B07	2006	Berlin	m	musician
B08	2006	Berlin	m	musician
B10	2006	Berlin	m	musician
B11	2006	Berlin	f	musician
B12	2006	Berlin	f	musician
B13	2006	Berlin	m	musician
B14	2006	Berlin	m	musician
B15	2006	Berlin	m	musician
B16	2006	Berlin	m	musician
B17	2006	Berlin	m	musician

B18	2006	Berlin	m	cultural organizer
B19	2006	Berlin	f	musician
B20	2006	Berlin	m	musician
K01	2004	Kraków	m	musician
K02	2004	Kraków	f	musician
K03	2004	Kraków	m	musician
K04	2004	Kraków	m	Catholic priest, cultural organizer
K05	2004 and 2005	Kraków	m	musician
K06	2004	Kraków	m	musician
K07	2004 and 2005	Kraków	m	musician
K08	2004	Kraków	f	musician
K09	2004	Kraków	m	musician
K10	2004	Kraków	m	cultural organizer
K11	2004	Kraków	m	cultural organizer
K12	2004 and 2005	Kraków	m	musician
K13	2006	Kraków	m	musician
K14	2006	Kraków	f	musician
K15	2006	Kraków	f	musician
K16	2006	Kraków	f	musician
K17	2006	Kraków	f	musician
K18	2006	Kraków	f	cultural organizer
K19	2006	Kraków	f	musician
K20	2006	Kraków	m	musician
K21	2006	Kraków	m	musician
K22	2006	Kraków	m	musician
K23	2006	Kraków	m	musician
K24	2006	Kraków	m	musician
K25	2006	Kraków	f	musician
K26	2008	Kraków	m	musician
K27	2006	Kraków	m	cultural organizer
K28	2006	Kraków	m	musician

INDEX